Praise for *Egypt and the Contradi*

"I read *Egypt and the Contradictions of Liber*
understanding one of the most significant events in our contemporary
history is in the caring and competent hands of some seminal critical
thinkers. Dalia F. Fahmy and Daanish Faruqi have brought together a
formidable volume challenging what they aptly call "Illiberal Intelligentsia"
and gauge the future of the Egyptian democracy beyond and through their
historic failures. What the community of critical thinkers gathered in this
volume discover and discuss is no mere indictment of the Egyptian liberal
intellectuals and their catastrophic failure at a crucial historic juncture,
but something far more deeply troubling in the very nature of unexam-
ined globalized liberalism. The result is a fiercely radical constellation of
critical thinking indispensable for our understanding not just of Egypt
and the rest of the Arab and Muslim world, but in fact the very legacy
of liberalism in the 21st century."

**Hamid Dabashi, Hagop Kevorkian Professor of Iranian Studies
and Comparative Literature, Columbia University**

"This edited volume is an essential contribution towards understanding
the current state of affairs in Egypt. The different chapters offer a sense
of the underlying dynamics at work within Egyptian society (among the
military, the Muslim Brotherhood, secularists and the youth). The reader
is invited to consider the complexity of the situation and what it will
take for Egyptian people to find their way towards freedom and justice."

**Tariq Ramadan, Professor of Contemporary Islamic Studies,
University of Oxford**

"An extraordinary and wide-ranging exploration of the Arab Spring's
excitement and reversal in Egypt. Compulsory reading to grasp the role
of Islam, secularism, authoritarianism and liberalism in contemporary
Egypt."

**Ebrahim Moosa, Professor of Islamic Studies, Keough School of
Global Affairs, University of Notre Dame**

"The question of democracy in Muslim societies has generated heated debate on the role of mainstream Islamist parties and democratization. Can they moderate their views? Will they respect electoral outcomes? Are they committed to political pluralism? The same questions, however, have been rarely asked of liberal and secular forces who occupy the same political space. This is precisely what is unique about this book. Focusing on Egypt's Arab Spring democratic transition, it examines the political behavior of Egyptian liberals during the transition period and after the 2013 military coup. In doing so, the editors and contributors make an important and exceptional contribution to understanding both the persistence of authoritarianism in the Arab-Islamic world and the obstacles to democracy. It is a must read volume that challenges stereotypes and deepens our grasp of the politics and societies of the Middle East."

Nader Hashemi, Director of the Center for Middle East Studies, University of Denver, and author of *Islam, Secularism, and Liberal Democracy: Toward a Democratic Theory for Muslim Societies*

"The heroic events of January and February 2011 seemed at first to rewrite the rules of Middle Eastern politics. One of the longest ruling autocrats in the Arab World fell not to a military coup, an assassination, or violent uprising, but to the immovable presence of the people demonstrating in public. The Tahrir Revolution was 'liberal' in the sense that its demands were for freedom, the rule of law, and social justice. Its promise was that these goals seemed to reflect a shared will uniting the secular and the Islamist, the masses and the middle class. Two short years later that promise was shattered in a supreme act of anti-political, counterrevolutionary violence. How did many Egyptian 'liberals,' who two years earlier stood side by side with Islamists against Mubarak in Tahrir, and one year earlier voted for Morsi for President, come to side with a return to military dictatorship over constitutional politics? *Egypt and the Contradictions of Liberalism* brings together many of the best scholars on Egyptian politics to answer just this question."

Andrew F. March, Associate Professor of Political Science, Yale University, and author of *Islam and Liberal Citizenship: The Search for an Overlapping Consensus*

Egypt and the Contradictions of Liberalism

—Illiberal Intelligentsia and the Future of Egyptian Democracy—

Edited by

DALIA F. FAHMY &
DAANISH FARUQI

Series: Studies on Islam, Human Rights, and Democracy
Series Editor: Khaled Abou El Fadl

ONEWORLD

A Oneworld Book

First published by Oneworld Publications, 2017

Copyright © Dalia F. Fahmy and Daanish Faruqi, 2017

ISBN 978-1-78074-882-5
eISBN 978-1-78074-883-2

Typeset by Silicon Chips

Printed and bound in Great Britain by Clays Ltd, St Ives plc

Oneworld Publications
10 Bloomsbury Street
London WC1B 3SR
England

Stay up to date with the latest books,
special offers, and exclusive content from
Oneworld with our monthly newsletter

Sign up on our website
www.oneworld-publications.com

To the people of Egypt

Contents

Section II: Liberalism and Egyptian Civil Society

Acknowledgments

In bringing this volume to completion after nearly two years of deliberation, design, and ultimately implementation, we as editors have become further emboldened in our core belief that undergirded the project when we first conceived it: that a topic as delicate as the contradictions of liberalism in Egypt *necessitated* a collaborative effort. Indeed, we cannot fathom the insights of this work having been properly articulated in a single-authored monograph; the breadth of the topic required casting a wider net than any one scholar or disciplinary perspective could possibly stand to offer. In that sense, we are deeply indebted to each of our contributors. As experts in a varied array of disciplinary perspectives, each offered insights that proved fundamental to the broader aims of our intervention, without which this book would have been wholly inadequate and incomplete. We are thus honored to have had the opportunity to partner with each of our distinguished colleagues. We were especially appreciative of the opportunity to have presented the broader theme of the book alongside a group of our contributors at a panel at the 2015 meeting of the Middle East Studies Association, and are thankful for the commentary and feedback we received from colleagues there – key among them from Stuart Schaar, a stalwart supporter of our project from its conception.

We would further like to express special thanks to Khaled Abou El Fadl as our series editor. Even when our project was at its most rudimentary conceptual stage, Dr. Abou El Fadl immediately proved deeply supportive of our vision, and spared no effort to work with us to refine the rough contours into a finished product. We are equally indebted to our remarkable team at Oneworld Publications, notably Novin Doostdar, Jonathan Bentley-Smith, and Paul Nash. From the submission of our original manuscript, they have proven deeply attentive to every aspect of our book's production, and it has been a pleasure to have worked with a publisher so dedicated to the success of its authors.

While both of the editors are united by a deep love for and dedication to *umm ad-Dunya*, we also remain cognizant of the clear idiosyncrasies of each of our approaches and experiences – one a political scientist whose primary area of research has been, and continues to be, Islamist movements in Egypt, the other a historian of Islamic political thought whose work has in recent years veered away from Egypt proper but who out of conviction forcefully returned to debates he originally inaugurated while beginning his career in Egypt some eight years ago. Accordingly, we felt it appropriate to augment our collective acknowledgments above with separate words of recognition for those who made our project possible.

Dalia Fahmy would like to thank the following for their insights on Egypt throughout the past few years: Gouda Abdel Khalek, Sahar Aziz, Nathan Brown, Daniel Brumberg, Eric Davis, John Esposito, Saad Eddin Ibrahim, Amaney Jamal, Karima Khorayyam, Marc Lynch, Timothy Mitchell, Eid Mohamed, Bessma Momani, Samer Shehata, John Voll, Moheb Zaki, and Wael Haddara. And for their support, she would like to thank the Department of Political Science and Dean David Cohen at Long Island University.

Daanish Faruqi would first like to express his sincere gratitude to the countless friends and colleagues made in Cairo during his stint as a researcher at the Ibn Khaldun Center for Development Studies in 2008 and 2009, key among them Moheb Zaki, Barbara Ibrahim, and Saad Eddin Ibrahim. Furthermore, he would like to thank the Duke University Graduate School of Arts and Sciences for financially supporting a research trip to Cairo in June 2015, as well as a series of colleagues and mentors at Duke University who proved deeply supportive of the project: Engseng Ho for his guidance as a dedicated supervisor, Anna Krylova for her camaraderie and intellectual support, and miriam cooke for her astute commentary on the first chapter, as well as for being such a demanding mentor to insist that what began as an unstructured set of ideas be cultivated into a finalized work of nothing short of the highest caliber. Finally, a special thanks to Bruce Lawrence, without whose assiduous mentorship, tutelage, and friendship this herculean endeavor would have never been possible.

All errors are ours alone.

1

Egyptian liberals, from revolution to counterrevolution

DAANISH FARUQI AND DALIA F. FAHMY

INTRODUCTION

Now six years since the popular uprising that ended the regime of longtime Egyptian dictator Hosni Mubarak, many have argued that the liberatory sentiment that stoked the Tahrir Revolution in the first place is barely recognizable. Following a year of the admittedly incompetent rule of Muslim Brotherhood-affiliated President Mohammad Morsi, the second uprising in July 2013 that brought down his rule ultimately gave rise to precisely the kind of authoritarianism Egyptian revolutionaries had been railing against in January 2011. Encapsulated most vividly by the Egyptian security forces' calculated slaughter of protesters on August 14, 2013 in Cairo's Rabaa Square,[1] the Egyptian police state

---

[1] Findings by Human Rights Watch, based on a year of investigation and research, conclude that key Egyptian leaders who oversaw the events at Rabaa are guilty of the "world's largest killings of demonstrators in a single day in recent history" and should accordingly be tried for crimes against humanity. See Editorial Board, "Egypt should be a pariah state for its bloody crackdown on dissent," *Washington Post*, August 12, 2014, http://www.washingtonpost.com/opinions/egypt-should-be-a-pariah-state-for-its-bloody-crackdown-on-dissent/2014/08/12/04a9cfd6-223a-11e4-86ca-6f03cbd15c1a_story.html; and Human Rights Watch, *All According to Plan: The Rab'a Massacre and Mass Killings of Protestors in Egypt*, HRW, August 12, 2014, https://www.hrw.org/report/2014/08/12/all-according-plan/raba-massacre-and-mass-killings-protesters-egypt

has returned with a vengeance. Under the stewardship of (now) President Abd al-Fattah al-Sisi, state repression has been escalated to levels hitherto unimaginable even during the Mubarak years, with not only suspected members of the Brotherhood, but Egyptian civil society more broadly, now subject to sweeping crackdowns.

As a preface, we cannot sufficiently emphasize that the ouster of Morsi was decidedly a *popular* coup. Even if the Tamarod (Rebel) movement that initially spearheaded the insurrection against Morsi in June 2013 ultimately exaggerated its claims to have collected twenty-two million signatures in opposition to Morsi's presidency, anti-Morsi sentiment in the months leading up to the June 30, 2013 uprising was deeply palpable. A sizeable constituency of the Egyptian public had indeed grown increasingly disillusioned with Morsi as their first elected leader, and feared his stewardship of the country now stood to violate the ideals of the uprising they had valiantly spearheaded in January 2011. Even the very revolutionary forces that were so instrumental in the fall of Mubarak concurred: major players in Egyptian civil society, including groups like Kifaya and the April 6th Youth Movement that played such a dominant role in the January 2011 uprising, had initially lent their support to the Tamarod campaign and its demand for early presidential elections.[2] In the face of such deep-seated anti-Morsi and anti-Brotherhood sentiment having permeated large contingents of Egyptian society, it is not altogether surprising that masses would enthusiastically cheer on the forcible removal of Morsi by the Egyptian military on July 3, 2013, or even then General Sisi's call later that month for a full "mandate" from the Egyptian people to combat terrorism – and thus embark on a systematic crackdown against Islamists tout court.[3]

Nonetheless, even if popular dissatisfaction with Morsi and the Muslim Brotherhood can conceivably excuse a critical mass of the Egyptian public for having lent its support to the early termination of the democratic experiment in Egypt, it does not sufficiently explain why a key contingent of Egypt's *liberals* succumbed to the same fate. Which is to say, an influential coterie of Egyptian liberal activists and intellectuals, who had earned their reputations as scions of protest and champions of democracy, civil

---

[2] Heba Afify, "The June 30 civilian alliance: A timeline of inception and erosion," *Mada Masr*, August 14, 2014, http://www.madamasr.com/sections/politics/june-30-civilian-alliance
[3] Kareem Fahim and Mayy El Sheikh, "Egyptian general calls for mass protest," *New York Times*, July 24, 2013, http://www.nytimes.com/2013/07/25/world/middleeast/egypt.html

society, and human rights during the Mubarak years, ultimately reneged on those commitments in the aftermath of the events of June 2013 and onward. Departing from their previous personas, these heretofore liberal figures instead lent support – in many cases enthusiastic support – to the new authoritarian order under President Sisi. All hail from different and varying perspectives, but are united by having been self-identified as liberal, secular democrats, and rather iconic figures of the idea of secular liberalism in Egypt more broadly. Yet paradoxically, these same figures came to enthusiastically support the coup against Egypt's first democratically elected president, and to continue that wave of support well into the point at which the new order under Sisi's rampant illiberal repression – against Muslim Brotherhood supporters and beyond – was made readily apparent.

Briefly, before fully proceeding, we should clarify what we mean here by 'liberal.' Here we rely primarily on the benchmark of self-identification, but even then, what is the 'liberalism' to which Egyptian figures under consideration subscribe? Broadly speaking, these figures employ the term to refer to a political philosophy more immediately rooted in seventeenth- and eighteenth-century Europe. Incubated in the context of feudalism and the arbitrary abuse of power by clerical authorities, liberalism as articulated by its most luminary figures such as John Locke, Adam Smith, Jean-Jacques Rousseau, and others, articulated a worldview in which individual freedom became sacrosanct:

> [They] envisioned a new world in which the arbitrary authority of the church and an arrogant aristocracy would cease to exist; a world in which reason and democracy would temper provincial ethnic and religious hatreds between states and races; a world of unfettered freedom, without radical differences in the distribution of wealth, in which an individual might better his lot through hard work and without fear of obstruction by the state.[4]

The individual thus became central to the liberal worldview, as a subject endowed with inviolable rights, and whose freedoms were to be protected at all costs, be it against the fetters of religious dogmatism or the invasive proclivities of the state apparatus. We will speak more about the history of liberalism as a philosophy in a subsequent section, but for now it should

---

[4] Stephen Eric Bronner, *Ideas In Action: Political Tradition in the Twentieth Century* (New York: Rowman and Littlefield, 1999), 26.

suffice to highlight its most salient attributes, in order to understand how the project reconstituted itself in Egypt, outside the immediately European cultural context in which it was originally conceived.

And in the Egyptian context, it is important to first preface that the liberals who form the basis of this study were not mere armchair intellectuals or fair-weather political activists. Figures of the persuasion we consider here had legitimately paid their dues in the pre-revolutionary context, many having faced serious persecution under Mubarak for their efforts at promoting democracy and the liberal rule of law. The prominent Egyptian journalist Ibrahim Eissa is a case in point: long a thorn in the side of the Mubarak regime, as editor of the opposition newspaper *al-Dustour*, Eissa was regularly harassed by the Egyptian courts for publishing allegedly subversive commentary – perhaps most famously in 2007, in which his article questioning then president Mubarak's failing health earned him a year-long prison sentence. Insinuating that the Egyptian president had health problems, the charges against him stipulated, was tantamount to harming national security.[5] Similarly, democracy and civil society activist Dr. Saad Eddin Ibrahim has been no stranger to the travesty of Egyptian justice, having spent several years languishing in Mubarak's prisons on the dubious charge of defaming Egypt through his advocacy work at the Cairo-based democracy think tank he had founded, the Ibn Khaldun Center for Development Studies.[6] The famed Egyptian novelist Alaa al-Aswany and founder of the March 9th Movement for University Independence Dr. Mohammad Abol Ghar also fall into this cadre of liberal reformers: Aswany was a founding member of the Kifaya, Egyptian Movement for Change, protest movement, while Abol Ghar served as a spokesman for the National Association for Change led by Mohamed El Baradei, and following the 2011 revolution co-founded the Social Democratic Party, "what many viewed as the most substantial political party for liberals."[7]

---

[5] Heba Afify, "Ibrahim Eissa is 'The Boss,' but at what cost?" *Mada Masr*, April 28, 2014, http://www.madamasr.com/sections/politics/ibrahim-eissa-%E2%80%9C-boss%E2%80%9D-what-cost

[6] Bari Weiss, "A democrat's triumphal return to Cairo," *Wall Street Journal*, February 26, 2011, sec. Opinion, http://www.wsj.com/articles/SB10001424052748703408604576164482658051692

[7] Joshua Hersh, "Portrait of a Cairo liberal as a military backer," *New Yorker*, August 17, 2013, http://www.newyorker.com/news/news-desk/portrait-of-a-cairo-liberal-as-a-military-backer

During their pre-revolutionary political careers, moreover, these liberal figures were quite nuanced in how they handled their associations with the Muslim Brotherhood. As avowedly secular figures, none was remotely sympathetic to Islamism as a political platform, but their opposition to the discourse of Islamism did not preclude them from accepting the Brotherhood as a reality in Egyptian political life. Ibrahim Eissa is perhaps more contentious than most liberals in this respect, having had a palpably antagonistic relationship with the role of religion in society even in his earlier career. As early as the nineties, Eissa published critiques of religious discourse, both in his expository writing in columns and books, as well as in a series of novels. But even then, as editor of *al-Dustour*, he allowed Muslim Brotherhood figures the opportunity to publish in his pages, and defended the group against state suppression. Arguing that the Brotherhood was "representative of Egypt's class and cultural map," in the immediate aftermath of the 2011 uprising, Eissa celebrated their electoral wins, declaring as recently as October 2011 that "[i]f millions of Egyptian voters were to give the Muslim Brotherhood the majority in the elections…this would be majorly and abundantly beneficial."[8] Thus, as much opprobrium as Eissa may have heaped on Islamism as an ideological discourse, he nonetheless respected the Brotherhood's role in Egyptian civil society.

Other liberals were even more forthcoming in their defense of the Brotherhood as a legitimate political force. Alaa al-Aswany in his pre-revolutionary writings stressed national unity despite ideological differences with the Brotherhood, reiterating in a column dated August 9, 2009, that it was the Mubarak regime that "has deliberately exaggerated the role and influence of the Muslim Brotherhood for use as a bogeyman against anyone who calls for democracy."[9] Even if the Brotherhood were to win fair elections, he maintained in a November 8, 2009 column, "wouldn't that be the free choice of Egyptians, which we should respect if we are true democrats?"[10] As for Dr. Saad Eddin Ibrahim, perhaps the defining aspect of his career both as a sociologist and as a democracy activist has been his long-standing commitment to the *domestication* of the Brotherhood. The quintessential Arab democrat, having refined his ideas on Islamist

---

[8] Afify, "Ibrahim Eissa is 'The Boss,' but at what cost?"
[9] Alaa al-Aswany, *On the State of Egypt: What Made the Egyptian Revolution Inevitable* (New York: Vintage, 2011), 96.
[10] Ibid., 9.

domestication through time spent with Brotherhood figures while in prison, Ibrahim has consistently maintained that allowing Islamists entry into the democratic process would liberalize their movement in the long term. Shortly after the 2011 revolution, Ibrahim analogized the Brotherhood to the Christian Democrats of Western Europe, arguing that "[t]hey started with more Christianity than democracy 100 years ago. Now they are more democracy than Christianity."[11]

Yet once the Muslim Brotherhood successfully entered the political arena, culminating in the election of Mohammad Morsi in June of 2012, these same figures radically shifted gears in their hitherto firm commitment to democratic reform. For all his bravado about considering a Brotherhood win in a fair election "majorly and abundantly beneficial," Ibrahim Eissa ultimately proved unwilling to abide by his own dictum. His journalistic work now degenerated from cutting-edge dissident commentary to sycophantic pro-military propaganda, Eissa firmly backed the overthrow of Morsi on the paranoid premise that, as he lamented in a conversation with Negar Azimi of the *New Yorker*, "[w]e don't want to turn into Iran."[12] Elsewhere, in an interview Eissa expresses no sympathy for protesters who support the Brotherhood – an oblique reference to protesters massacred in Rabaa and al-Nahda squares – stating "[t]here is no such things as rights for terrorists[.]"[13]

So profound was his descent from being a champion of liberal values to his new persona as a political reactionary, Eissa went as far as to applaud the arrest of the April 6th Youth Movement founder Ahmed Maher, questioning the movement's patriotism. The very political movement that played a defining role in the overthrow of Mubarak, Eissa now maintains, is so insufficiently loyal to Egypt as to warrant its founder languishing in prison for the next three years. Maher eventually responded, penning a bitter letter from prison to his erstwhile ally and comrade in the revolution: "Addressed to 'Hima,' the affectionate nickname activists used to have for Eissa, the letter states: 'He says that we are wavering, even though our

---

[11] Weiss, "A democrat's triumphal return to Cairo."

[12] Negar Azimi, "The Egyptian Army's unlikely allies," *New Yorker*, January 8, 2014, http://www.newyorker.com/news/news-desk/the-egyptian-armys-unlikely-allies

[13] Quoted in Mayy El Sheikh, "A voice of dissent in Egypt is muffled, but not silent," *New York Times*, May 2, 2014, http://www.nytimes.com/2014/05/03/world/middleeast/an-egyptian-voice-of-dissent-is-muffled-but-not-silenced.html

positions are constant and his change every few months. Not only his positions – Eissa's core values change, his principles and convictions.'"[14]

Other liberal figures in this vein similarly followed suit. Alaa al-Aswany's ballyhooed portrayals of then General Abd al-Fattah al-Sisi as "a national hero" were matched only by his disdain for the Brotherhood, as he revealed in conversation with the *New Yorker*: "They are like a bad version of Don Quixote because they live in history. They believe they were chosen by God to restore the glory of their religion. This type of fascism is very, very dangerous!"[15] Not to be outdone in braggadocio on behalf of the counterrevolutionary regime, Mohammad Abol Ghar unreservedly justified this circumvention of the democratic process by invoking alleged corollaries in American history: "'Would the Americans have been willing to wait four years for Nixon to finish his term?' Aboul-Ghar asked…'And remember, Nixon did much less than Morsi did.'"[16]

And as for Saad Eddin Ibrahim, even the Arab world's arguably most prominent democrat, who only years earlier had aggressively lobbied on Capitol Hill to convince American lawmakers to force the Mubarak regime to grant political space for the Brotherhood, ultimately capitulated to lend his enthusiastic support to the overthrow of Morsi, going so far as to support then General Sisi's presidential ambitions. Ibrahim proved wholly unapologetic for this seeming about-face, citing that experience has matured his political thinking: "I have no regrets whatsoever," said the seventy-five-year-old director of the Ibn Khaldun Center – which has backed democracy since he founded the group in 1988 – of his advocacy for the once powerful Islamist group he now opposes. "My perspective evolved."[17]

Interestingly enough, though, in the years following the events of July 2013, several of these same liberal figures have increasingly backtracked from or made concessions to their otherwise stalwart support of the military establishment. In the case of Saad Eddin Ibrahim, it seems that he has had a bona fide change of heart; in an interview in November 2015, Ibrahim adopts a style far more reminiscent of his pre-2013 persona,

---

[14] Afify, "Ibrahim Eissa is 'The Boss,' but at what cost?"

[15] Azimi, "The Egyptian Army's unlikely allies."

[16] Hersh, "Portrait of a Cairo liberal as a military backer."

[17] Matt Bradley, "Military Regime Draws Support From Egypt's Liberals," *Wall Street Journal*, January 12, 2014, sec. World, http://www.wsj.com/news/articles/SB10001424 0527023038197045793166684260794724?mg=reno64-wsj&url=http://online.wsj.com/article/SB10001424405270230381970457931 6684260794724.html

now urging the Sisi regime to reconcile with the Muslim Brotherhood, emphasizing that "[t]he state should embrace these people one way or another. They are political cadres, and are not ignorant. Conflict with them will exhaust resources and shed the blood of citizens. It threatens us with a civil war and therefore reconciling with the Brotherhood is a must before matters develop into what is worst."[18]

Similarly, Alaa al-Aswany has become increasingly critical of the Sisi regime in his writings, to the point that the state has censored both his public seminars in Cairo and his writings in state-run media. Yet Aswany has been more reserved than Ibrahim, maintaining that he continues to support the state's "fight against terrorism," with the caveat that this does not justify dictatorship.[19] If Aswany's case is any indication, liberal support for the military apparatus is no guarantee of immunity against that apparatus turning its guns on its very enablers – a fate that has also recently befallen Ibrahim Eissa, who in early January 2016 was under criminal investigation by Egyptian prosecutors for allegedly insulting the judiciary in an article published in the *Al-Maqal* newspaper he edits.[20] Now cognizant of his own vulnerability, even as a stalwart supporter who initially hailed Sisi's rise as "a day of joy, a day of victory, a day of dignity, a day of pride, the day Egypt and its people were victorious," Eissa has since begun to more directly challenge his erstwhile hero: "What happened exactly to make our nation turn around with you to the ear of searching consciences, putting minds on trial and imprisoning writers and authors?"[21]

Still, other liberal figures have been less sanguine, having held firm in their belief that the existential threat posed by the Muslim Brotherhood and by "terrorism," nebulously defined, necessitates the current regime's

---

[18] "Sa'ad Al-Din Ibrahim: Either we reconcile with the Muslim Brotherhood or go to civil war," *Middle East Monitor*, November 15, 2015, https://www.middleeastmonitor.com/20151115-sa-ad-al-din-ibrahim-either-we-reconcile-with-the-muslim-brotherhood-or-go-to-civil-war

[19] Marcia Lynx Qualey, "Egypt shuts down novelist Alaa Al-Aswany's public event and media work," *Guardian*, December 11, 2015, sec. Books, http://www.theguardian.com/books/2015/dec/11/egypt-shuts-down-novelist-alaa-al-aswanys-public-event-and-media-work

[20] "Egypt sentences journalists to prison for 'publishing false news' – Committee to Protect Journalists," accessed January 19, 2016, https://www.cpj.org/2016/01/egypt-sentences-journalists-to-prison-for-publishi.php

[21] Quoted in Ahmed Aboulenein, "As hard times hit, Egyptians at last find fault with Sisi," Reuters, March 11, 2016, http://www.reuters.com/article/us-egypt-politics-idUSKCN0WD15X

crackdown on Egyptian civil society. On this, Mohammad Abol Ghar is quite forthcoming, declaring in a November 2015 interview that all Egyptians are united behind the state, and that the democratic process can and should allow the Egyptian people the right to curtail rights and freedoms as the national interest dictates:

> Democracy means communal participation in decision-making, which is different from talking about 'rights and freedoms.' And if democracy is achieved, then the Egyptian masses [have the prerogative to] decide at a certain moment that we cannot grant freedoms one hundred percent in the name of [achieving] the national interest, as circumstances require.[22]

More recently, in March 2016, Abol Ghar authored a column lamenting the state of the country, in which he goes as far as to accuse Sisi of presiding over a broken political process, and over a police force that cavalierly beats and tortures. But his ire here directed at his former "Redeemer and Savior" is largely economic, decrying the devaluation of the Egyptian pound in contradistinction to the dollar, and Sisi's recklessness in commissioning large projects (ostensibly referring to the Suez Canal expansion) without having done the due diligence to assess their economic viability.[23] While Abol Ghar does offer some interspersed critiques of political repression, the tenor of his missive here suggests that, per his December 2015 article, circumscribing political freedoms would nonetheless still qualify as within the ambit of national interest, were Sisi's repressive rule to have brought economic prosperity to the country. Only in the face of the threat of economic failure, and the concomitant departure of foreign companies and international credit lines, **does** Abol Ghar begin to reconsider his commitments to political and intellectual freedom – and by extension, to the core vision undergirding the Egyptian revolution of 2011, and to the principles that he himself articulated in his advocacy for academic freedom through the March 9th Movement for University Independence, and in his work as spokesman for the National Association for Change alongside El Baradei.

---

[22] Karima 'Abd al-Ghani, "Abol Ghar li'al-Ahram': Qalb al masriyiin jami'an ma' al-dawla," *Al-Ahram Online*, November 13, 2015, http://www.ahram.org.eg/NewsQ/453551.aspx
[23] Mohammad Abol Ghar, "Hazin 'alaika ya watani," *Al-Masry al-Youm*, March 7, 2016, http://www.almasryalyoum.com/news/details/906019

What happened, then, to the liberal experiment in Egypt? How could intellectuals and activists so demonstrably committed to the cause of civil society, freedom, and democracy in Egypt – indeed, to the very impulses that inspired the 2011 uprising – come to abandon those commitments? How could the guardians of liberal values in Egypt ultimately embolden the nation's recidivism into authoritarian rule? Or, put another way, how could liberals in Egypt ultimately give rise to outright *illiberal* proclivities? It is this question that *Egypt and the Contradictions of Liberalism* seeks to critically address.

Having said that, doing full justice to the issue of Egypt and the contradictions of liberalism requires a systematic approach that goes beyond the career of this or that contemporary liberal figure. Liberalism in Egypt was and remains part of a deep historical trajectory stretching back to the late nineteenth and early twentieth centuries, which produced an intellectual and philosophical legacy that continues to inform even the liberals of today. Moreover, the key intellectuals and activists associated with early Egyptian liberalism attempted to cement their political project through the cultivation of liberal *institutions*, the legacy of which bears direct ramifications for the failures of the contemporary liberal project. Thus, to fully disentangle the illiberal proclivities of modern Egyptian liberalism, we must situate it in the intellectual history of the Egyptian liberal tradition more broadly, and, equally important, with the institutional legacy that tradition produced. It is to this question that we shall now turn.

THE GENEALOGIES OF EGYPTIAN LIBERALISM

In May 2003, two months after officially being cleared by the Egyptian Court of Cassation of all charges against him and subsequently released from prison, Saad Eddin Ibrahim spoke at the National Endowment for Democracy in Washington DC about his experiences under incarceration. Despite having languished in Mubarak's prisons to the point that his health had been irreparably damaged, Ibrahim delivered a message of optimism, assuring his audience that a democratic Egypt was wholly within the realm of possibility – because Egyptian society had an immanent tradition that articulated precisely the values of freedom and justice on which a democratic order is ultimately based. Referring to the Liberal Age – a term he borrows from the intellectual historian Albert Hourani[24] – Ibrahim harkens back to a period of nascent intellectual freedom and prosperity in Egypt stretching from, by his chronology, 1850 until its untimely demise with the rise of Nasser in 1952. Despite its early termination, Ibrahim maintains that the Liberal Age planted the seeds for the cultivation of democratic governance and a robust civil society in Egypt. Reviving this immanent discourse of the Liberal Age, then, is Ibrahim's solution to the authoritarian impasse facing Egypt:

> When we founded the Ibn Khaldun Center and as we guided its work throughout the late 1980s and 1990s, we had the Liberal Age very much in mind. We saw ourselves not as builders from scratch, but as revivers of a great (but not perfect) tradition that had existed not only in our own country but also in Syria, Iraq, Iran, Morocco, and elsewhere. We were and remain determined that this liberal tradition – and the Egyptian Court of Cassation, as witnessed in our legal case, is part of this legacy – will not be forgotten. We believe that if these ideas receive the exposure they deserve, the memory of this tradition and, more importantly, the still-living relevance of its core teachings on rights, freedom, transparency, and justice can play a large role in showing that democracy does indeed have a reasonable chance of putting down roots and growing in the Middle East.[25]

The Liberal Age began as part of a broader movement known as the Arab Renaissance, or the Nahda, largely in response to European material ascendancy over Muslim lands. Initially, the Nahda gave rise to a form of Islamic liberalism, with figures like Jamal al-Din al-Afghani (d. 1897) and Muhammad Abduh (d. 1905) seeking to reorient the Islamic tradition to its rationalist roots, thus making Islam more congruent with the needs of the modern world. Islamic liberalism then gave rise to a "humanist liberalism," built on largely European auspices.[26] Many leading early liberals

---

[24] See Albert Hourani, *Arabic Thought in the Liberal Age: 1798–1939* (Cambridge: Cambridge University Press, 1983).

[25] Saad Eddin Ibrahim, "Reviving Middle Eastern liberalism," *Journal of Democracy* 14, no. 4 (October 2003): 9–10.

[26] Jamal Mohammed Ahmed, *The Intellectual Origins of Egyptian Nationalism* (New York: Oxford University Press, 1960), 43.

like Ahmad Lutfi al-Sayyid (d. 1963), Taha Husayn (d. 1973), and others began as students of Abduh on the one hand, and went on to study in Europe on the other hand. For whatever the divergences in their positions, a critical mass of this early generation of Egyptian liberals were formatively shaped by insights they acquired in Europe: Taha Husayn went so far as to insist that "[i]n order to become equal partners in civilization with the Europeans, we must literally and forthrightly do everything that they do."[27] It is under these auspices, having imbibed the tenets of liberal philosophy in Europe, that liberal thinkers in Egypt attempted to forge a new vision for an Egyptian consciousness, as the basis for what became early Egyptian territorial nationalism. It is this vision, moreover, that Ibrahim is seeking to revive as a basis of democratic reform.

Given the centrality of European liberal thought to the Egyptian encounter with liberalism, moreover, it behooves us to briefly consider the experience of liberalism in Western history, in order to do full justice to the Egyptian Liberal Age it helped inspire. Again, liberalism as a political philosophy ultimately ascribed primacy to the individual against the caprices of the arbitrary exercise of power, namely from feudal authorities on the one hand and an overzealous church on the other. Early liberal thinkers thus grounded the political community they envisioned not in some placation to history, myth, or religious dogma, but instead to universal values predicated on reason, that "made certain abstract assumptions about human nature, linked them with the interests that might bring individuals together in a political community, and drew the institutional consequences."[28]

For Thomas Hobbes (d. 1679), these liberal universals were articulated through a hypothetical "state of nature" that otherwise sought to wreak havoc on the lives of individuals caught in its crosshairs. As rational actors interested in self-preservation, Hobbes maintained, individuals would willingly surrender autonomy to a powerful sovereign, which would in turn be tasked with ensuring the safety necessary for the individuals under its stewardship, such that they can properly maximize their own liberties unencumbered by the threat of the ongoing anarchy of the state of nature. The sovereign for Hobbes is depersonalized, such

---

[27] Taha Husayn, *The Future of Culture in Egypt* (Washington, DC: American Council of Learned Societies, 1954), 15, quoted in Elizabeth Suzanne Kassab, *Contemporary Arab Thought: Cultural Critique in Comparative Perspective* (New York: Columbia University Press, 2010), 42.

[28] Stephen Eric Bronner, *Reclaiming the Enlightenment: Toward a Politics of Radical Engagement* (New York: Columbia University Press, 2004), 43.

that public existence is made wholly distinct from private existence: "The state stands over and apart from the personal interests defining civil society while law becomes external to the individuals who make up the community."[29] The depersonalized state, thus, can serve as an impartial arbiter of grievances and disputes among individuals, who are all (*de jure*) equal before a liberal rule of law applied uniformly to each constituent of the political community.

The dilemma in Hobbes's vision was that it gave rise to absolutism; his understanding of sovereignty was so all-encompassing that he opposed the ability of individual liberal subjects to make claims against the state. Put another way, Hobbes's sovereign was one largely unencumbered by accountability to the individuals under its jurisdiction, so long as it continued to fulfill its perfunctory obligation to guarantee their immediate safety. John Locke (d. 1704) recalibrated the liberal community to ground citizenship not on self-preservation, but on property rights; so long as citizenship was based on property, he surmised, individuals as rational actors would largely go about their business, and through self-interest would maximize their own liberties. The state's sovereignty, then, would be circumscribed, engaging only in central administration while leaving private interests governed by civil society otherwise unhindered.

Moreover, Locke saw the sovereign as accountable to the governed, through an emphasis on constitutionalism and legislature clearly delineating equality under the law and formal recognition of reciprocity. The liberal rule of law, as envisioned by Locke, was not a tool of constraint, but one operating in the *preservation* of freedom, which "anchors the particular, protects the exercise of 'difference,' rather than serves as the justification for squashing it."[30] This concern with the protection of difference is perhaps most palpable in Locke's famous *Letter on Toleration* (1690), in which he emphasizes religious tolerance as the only prudent option available in light of sectarianism produced by the Protestant Reformation on the one hand, and the dogmatism of the Catholic Church on the other.

The liberal vision, as articulated by its key theorists such as Locke, was predicated on "the moral responsibility of the individual for his or her fate, the radical implications of the division between church and state,

---

[29] Ibid., 45.
[30] Ibid., 49.

and the insistence that the grievances of the weak and exploited demand the institutional possibility of redress."[31] That said, the blueprint for this formula was certainly recalibrated with each passing generation of liberal theorists – T. H. Green (d. 1882), in contradistinction to figures like Locke, saw a role for state intervention in the advancement of liberty, Jean-Jacques Rousseau (d. 1778) grounded citizenship not in property rights but on what he termed the "general will," to name a few tangents on which the liberal vision has traversed. But these broader commitments, to the advancement of the liberty of the individual, to an articulation of state sovereignty specifically as a means of preserving individual liberty, and to the rule of law, have continued to play a formative role in the liberal worldview. And it is precisely these commitments, as Saad Eddin Ibrahim articulates, that helped inform the Liberal Age in Egypt.

Two of Ibrahim's observations here prove especially salient. First, the Liberal Age left behind an inheritance of *ideas*, replete with "core teachings on rights, freedom, transparency, and justice." Perhaps most central to that intellectual legacy, for our purposes, was a commitment to *secularism*. Keeping in mind the centrality of the separation of religion and the state in the European liberal worldview – owing in large part to the environment of religious sectarianism in which figures like John Locke immediately found themselves – it makes perfect sense that Egyptian figures deeply informed by European liberal thought would adopt a similar attitude toward religion. Thus, relying on antecedents in European liberal philosophy, major figures of the early Liberal Age largely rejected religion as a legitimate basis of political action. Figures like Lutfi al-Sayyid were quite obstinate in this respect, explicitly seeking to delink the Egyptian nationalist movement from the Arab and Islamic intellectual heritage altogether; this militant strand of secularism in early Egyptian liberal thought ultimately coalesced in the revival of Pharaonism as the basis of Egyptian territorial nationalism – which also served as a basis of situating Egypt as a legitimate heir to Western civilization, given ancient Egypt's connections to the Hellenic world.[32]

Having said that, this rigid commitment to secularism should not be viewed as a purely uninterrupted linear development in Egyptian liberalism. Indeed, as much as figures like Lutfi al-Sayyid wholly excised

---

[31] Ibid., 51.

[32] For more on early Egyptian liberal flirtations with Pharaonism as the basis of Egyptian nationalism, see Israel Gershoni and James P. Jankowski, *Egypt, Islam, and the Arabs: The Search for Egyptian Nationhood, 1900–1930* (New York: Oxford University Press, 1986).

religion from their political project, contemporaneous Egyptian figures associated with the Liberal Age like Qasim Amin (d. 1908), Huda Sha'rawi (d. 1947), Saad Zaghlul (d. 1927), and others attempted to articulate campaigns of some kind of liberal reform, while giving at least a perfunctory acknowledgment to Egypt's Arab and Islamic heritage. Others conceived their political projects under explicitly secular auspices, to later incorporate Islamic themes (*Islamiyyat*) into their writings – most famously Muhammad Husayn Haykal (d. 1956).[33] Moreover, subsequent generations of liberals proved more ambitious than their predecessors in this respect, with liberals of the generation following 1967 having been willing to actively engage rather than cavalierly elide the Arab-Islamic heritage (*turath*): "In contrast to the earlier liberal writers, their defiant discourse sought the deconstruction of Islamic tradition and the establishment of a dynamic civic polity by focusing explicitly on the core of Muslim consciousness – the Qur'an – and transforming it from a divine and legal text into a more historical text."[34]

Suffice to say, rather than constituting a narrow linear trajectory, Egyptian liberalism's relationship with religion has evolved with each passing generation. Nonetheless, liberalism in Egypt from its early antecedents to the present has remained largely committed to some understanding of secularism – which by extension deeply informs liberal antagonism toward Islamism and the Muslim Brotherhood. To be fair, some of these fears were well founded, as liberal figures did indeed find themselves caught in Islamist crosshairs throughout modern Egyptian history – the murder of Egyptian secularist Farag Foda in 1992 by members of al-Gama'aa al-Islamiyya would be a case in point. But what is especially germane for our purposes in this discussion is that the early Liberal Age's commitments to wholly excising religion from public life continued to play a palpable

---

[33] Haykal's turn to *Islamiyyat* became the subject of considerable contention in Western historiographical debates. Most notably, Nadav Safran categorized Haykal's embrace of Islamic themes as indicative of a "crisis of orientation," whereby Egyptian liberalism was being thrown off course from its secular foundations to instead come to embrace reactionary religious proclivities. That thesis has been thoroughly problematized in subsequent generations of scholarship – and is addressed in detail in Joel Gordon's chapter in this volume, "Egypt's New Liberal Crisis." For more on the original "crisis of orientation" thesis, see Nadav Safran, *Egypt in Search of Political Community: An Analysis of the Intellectual and Political Evolution of Egypt, 1804–1952* (Cambridge, MA: Harvard University Press, 1961).

[34] Meir Hatina, "Arab Liberal Thought in Historical Perspective," in *Arab Liberal Thought After 1967: Old Dilemmas, New Perceptions*, ed. Meir Hatina and Christoph Schumann (New York: Palgrave Macmillan, 2015), 28.

role in informing the acrimonious relationship contemporary liberal figures in Egypt have tended to have with Islamists – even despite scions of the broader European liberal tradition such as Locke emphasizing the *protection* of difference through religious tolerance.

The second of Ibrahim's insights here that prove formative to our analysis is the centrality of *institutions* as part of the legacy of the Liberal Age. Much like John Locke and other European liberals who stressed constitutionalism and a transparent legislative process, Ibrahim recognizes the necessity to ground Egyptian liberalism in tangible institutional structures and processes. He refers to the Egyptian Court of Cassation, which ultimately granted him his freedom, as emblematic of the liberal tradition. That court was part of a broader attempt by early liberals to indigenize their liberal project through a palpable institutional presence, central to which is an independent liberal judiciary. Similarly, the Liberal Age witnessed the establishment of liberal political parties, most notably Lutfi al-Sayyid's Umma Party in 1907, the leadership of which went on to form the Wafd Party in 1919.

Moreover, in addition to investing in structures of the state, early liberal figures were central to the cultivation of an Egyptian civil society, through which the tensions between state and society could ultimately be self-regulating. Education, in particular, was considered central to the liberal project, not only as a means of discursive instruction but also "a vital part in teaching the civic virtues and creating the conditions in which a democratic government can exist."[35] Recognizing the potential of the Egyptian educational system as a locus by which the liberal project can permeate Egyptian society, Taha Husayn and Ahmad Lutfi al-Sayyid worked assiduously in education reform, to the extent that both men ultimately served as Ministers of Education. Education aside, the media was a central outlet for the cultivation of civil society during the Liberal Age. The Egyptian press in the late nineteenth and early twentieth centuries witnessed one of its most creative periods, with the establishment of *Al-Ahram* (1876), *al-Muqattam* (1889), *al-Muqtataf* (1884), and others. In particular, the Umma Party's newspaper *Al-Jarida*, under the leadership of Lutfi al-Sayyid, was perhaps the most formative organ for molding the first generation of early liberal thinkers, to the extent that he would be affectionately referred to as the *ustadh al-jil*, or teacher of the generation.

---

[35] Hourani, *Arabic Thought in the Liberal Age*, 336.

Additionally, liberal thought became institutionalized through think tanks and non-governmental organizations advocating liberal policy reform. The Society of National Renaissance (Jama'at al-Nahda al-Qawmiyya) – founded in part by Lutfi al-Sayyid – was a case in point, particularly through the person of Merrit Butrus Ghali (d. 1991), whose key text *The Policy of Tomorrow* formed the basis of the Society's program of liberal political and agrarian reform.[36] Moreover, the Society came to have a considerable impact on Egyptian liberal journalism; under the editorship of Zaki Abd al-Qadir, its monthly publication *al-Fusul* would serve as the clearinghouse for the next generation of prominent liberal journalists, who would later acquire fame as leading opinion makers in *Ruz al-Yusuf* – a journal that under the leadership of Ihsan Abd al-Quddus (d. 1991) "became one of the strongest forces for liberal and socialist reform in the 1950s."[37]

And this institutional legacy continued to have an impact on subsequent generations of Egyptian liberals, to the present. Indeed, it is no accident that Ibrahim Eissa began his career in the nineties at *Ruz al-Yusuf*, even decades following its establishment considered "one of the country's oldest, most prestigious papers at the time, known as a school for liberal intellectuals and artists."[38] As for the legacy of liberal think tanks and NGOs, Saad Eddin Ibrahim's Ibn Khaldun Center for Development Studies is modeled on precisely these auspices laid out by earlier generations of liberal thinkers. And with respect to education, Mohammad Abol Ghar founded his March 9th Movement for University Independence with the Liberal Age quite literally in mind, having selected the namesake precisely to coincide with the date in 1932 in which Ahmad Lutfi al-Sayyid resigned from his post as rector of the Egyptian University (since renamed Cairo University) in protest at the Wafdist Ministry of Education censorial decree to remove Taha Husayn as Dean of Arts.[39]

---

[36] Roel Meijer, *The Quest for Modernity: Secular Liberal and Left-Wing Political Thought in Egypt, 1945–1958* (New York: Routledge, 2002), 42.

[37] Ibid., 61.

[38] Afify, "Ibrahim Eissa is 'The Boss,' but at what cost?"

[39] Wael Rabi'a, "12 'aman 'ala tadshin 'haraka 9 maris majmu'at al-'aml min ajl istiqlal al-jami'at," *Al-Youm al-Sab'a*, March 9, 2015, http://www.youm7.com/story/2015/3/9/%D8%A8%D8%A7%D9%84%D8%B5%D9%88%D8%B1-12-%D8%B9%D8%A7%D9%85%D9%8B%D8%A7-%D8%B9%D9%84%D9%89-%D8%AA%D8%AF%D8%B4%D9%8A%D9%86-%D8%AD%D8%B1%D9%83%D8%A9-9-%D9%85%D8%A7%D8%B1%D8%B3-%D9%85%D8%AC%D9%85%D9%88%D8%B9%D8%A9-%D8%A7%D9%84%D8%B9%D9%85%D9%84-%D9%85%D9%86-%D8%A3%D8%AC%D9%84-%D8%A7%D8%B3/2098697#.Voz0cZOLRE7

Much like Husayn before him, who viewed the university in particular as a forum that must remain wholly independent in order to cultivate a fully autonomous intellectual community,[40] Abol Ghar's initiative was designed specifically "to defend academic freedom and to protect universities from the intervention of state security agencies, as well as academic corruption and discrimination."[41] His decision to co-found the Social Democratic Party following the 2011 revolution, moreover, is a further testament to the institutional legacy of the early Liberal Age on contemporary liberals.

Addressing the failures of the contemporary liberal project in Egypt, then, necessitates being acutely aware of both the intellectual *and* the institutional legacy of the early Liberal Age from which it derives. Put another way, addressing the contradictions of liberalism in Egypt requires that we take into account the distinctly *Egyptian* institutional, social, and intellectual context in which the liberal experiment operates. We have arranged the volume accordingly.

STRUCTURE OF THE ARGUMENT

We begin the book with Section I, which deals with the issue of liberalism and the Egyptian state. Chapter 2 by Dalia Fahmy addresses the *structural* illiberalism of Egyptian party politics, as evidenced most recently by the fecklessness of the new spate of liberal and leftist parties to emerge following 2011 as robust opposition blocs to counter the praetorian state. Mohammad Abol Ghar's Social Democratic Party, and its failure to make any meaningful electoral gains, would be a case in point of this phenomenon.

Similarly, Chapter 3 by Hesham Sallam deals with the issue of structural constraints from the perspective of socialist-leaning leftist currents in Egypt, and how the institutional legacies of the Nasser and Sadat eras have come to bear on how those movements engage with Islamist currents.

---

[40] In contradistinction to the secondary education system, for which Husayn proposed considerable direct reforms and state interventions – notably the introduction of classical languages like Latin and Greek – he viewed the university as a forum that must remain wholly independent, in order to cultivate a fully autonomous intellectual community. See Hourani, *Arabic Thought in the Liberal Age*, 337.
[41] "Mohamed Abul-Ghar," *Jadaliyya*, November 18, 2011, http://www.jadaliyya.com/pages/index/3173/mohamed-abul-ghar

State interventions during the 1960s and 70s, Sallam maintains, created an asymmetrical playing field between leftist and Islamist currents that ultimately made credible pact-making between the two highly tenuous at best; the willingness of leftist and liberal actors in endorsing the military ouster of Morsi in 2013, then, is a testament to the enduring character of that legacy. Finally, Sahar Aziz continues this thread, and closes this section, in Chapter 4 by emphasizing the structural illiberalism of the Egyptian judiciary and its role in circumventing revolutionary changes to governance following the January 25, 2011 uprising. Particularly during the last decade of Mubarak's rule, the Egyptian judiciary was increasingly disentangled from its nineteenth-century liberal roots; this deliberalization of the judiciary ultimately gave rise to a court-centered counterrevolution, which began the very day Hosni Mubarak stepped down on February 11, 2011.

Section II continues to analyze liberalism from an institutional perspective, but shifts gears to address civil society. In Chapter 5, Ann Lesch analyzes the difficulties facing the NGO community in the context of the authoritarian state's effort to monopolize the religious and moral spheres and control public space. NGOs are viewed with suspicion, along with the press, social media, universities, independent trade unions, and independent political movements. Despite the severe crackdown, courageous human rights groups seek to defend citizens' rights and press to implement constitutionally guaranteed freedoms.[42] In Chapter 6, Mohamad Elmasry addresses civil society through the prism of the media. The illiberal turn of Ibrahim Eissa, for instance, is not an entirely isolated phenomenon, but is indicative of the Egyptian media's broader failure as a truly liberal institution. Analyzing the trajectory of the Egyptian media and political discourse in the lead up to and aftermath of July 3, 2013, Elmasry argues that the Egyptian press constructed a hegemonic discourse of the Muslim Brotherhood and of then President Mohammad Morsi as not simply incompetent but as a sinister and existential threat to the wholesomeness of Egyptian society. This hysterical caricature, Elmasry submits, provided the necessarily ammunition for public support not only of the coup, but

---

[42] For more on the constant threats under which human rights NGOs in Egypt presently operate more broadly, please see the most recent report from Human Rights Watch, *Egypt: Rights Defenders at Risk of Prosecution*, HRW, March 23, 2016, https://www.hrw.org/news/2016/03/23/egypt-rights-defenders-risk-prosecution

also of the violent elimination of the Muslim Brotherhood from public and private life post-coup.

Finally, in Chapter 7, Abdel-Fattah Mady closes this section on liberalism and civil society, by investigating the role of the Egyptian student movement as a purveyor of progressive political change, from the early twentieth century to the present. Given the emphasis by liberal figures from Taha Husayn to Mohammad Abol Ghar most recently on the centrality of the role of education to disseminate liberal values – and by extension on the preservation of university independence under those auspices – it is unsurprising that university activism has played such a demonstrable role as a site of civic debate and protest. In examining university activism from its auspices to the current crackdown on student movements under the rule of Sisi, Mady concludes with implications for the future role of student activism in the preservation of civil society, and the cultivation of bona fide democratic alternatives in Egyptian political and civic life.

Now moving on from an institutional to an ideological analysis of the liberal project, Section III shifts gears by considering the place of religion, and by extension of secularism, in the liberal imagination. In Chapter 8, Khaled Abou El Fadl addresses the role of secularized intelligentsia in Egypt as a self-appointed *avant garde* tasked with leading their society toward progress and away from cultural backwardness and reactionary religious sentiment. Armed with a distinctly Western epistemological framework, the secular intelligentsia from the colonial period onward has relied excessively on the repressive apparatus of the praetorian state to maintain its privileged status in Egyptian society on the one hand, and to stave off the putative threat of Islamism on the other. Its support of the 2013 coup, Abou El Fadl argues, is yet the latest manifestation of that paradigm in action.

Building on this theme, Ahmed Abdel Meguid and Daanish Faruqi argue in Chapter 9 that Egyptian liberals, for all their claims to be diametrically opposed to the Islamist project on the basis of secular ideals, nonetheless coalesce with their very adversaries on one fundamental basis: both a distinct current of the Egyptian liberal project on the one hand, and of the Muslim Brotherhood experiment on the other hand, ground the polities they envision in an all-encompassing inviolable sovereign conception of the *state*, that becomes the sole and ultimate arbiter of the Egyptian social contract. This ideological statist posturing is paradoxical, moreover, both to liberalism's ostensible emphasis on individual liberties and personal autonomy, as well as the largely decentralized model of governance typical of medieval Islamic society. Ultimately, Abdel Meguid and Faruqi argue, the chauvinism of the Muslim Brotherhood while in office, as well as the intransigence of Egyptian liberals in giving rise to a military-led counterrevolution and the consequent abortion of the democratic experiment in Egypt, directly result from the ideological statism embedded in both political projects.

In Section IV, we end the volume with analyses of Egyptian liberals in comparative perspective in the aftermath of the events of 2013. In Chapter 10, Emran El-Badawi juxtaposes the career of famed Egyptian literary critic Gaber Asfour against that of exiled Syrian liberal academic Burhan Ghalioun, and the role both played as secular liberal intellectuals and political activists in the Arab Spring uprisings in their respective nations. In detailing Asfour's having succumbed to being coopted by the military autocracy, and Ghalioun opting for overseas mobilization as the first chair of the Syrian National Council (SNC) –only for its lack of strategy and internal fractiousness to necessitate his resignation – El-Badawi attempts to articulate the limitations of Arab liberalism, "the seeds of which were sown by their literati ancestors two centuries ago."

In Chapter 11, Joel Gordon continues with another comparative analysis, this time juxtaposing Egyptian satirist Bassem Youssef with novelist and activist Alaa al-Aswany. Attempting to situate contemporary Egyptian liberal thought into a broader historical trajectory, Gordon puts both figures in conversation with Western orientalist readings of early twentieth-century Egyptian liberalism, which described efforts by early liberals like Taha Husayn and Muhammad Husayn Haykal to incorporate religious themes and Islamic history (*Islamiyyat*) into their liberal project as indicative of an insidious "crisis of orientation"[43] – a rigid secular-religious binary that was thoroughly criticized by later generations of scholars. As evidenced by the work of Youssef and Aswany, Gordon argues for an emergence of a new "crisis of orientation," in which leading liberal voices in Egypt have seemingly embraced this very binary of secular progress versus religious reaction, while playing a major role in the divisive politics that characterized politics in the period of the January 2011 uprising and the July 2013 ouster of Mohammad Morsi. This new crisis in turn led

---

[43] See most notably Nadav Safran, *Egypt in Search of Political Community: An Analysis of the Intellectual and Political Evolution of Egypt, 1804–1952* (Cambridge: Harvard University Press, 1961).

many secular liberals, facing the alleged threat of 'Brotherhoodization' to a reactionary embrace of the *ancien régime*.

We close this section with a unique vista into the Egyptian liberal predicament, by one of its most luminary representatives.[44] Alongside Hossam Bahgat, Amr Hamzawy has the honor of having been deemed one of "the only [two] true liberals in Egypt" by Steven Cook of the Council on Foreign Relations.[45] Indeed, he has earned the distinction, as perhaps the only prominent liberal in Egypt to condemn the military ouster of Morsi and the subsequent crackdown of civil society, going so far as having "called the celebration of the military takeover 'fascism under the false pretense of democracy and liberalism.'"[46] Previously subjected to a travel ban for his outspoken criticism of the military regime, Hamzawy has since left Egypt altogether, now serving as a visiting scholar at the Center on Democracy, Development, and the Rule of Law at Stanford University.

In Chapter 12, Hamzawy diagnoses Egyptian liberals as having internalized a series of anti-democratic deceptions that in turn emboldened them to support the military incursion into the democratic process. From sequentialism, the idea that democracy requires a series of incremental prerequisites, to the nebulous notion of national necessity, to the subordination of society and citizens to the state, these anti-democratic deceptions by Egypt's liberals in turn made it feasible for the return of a military strongman to terminate Egypt's short-lived democratic experiment.

Finally, we bring the volume to a close with an equally illuminating insider account of the liberal predicament in Egypt. A professor of political science at the American University in Cairo and a staunch opponent of the July 3, 2013 military coup, Emad El-Din Shahin's role as one of Egypt's public intellectuals was tragically compromised by a politically motivated case brought against him in January 2014. Accused of espionage, of leading and offering material support to an illegal organization, and of harming national unity, among a litany of equally dubious charges,

---

[44] See, for instance, Sharif Abdel Kouddous, "A voice for democracy against Egypt's 'Fascist Buildup,'" *The Nation*, February 12, 2014, http://www.thenation.com/article/voice-democracy-against-egypts-fascist-buildup/

[45] Max Fisher, "What's the Matter with Egypt's Liberals?" *Washington Post*, August 12, 2013, https://www.washingtonpost.com/news/worldviews/wp/2013/08/12/whats-the-matter-with-egypts-liberals/

[46] David D. Kirkpatrick, "Egyptian liberals embrace the military, brooking no dissent," *New York Times*, July 15, 2013, http://www.nytimes.com/2013/07/16/world/middleeast/egypt-morsi.html?pagewanted=all&_r=1&mtrref=undefined

Shahin was tried *in absentia* and was summarily sentenced to death in May 2015. Shahin has since sought academic exile in the United States, and is presently serving as the Hasib Sabbagh Distinguished Visiting Chair of Arabic and Islamic Studies at Georgetown University.

In his conclusion, Shahin takes stock of the totality of critiques of Egyptian liberalism articulated throughout this volume, and tries to offer a series of proposals on how liberalism can overcome its present impasse. Rather than cynically dismissing Egyptian liberalism as an abject failure, he insists that Egypt *needs* a robust liberalism with long-term viability. Cultivating that viability, though, will require that liberals in Egypt reconstitute their project in a way that does sufficient justice to Egyptian social and cultural identity, and that overcomes its elitist and authoritarian proclivities. While Shahin cautions that ignoring these imperatives will ensure that liberals will continue to fail miserably in electoral politics, he ends with the optimistic reminder that resuscitating liberalism in Egypt remains within reach.

CONCLUSION: IS LIBERALISM CONTRADICTORY?

As this is a volume dedicated to exploring illiberal currents among Egyptian liberals, we must at least briefly pause to consider whether this is a phenomenon that has valence beyond Egypt proper. Which is to say, are these contradictory tendencies better ascribed to liberalism as a philosophical and political doctrine more broadly? Indeed, a fair amount of ink has been spilled on the very issue of illiberalism within the liberal paradigm – particularly as it pertains to empire. After all, liberal ideas as they emerged in the West "did not seem particularly liberal to the peoples subjugated by British, French, and American imperialism in the 18th and 19th centuries."[47] How, then, does one reconcile the fact that key liberal figures like John Stuart Mill, Alexis De Tocqueville, and others, for all their placations of individual freedoms and the liberal rule of law, were also enthusiastic supporters of the imperial projects their nations were spearheading?

Perhaps most famously, Uday Mehta's thesis proposes that this tension is not a contradiction at all, but that imperialism in fact was a

---

[47] Pankaj Mishra, "Bland fanatics," *London Review of Books*, December 3, 2015, http://www.lrb.co.uk/v37/n23/pankaj-mishra/bland-fanatics

necessary byproduct of liberal assumptions about reason and historical progress – assumptions that could not help but lead to views of non-Western milieus like India – or Egypt, as the case may be – as backward and in need of imperial stewardship to properly liberalize.[48] Others like Pankaj Mishra have gone further, arguing that "contradictions and elisions haunted the rhetoric of liberalism from the beginning," and that those contradictions go beyond the contours of the imperial project. Referring to the Cold War period, Mishra notes that many of the same Western liberals who promoted a liberal market economy and equal rights as the formula for prosperity nonetheless benefited from long-established histories of economic protectionism and pervasive racism in their own nations. A deeply illiberal anti-communism, Mishra continues, eventually reincarnated itself as neo-liberalism, replete with the economic havoc it wreaked on the Global South. These contradictions are not accidental, Mishra maintains, but are necessarily outcomes of the anachronistic assumptions of the liberal project, "derived from a sanguine 19th century philosophy of history and progress" that has no space for the non-West.[49]

This literature indeed has implications for the liberal project in Egypt. If, in fact, liberalism is doctrinally incapable of dealing with cultural difference, then its putative failure in a non-Western context like Egypt may not be altogether surprising. But to play devil's advocate, this body of literature has been met with some serious pushback. Works like Jennifer Pitts's thesis argue that, while mid-nineteenth-century liberal thinkers certainly did support the conquest of non-European peoples, this posturing was actually a *departure* from the liberal tradition as articulated by the late eighteenth-century thinkers figures such as Mill and Tocqueville saw as their intellectual ancestors.[50] Sankar Muthu goes further by articulating how an array of European political thinkers in the late eighteenth century such as Denis Diderot, Immanuel Kant, and others – themselves prominent figures in the liberal canon – attacked the very foundations of the imperial project as manifestly unjust. Committed to an understanding of human beings as necessarily diverse cultural agents, Muthu maintains, these thinkers cultivated a political project

---

[48] Uday Singh Mehta, *Liberalism and Empire: A Study in Nineteenth-Century British Liberal Thought* (Chicago: University of Chicago Press, 1999).

[49] Mishra, "Bland fanatics."

[50] Jennifer Pitts, *A Turn to Empire: The Rise of Imperial Liberalism in Britain and France* (Princeton: Princeton University Press, 2006).

that allowed non-European peoples the autonomy to order and arrange their own societal milieus.[51]

Suffice to say, against the backdrop of two radically competing appraisals, the scholarly literature gives us no clear answer as to where liberalism's track record ultimately lies. But that should not deter us, because ultimately this volume is not the appropriate forum to make a definitive ontological claim about liberalism as a political philosophy in the first place – at least with finality. Insofar as this is a study of *Egypt and the Contradictions of Liberalism*, taking liberalism to task tout court would be far too ambitious for the purposes of this exercise. That said, investigating the historiography of European liberalism does allow us to conclude comfortably that the liberal project in its outcomes was beset with contradictions, irrespective of whether or not those contradictions are inherent to the ontological claims of liberal philosophy as such. Even outside the imperial context, within the European metropole these contradictions have continued to beset the revolutionary claims of the liberal project.

After all, liberalism was once a bona fide revolutionary phenomenon, having been central to the revolutions of 1848 throughout Europe, in which liberal bourgeoisie confronted counterrevolutionary efforts by aristocratic supporters of the Restoration. Thus, liberals were key to the preservation of the values embodied in the French Revolution. But when working people sought to radicalize the demands for a democratic republic with a concomitant demand to mitigate the inequities of the market, aristocratic liberals backtracked – paradoxically enough – to support the counterrevolution: "Especially with the rise of a mass-based social democratic labor movement, which sought universal suffrage and thereby threatened private property, liberals realigned themselves with the aristocratic enemies of the original revolution and helped repress the new uprisings. Their own political power was crushed, but the market was saved." It is in this sense that, despite liberalism's revolutionary ambitions, "[b]y the second half of the nineteenth century, especially in Europe, liberalism had become the ideology of the bourgeois gentleman."[52]

Is the experience of Europe in 1848 an ominous sign of things to come in Egypt? Should the capitulation by Egyptian liberals in the aftermath of the events of July 3, 2013 be read as indicative of an abandonment by

---

[51] Sankar Muthu, *Enlightenment Against Empire* (Princeton: Princeton University Press, 2003).

[52] Bronner, *Ideas In Action*, 27.

Egyptian liberalism of its revolutionary ambitions, and its domestication into the ideology of the bourgeois Egyptian gentleman? Not necessarily. Indeed, the European experience was one of a vacillation between revolution and counterrevolution, in which the immediate aftermath of mass revolts said very little about the legacies those upheavals would ultimately leave behind. While the security state under Sisi may appear to have the upper hand in Egypt as of this writing, the story of the Egyptian revolution of 2011 remains a work in progress. Irrespective of the ground lost to the ideals of that initial uprising since the return of military rule in 2013, dissensions in Egyptian society run as deep now as, if not deeper than, before the events of 2011 – as evidenced perhaps most recently by mass protests throughout the nation following the Sisi administration's decision to grant territorial control of Tiran and Sanafir, strategically important islands off Egypt's Red Sea coast, to Saudi Arabia in April of 2016.[53] Remaining faithful to a *longue durée* approach to history, in which long-term historical structures play a more palpable role in the ebb and flow of history than individual events themselves, we can and should view the Egyptian revolution as an unfinished project that can just as easily culminate in the fulfillment of the ideals of freedom and dignity that sparked the initial protests in January of 2011 as to their abandonment.

Similarly, the story of liberalism in Egypt remains an unfinished project, one that can just as conceivably be elevated into an emancipatory political force as it could be domesticated into a desiccated relic of Egyptian elites. Which is to say, the contradictions of liberalism in Egypt are not necessarily binding, and with sufficient wherewithal from those who carry its banner the liberal project in Egypt can indeed be reconstituted to overcome its present impasse. Whether that will in fact transpire remains to be seen. But as we shall demonstrate in the pages that follow, discerning the ultimate fate of Egyptian liberalism requires taking ample stock in the specific contours of the liberal project in its *Egyptian* context – historically, institutionally, and culturally. And in so doing, we can credibly end by saying that the fate of the liberal experiment in Egypt will wholly depend on the extent to which Egyptian liberals are willing to articulate their political project in a way that does sufficient justice to the *immanent* social and cultural realities of Egyptian culture and society. If *Egypt and the Contradictions of Liberalism* is to offer only

---

[53] Jared Malsin, "The fate of two deserted islands has Egyptians taking to the streets again," *Time*, April 15, 2016, http://time.com/4296334/egypt-protests-tiran-sanafir-islands/

one formative lasting critique, it is that the contradictions of the liberal experiment in Egypt can only be overcome by realigning the project to speak to the needs of the Egyptian people in a cultural, social – and yes, religious – idiom that they find congruent.

It would thus be fitting to end this chapter with a bezel of wisdom from the late Pakistani-American intellectual activist Eqbal Ahmad, whose astute analyses of the politics of the Muslim world have proven increasingly timely with each year since his death in 1999.[54] Indeed, in his study of *Islam, Secularism, and Liberal Democracy*, Nader Hashemi relies on the same sage advice as an interpretative lens to the "Muslim political drama" as it comes to fruition: "As the late Eqbal Ahmad once observed, a primary lesson to be learned from the European experience of political modernization that is relevant to a Muslim context is that 'no significant political change occurs unless the new form is congruent with the old. It is only when a transplant is congenial to a soil that it works.'"[55] Ultimately, then, if liberalism in Egypt is to overcome its contradictions, the onus is on Egyptian liberals to reconfigure their project such that it becomes congenial to Egyptian soil. We can only hope they will take that necessary initiative.

---

[54] For more on the life and career of Eqbal Ahmad, see the magisterial recent study of his life by one of his closest friends: Stuart Schaar, *Eqbal Ahmad: Critical Outsider in a Turbulent Age* (New York: Columbia University Press, 2015).

[55] Nader Hashemi, *Islam, Secularism, and Liberal Democracy: Toward a Democratic Theory For Muslim Societies* (Oxford: Oxford University Press, 2009), 102.

SECTION I

Liberalism and the Egyptian state

2

Egypt's structural illiberalism

How a weak party system undermines participatory politics

DALIA F. FAHMY

S trong and robust political parties are key tools for ensuring
state political development. In granting a structure to political participation, its organization, and its expansion, political
parties help ensure the overall stability of a liberal democratic state.[1]
Regrettably, however, this is not the case in Egypt, where weak institutions
have considerably hampered democratic consolidation. In particular, the
Egyptian legislative assembly, as the site for the cultivation of laws regulating political party formation, has proven complicit in outright enfeebling
Egyptian political institutions rather than emboldening them. Rather
than being an outlet for civilian voices, political parties in Egypt instead
remain deeply circumscribed, and ultimately ineffectual. Put another way,
despite the key role of a multiparty system in the preservation of a liberal
democratic political order, the dysfunctional nature of party politics in
Egypt has instead promoted an *illiberal* political order, enshrined and
perpetuated at a systemic level. This chapter thus analyzes the structural
illiberalism of Egyptian politics, by paying close attention to the weakness
of the Egyptian political party system. In so doing, it will elucidate how
the failure of political mobilization in Egypt to make significant gains is

---

[1] Samuel Huntington, *Political Order and Changing Societies* (New Haven: Yale University
Press, 1968), 401.

EGYPT AND THE CONTRADICTIONS OF LIBERALISM

largely grounded in the systemic failure of party politics as a mouthpiece for the political aspirations of the Egyptian masses.

THE PARTY SYSTEM IN EGYPT

Throughout its modern history, Egypt has proven largely incapable of providing a meaningful outlet to political opposition. Since the overthrow of the monarchy in 1952 by Gamal Abdel Nasser (d. 1970) and the Free Officers Movement, the Egyptian state was ushered in as a secular nationalist *republic*. Yet despite the demands on a bona fide republican government to vest power in the governed through elected representatives, the Egyptian republic from its inception gave rise to a series of structural conditions that both undermined and circumscribed political contestation.

The first such juncture dovetailed with the rise of Nasser, and the subsequent transformation of Egypt from a monarchy to a revolutionary government. To fulfill the ambitions of the revolution he inaugurated, Nasser decided it was necessary to disband all political parties by executive decree, both to undermine the stronghold of the old elites and to eliminate any vestiges of political opposition to his movement.[2] Accordingly, in 1957 Nasser established the National Union (*Al-Ittihad al-Qawmi*, or NU), a political organization tasked with mobilizing the Egyptian masses without allowing for the creation of an opposition. Adopting a Communist party model, Nasser's NU was a hierarchical organization in which authority and political directives would be administered in a top-down fashion.[3] Through the NU, Nasser was able to consolidate both his political and institutional influence, resulting in hegemonic control of the body politic while structurally eliminating potential opposition.

In 1962, Nasser reconstituted the NU, a non-party political organization, into the Arab Socialist Union (ASU), as the country's sole political party. Established in large part as an attempt to unify the country after Egypt's short-lived political union with Syria (the United Arab Republic, or UAR) had prematurely collapsed. However, owing to its being a product of Nasser's top-down model of political hegemony, the ASU proved unable to effectively mobilize the Egyptian masses into party politics.

---

[2] Tamir Moustafa, "Law versus the state: The judicialization of politics in Egypt," *Law & Social Inquiry* 28, no. 4 (2003): 888.

[3] Ninette Fahmy, *The Politics of Egypt* (London: RoutledgeCurzon, 2002), 57.

Seeking to control the masses rather than incorporate them in the political process, the ASU could not galvanize Egyptians to meaningfully engage in participatory politics.

The second major political juncture transpired under the administration of President Anwar Sadat (d. 1981). Having been appointed general secretary of the NU under Nasser, Sadat was no doubt well vested in its successor organization the ASU by the time he assumed the presidency. However, in contradistinction to his predecessor, Sadat quickly distanced himself from the staunch socialist roots that had undergirded the ASU, embarking instead on a policy of open-door economic liberalization (al-Infitah).[4] To consolidate his own power, Sadat granted the Egyptian parliament stewardship over the organization, which carried the dual benefit of emphasizing his commitment to liberal reform, while simultaneously undermining the effectiveness of the ASU as a putative rival. The ASU subsequently gave rise to three competing political platforms – left, center, and right – which by 1978 were established as bona fide independent political parties, leading to the disbanding of the ASU.[5] Only one of these parties, however, maintained significant currency in Egyptian political life. The National Democratic Party (NDP), the party formed of the centrist wing of the ASU, emerged as disproportionately the most powerful of the three newly established political parties. Moreover, under Sadat, the NDP protected the interests of the elites who benefited from his open-door economic policy, to the detriment of the Egyptian masses that had been politically marginalized for a generation. Thus, participatory politics under Sadat remained deeply underdeveloped.

President Sadat's assassination in 1981, and his succession by President Hosni Mubarak, gave rise to the third major juncture in Egyptian party politics. Upon assuming power, Mubarak took stewardship of the NDP, but quickly removed Sadat loyalists from its apparatus – particularly those connected to rampant corruption associated with Sadat's open-door economic liberalization policy, which flooded the Egyptian market with foreign goods and opportunities for crony capitalism. Replacing them with his own clients, Mubarak went as far as promoting several Nasserites as a counterbalance against Sadat-era elites. In so doing, he was able to ensure the continuation of the NDP as an "enclave of bourgeois

---

[4] Hamied Ansari, *Egypt, the Stalled Society* (New York: State University Press of New York Press, 1986), 85.
[5] Fahmy, *The Politics of Egypt*, 61.

exclusivity."[6] Under this political juncture during the Mubarak administration, moreover, the NDP became a de facto single party in a system that was only multiparty by formality, in which the licensing of new parties became tightly controlled and circumscribed. This stymied environment of party politics continued unabated until the January 25, 2011 revolution.

This brief history of Egyptian political party structures, and their transformation across three different trajectories, demonstrates one consistency: Egyptian party politics have ultimately failed by the system's very design. From its auspices under Nasser, to its developments under Sadat and then Mubarak, the party system has repeatedly circumscribed genuine democratic participation from the Egyptian masses. Put another way, despite the purported role of political parties in institutionally cementing a liberal political order, in Egypt the party system was structurally predisposed to enshrine an illiberal body politic.

ELECTIONS IN EGYPT AND WHY THEY MATTER

Democratic theory overwhelmingly maintains that political parties are the primary fulcrum of substantive democracy.[7] Strong sustainable democracy, the preponderance of literature finds, is wholly dependent on well-functioning political parties that articulate the diverse interests of a body politic, effectively recruit representative candidates, and develop competing policy proposals that provide the electorate with robust political options.[8] In fact, according to democratic theorist Robert Dahl, political parties are central to the cementing of democratization, or democratic consolidation: under a full polyarchy – a term Dahl uses to refer to a political system characterized by rule by a small group of competing elites, themselves elected into their roles by mass participation – democratic consolidation is recognized after two consecutive elections take place.[9]

---

[6] Hamied Ansari, "Mubarak's Egypt," *Current History* (January 1985): 23, 24.

[7] Raymond Wolfinger and Steven Rosenstone, *Who Votes?* (New Haven: Yale University Press, 1980); and Samuel Huntington, *The Third Wave: Democratization in the Late Twentieth Century* (Norman: University of Oklahoma Press, 1993).

[8] Guillermo O'Donnell, "Illusions about consolidation," *Journal of Democracy* 7, no. 2 (1996): 42–51; and Juan Linz and Alfred Stepan, *Problems of Democratic Consolidation: Transition and Consolidation* (Baltimore: Johns Hopkins University Press, 1996).

[9] For more on polyarchy, see Robert A. Dahl, *Polyarchy: Participation and Opposition* (New Haven: Yale University Press, 1972).

At face value, this should bode well for Egypt, which held its first recorded parliamentary elections in November 1866, and its first multi-party elections in 1976.[10] Since then, eight parliamentary elections have been held: 1979, 1984, 1987, 1990, 1995, 2000, 2005, and most recently in 2010. Yet despite the semblance of regular and consecutive elections, Egyptian elections have proven far from truly free, fair, or competitive. And while competing political parties and groups do carry a range of ideological orientations, from secular liberals and leftist socialists to Islamists, ultimate control of the Egyptian parliament has remained firmly in the hands of the ruling NDP. Furthermore, the NDP-controlled parliament has effectively functioned as a rubber stamp to the executive branch, which is able to utilize state bureaucracy and security organs to implement its narrow political agenda.[11] Accordingly, while the preponderance of regular elections in Egypt at the surface level portends Egypt's transformation into a full polyarchy, the superficiality of those elections reveals a considerable deficit in democratic consolidation.

In fact, the deficit of bona fide democratic consolidation in Egypt speaks to an equally pressing phenomenon: democratic decay. As Levine and Crisp point out, "hard-won stability can be put in jeopardy by rapid social change, institutional rigidity, and organizational complacency."[12] And when considering the onerous constraints under which opposition parties in Egypt operate – working against the backdrop of the pendulum swing of democratic consolidation, through formal yet wholly superficial elections and institutions – that potential for democratic decay becomes altogether apparent. For these political institutions do not perform the same function in an authoritarian context as they would under a bona fide democracy. The primary aim of political institutions under an authoritarian regime is to ensure that state–society relations "can be controlled, where demands can be revealed without appearing as acts of resistance, where issues can be hammered out without undue public scrutiny, and where resulting agreements can be addressed in a legitimate forum and

---

[10] Eric Davis, *Challenging Colonialism: Bank Misr and Egyptian Industrialization, 1920–1941* (Princeton: Princeton University Press, 1983).

[11] For more on the instrumental use of such state institutions, see Mona Makram-Ebeid, "Egypt's 2000 Parliamentary Elections," *Middle East Policy* 8, no. 2 (2001): 32–43.

[12] Daniel H. Levine and Brian F. Crisp, "Venezuela: The character, crisis, and possible future of democracy," in *Democracy in Developing Countries: Latin America*, 2nd ed., ed. Larry Diamond et al. (Boulder: Lynne Rienner, 1999), 369.

publicized as such."[13] Accordingly, the function of such institutions under authoritarian regimes is not to check the authority of the executive, but is rather to control society at large by circumscribing formal avenues of participation.

In this respect, political participation in formal institutions gives rise to greater social control, through a limited space of contentious politics in a controlled environment. By their very design, political institutions are meant to encourage some degree of mass participation, yet paradoxically, such institutions in an authoritarian context aim to coopt dissenting voices by domesticating them into the establishment, by repressing them, or by haphazardly changing institutional arrangements. Why, then, would regime opponents willingly engage the formal political arena?

Typically, regime opponents in authoritarian political systems enter into politics to "inflict costs on their leaders for failing to uphold their… commitments."[14] But in the case of Egypt, there is an additional motivation for oppositional figures to enter the formal political arena: in so doing, not only can oppositional movements demand greater accountability from the regime, but they also can utilize the formal structures of the state to increase their own visibility and legitimacy to the public, and ensure their future institutional access. And in the case of the Muslim Brotherhood, as we shall see shortly, this desire for public legitimacy proves especially palpable.

Moreover, much of the literature on institutions under authoritarian regimes is rather dismissive, seeing institutions like the parliament as forums that do little more than distribute rents or as irrelevant in terms of making policy concessions.[15] When institutions are seen as insignificant, or little more than rubber stamps of the regime that stewards them, their

---

[13] Jennifer Gandhi and Adam Przeworski, "Cooperation, cooptation and rebellion under dictatorships," *Economics and Politics* 18, no. 1 (2006): 14.

[14] Jason Layall, "Pocket protests: Rhetorical coercion and the micro politics of collective action in semi-authoritarian regimes," *World Politics* 58, no. 3 (2006): 383.

[15] Leonard Binder, *Iran: Political Development in a Changing Society* (Berkeley: University of California Press, 1964); Ruth Berins Collier, *Regimes in Tropical Africa: Changing Forms of Supremacy, 1945–1975* (Berkeley: University of California Press, 1982); Aristide R. Zolberg, *One-Party Government in the Ivory Coast* (Princeton: Princeton University Press, 1969); Juan Linz and Alfred Stepan, "Opposition To and Under an Authoritarian Regime: The Case of Spain," in *Regimes and Oppositions*, ed. Robert Dahl (New Haven: Yale University Press, 1973); and Guillermo A. O'Donnell, *Modernization and Bureaucratic-Authoritarianism: Studies in South American Politics* (Berkeley: Institute of International Studies, 1979).

inner workings are largely elided. However, as the activity of the Muslim Brotherhood within state institutions has shown over the past decade, paying close attention to the inner workings of state institutions under authoritarian regimes is essential to understanding political participation under such regimes. In particular, looking at cooperation, strategies, and compromises made within institutions like the parliament highlights the conditions that may lead to future cooperation within authoritarian regimes. Thus, the parliament can emerge as a site of political contestation. It is to that question that we shall next turn.

THE PARLIAMENT AS A SITE OF CONTESTATION

Parliaments and parliamentary elections are essential not only as perfunctory components of government, as they are "essential for the formulation of national policies," but also because they constitute the very space through which national policy is ostensibly benchmarked against the national interest.[16] Maye Kassem problematizes this assumption by claiming that parliaments serve the regime in power by essentially serving as a mechanism of social control.[17] But even then, parliaments are increasingly becoming the preferred site by which political opposition groups seek to launch their challenge to the standing regime. Baaklini, Denoeux, and Springborg identify the characteristics of contentious relations between regime and opposition in Egypt thus: "The first is that access to parliament is the principal point of contention between government and opposition... [and] presidential legitimacy is largely a function of the representation of the opposition within the legislature: the fewer opposition MPs in Parliament, the lower the level of presidential legitimacy."[18]

Thus, irrespective of the structural limitations of the formal political channels in an authoritarian context, opposition movements in Egypt continue to have much at stake in the parliament as their preferred site of contestation: doing so allows them to challenge the regime on substantive

---

[16] For more on the role of such legislative bodies, see Barrington Moore, *Soviet Politics: The Dilemma of Power: The Role of Ideas in Social Change* (New York: Harper Torchbooks, 1965), 260–7.

[17] Maye Kassem, *Egyptian Politics: The Dynamics of Authoritarian Rule* (Boulder: Lynne Rienner, 2004).

[18] Abdo Baaklini, Guilain Denoeux, and Robert Springborg, eds., *Legislative Politics in the Arab World: The Resurgence of Democratic Institutions* (Boulder: Lynne Rienner, 1999), 229.

issues, as well as transform from loosely affiliated protest movements to a bona fide opposition party. Moreover, opposition movements' entry into parliamentary politics stands to have an impact at an institutional level, forcing structural change.

Until 2015, the Egyptian parliament was bicameral, consisting of the Majlis al-Sha'b ("People's Assembly," a 454-seat lower house)[19] and the Majlis al-Shura ("Consultative Council," a 264-seat upper house).[20] The members of each house are elected for a period of five years, the Majlis al-Sha'b in a central vote and the Majlis al-Shura in three electoral rounds within one term, during each of which roughly one-third is elected.[21] Constitutionally, the Majlis al-Sha'b is by far the more powerful of the two chambers. Founded in 1980, the Shura Council has limited legislative powers in contradistinction to the Majlis al-Sha'b, which maintains the final decision in passing legislation.

The Shura Council in particular remained a key site for political cooptation, often having been described as a "retirement haven for burned-out top-level bureaucrats, ministers, and politicians."[22] Consequently, in the 2010 mid-term Shura Council Elections, the ruling party won ninety percent of the seats, with only eight seats going to members of the thirteen competing parties, and none of the fourteen fielded Muslim Brotherhood candidates winning a seat.[23] Thus, the Shura Council, while an ineffective political institution, served as a symbolic victory for the regime during its successive electoral victories. Ridden with electoral corruption and cooptation, it was ultimately seen as detrimental to the viability of political parties.

On the other hand, opposition political struggles became deeply concerned with representation in the Majlis al-Sha'b. This is not altogether surprising, as the fate of political parties is intricately linked with this

---

[19] The People's Assembly has 444 elected members plus an additional 10 appointed by the President.

[20] Maye Kassem, *The Guise of Democracy: Governance in Contemporary Egypt* (Ithaca: Ithaca Press, 1999), 35–9.

[21] The total number of members in the Shura Council is 264, where the president appoints a third of them. The other two-thirds are elected every three years.

[22] Robert Springborg, *Mubarak's Egypt: Fragmentation of the Political Order* (Boulder: Westview Press, 1989), 137.

[23] Ethar Shalaby, "Egypt's Shura Council Elections start off amid violations," *The Egyptian Dialogue Institute*, http://dedi.org.eg/index.php/top-news/420-egypts-shura-council-elections-start-off-amid-violations

institution, the more powerful of the two branches of the Egyptian parliament. The Muslim Brotherhood in particular relied on this branch of parliament as its site of contestation, recognizing the potential cachet of electoral victories there – like the victory it attained during the 2005–10 parliamentary session. Even given its institutional limitations, and the difficulty of marshaling meaningful legislation that would ultimately see the light of day, Brotherhood victories in parliament – the Majlis al-Sha'b in particular – were key symbolic capital. As it developed from a social movement to an overtly political one, the Brotherhood accordingly placed great emphasis on participation in parliamentary elections.

For unlike other opposition groups, the Brotherhood had to contend with a long history of forced repression at the hands of the Egyptian state apparatus, as well as with its reputation as a deeply secretive clandestine organization; thus, public legitimacy was paramount for its future political viability. Through the popular mass support it had historically established through its vast social networks, the Brotherhood was able to utilize the parliament as precisely the site through which it could cultivate this public legitimacy. Following the ouster of Mubarak, moreover, the Brotherhood similarly regarded the parliament as the basis of its political project, but this time it sought more than public legitimacy; in a newly opened political space, the Brotherhood sought tangible political power in the post-revolutionary order.

POLITICAL PARTIES AFTER THE REVOLUTION: A LIBERAL POSSIBILITY

The January 25, 2011 Egyptian revolution, culminating in the ouster of President Hosni Mubarak, ushered in a world of new possibilities for competitive politics. For not only did the revolution put an end to Mubarak's long reign, but it also sought to resuscitate the political contestation and mass participation that had been so thoroughly repressed under Mubarak, through the introduction of robust alternative political voices. Thus, the revolution gave rise not only to institutional changes in the political apparatus, such as the new Law on Political Parties, but also forced traditional political parties – both religious and secular – to reconstitute themselves to articulate alternative political platforms.

All of these overtures to robust contentious politics were previously impossible under Mubarak's stewardship. In 2007, the Political Parties

Court rejected the legalization of twelve parties – eleven of which were considered secular – on the nebulous basis that they all offered similar political platforms, and that they failed to garner the necessary signatories required from each of Egypt's twenty-nine provinces.[24] This excessive bureaucratic burden left secular political parties, whether liberal or social- ist in ideological orientation, struggling for meaningful representation in a deeply circumscribed political environment – particularly when pitted against the increasingly hegemonic National Democratic Party, which by the Mubarak years had metastasized into Egypt's de facto single party.

Furthermore, these arbitrary constraints on political participation posited secular parties against the Muslim Brotherhood, the regime's single most organized opposition movement, to vie for popular support. Secular parties in Egypt lacked the organizational structure and social support the Brotherhood enjoyed even under political constraints. Consequently, secular parties under Mubarak – which included over a dozen registered political parties in 2006 – faced two distinct challenges: institutional constraints placed by the regime, and organizational limitations. These challenges ultimately made it painstakingly difficult for secular parties to make considerable gains in Egyptian political life: for instance, during the much lauded 2005 multiparty parliamentary elections, which resulted in the Muslim Brotherhood winning twenty percent (eighty-eight) of the contested seats, the registered secular Wafd and al-Ghad parties, and the two leftist parties of Al-Tagammu' and the Arab Nasserist parties, collectively could only secure five percent.[25]

With the 2011 revolution, this all stood to change. On March 28, 2011, the Supreme Council of the Armed Forces (SCAF) revealed the new Law on Political Parties. Exponentially more lenient and inclusive – not to mention more bureaucratically tame – than its predecessor legislation, this new law requires parties applying for registration to gather a more modest five thousand signatures, and only ten of Egypt's twenty-nine provinces need be represented. Moreover, it guaranteed that all applications for party registration will be reviewed within thirty days. This new law was seen as liberating parties from the political limbo in which they were

---

[24] Marina Ottaway and Amr Hamzawy, "Fighting Two Fronts: Secular Parties in the Arab World," in *Getting to Pluralism: Political Actors in the Arab World*, ed. Marina Ottaway and Amr Hamzawy (Washington DC: Carnegie Endowment for International Peace, 2009).
[25] Hossam Tammam, "The Muslim Brotherhood and the Egyptian regime: The test of parliamentary elections as a condition for political transition," *Arab Reform Bulletin*, 38 (April 2010).

entrenched under Mubarak. In the first few weeks following its passage, dozens of informal political parties and movements submitted applications requesting formal party status recognition – thereby suggesting that Egypt had successfully maintained a latent political vibrancy that now stood to come to full fruition on the national scene. One such party was the newly formed Egyptian Social Democratic Party (SDP), founded in part by the prominent Egyptian liberal human rights activist and political scientist Amr Hamzawy, which was comprised of hundreds of professionals and university professors.[26] Hamzawy envisioned the new party garnering the support of the Egyptian masses, both Muslim and Coptic, and being represented by prominent secular figures such as Emad Gad and Fatima Naaot, to help articulate a new vision for a post-revolutionary Egypt.

Other secular, liberal, and leftist currents in Egyptian politics followed suit. On March 31, 2011, the secular Wafd Party hosted a symposium for all Egyptian secular parties, both old and new, to join forces and establish a broad coalition in order to command greater political representation in the upcoming parliamentary elections, slated to occur in September of that year.[27] Similarly, on March 19, 2011, seventy-three members of Egypt's oldest leftist party, Al-Tagammu', walked out of the party's conference in protest, accusing its leadership of being too closely tied to Mubarak-era remnants, and calling for the formation of a new party. They in turn joined the Popular Alliance, a new coalition attempting to bring Egypt's fragmented leftist parties under a single umbrella organization independent of past political allegiances, with economic freedom and social justice as their new platform for social democracy.

Thus, in the month following the ouster of Mubarak, it appeared that for the first time since President Gamal Abdel Nasser's overthrow of the Egyptian Monarchy in 1952 that Egypt's secular parties and groups were emerging as alternative voices in the Egyptian political landscape. And while Egypt's party formation remained a work in progress and had yet to be finalized in the aftermath of revolutionary upheaval, it genuinely seemed that the newly resuscitated Egyptian leftist and secular political

---

[26] Hamzawy later resigned from the Egyptian Social Democratic Party in April 2011, in order to form the Freedom Egypt Party on May 18, 2011. For more on Amr Hamzawy, please see his contribution to this volume in Chapter 12, titled "Egyptian Liberals and their Anti-democratic Deceptions: A Contemporary Sad Narrative."

[27] Hill Evan, "Explainer: Egypt's crowded political arena," Al Jazeera, November 17, 2011, http://www.aljazeera.com/indepth/spotlight/egypt/2011/11/2011111510295463645.html

forces were embracing a new era of political contestation, which would come to fruition in the forthcoming September parliamentary elections.

Furthermore, just as the revolution ushered in a new era for leftist and secularist parties, it similarly caused a fundamental shift in Islamist political activism. More specifically, the revolution ended the reign of the Muslim Brotherhood as the sole opposition party vying for political power and representation in Egypt, and replaced it with a series of alternative voices articulating competing interpretations of a Muslim democratic platform – the political ideological position of the Brotherhood since 2005. In fact, the very first political party to gain judicial recognition in post-revolutionary Egypt was precisely modeled on such auspices. The Al-Wasat (Center) Party, founded by Abul Ela Madi and several other former members of the Muslim Brotherhood, was previously criminalized under Mubarak, only to gain formal recognition on February 19, 2011 in the early phase of the post-Mubarak era.[28] The Al-Wasat Party's political vision, moreover, was motivated as an ideological alternative to the Brotherhood, hence its emphasis on inclusion of Copts and women among its leadership. Al-Wasat Party membership proved integral to the 2004 popular uprising that led to the establishment of the Egyptian Movement for Change, or Kifaya.[29]

In the aftermath of revolutionary upheaval, the Brotherhood was caught between the dual commitments it had been vacillating between over the past decade, whether to remain engaged in politics, or to return to its roots in *da'wa* (religious outreach).[30] The latter approach involves a movement informed less by political activism than by being driven by the social sphere, aiming to foster a more pious Muslim community through preaching, social services, and integrity by example. This tension in the Brotherhood's vision had been culminating for some time, but now in the post-revolutionary context was leading the organization to rethink outright the project's broader meaning.

---

[28] "Wasat Party," *Jadaliyya*, November 18, 2011, http://www.jadaliyya.com/pages/index/3152/al-wasat-party

[29] Virginie Collombier, "Politics without parties. Political change and democracy building in Egypt before and after the revolution," *EUI Working Papers*, European University Institute, 2013, http://cadmus.eui.eu/bitstream/handle/1814/29040/MWP_2013_35_Collombier.pdf

[30] See Abdullah Al-Arian, *Answering the Call: Popular Islamic Activism in Sadat's Egypt* (New York: Oxford University Press, 2014).

Divisions within the Brotherhood, moreover, were further exacerbated by the organization's youth, whose direct participation in the
January 2011 protests not only was essential to the revolution's success,
but also gave them a hitherto unimagined political legitimacy. As a
result, the Brotherhood found itself attempting to hold on for dear
life to its rebellious activist youth, who after having earned their battle
scars during the revolution began to see their elders in Brotherhood
leadership as increasingly out of touch with Egypt's social and political
realities. As younger Islamists began to distance themselves from the
Brotherhood's overtly Islamist political identity, moving instead toward
a pluralistic framework wherein the movement's past signifies a moment
in the strategic evolution of Islamism that is now over, the Brotherhood
found itself in a key predicament – it was no longer the single voice of
political Islam in Egypt.

The movement thus had to respond accordingly. On February 23,
2011, the Muslim Brotherhood's Guidance Bureau (*Maktab al-Irshad*)
announced that it would establish a political party wholly distinct from
the movement, called the Freedom and Justice Party (FJP). The new party
would be led, moreover, by Saad Al-Katatni, former head of the Muslim
Brotherhood's parliamentary bloc from 2005 to 2010.[31] While initially
the party remained banned, due to its articulation of religion as its source
of guidance – a disqualifier for a political party from the perspective of
Egyptian constitutional law – on March 29, 2011, the party invited Coptic
Christians to join its membership. In emphasizing exclusivity, it was in
turn emphasizing that it was *not*, in fact, a party rooted in religion – and,
more specifically, that it was not an arm of the Muslim Brotherhood
as such. Accordingly, the FJP was then able to successfully register as a
political party, gaining legal status on June 6, 2011.[32]

Moreover, even within the Brotherhood, there emerged *competing*
articulations of its Islamist project, which went on to manifest themselves into bona fide political parties. On March 26, 2011, high-ranking
Brotherhood Guidance Bureau member Abdel Moneim Abul Fotouh
announced to a gathering of Brotherhood youth that he would be forming

---

[31] "Egypt's El-Katatni becomes new head of Muslim Brotherhood's FJP," *Al-Ahram Online*,
http://english.ahram.org.eg/NewsContent/1/64/56019/Egypt/Politics-/BREAKING-
Egypts-ElKatatni-becomes-new-head-of-Musl.aspx
[32] Said Shehata, "Profile: Egypt's Freedom and Justice Party," *BBC News*, November 25,
2011, http://www.bbc.com/news/world-middle-east-15899548

a more liberal Islamic party.[33] This party would still reflect the core ideals of the Muslim Brotherhood, namely piety and social justice, but it would move ideologically beyond the Muslim Brotherhood and embrace "liberal Islamism" as reflected in Turkey's Justice and Development Party (AKP). Another high-ranking Muslim Brotherhood member, Ibrahim al-Zafaarani, who is widely respected by the Brotherhood's youth, announced the establishment of the Nahda Party ("Revival Party") that aims to become a party rooted in Islam, with political pluralism and democracy as its main goals. Much like secular political forces, political Islam now gained a multitude of overlapping and competing articulations in the Egyptian political marketplace.

In the six weeks after the January 2011 revolution, then, new political ideas and values emerged, which coalesced in the establishment of new and different forms of political party articulation. In this milieu, ordinary Egyptian citizens finally gained nascent faith in the political process, and in the parliament as the primary site for political contestation and representation. Absent the structural conditions that limited such possibilities and aspirations under Nasser, Sadat, and Mubarak, participatory politics finally seemed possible, a fulfillment of the demands of the revolution. Authoritarian rule, it seemed, had finally been replaced by a nascent political landscape whose finer details were yet to be established, but was well on its way to liberal political pluralism. Regrettably, though, this would not last.

PARTICIPATORY POLITICS UNDER SCAF AND THE RISE OF THE MUSLIM BROTHERHOOD

Pending the establishment of a new civilian government, state authority post-revolution remained in the hands of the Supreme Command of the Armed Forces (SCAF). With the military in power, Egyptians seemed divided over the timing of future elections. The secularists and revolutionary coalitions wanted to postpone elections, giving them time to organize and campaign, but the Muslim Brotherhood, under the newly formed FJP, wanted elections held as quickly as possible. While the

---

[33] Shadi Hamid, "Brother President: The Islamist agenda for governing Egypt," *Brookings Institute*, August 26, 2012, http://www.brookings.edu/research/articles/2012/08/26-brother-president-hamid

Brotherhood purported to be pushing for early elections in order to quickly remove SCAF from power and return to civilian rule, many Egyptians perceived this move as an act of collusion between the Brotherhood and SCAF, whereby the Brotherhood as the largest organized political group in the country would surely win a majority of parliamentary seats – with SCAF approval. Secularist political forces, moreover, also sought to postpone parliamentary elections under the drafting of a new constitution, fearing that an Islamist-dominated parliament would give rise to an Islamist-dominated constitutional assembly responsible for drafting Egypt's post-revolutionary constitution – thus raising fears of the constitutionally mandated Islamization of Egyptian society. SCAF ultimately chose to hold the constitutional drafting period between the parliamentary and presidential elections.

Egyptian parliamentary elections are unique in that they are directly supervised by the judiciary. And given the vastness of the country on one hand, and the limited number of judges on the other, SCAF opted to hold elections over a period of four months. During that period, several smaller parties joined the Brotherhood-affiliated FJP to form the Democratic Alliance; after two rounds of elections, it became clear that the Democratic Alliance would be in the majority, winning over fifty percent of parliamentary seats.[34] In this respect, the Brotherhood made a major strategic mistake, in openly presenting itself as the largest, most organized, and most publicly visible group during the parliamentary campaigning period – followed only by the religiously conservative and hard-line Salafi Nur Party.

But why would being electorally ambitious be a strategic mistake? The reason is that this posturing is directly at odds with the Brotherhood's historical record of maintaining modest electoral objectives, contesting no more than a third of parliamentary seats. According to former Secretary General of the Brotherhood and the current interim General Guide, Mahmoud Izzat, "we are not after power, rather we want to have influence in parliament, to reflect the will of the people that elect us to those positions."[35] These more modest parliamentary gains would allow the Brotherhood to meet the minimum threshold necessary to veto any constitutional changes, while at the same time prevent it from

---

[34] "Elections Summary," *Tahrir Institute for Middle East Policy*, December 21, 2015, http://timep.org/pem/elections-summary/elections-summary/
[35] Personal interview with *Mahmoud Izzat*, Secretary General of the Ikhwan, July 11, 2008.

appearing hegemonic in its political ambitions to the Egyptian public. As Carrie Wickham explains, the Brotherhood's strategy during several decades in which it was officially barred from political participation "can be likened to the swing of a pendulum, seesawing between moments of self-assertion and moments of self-restraint," in which "its leaders continually recalibrate[ed] the terms of their engagement in an effort to expand their influence without jeopardizing the group's survival."[36] In the post-revolutionary context, though, it seemed that the Brotherhood had started to pivot more significantly toward self-assertion, to the detriment of self-restraint.

Accordingly, the post-revolutionary public perception of the Brotherhood was an organization committed to political dominance. This perception no doubt intensified after the formal declaration of the FJP as a separate political party, after which it began a protracted campaign of self-promotion. Prior to parliamentary elections, polls were placing Brotherhood FJP support at twenty to thirty percent. However, after a few short weeks of heavy campaigning, through extensive reliance on the Brotherhood's vast social networks, the country was plastered with images of candidates campaigning under the FJP banner.[37] Attempting to make sense of this barrage of FJP images – which, interestingly enough, bore little religious symbolism as such– the Egyptian public nonetheless felt it was receiving mixed messages as to who was ultimately in charge of this new political party.[38] Although the FJP had established itself as a political entity wholly separate from the Muslim Brotherhood, and maintained a separate headquarters in Cairo's Muqqatam district, its statements issued relating to the parliamentary elections were released from the Office of the Muslim Brotherhood Guidance Bureau, in the Minyal district. Thus, it was clear to the public that the FJP and the Muslim Brotherhood were part of the same entity, and that the

---

[36] Carrie Rosefsky Wickham, *The Muslim Brotherhood: Evolution of an Islamist Movement* (Princeton: Princeton University Press, 2015), 96.

[37] Amr Darrag, "Politics or piety? Why the Muslim Brotherhood engages in social service provision," in *Islamists on Islamism Today*, a series within Brookings's *Rethinking Political Islam* project, Brookings Institution, April 2016, http://www.brookings.edu/research/papers/2016/04/muslim-brotherhood-social-service-darrag

[38] Dalia Fahmy, "The rise and fall of the Muslim Brotherhood: Between opposition and power," in *Through Egyptian Eyes: The Egyptian Revolution and the Struggle for Democracy Under Three Regimes*, ed. Bessma Momani and Eid Mohamed (Indiana University Press, forthcoming).

Brotherhood Guidance Bureau was running the FJP as a political wing of its own organization.

Moreover, the Brotherhood further undermined its historical legacy of electoral minimalism, of not contesting more than thirty to forty percent of parliamentary seats – which had allowed it to successfully secure a place in Egyptian politics without being perceived by the public as a usurping power – in the run-up to parliamentary elections. The Brotherhood Guidance Bureau attempted to assuage popular concerns with announcements assuring that the Brotherhood sought participation rather than domination, with Brotherhood General Guide Muhammad al-Badie going so far as to announce both on the Brotherhood's website and in speeches during April 2011 that the Brotherhood "was from the people, with the people, and for the people," and wanted to affect change in the parliament rather than dominate it.[39] But those announcements did little to appease the public – particularly given the Brotherhood's subsequent power plays in the election process through its FJP conduit. For instance, on April 30, the FJP announced it would not contest more than forty-five to fifty percent of seats – a departure from its historical legacy of restraint, in contesting no more than thirty to forty percent of seats.[40] This announcement, particularly when coupled with the entry of the Salafi Nur Party into the competition, was perceived as threatening to undermine the loosely allied liberal coalitions.

And the Brotherhood did not stop there. Insisting that liberals were not willing to fill party lists and cooperate with them, lest they risk appearing complicit in Islamist-led coalitions,[41] the FJP by mid-October 2011 announced that it would address the deficit of sufficient candidates on certain lists by increasing the proportion of seats they were contesting to sixty percent.[42] A few days later, the FJP announced that it would field candidates in every race, contesting 100% of seats in the parliament.[43]

---

[39] "MB Chairman: We seek to participate, not dominate elections," *Ikhwanweb*, April 20, 2011, http://www.ikhwanweb.com/article.php?id=28432

[40] "Jama'atu-l-ikhwan tunafis'ala 50 percent min maqa'id al-barlaman wa'an taqdim al-hizb murashahh li-ri'asati-l-jumhuriyya amrun mahhalu-niqash," http://elmokhalestv.com/index/details/id/3124

[41] Personal interview with Abdel-Mowgoud Dardery, New York, March 11, 2016.

[42] "Al-ikhwan tunafis'ala akthar min 60 percent min maqa'id al-barlaman," http://www.nmisr.com/vb/showthread.php?t=360601

[43] "Qawa'im al-ikhwan tunafis'ala jami' al-maqa'id al-barlamaniyyah," http://www.alqabas.com.kw/node/23510

Ultimately, the FJP won 47.2% of the seats, and 24.7% went to the Salafi Nur Party, resulting in Islamist control of 72% of the parliament.[44] Suffice to say, the Brotherhood's historical policy of self-restraint in years past now gave rise to a more firm articulation of self-assertion.

Non-Islamist parties, by contrast, won 114 seats in the parliament (23.3% in total). The largest non-Islamist entity was the Wafd Party, with forty-one seats, followed by the SDP, with sixteen seats, and the Free Egyptians Party (FEP) – a new secular liberal party founded in part by Egyptian business tycoon Naguib Sawiris on April 3, 2011 – with fifteen. The SDP and the FEP, moreover, both campaigned with the leftist Al-Tagammu' as part of the Egyptian Bloc, an electoral alliance formed in August 2011 specifically as a bulwark against electoral gains by the Brotherhood. The FEP in particular was seen as the coalition's primary liberal contingent, close in content and platform to the Wafd Party, itself a remnant of Mubarak-era politics that has an extensive history in early Egyptian liberal nationalism. The SDP, by contrast, under the steward-ship of gynecology professor and social justice activist Mohammad Abol Ghar, attempted to represent a new voice in the Egyptian political land-scape, basing its platform on European-style social democratic principles. However, barring the Wafd Party, which still had strong institutional ties to the Delta, these new secular, liberal, and leftist parties were reluctant to participate in coalitions, and ultimately remained deeply weak and unorganized.

Islamists' success in the parliamentary elections was quickly met with a direct response from the ruling SCAF, which appointed a new Advisory Council populated with liberals and secularists, and heads of political parties who had not fared well in the elections. Moreover, SCAF selected Dr. Kamal al-Ganzouri, a prime minister from 1996 to 1999 under Mubarak. After initially joining the Advisory Council, the FJP withdrew its participation, seeing it as an appointed body created specifically as a counterbalance to the parliament – the truly representative body of the Egyptian people. Thus, the Brotherhood and the FJP found themselves caught between two tensions: on the one hand, they faced animus from the masses who grew increasingly suspicious at their full-throttle domination of the parliamentary elections, despite decades of electoral minimalism. And on the other hand, they faced equal pressure from a transitional

---

[44] Historically, the Brotherhood controlled 15.8% in 2000, and 22% in 2005.

authority seeking to systematically undermine any perceived political gains it stood to make as a new dominant opposition.

SCAF did not take the Brotherhood's electoral gains lightly, particularly given that it controlled both the upper and lower houses of parliament, and was now after the presidency. Accordingly, SCAF threatened to dissolve Parliament in order to check the ambitions of an increasingly powerful Brotherhood. Revolutionary groups, moreover, themselves feeling ever more insecure in the face of Brotherhood control over two branches of government, increasingly echoed this sentiment. The High Constitutional Court ultimately concurred and dissolved parliament on June 14, 2012, two days before the presidential election.[45] It was becoming clear that transition to civilian rule was simply not part of SCAF's strategic agenda.

According to Amr Hamzawy, speaking in his capacity as a former member of the upper house, "dissolving the parliament was the first real attack on democracy."[46] But in the run-up to the presidential elections, SCAF demonstrated that it was only the first of several attacks on the democratic process. On June 14, the military occupied the parliamentary building, claiming all legislative powers for itself.[47] The Ministry of Justice then reinstituted the emergency laws that had been lifted after Mubarak's fall. And on June 17, during the final round of presidential elections, SCAF issued a constitutional declaration transferring much of the powers vested in the presidency to itself, stripping the president of his role as commander-in-chief of the armed forces, and placing it instead in the hands of SCAF leader Field Marshal Mohammad Hussein Tantawi. It similarly dissolved the 100-member constitutional writing committee recently appointed by parliament, granted itself veto power over any presidential decree, and appointed one of Tantawi's assistants, another military general, as Chief of Staff to the President.[48] Ultimately,

---

[45] David Hearst and Abdel-Rahman Hussein, "Egypt's supreme court dissolves parliament and outrages Islamists," *Guardian*, June 14, 2012, http://www.theguardian.com/world/2012/jun/14/egypt-parliament-dissolved-supreme-court
[46] Public interview with Amr Hamzawy by Sarah Leah Whitson (Human Rights Watch), New York City, March 10, 2016.
[47] Matthew Weaver and Brian Whitaker, "Egypt reels from 'judicial coup,'" *Guardian*, June 15, 2012, http://www.theguardian.com/world/middle-east-live/2012/jun/15/egypt-reels-judicial-coup-live
[48] "Arab Uprisings; Morsi's Egypt," *POMEPS Briefings*, August 20, 2012, http://pomeps.org/wp-content/uploads/2012/08/POMEPS_BriefBooklet13_Egypt_Web.pdf

SCAF methodically neutered the office of the presidency, such that, upon taking up the role on June 30, 2013, newly elected Muslim Brotherhood-affiliated President Mohammad Morsi took on an office that had become a surrogate to the powers of the military apparatus.

And throughout SCAF's systematic attempts to undermine the Egyptian political process, liberal and leftist parties largely stood by and refused to intervene – despite purporting to speak on behalf of liberal values eschewing excessive government intervention, the primacy of the rule of law, and a transparent electoral process. Their complicity in the SCAF-led denuding of a liberal parliament, then, evokes serious questions of how committed liberal forces in Egypt ultimately were to liberal politics; would these groups and parties only endorse participatory politics if it conformed precisely to their vision and platform, to the detriment of all others? With tacit approval from liberals, secularists, revolutionaries, and Mubarak-era loyalists alike, the parliament remained dissolved during the entirety of Morsi's presidency, thus derailing party politics in Egypt during that entire period. The parliament would return only after those same figures returned to the streets to facilitate the military ouster of Egypt's first democratically elected civilian president on July 3, 2013.

THE 2015 PARLIAMENT: THE POLITICAL CONSOLIDATION OF AUTHORITARIAN RULE

Under General and now President Abd al-Fattah al-Sisi, the Egyptian parliament was finally reinstated, convening for the first time in three years on January 2016. However, this new parliament was summarily stripped of its dynamism. Gains made in the immediate aftermath of the January 2011 revolution had been radically scaled back, to the point that the current parliament, far from being the site of political participation, contestation, and government oversight, had degenerated into an even weaker system than under Nasser. Sisi's administration effectively neutered the political potential of the parliament through constitutional fiat. Granted, the referendum-endorsed January 2014 constitution does ensure a degree of legislative power and legislative oversight. Nonetheless, it also states that the parliament can be dissolved if it rejects the contingent of parliamentary candidates reserved by presidential appointment – a process I will explicate in more detail shortly. Similarly, it grants the President the authority to declare a state of emergency without parliamentary approval, and strips the Egyptian parliament of the authority to review appointments or budgets of key government ministries, including the Ministries of Defense, Interior, and Justice.[49]

On the electoral level, moreover, the 2014 constitution eliminated the upper house of parliament altogether, replacing it with a unicameral legislature under the stewardship of a new House of Representatives. It increased the full roster of parliament by 20% to 596 seats, and mandated that 75% of those seats be reserved for candidates without party affiliation – thereby ensuring that no single party can have a significant parliamentary majority. It further mandated that only twenty percent of parliamentary seats (120 seats) be assigned to party lists – thus assuring the marginalization of small parties.[50] Moreover, it mandated that the remaining five percent of seats (twenty-eight members) be appointed by the president himself. Ultimately, then, the post-2014 parliament by constitutional design would serve as little more than a rubber stamp of executive authority, having been systematically stripped of its functional powers.

Within this new parliamentary milieu, party politics became exponentially more circumscribed. Of the 120 seats available to party lists, Sisi himself called for the creation of a unified electoral list – which would in effect undermine the competitive nature of the electoral process.[51] In response to that call emerged the "For the Love of Egypt" coalition, a political alliance that, while denying any formal ties to Sisi or the state security apparatus, was decidedly pro-Sisi. The For the Love of Egypt bloc went on to win all 120 seats, which effectively allowed for the swift transition of Sisi's rule to now usurp full legislative power in addition to his already expansive executive powers. In the parliament currently serving in Egypt, political opposition has all but disappeared from the electoral process.

The three most significant political parties to compromise the For the Love of Egypt alliance, moreover, are especially telling: a weakened

---

[49] Beesan Kassab, "Why is Sisi afraid of the constitution and parliament," *Mada Masr*, September 15, 2015, http://www.madamasr.com/sections/politics/why-sisi-afraid-constitution-and-parliament

[50] Rania Al-Malky, "In Egypt a house of (un)representatives?" *Middle East Eye*, July 30, 2015, http://www.middleeasteye.net/fr/node/45512

[51] "Parties consider Sisi's call for a unified electoral list unfeasible," *Mada Masr*, January 14, 2015, http://www.madamasr.com/news/politics/parties-consider-sisi%E2%80%99s-call-unified-electoral-list-unfeasible

Wafd Party, the country's oldest secular liberal party and a mainstay of Mubarak-era politics; the new Nation's Future Party, founded by twenty-four-year-old anti-Brotherhood former student activist and coup supporter Mohamed Badran;[52] and the FEP, a party that, despite its aspirations as a new secular liberal voice in Egyptian politics, had at this point been largely constituted by Mubarak-era NDP loyalists. For the Love of Egypt, then, was comprised largely of the very forces that purported to offer a liberal alternative to both Mubarak-era politics on the one hand, and the Brotherhood on the other. And much as those liberal and leftist forces largely rejected participation in Brotherhood-led coalitions and party lists during the SCAF-led parliamentary period, and as much as they largely acquiesced to the SCAF-led dismantling of the parliament, the same forces ultimately became enthusiastic Sisi loyalists, thus helping give rise in the country's swift return to authoritarianism.

CONCLUSION

Since the start of electoral rule in Egypt in 1952, structural and institutional constraints have fundamentally compromised the development of a strong body politic. Liberals, leftists, and Islamists alike have been forced to carve out spaces for themselves in an increasingly tenuous environment, first under the outright elimination of party politics under Nasser, then under single-party rule under Sadat, limited party contestation under Mubarak, and the ostensible return to party elimination under Sisi. And for whatever gains made by opposition groups in Egypt under deeply circumscribed circumstances, strong and sustainable democracy remains wholly dependent on well-functioning political parties, which in turn have several functions: articulating the diverse interests of the representative population, recruiting representative candidates for direct leadership, and developing compelling policy proposals that provide the body politic with an array of choices for their political future.

In the immediate aftermath of the January 2011 revolution, it seemed that such an environment of robust party politics was finally on its way to being established. But following the dismantling of that process, first by

---

[52] Sarah El Sirgany, "The 24 year old party leader who seeks to rule Egypt," Atlantic Council, October 19, 2015, http://www.atlanticcouncil.org/blogs/menasource/the-24-year-old-party-leader-who-seeks-to-rule-egypt

SCAF and then by President Sisi, a healthy system of party politics is not merely absent, but has been rendered constitutionally impossible. Rather than the parliament being a site of contestation, it has degenerated into a site for an authoritarian regime to manipulate in order to consolidate its rule, thus rendering political contestation impossible. The demands of the January 2011 revolution can never be actualized without being grounded in strong and robust liberal political institutions. Political parties are paramount in this respect. Thus, a return to the democratic opening witnessed in 2011 will necessitate a resuscitation of party politics, and the return of parliament as a genuine site for political contestation.

3

Nasser's comrades and Sadat's brothers

Institutional legacies and the downfall of the Second Egyptian Republic[1]

HESHAM SALLAM

The coup of July 3, 2013 brought a decisive end to Egypt's brief experiment with elected civilian governance that followed the downfall of President Hosni Mubarak in February 2011. The coup paved the way to a military-sponsored authoritarian regime under the leadership of Abd al-Fattah al-Sisi, an army general who was elected president in 2014 in a ceremonial poll that failed to garner any credibility. Shortly after the coup Egypt's new rulers pledged to restore the electoral process and civilian rule. Instead, they worked swiftly to limit political space. They employed arbitrary detentions and deadly violence against their opponents, while simultaneously placing vast formal and informal restrictions on expressions of political dissent.

Early attempts to understand the downfall of the Second Egyptian Republic[2] focused largely around the events that immediately preceded

---

[1] The author would like to thank Ziad Abu-Rish, Joel Beinin, Adel Iskandar, Nancy Okail, and Ahmad Shokr for their comments on earlier versions of this essay.

[2] "The Second Egyptian Republic" is used in this essay to refer to Egypt's brief experiment with elected governance between the end of 2011 and the coup of July 2013. I use the term while acknowledging the limitations placed on elected institutions during that period and the different manifestations of continuity between the Mubarak era and the political framework that surfaced following his ouster. For example, the anti-democratic privileges of the military establishment and other entrenched bureaucratic powers remained largely intact even after Mubarak's downfall, and were not subjected to any meaningful checks from elected institutions.

the ouster of President Mohammad Morsi. One set of views attributed the end of Egypt's post-Mubarak transition to a coalition composed of entrenched bureaucratic interests that sought to protect their anti-democratic privileges from elected institutions. These include the army, the policing establishment, and the judiciary. Joining them were opponents of the Muslim Brotherhood among liberal and leftist political forces, who collaborated with and legitimized the military's ouster of Morsi. Significant within that story is the refusal of the community of so-called secular political actors to accept electoral defeat, play by the rules of political game, and recognize the legitimacy of the elected president.

An opposing perspective lays the blame on the Muslim Brotherhood-affiliated president. Morsi, the argument goes, exploited his electoral mandate to undermine the opposition by monopolizing political power and imposing a non-consensual constitutional framework. Central to this narrative is the notion that the Brotherhood was using democratic institutions to advance an anti-democratic, sectarian agenda that was progressively shifting the non-religious character of the Egyptian state and undermining civil liberties.

In sum, both perspectives present the democratic commitments of particular actors (or, more accurately, the lack thereof) as the central driving force behind the downfall of the Second Egyptian Republic. The first argues that the democratic transition fell apart because secular forces were not democrats, whereas the second view claims it was the Brotherhood that betrayed democratic values and norms. Setting aside the merits of each of the two sets of claims, they both overlook the pre-existing structural conditions that shaped the prospects for pact-making between Egypt's various political forces and the direction that post-2011 transition eventually took. The aim of this chapter is to shed light on the enduring institutional legacies that affected the configuration of power inside Egypt's contemporary political arena, and, relatedly, the fate of the Second Republic.

The chapter argues that decades-old institutional legacies have structured Egypt's political field in ways that encourage defections from pacted transitions in the present moment. Significant state interventions during the 1960s and 70s have set Islamist and leftist currents on two divergent paths of institutional development. It is in that particular divergence that one could trace the origins of the major asymmetries in the current Egyptian political arena: an organized, autonomous, electorally dominant Islamist current, versus a fragmented, state-coopted left with little electoral agility. In the context of post-Mubarak Egypt, these imbalances have limited the viability of credible pact-making between the Muslim Brotherhood and its opponents, and reinforced the conflicts that led to the failure of the transition.

The first section makes the case for conceptualizing the downfall of the Second Egyptian Republic as the failure to achieve what is known as "contingent consent" among the country's warring political forces in the aftermath of Mubarak's ouster. It also explains why the asymmetrical structure of the political field was not conducive to emergence of credible pacts between the Muslim Brotherhood and their opponents. The argument of this chapter is that state interventions during the 1960s and 70s have limited the scope of possibilities in post-Mubarak Egypt. Thus, the second section seeks to understand the ways in which these interventions have contributed to the uneven configuration of power inside the contemporary political arena. It explains the impact of relevant state policies on the divergent trajectories of institutional development of Islamist and leftist movements in Egypt.

THE FAILURE OF CONTINGENT CONSENT

The earliest literature on transitions from authoritarian rule emphasized the centrality of pacts among warring political factions as a possible mode of transitioning toward democracy. A pact is a formal or informal "agreement among a select set of actors which seeks to define...rules governing the exercise of power on the basis of mutual guarantees for the 'vital interests' of those entering into it."[3] In some contexts that could mean members of the old regime would not be prosecuted, private property would not be appropriated, traditional institutions would be preserved, and representation for particular social groups would be guaranteed.

Such pacts, as Guillermo O'Donnell and Philippe Schmitter note, often have direct bearing on formal and informal rules of electoral contestation. Pacts ensure that actors capable of impeding a transition are offered sufficient assurances that their interests would be shielded from the

---

[3] Guillermo O'Donnell and Philippe C. Schmitter, *Transitions from Authoritarian Rule: Tentative Conclusions About Uncertain Democracies* (Baltimore: Johns Hopkins University Press, 1986), 37.

uncertainties of electoral outcomes.[4] "If a peaceful transition to democracy is to be possible," writes Adam Przeworski, "the first problem to be solved is how to institutionalize uncertainty without threatening the interests of those who can still reverse this process."[5] Founding elections, therefore, provide an opportunity to institutionalize the compromises necessary for securing the buy-in of relevant political actors.

Central to whether or not these institutionalized compromises will succeed in building consensus around the democratic process is the notion of contingent consent, which is particularly relevant to parties that compete in elections. Contingent consent is the understanding that election losers will accept defeats so long as it is established that today's winners will not use their position of superiority to impede their opponents' ability to assume office in the future.[6] Thus, the challenge confronting political parties is designing rules of political competition in ways that could facilitate such an understanding.[7] These rules are necessary to sustain a viable "democratic bargain" in the long run, because in their absence losers are more likely to defect from peaceful political competition and undermine the stability of the political system from without. "Political forces comply with present defeats," writes Przeworski, "because they believe that the institutional framework that organizes the democratic competition will permit them to advance their interests in the future."[8] How do these theoretical discussions inform our understanding of the failure of Egypt's transition?

On the one hand, the Muslim Brotherhood-led parliament (and later presidency) catered to a certain degree to the interests of powerful political actors such as the military and other security agencies.[9] In fact,

---

[4] Ibid., 40–5.

[5] Adam Przeworski, "Some Problems in the Study of the Transition to Democracy," in *Transitions from Authoritarian Rule: Comparative Perspectives*, ed. Guillermo O'Donnell, Philippe C. Schmitter, and Lawrence Whitehead (Baltimore: Johns Hopkins University Press, 1986), 60.

[6] O'Donnell and Schmitter, *Transitions from Authoritarian Rule*, 59.

[7] Ibid., 60–1.

[8] Adam Przeworski, *Democracy and the Market* (New York: Cambridge University Press, 1991), 19.

[9] The one exception to that trend was the judiciary, which had a much more contentious relationship with Morsi and the Muslim Brotherhood, more generally. For a summary of political confrontations between them, see Nouran El-Behairy, "Timeline of Morsi and the Judiciary: One year in power," *Daily News Egypt*, June 29, 2013, accessed September 12, 2015, http://www.dailynewsegypt.com/2013/06/29/timeline-of-morsi-and-the-judiciary-one-year-in-power/

one could argue that much of the political framework in Egypt during that period was grounded in a pact between the military and the Muslim Brotherhood. Within that framework, the generals ceded some political space for a Muslim Brotherhood-led civilian government with the understanding that elected officials would not infringe upon the autonomy and institutional interests of the military. Thus, as the Muslim Brotherhood was scoring important electoral gains, its leaders signaled on multiple occasions that military officials would not be prosecuted for crimes they were suspected of committing during and after the January 25, 2011 uprising. The 2012 Brotherhood-supported constitution, moreover, kept intact the military's political and fiscal autonomy and other important privileges the institution long enjoyed.[10] Although the Brotherhood's stance toward the police was more ambiguous at times, talk of enacting meaningful reforms to the policing establishment had dissipated after Morsi assumed the presidency and no meaningful steps were pursued toward that end.[11]

At the same time, however, the transitional framework was far less successful in producing some sort of agreement over the rules of political competition among prominent political factions. Although the transition yielded an elected leadership and a new constitution, a large part of the political community continued to question the legitimacy of the president and the constitution that the ruling coalition endorsed. That is, the transition failed to generate contingent consent.[12]

There were promising signs of collaboration within Egypt's political community prior to the 2012 presidential elections. After the first round of voting, two candidates advanced to the runoff, namely Ahmad Shafiq, Mubarak's last prime minister who was widely viewed as the representative of the old regime, and Mohammad Morsi, a longtime Muslim Brotherhood

---

[10] See Hesham Sallam, "Obsessed with Turkish models in Egypt," *Jadaliyya*, June 30, 2013, accessed September 12, 2015, http://www.jadaliyya.com/pages/index/12517/obsessed-with-turkish-models-in-egypt/; and "Morsi past the point of no return," *Jadaliyya*, December 8, 2012, accessed September 12, 2015, http://www.jadaliyya.com/pages/index/8881/morsi-past-the-point-of-no-return/

[11] See Yezid Sayigh, *Missed Opportunity: The Politics of Police Reform in Egypt and Tunisia* (Washington, DC: Carnegie Endowment for International Peace, 2015), accessed September 12, 2015, http://carnegieendowment.org/files/missed_opportunity.pdf/

[12] The discussion that follows is informed by Hesham Sallam, "Egypt: Transition in the midst of revolution," in *Elections and Democratization in the Middle East: The Tenacious Search for Freedom, Justice, and Dignity*, ed. Mahmoud Hamad and Khalil al-Anani (New York: Palgrave Macmillan, 2014), 35–66.

leader. In an effort to ensure that elections would not bring to power remnants of the Mubarak regime, liberal and leftist groups agreed to back Morsi under the condition that, if elected, he would share power with his rivals in a national salvation government.[13] Ultimately, Morsi won the vote and was declared president, albeit only after agreeing to abide by a military-sponsored constitutional declaration that guaranteed the military's autonomy and control over national security policy.

It was not long, however, before liberal and leftist forces began clashing with the newly elected president over what they saw as a series of betrayed promises for meaningful power-sharing and national cooperation. These differences only exacerbated preexisting tensions over the work of the Constituent Assembly, the body tasked with drafting Egypt's new constitution. By virtue of the majority it secured in parliament in early 2012, the Brotherhood held the upper hand in deciding upon the composition of the Assembly.[14] As constitution writing proceeded, non-Islamist political groups accused the Brotherhood and its allies among members of the Islamist current of trying to dominate the constitution-writing process to place limits on individual rights, religious freedom, and freedom of speech.[15] Thus, defections from the Assembly began mounting that summer and by the fall of 2012 almost a third of its participants had withdrawn in protest at what they saw as the Brotherhood's domineering role in constitution drafting.

The conflict between Morsi and the opposition reached new heights in late November 2012, when the president adopted a series of controversial decisions that pushed the confrontation between the two sides into open warfare. In an attempt to preempt an alleged imminent ruling by the judiciary to dissolve the Constituent Assembly, Morsi announced a constitutional declaration that made presidential decisions immune

---

[13] Salma Shukrallah, "Once election allies, Egypt's 'Fairmont' opposition turn against Morsi," *Al-Ahram Online*, June 27, 2013, accessed September 12, 2015, http://english. ahram.org.eg/NewsContent/1/152/74485/Egypt/Morsi,-one-year-on/-Once-election-allies,-Egypts-Fairmont-opposition-.aspx/

[14] For background on the formation of the Constituent Assembly and the politics surrounding it, see International Commission of Jurists, *Egypt's New Constitution: A Flawed Process; Uncertain Outcomes* (Geneva: International Commission of Jurists, 2012), accessed September 12, 2015, http://www.refworld.org/pdfid/530ef8a34.pdf/

[15] For more on these controversies and allegations, see Lina Attalah, "The draft constitution: Some controversial stipulations," *Egypt Independent*, December 1, 2012, accessed September 12, 2015, http://www.egyptindependent.com/news/draft-constitution-some-controversial-stipulations/

from judicial review, and replaced the Mubarak-era prosecutor general. The opposition staged a series of protests and sit-ins demanding that the decrees be revoked, charging that the president was setting the stage for a return to autocracy. Morsi remained defiant, and within weeks the Constituent Assembly completed its work and sent the draft constitution to a national referendum. The constitution was passed and signed into law despite the strong objections of large swaths of the political community.

While the Muslim Brotherhood finally managed to fill the constitutional vacuum that Mubarak left behind in February 2011, the new political order it erected did not garner much support outside of the ruling coalition.[16] The National Salvation Front (NSF), a broad alliance encompassing major opposition groups and figures,[17] continued to question the legitimacy of the political system, and vowed to bring down the constitution. Efforts to bridge the differences between the president and his challengers failed, and the opposition signaled that it would boycott any prospective elections. In justifying its rejectionist stance, the NSF claimed that the Brotherhood was seeking to entrench its own power inside state institutions in order to ensure that its opponents would have no chance to make it to power or participate in governance in the future. "How can we trust talk about the integrity of the elections if the state is determined to seize power," said Sameh Ashour, spokesperson of the NSF.[18] Put simply, the opposition was not willing to recognize the authority of the president or play by the rules of the new constitution, because they believed the political system was designed to marginalize them and shut them out of political power permanently. The new political order failed to generate contingent consent.

Just as these conflicts continued to brew with no end in sight, popular calls for Morsi to step down and make way for early presidential elections began gaining momentum and became more organized.[19] Opposition

---

[16] On the disconnect between formal and contentious politics in Egypt during that period, see Sallam, "Egypt: Transition in the Midst of Revolution."

[17] For more on the NSF and its composition, see "Profile: Egypt's National Salvation Front," *BBC News*, December 10, 2012, accessed September 12, 2015, http://www.bbc.com/news/world-middle-east-20667661/

[18] *Al-Masry al-Youm*, "NSF to Boycott Parliamentary Elections," *Egypt Independent*, February 26 2013, accessed September 8, 2015, http://www.egyptindependent.com/news/nsf-boycott-parliamentary-elections/

[19] For more background on these efforts, see Adel Iskandar, "Tamarod: Egypt's revolution hones its skills," *Jadaliyya*, June 30, 2013, accessed September 12, 2015, http://www.jadaliyya.com/pages/index/12516/tamarod_egypts-revolution-hones-its-skills/

leaders and protest movements endorsed these calls, setting the stage for a series of national protests, which broke out in June 2013 demanding Morsi's resignation. Under the pretext of these protests, the military intervened on 3 July 2013 to oust Morsi in an apparent coup, announcing a new roadmap supposedly designed to reset Egypt's transition. And thus was the end of Egypt's Second Republic, and the beginning of a new authoritarian era that arguably remains in place until today.

INSTITUTIONAL LEGACIES AND THE LIMITATIONS OF AGENCY-CENTERED NARRATIVES

Indeed, it is tempting to scrutinize the events that led to the coup and consider how that outcome could have been averted. What sorts of compromises could have been made to build common ground between the Brotherhood and the opposition and break the gridlock of 2012–13? Would an alternative set of electoral laws or constitutional design have made a difference? Would the state of polarization have been the same had the Constituent Assembly's composition been more balanced?

These questions, and the line of reasoning they evoke, however, overlook the structural conditions that limited the viability of cooperation between the ruling party and the opposition. The political field inherited from the Mubarak era was structured in such a way that it made the production of contingent consent extremely difficult and defections from the democratic process more likely. Specifically, the asymmetries between the Islamist current and other non-Islamist groups created a reality in which election losers had no reason to believe that they had any chance of winning future elections through democratic means. Under such conditions, their continued compliance with the underlying political rules of the game was difficult to secure.

Contingent consent is grounded in the idea that losers will accept defeat on the assumption that they are capable of being tomorrow's winners. Yet in post-Mubarak Egypt, that proposition was simply not credible in light of the organizational inequities between the new ruling party and its opponents. In theory, political institutional design can be modified to increase the probability that electorally weaker parties would secure meaningful representation. Yet the greater the organizational disparities among parties competing for office, the more limited the available range of possible institutional arrangements that could guarantee some form of peaceful power-sharing between them. These realities became unambiguously clear as the Brotherhood dominated successive votes in 2011 and 2012 under different electoral formulas. That is to say, the perceived absence of an electorally viable alternative to the Brotherhood simply reinforced the belief that the majority coalition was here to stay, and that the democratic process had little to offer the opposition by ways of access to decision-making. There may have been normative reasons for why continuing to play by the rules of the democratic game was imperative, but the strategic case for doing so based solely on the possibility of future electoral payoffs was tenuous.

Most observers acknowledge the existence of these disparities. Many attribute them to short-term factors pertaining to the incompetence of secular parties and their unwillingness to engage constituents outside their own headquarters. Similar arguments revolve around the political immaturity of leftist protest movements that came to the surface in the wake of the January 25 revolution. "If these youth would only stop protesting and start organizing as political parties and prepare for elections," the conventional argument went, "they would have been able to pose a more credible alternative to Islamist currents." Besides proceeding on factual inaccuracies, these explanations lack any historical reference. The contemporary imbalances in the political arena did not emerge on a blank slate and cannot be reduced to the short-term failings of a particular group of individuals. Simply put, history did not begin on January 25, 2011. It is the argument of this chapter that the current asymmetries between Islamist and leftist movements must be understood as one of the long-term effects of policies that the state pursued in the 1960s and 70s. These policies set Islamist and leftist currents on two different trajectories of institutional development in ways that had significant implications for post-2011 Egyptian politics. Specifically, by contributing to the weakness of leftist currents vis-à-vis their Islamist counterparts, these policies made production of contingent consent more difficult in the contemporary moment. Indeed, this chapter focuses on leftist currents and does not cover evolution of other political players, such as liberal parties. Yet two points must be considered. First, the experience of the left, particularly as it relates to the various state-imposed constraints it faced, is symptomatic of a broader set of problems that confronted liberal groups as well. That is, the left's experience is representative of the challenges that other non-Islamist currents had to grapple with and that continue to haunt them. Second, the organizational fragility of the left is something that has weakened liberal parties in the contemporary moment to the extent that it ruled out the possibility of effective alliances with leftist groups in the face of Islamist electoral dominance.

THE ORIGINS OF THE POLITICAL FIELD

The rest of this chapter summarizes two sets of state interventions that occurred in the 1960s and 70s, and that are central to the abovementioned, contemporary imbalances between Islamist and non-Islamist political forces. These policies have set leftist and Islamist political currents on two different institutional developmental trajectories, and in ways that have affected the long-term balance of power between them.

Characterizing the left's trajectory were restrictive, repressive policies during the formative period of the 1970s, and the complete absence of autonomy from the state due to two important events. The first was state pressure during the 1960s to force major communist groups to dissolve their structures and join the ruling party. Eventually, the communists capitulated to President Gamal Abdel Nasser (r. 1954–70), terminating their political organizations. That development was a major setback to the Egyptian left in more than one respect. It injected enduring disunity within it and limited the prospects for cooperation between veteran communists and the younger generation of leftist activists during the 1970s. It also hindered the autonomy of leftist political organizations by generating a legacy of collaboration between the ruling establishment and communist leaders who had joined the Arab Socialist Union (ASU)'s secret vanguard arm. The second event was the decision of significant sectors of the communist movement to submit to regime pressure in the 1970s and participate in state-managed political contestation, mainly through Al-Tagammu' Party.[20] That decision exposed the left to chronic state intervention for decades to come and limited the possibilities for developing autonomous political organizations.

The Islamist movement that emerged at the forefront of political activism in the 1970s took on a strikingly different trajectory, largely due to what this chapter describes as "Islamist incorporation" policies. The latter denotes a set of policies that the late President Anwar Sadat (r. 1970–81) pursued to open political space toward Islamist groups with the goal of

---

[20] The party is formally known as *Al-Tagammu' Al-Watani Al-Taqadomi Al-Wahdawi* or the National Progressive Unionist Party (NPUP). The party is widely dubbed "Al-Tagammu."

undermining his leftist and Nasserist opponents. Wittingly or not, these policies provided the Muslim Brotherhood and its would-be leaders within the Islamist student movement with space to develop political organizations that were autonomous from the state and less prone to state intervention than formal political parties were. It was in that context that the aging leaders of the Brotherhood, whom Sadat released from prison, were able to join forces with a younger generation of Islamist student activists and lay the groundwork for the Brotherhood's existing political organization. There was no similar organizational umbrella that was able to accommodate and unite the dynamic leftist currents within the student movement for the reasons mentioned above; thus, the stark contemporary disparities in political organization across the Islamist-non-Islamist divide.

The subsequent sections explain the major elements of each of these two distinct developmental trajectories and how they contributed to the underlying imbalances in Egypt's political arena.

Islamist trajectory: Islamist incorporation and autonomous organization

The Brotherhood 1971: The uncertain future

The 1970s was a formative period in the history of the Muslim Brotherhood's development. One could argue that it was during that decade that the movement began to build the incredible organizational capacity it enjoyed on the eve of Mubarak's downfall in 2011. That view may be at odds with the popular belief that the Muslim Brotherhood has been organizing for over eighty-five years. Taking at face value the idea that the Brotherhood has been in operation since its establishment in 1928, many observers are inadequately attentive to the reality that the group's fate was uncertain after its virtual disappearance in the wake of the crackdown it endured during the 1950s and 60s. Instead, they assume that, after their release from Sadat's prisons in the early 1970s, the Muslim Brotherhood leaders were simply resuming the movement's pre-1952 legacy, picking up from where their predecessors had left off.

There is clear evidence, however, that this neat narrative eschews the extent to which the Brotherhood's return to political life in the 1970s was by no means inevitable. If anything, the view in 1971 suggested that all the odds were heavily stacked in favor of the movement's collapse and disintegration. After remaining in Nasser's prisons for almost two decades, the Muslim Brotherhood of the early 1970s enjoyed only a limited follow-ing with a membership that did not exceed a few hundred individuals.[21] Nasser's repression, as longtime Muslim Brotherhood member Farid Abdel-Khaleq explains, created a huge void inside the organization and led to its complete loss of contact with an entire generation.[22] Additionally, the Muslim Brotherhood was still suffering from the internal discord that followed the 1949 death of its founder Hassan al-Banna.

This is to say that the old leaders of the Muslim Brotherhood who sought to bring the movement back to the political map in 1971 were embarking upon an unusually ambitious endeavor. These leaders were inheriting a highly incoherent and factionalized organization, and not, as many assume, a well-structured group that was prepared to live up to the glorious legacy its earliest founders had left behind. How is it then that the Brotherhood was able to beat these extremely unfavorable odds and reconstitute itself successfully? Much of the answer, as this chapter explains, lies in Sadat's Islamist incorporation policies. On one level, Sadat provided the Brotherhood with much needed political space in the hopes that it could grow into a credible counterweight to his leftist opponents. Equally important, the Brotherhood reaped indirect (but important) benefits from the tacit support that the Sadat regime channeled to Islamist activists at public universities. Specifically, the Muslim Brotherhood found in the Islamist student movement a highly organized community of committed, energetic activists who had the will and capability to bring Hassan al-Banna's group back to public life. And within this partnership grew the seeds of the Muslim Brotherhood's second founding. Echoing this same conclusion is his-torian Abdullah Al-Arian's recent study on 1970s Islamist activism at Egyptian public universities. He argues that the reconstitution of the Muslim Brotherhood "could not have been achieved without the active incorporation of the Islamic student movement."[23] The next subsection explains what is it exactly about Sadat's Islamist incorporation policies that made that second revival possible.

---

[21] See testimony of former Muslim Brotherhood leader Abdel-Sattar Al-Meleegy in Abdullah A. Al-Arian, *Answering the Call: Popular Islamic Activism in Sadat's Egypt* (New York: Oxford University Press, 2014), 101.

[22] Farid Abdel-Khaleq, *Al-Ikhwan al-muslimun fi mizan al-haq* (Al-Qahirah: Dar Al-Sahwa lil-Nashr, 1987), 143–6.

[23] Al-Arian, *Answering the Call*, 148.

Sadat, de-Nasserization, and Islamist incorporation

Islamist incorporation is understood here as a deliberate effort on the part of the state to allow for the participation of Islamist groups in formal political life. Participation could take on multiple forms, including contestation of national elections or elections in state-managed professional, student, and labor associations, and participation in cabinets and legislatures. In the context of 1970s Egypt, Islamist incorporation manifested itself in various state-sponsored initiatives, as well as direct and tacit support for the public engagement of the Islamist student movement and the Muslim Brotherhood.

The context of these policies was the rising challenge to Sadat from among leftists and Nasserists in formal politics, university activism, and the labor movement. Driving that opposition was a set of de-Nasserization initiatives that Sadat undertook on the economic and foreign policies fronts.[24] Among the most controversial of them were his plans to pursue economic liberalization schemes in ways that would have limited the role that the state had taken on under Nasser as the protector of distributive justice. Fearful of the subversive potential that leftist movements posed, particularly with respect to mobilizing the losers of economic reform in opposition to the regime, Sadat pursued a number of steps to marginalize his most vocal opponents. Among them were Islamist incorporation policies. That is, Sadat sought to provide Islamist currents with greater political and cultural space, believing that they would usefully act as a counterweight to communist and Nasserist activists who opposed his policies.

These Islamist incorporation policies were crucial to the success of the Muslim Brotherhood in reconstituting itself and resurrecting its organizational structures after suffering two decades of marginalization under Nasser's rule. Two elements of Islamist incorporation were critical to the Brotherhood's reemergence as an autonomous political organization: (1) the regime's tacit and direct support to Islamist student activism at universities campuses; and (2) Sadat's support for the reintegration of the Muslim Brotherhood into public life.

---

[24] For more detailed accounts of these developments, see John Waterbury, *The Egypt of Nasser and Sadat: The Political Economy of Two Regimes* (Princeton, NJ: Princeton University Press, 1983); and Mark N. Cooper, *The Transformation of Egypt* (Baltimore: Johns Hopkins University Press, iBooks, 1982).

Islamist incorporation and university activism

The idea of promoting Islamist student activism took hold within the country's top leadership in 1972 in the wake of the intensifying opposition from Nasserist and communist students on campus.[25] Indeed, the ASU made concerted efforts during the 1970s to implant on university campuses an Islamist current that it could control and use to rein in Sadat's leftist opponents. But, in reality, the ASU was never quite able to realize this ideal vision due to a variety of practical challenges.[26] Ultimately, the regime ended up settling for an alternative set of strategies, which were rather subtle and did not afford it the same degree of control it initially envisioned. The regime began extending (from afar) a helping hand to Islamist student groups that had developed autonomously of the state. It is within this context that one could understand the emergence of *al-jama'at al-islamiyya fil jami'at,* or the Islamic Groups at the Universities (IGUs).[27]

IGUs represented by far the most significant national student movement in the 1970s. The roots of the IGUs date back to the 1970–1 academic year, when a few medical students formed a small student group

---

[25] The emergence and evolution of that policy is well documented in four critical insider accounts, namely those of Sadat senior advisor and Governor of Assiut Mohamed Othman Ismail (see Atef Abdel-Ghany, *Mohamed Othman Ismail yatadhakar: Al-Wazir alathi kalafahu Al-Sadat betakween al-jamaat al-islamiyya,* Al-Qahirah: Atef Abdel-Ghany, 2000); Sadat's advisor and friend Mahmoud Gamee ('*Arift Al-Sadat,* Al-Qahirah: Al-Maktab Al-Misri Al-Hadith, 2004); former minister of interior Hassan Abu-Basha (*Fi al-amn wal-siyasya,* Al-Qahirah: Dar Al-Hilal, 1990, accessed April 5, 2015, http://www.ikhwanwiki.com/index.php?title= والسياسة_الأمن_في), who headed domestic security services under Sadat; and Fouad Allam (*Al-Ikhwan wa ana: min al-manshiyya ila al-manassa,* Al-Qahirah: Akhbar Al-Youm, 1995), a longtime security official.

[26] See testimony of Mohamed Othman Ismail in Abdel-Ghany, *Mohamed Othman Ismail yatadhakar,* 80.

[27] The history of IGUs is detailed in the firsthand account of Abdel Moneim Abul Fotouh (*Shahid 'ala tarikh al-haraka al-islamiyya fi misr: 1970–1984,* Al-Qahirah: Dar Al-Sherouk, 2010) and Al-Sayyid Abdel-Sattar Al-Meleegy (*Tajribati Ma'a Al-Ikhwan,* Al-Qahirah: Al-Markaz Al-'Ilmsi lil-Behouth wal-Dirasat, 2009, accessed April 3, 2015, http://www.ikhwanwiki. com/index.php?title=%D8%AA%D8%AC%D8%B1%D8%A8%D8%AA%D9%8A_%D9 %85%D8%B9_%D8%A7%D9%84%D8%A5%D8%AE%D9%88%D8%A7%D9%86_% D9%85%D9%86_%D8%A7%D9%84%D8%AF%D8%B9%D9%88%D8%A9_%D8%A 5%D9%84%D9%89_%D8%A7%D9%84%D8%AA%D9%86%D8%B8%D9%8A%D9% 85_%D8%A7%D9%84%D8%B3%D8%B1%D9%8A), as well as the accounts of various Islamist student leaders, including Essam El-Erian, and Abul Ela Madi, and others. See their testimonies in Sameh Eid, *Al-Islamiyyoun yatahadatoun* (Al-Giza: Dar Hala, 2013). Also see Al-Arian, *Answering the Call.*

under the name of "The Religious Society" (*al-jami'yya al-diniyya*) at Cairo University. Among the group's leaders was Abdel Moneim Abul Fotouh, who would later become an iconic figure in the history of the Muslim Brotherhood and of student activism in Egypt. The group initially worked on a small scale with the goal of promoting religious values and ideas on campus. Eventually, the organization expanded, and, under the name of the Islamic Group (IG), won successive student union elections, and developed a national network of Islamist student groups.

By the mid-1970s, IG was now organizing regular student camps. Usually held on campus during the summer or winter breaks, these were weeks-long conventions that brought together thousands of students with the goal of promoting knowledge on subjects related to Islamic thought. Featuring speaking engagements by prominent Islamic scholars, these camps provided an effective way for recruiting new members en masse and inducting them into Islamist norms and principles. In addition, they offered Islamist student activists a rare opportunity to network and collaborate with like-minded students who belonged to other academic divisions or different universities altogether. It was in this environment that IG's model diffused to distant universities, and the Cairo University contingent was able to join forces with similar groups across the country through well-institutionalized, formal bodies.

By the fall of 1978, the control of Islamist currents over university student activism was complete. Islamists came to dominate student union elections at eight out of the twelve public universities that existed in Egypt at the time. That same year, Islamist candidates won a majority of seats in the National Student Union. The post of vice-president went to an engineering student from Al-Minya University named Abul Ela Madi, who would later assume a central role in the Muslim Brotherhood before he left to form the Al-Wasat Party in 1995.[28]

Refuting widespread claims, leaders of the IG of Cairo University insist that they never struck "deals" with the ruling party or collaborated with it in any formal capacity. "I hereby testify before God that we did not strike any deals with the regime or anyone," says Abdel Moneim Abul Fotouh, asserting that, if any such deals were actually made, he would have been privy to them.[29] At the same time, there are clear indications that the regime

---

[28] Abul Ela Madi, "Hikayati ma'a al-ikhwan wa qisat al-wasat," *Masress*, January 4, 2006, accessed April 5, 2015, http://www.masress.com/almesryoon/9998/
[29] Abul Fotouh, *Shahid 'ala tarikh al-haraka al-islamiyya fi misr*, 52.

welcomed the formation of IGUs with open arms, allowing these groups to expand and flourish as part of a broader Islamist incorporation strategy. Facing criticism from the left, Abdel-Sattar Al-Meleegy writes, "[Sadat] resorted to the well-known political game of using one political current to undermine another, giving a blind eye for the growing Islamist current in order for it to prevail at universities and replace the communist one."[30] Abul Fotouh admits that the level of freedom that Islamist currents enjoyed under Sadat was unprecedented, and would remain so under Mubarak's rule.[31]

But there was more to the regime's support for IGUs than just standing passively on the sidelines to clear the way for Islamist student activism. The state's proactive support was often apparent. For instance, members of the ruling establishment were featured prominently on the programs of Islamist student camps. And beyond the government's own endorsement of the "Islamization" of campus politics, state-appointed senior university administrators lent IGUs much support.[32] The support of university administrators and their willingness to facilitate the activities of IGUs were arguably indispensable to the success of the Islamist student movement. Both Abul Fotouh and El-Erian, who helped build the IG's network at Cairo University's Medical School, acknowledge that, before entering the student union and gaining access to the funding and resources that came with it, their group suffered extreme financial constraints.[33] Assuming control of the union, they explain, provided them with office space, as well as logistical and financial support from the university. It was only then that the same organization that could barely afford the cost of printing paper a few years earlier was now able to print books en masse and sponsor conferences and gatherings for thousands of students.

All the official activities that IG leaders report in their memoirs reveal a hefty set of costs that would have been nearly impossible to cover, without the financial backing of the university: pilgrimage trips to Saudi Arabia,[34]

---

[30] See Al-Meleegy, *Tajribati Ma'a Al-Ikhwan*. The same interpretation is apparent in Abul Fotouh's own testimony on the history of the 1970s Islamist student movement. See Abul Fotouh, *Shahid 'ala tarikh al-haraka al-islamiyya fi misr*, 54.

[31] Ibid., 57, 127.

[32] "Sufi Abu-Taleb who was the Vice-President of [Cairo] University until my graduation in 1977 never turned down any of the requests I made as the leader of the Student Union," says Abul Fotouh. Abul Fotouh, *Shahid 'ala tarikh al-haraka al-islamiyya fi misr*, 110.

[33] Ibid., 33, 41, 49; see also Essam El-Erian's testimony in Eid, *Al-Islamiyyoun yatahadatoun*, 86–7.

[34] Ibid., 103.

publishing and printing book series,[35] selling subsidized textbooks to students, sponsoring student trips to Luxor and Aswan,[36] and selling hijabs to female students as part of a veiling promotion campaign.[37] Footing the bill for all these expenses was a receptively sympathetic university administration. More significantly, the famed student camps that expanded the regional and national networks of IGUs were convened on campus under the auspices of the university, which generously provided space and meals for thousands of students for at least two weeks.[38]

The vast discretionary power that this arrangement afforded the regime vis-à-vis IGUs became unquestionably clear when Islamist currents incurred Sadat's wrath. Abul Fotouh notes that the cooperative attitude that university administrators had shown Islamist student groups for nearly a decade disappeared once their affiliates heightened their criticism of Sadat's foreign policies toward the end of the 1970s. Instead, administrators began hampering IGUs' activities by withholding funding, intensifying bureaucratic red tape and inflexibility, tightening regulation of student residences, limiting services and meals for student events, and, most painfully, cancelling student summer camps.[39]

In short, the 1970s witnessed a concerted effort on the part of the regime to promote Islamist student groups as a counterweight to Sadat's Nasserist and Marxist opponents at public universities. This policy would play a major role in supporting the coinciding efforts of Muslim Brotherhood leaders to resurrect their organization after suffering two decades of marginalization under Nasser.

Sadat, IGUs and the reemergence of the Muslim Brotherhood

Sadat's direct contribution to the Muslim Brotherhood's reemergence on the political scene was quite evident. Besides releasing them from prison, the president instructed authorities to reinstate recently released inmates

---

[35] Ibid., 97.

[36] Ibid., 85.

[37] Montasser Al-Zayat testimony in Eid, *Shahid 'ala tarikh al-haraka al-islamiyya fi misr*, 33.

[38] Abul Fotouh, *Shahid 'ala tarikh al-haraka al-islamiyya fi misr*, 46. In outlining the procedures for convening these camps, Abdel-Sattar Al-Meleegy reveals the central role that the university administration used to play in supporting such events, Al-Meleegy, *Tajribati Ma'a Al-Ikhwan*.

[39] Ibid., 111.

to their old jobs, and to relax security surveillance over their activities.[40] Additionally, Sadat permitted the Brotherhood to publish its magazine *Al-Dawa*, which offered the group an institutional base to coordinate and organize its activities. Most importantly, however, it was that open political environment that allowed the Muslim Brotherhood's aging leadership to enlist the support of the Islamist student movement and channel their dynamism and vitality into the Brotherhood. The lifeline that this younger generation of Islamist activists afforded the Brotherhood came at a moment when the movement's fate was uncertain.[41]

Within that open environment, the Muslim Brotherhood and the Islamist student movement began forging institutional ties. Shortly after his release from prison in 1974, Muslim Brother Kamal Al-Sananiri established contact with Abdel Moneim Abul Fotouh, one of the organizers of the national Islamist student movement.[42] According to Essam El-Erian, it was during that period that the core leaders of the IG started deliberating over the future of their organization, specifically whether or not they would seek to form an independent group or enter into the Muslim Brotherhood. One of the major reasons they eventually opted to join the Brotherhood, he explains, was the rapport they established with its members and preachers, whom they often hosted as speakers at their camps and lectures.[43]

Although they embraced the leadership of the Muslim Brotherhood as early as 1975, the Islamist student organizers chose to keep that affiliation under the surface for years in order to avoid raising public concerns or provoking the ruling establishment.[44] It was only in 1979 that the national leaders of the student movement began actively calling on their colleagues to join the Muslim Brotherhood formally, according to Abul Ela Madi.[45] Indeed, the extent of the government's surveillance of the Brotherhood and the Islamist student movement at that time is unknown. But there is little

---

[40] According to Abdel-Sattar Al-Meleegy, Brotherhood figures have acknowledged these gestures in various accounts. See Al-Meleegy, *Tajribati Ma'a Al-Ikhwan*. The second claim is consistent with the testimony of Fouad Allam. See Allam, *Al-Ikhwan wa ana*, 251.

[41] Al-Arian, *Answering the Call*, 140, 104, 109.

[42] Abul Fotouh, *Shahid 'ala tarikh al-haraka al-islamiyya fi misr*, 74–5.

[43] See El-Erian's testimony in Eid, *Al-Islamiyyoun yatahadatoun*, 91.

[44] See Abul Fotouh, *Shahid 'ala tarikh al-haraka al-islamiyya fi misr*, 88–9; see also El-Erian's testimony in Eid, *Al-Islamiyyoun yatahadatoun*, 97.

[45] Quoted in Abdel-Reheem Aly, *Al-Ikhwan Al-muslimun: Azmat tayyar al-tajdid* (Al-Qahirah: Markaz Al-Mahrousa, 2004), 169.

doubt that Sadat's decision to relax security interferences with Islamist currents helped keep that significant development off the regime's radar.

In granting license to *Al-Dawa* in 1976, Sadat was allowing the Brotherhood not only a voice, but also a critical institutional base, which was key to advancing the movement's reemergence on the political scene. Throughout the 1970s, *Al-Dawa's* headquarters became the de facto home base for the Brotherhood and the focal point of its organization efforts.[46] The magazine, moreover, was one of the major points of collaboration between the young student activists and the Muslim Brotherhood's older leaders. Furthermore, Abul Fotouh recalls that *Al-Dawa's* contributions played a major role in convincing him and his colleagues that joining the Muslim Brotherhood was the way to go.[47]

Besides channeling energy into *Al-Dawa*, the incorporation of the Islamist student movement into the Muslim Brotherhood afforded the group a national organizational structure capable of undertaking grassroots activism. The astounding resurgence of the Muslim Brotherhood as a coherent organization in the 1970s and 80s was primarily the product of its partnership with the vibrant Islamist student movement that grew under the auspices of Islamist incorporation policies.[48] At a time when the Brotherhood's historic figures, including Mustafa Mashhur and Al-Sananiri, were failing to bring new blood into the group, Madi explains, student organizers, such as Abul Fotouh and others, were able to recruit thousands of new members.[49] The Brotherhood's student movement generation was left in charge of the effort to bring the group back to public life, especially after Al-Sananiri's death in 1981, and Mashhur fleeing Egypt that same year. For instance, among those tasked with reconstituting the Brotherhood's networks nationwide were former student activists such as Abul Fotouh, Abdel-Sattar Al-Meleegy, and Anwar Shehata. Al-Meleegy, along with fellow recent graduates Helmy al-Gazzar and Madi, took responsibility for managing the Brotherhood's university chapters.[50]

---

[46] Al-Meleegy, *Tajribati Ma'a Al-Ikhwan.*

[47] Abul Fotouh, *Shahid 'ala tarikh al-haraka al-islamiyya fi misr*, 103.

[48] Abul Fotouh's firsthand account of the history of the Islamist movement makes this point very decisively. Ibid., 91–2.

[49] Quoted in Aly, *Al-Ikhwan Al-muslimun*, 169.

[50] See Mohamed Habib, *Dhikrayat duktur Mohamed Habib: 'an al-hayah wal-da'wa wal-siyasa wal-fikr* (Al-Qahirah: Dar Al-Sherouk, 2012), 170; Al-Meleegy, *Tajribati Ma'a Al-Ikhwan.*

Not long after their release from prison in 1982, many of these recent, young recruits began discussing how to pursue their political engagement now that their college activism came to a close with graduation. These deliberations eventually led to the Brotherhood's decision to contest elections in multiple professional syndicates, where it secured significant representation, starting with the medical doctors' and the engineers' syndicates.[51] Subsequently, members of the student movement generation, including Abul Fotouh, Mukhtar Nouh, Mohamed Abdel-Qouddous, and Badr Mohamed Badr, were tasked with coordinating the Brotherhood's engagement inside professional syndicates.[52] That community of students, including Mukhtar Nouh, Essam El-Erian, and Mohieddin Issa, also played a visible role in parliament after the Muslim Brotherhood became the largest opposition bloc in the legislature in 1987. Although many of these figures would later suffer marginalization, their central role in writing a new history for the Muslim Brotherhood was unmistakable. Equally significant, for the purpose of this chapter, is the role of Islamist incorporation policies in making this possible by supporting the emergence of the Islamist student movement, which became the organizational backbone of the Muslim Brotherhood.

One distinctive aspect in how the Brotherhood reconstituted itself during that formative period is the organizational autonomy it enjoyed vis-à-vis the state. State policies supported the resurrection of the Brotherhood, yet without coopting the movement into state bodies, as was the case with the communist movement and its successors. Indeed, regime figures tried to establish Islamist groups on university campuses as part of a secret ASU arm. Yet they failed to do so, and instead had to settle for supporting the more independent IGUs, which later played an important role in the reconstitution of the Muslim Brotherhood. Additionally, Sadat offered to allow Brotherhood leaders into the ruling party, and in another instance, an opportunity to obtain legal status. Aware of the potential state interferences associated with operating under state regulation, Brotherhood leaders turned down these offers.[53]

---

[51] See Abul Fotouh's comments in Aly, *Al-Ikhwan Al-muslimun*, 163.

[52] Al-Meleegy, *Tajribati Ma'a Al-Ikhwan*.

[53] See the testimony of Saleh Abu-Ruqayiq in Hassanein Koroum, *Al-taharukat al-siyasiyya lil-ikhwan al-muslimin 1971–1987* (Al-Qahirah: Al-Markaz Al-Arabi Al-Dawli Lil-I'lam, 2012), 31–9. Late Muslim Brotherhood Guide Mamoun Al-Houdaibi admits in a 1998 interview that Sadat did in fact make that offer, but that this would have given the government much discretion in intervening in its internal affairs. See Adel Al-Ansary,

In contrast, the Brotherhood's leftist counterparts, as the next section explains, developed under the guardianship of the state, which ruled out the emergence of a strong, autonomous political organization on the left side of the political spectrum.[54]

Leftist trajectory: A history of capitulations

Communist activism on the eve of Nasser's state socialism

Communist activism has a long history in Egypt. Documented presence of communist cells dates back to at least 1894. More formal structures came into being in 1921 with the establishment of the Egyptian Socialist Party, which was later renamed the Egyptian Communist Party. The group, however, suffered from state repression until it was virtually nonexistent by the late 1920s.[55] The 1930s and 40s witnessed the reemergence of communist organizations, though they suffered from chronic fragmentation. Some promising signs surfaced in 1947 when two of the most influential communist groups joined forces to become Hadeto, which would comprise almost ninety percent of the entire communist movement.[56] Yet, within its first year, disunity began haunting the group, leading to defections and splintering.[57]

In spite of unfavorable conditions, including state-led repression, the tide of communist activism appeared unstoppable. Hadeto's influence was on the rise again, as its membership doubled between 1947 and 1952.[58] The group also enjoyed some presence inside the military and, more

---

Al-Ikhwan al-muslimun: 60 qadiyya sakhina (Al-Qahirah: Dar Al-Tawzee wal-Nashr Al-Islamiyya, 1998), 42.

[54] Beinin argues the absence of independent political groups within the Egyptian left was detrimental to the ability of the workers movement to push the post-2011 transition toward a more democratic outcome comparable to that of the Tunisian transition. Joel Beinin, *Workers and Thieves: Labor Movements and Popular Uprisings in Tunisia and Egypt* (Stanford, CA: Stanford University Press, ebook, 2015), 334–6.

[55] Tareq Y. Ismael and Rifaat El-Sa'id, *The Communist Movement in Egypt, 1920–1988* (Syracuse: Syracuse University Press, 1990), 12–31.

[56] Rami Ginat, *A History of Egyptian Communism: Jews and Their Compatriots in Quest of Revolution* (Boulder: Lynne Rienner Publishers, 2011), 277–83.

[57] Ismael and El-Sa'id, *The Communist Movement in Egypt*, 67.

[58] Ismael and El-Sa'id, *The Communist Movement in Egypt*, estimate membership at three thousand in 1952, whereas Curiel reports one thousand and four hundred members in 1947. Quoted in Ginat, *A History of Egyptian Communism*, 279.

significantly, among the Free Officers Movement, and thus it was initially supportive of the July 23, 1952 revolution. It was not long, however, before relations between the communists and the country's new military leaders soured in large part due to state repression of labor activism.

On January 8, 1958, the three major communist groupings in the country, including Hadeto, announced they would rally under a single organization known as the Communist Party of Egypt (CPE). That unity was once again short-lived due to disagreements over the relative share of power between the three factions and persistent differences regarding how to manage relations with Nasser. Eventually, the group split in January 1959 when the Hadeto contingent announced it would form its own party.[59] The split between these groups coincided with a crackdown against communist organizations, which left thousands of activists in prison from 1959 until the mid-1960s.[60]

State socialism and the cooptation of the communist movement

Nasser later reversed the regime's repressive orientation toward the communist movement during the first half of the 1960s, releasing them from prisons and coopting them into the ruling establishment. Central to that change of heart was Egypt's turn to "state socialism" during that same period. On the political side, the shift was associated with an effort to confront and balance against a variety of bureaucratic and private interests that managed to maintain pockets of influence inside the state apparatus despite the 1952 revolution. Toward that end, Nasser formed the ASU's "Vanguard Organization" (VO), which was designed to keep in check opportunistic and subversive forces inside the state apparatus. The

---

[59] Ibid., 109–21.

[60] Paving the way to that wave of repression was Nasser's suspicious attitude toward communist activists due to their support for Iraq's President Abdul-Kareem Qassem, who refused to accede to Egypt's leadership and join the United Arab Republic (UAR). That communists in both Syria and Iraq resisted the UAR idea only made Nasser more dubious of their Egyptian counterparts. The beginning of the end for the CPE, however, was turning down Nasser's request to instruct members to join the ruling party, after which a wide series of arrests followed, making the Egyptian communist movement virtually disappear for years. See Joel Beinin, *Was the Red Flag Flying There?: Marxist Politics and the Arab-Israeli Conflict in Egypt and Israel, 1948–1965* (Berkeley: University of California Press, 1990), 205–7.

VO was also one of the main instruments through which the president sought to coopt senior communist leaders.

The establishment of the VO came about in late 1963,[61] when Nasser summoned to his home a number of political leaders and advisors to devise a strategy for building a secret organization inside the ruling party.[62] Also conceived within that meeting was the beginning of Nasser's efforts to coopt members of the communist movement into the ruling party and the state apparatus. Informing that move was a desire to inject into the VO individuals who displayed both revolutionary purity and a commitment to the socialist transformation.[63] Unsurprisingly, therefore, the earliest VO cells featured a variety of communist activists.[64]

By the spring of 1964, months after the launching of the VO, all communists that were detained in 1959 had been released from prison. Meanwhile, Nasser ordered senior officials to facilitate the work of the communist contingent inside the VO, which reached 250 members within a short period of time.[65] Certainly, the communists were by no means the dominant force inside the VO, but their presence was quite pronounced, especially during its formative stages.[66]

The dissolution of the communist parties

The rapprochement between the communists and Nasser, however, came at a heavy price, one that proved to be a major setback for the independence of leftist political activism in the long run. As a condition for their reintegration into political life and their entry into the ruling party, Nasser

---

[61] The details of that discussion were conveyed in two different independent firsthand accounts, namely those of Nasser's aide Sami Sharaf (*Sanawat wa ayyam ma'a Gamal Abdel Nasser, al-juzu al-awwal*, Al-Qahirah: Al-Firsan lil-Nashr, 2004); and Ahmad Fouad in Ahmed Hamroush, *Shehoud thawrat youlyo* (Al-Qahirah: Maktabet Madbouly, 1984).

[62] Sami Sharaf, *Sanawat wa ayyam ma'a Gamal Abdel Nasser, al-juzu al-thani* (Al-Qahirah: Maktabet Madbouly, 2005), 169; Ahmed Hamroush, *Thawrat 23 youlyo* (Al-Qahirah: Al-hay'aa al-'amah lil-kitab, 1992), 611.

[63] Ibid., 611.

[64] Sami Sharaf, "Abdel Nasser wal-tanzim al-siyasi," in *Sanawat wa ayyam ma'a Gamal Abdel Nasser, al-juzu al-thani* (undated document), accessed April 15, 2015, http://hakaek-misr.com/yahiaalshaer.com/SAMY/Book-2-POLORG-XX.html/

[65] Hamroush, *Thawrat 23 youlyo*, 614.

[66] Hamada Hosni, *Abdelnaser wal-tanzeem al-talee'i al-serri 1971–1963* (Al-Qahirah: Maktabet Beirouth, 2007), 68.

demanded that communist leaders dissolve their organizational structures. In spite of internal resistance, the CPE decided to comply and dissolved itself in early 1965. The other Communist Party of Egypt, which included the Hadeto faction, had dissolved itself a month earlier.[67]

There is wide consensus that communist groups' self-dissolution in 1965 was a huge setback for the long-term development of leftist political organizations in Egypt. The wounds of that controversial measure continued to haunt leftist political groups for decades and arguably until this day.[68] In the 1970s, it hampered the ability of veteran communist leaders to recruit into their political organizations the younger generation of leftist activists that emerged on college campuses in the wake of Sadat's de-Nasserization initiatives. In its 1981 program, the Egyptian Communist Party, which was reconstituted in 1975, admits to the disastrous consequences of the 1965 dissolution, recognizing the chasm it created between older and younger generations inside the communist movement.[69] It is quite telling that during the 1970s many younger activists dismissed the newly formed Al-Tagammu' and refused to join the party on the grounds that they deemed its cofounders guilty for dissolving the communist parties in 1965.[70]

Beyond the internal discord it introduced inside the Egyptian left, the dissolution of the two communist parties in 1965 brought a conclusive end to the organizational independence of the communist movement from the state. It turned a once promising political movement into, at best, a subordinate partner inside the ruling establishment, or, at worst, a group of underworked bureaucrats.[71]

A limited number of old guard communists, along with some newer cadres of leftist activists, tried to resist the dissolution decision and maintained underground organizations. Some of them showed some promising potential and succeeded in building a presence within the

---

[67] For a more detailed account of that history and the factors behind the dissolution decision, see Beinin, *Was the Red Flag Flying There?*; and Ismael and El-Sa'id, *The Communist Movement in Egypt*.

[68] See Revolutionary Socialists' 2006 vision for change, which references those decisions. Revolutionary Socialists, *Al-Ishtirakiyya allati nudaf'i 'anha* (Al-Qahirah: Markaz Al-Dirasat Al-Ishtirakiyya, 2006), 35.

[69] Quoted in Ismael and El-Sa'id, *The Communist Movement in Egypt*, 140.

[70] See Rifaat Al-Said, *Mujarad dhikrayat al-juzuu al-taleth* (Demashq: Dar Al-Mada, 2000), 42.

[71] See Hamroush, *Thawrat 23 youlyo*, 615.

student movement during the 1970s. Yet, in contrast with their Islamist counterparts, none of the groups was ultimately able to channel their efforts into enduring political organizations due to successive waves of state repression during the 1970s and internal splits.[72]

On the other hand, those who accepted the dissolution decision and made their peace with the Nasserist regime found a place inside the ruling establishment through the ASU and its VO, as well as state media and cultural institutions. The communists agreed to join the ruling party on the assumption that they would get to play a prominent role in leadership circles and advance their agendas from positions of influence. Later on, well after dissolving their organizations and joining the ASU, the communists realized the political leadership was determined to keep them in subordination at all times and shut them out of positions of influence.

Indeed, Marxist perspectives became more pronounced inside state media institutions. Nonetheless, the representation of Marxist figures in positions of leadership in state media and other state bodies remained rather limited.[73] The situation was no different inside the ASU. Notwithstanding the regime's initial interest in recruiting the support of the communists inside the VO, at no point were they granted influential posts inside the ASU.[74] These trends collectively underscore the limited role that Nasser envisioned for the affiliates of the communist movement. That is, he wanted to employ them as an instrument of control in the service of the state in containing the influence of rival bureaucratic powers and private capital, but without giving the radical left or the social classes it sought to represent a real shot at sharing power.[75]

---

[72] For more on these organizations, see Ismael and El-Sa'id, *The Communist Movement in Egypt*, 127–50; Rifaat Al-Said, *Al-Tayyarat al-siyasiyya fi misr, ru'ya naqdiyya: Al-Markeseyoun, al-ikhwan, al-nasiryoun, al-tagammu'* (Al-Qahirah: Al-hay'aa al-'amah lil-kitab, 2002), 83–5; Al-Ahram Center, *Al-Taqrir Al-Istratiji Al-'Arabi 1987* (Al-Qahirah: Markaz Al-Dirasat Al-Siyasiya wal-istratijiyya, 1987), 371–7.

[73] See Sharaf, *Sanawat wa ayyam ma'a Gamal Abdel Nasser, al-juzu al-thani*, 389–90; Sherif Younis, *Nidaa' Al-Sha'b: Tarikh naqdi lil-'idiolojiyya al-nasiriyya* (Al-Qahirah: Dar Al-Sherouk, 2012), 580.

[74] Hamroush, *Thawrat 23 youlyo*, 627; Ismael and El-Sa'id, *The Communist Movement in Egypt*, 128.

[75] Hamroush himself cites evidence in support of that argument. See Hamroush, *Thawrat 23 youlyo*, 621–2.

The Egyptian left and the legacy of the VO

Although the VO was officially terminated in the wake of Sadat's infamous showdown with the "centers of power," the legacy of the VO's network continued to live on well into the Mubarak era. Not only did the VO's cadre come to control the ruling NDP throughout much of the 1980s and 90s, but it also exerted much influence inside opposition groups, including the socialist Al-Tagammu'. The old VO networks that once tied NDP personnel and opposition leaders offered the regime an additional channel for pressuring opposition parties into compliance. Much like most of the opposition parties that emerged under Mubarak, Al-Tagammu' exhibited the pathologies of association with the former VO, given that its leaders were once part of the VO culture of cooperation with the ruling party and security agencies. Specifically, many of Al-Tagammu''s founding and long-standing leaders were tied to the VO at one point or another.[76] Practically speaking, these individuals were tasked with submitting secret reports to officials about activities they deemed subversive, especially at their site of employment. In more cynical terms, they served as spies for the ASU.[77] That legacy of covert collaboration with the ruling party would haunt Al-Tagammu' during the 1980s and would facilitate the process by which the regime managed to coopt the party and temper its oppositionist orientations.[78]

Al-Tagammu' and the second capitulation: The prison legality

A second major development that further hindered the efforts of Egyptian leftists to build independent political organizations pertained to the formation of the Al-Tagammu' Party in the mid-1970s. The context for Al-Tagammu''s formation was a set of reforms that Sadat pursued in the 1970s with a view to contain political actors capable of exploiting the grievances of organized labor to mobilize opposition against the regime.

---

[76] Hosni, *Abdelnaser wal-tanzeem al-talee'i al-serri 1971–1963*, 52–7; Hamroush, *Shehoud thawrat youlyo*, 22; Sharaf, "Abdel Nasser wal-tanzim al-siyasi"; Ismael and El-Sa'id, *The Communist Movement in Egypt*, 123.

[77] See Hazem Kandil, *Soldiers, Spies, and Statesmen: Egypt's Road to Revolt* (London: Verso, 2012), 59–60; Hamroush, *Thawrat 23 youlyo*, 629, 631.

[78] For a detailed firsthand account of that history, see Hussein Abd al-Raziq, *Al-Ahaly: Sahifa taht al-hisar* (Al-Qahirah: Dar Al-'Alam Al-Thaleth, 1995).

The obvious contenders for such a role were those whom the president had just demoted from the ruling coalition, notably Nasserists, along with a host of communist groups that saw the political decline of the ASU and state socialism as an opportunity to reconstitute their networks. Sadat had hoped that those forces could somehow be coopted and kept in check through the left *minbar* (platform) of the ASU, which would later become Al-Tagammu' Party.[79]

The diverse communities of leftists that formed Al-Tagammu' at Sadat's invitation were certainly successful in carving out valuable space for the progressive left within the emergent political arena. Opponents of Sadat's political and economic reforms now had a clear, recognizable home base at Al-Tagammu', even if many relevant activists were still dubious about the credibility of the organization. At the same time, by assuming the role of a formal opposition, the founders of Al-Tagammu' were in effect accepting a number of institutional constraints that proved highly crippling in the long run. These institutional hindrances serve as a useful contrast to the wide space that the state granted Islamist political currents during that same period. These seemingly benign disparities would have long-lasting implications for the future balance of power between the Muslim Brotherhood and leftist currents.

Just like any other licensed political party, the founders of Al-Tagammu' ceded a great deal of autonomy to the state by agreeing to operate under a highly unfavorable legal framework, particularly Law 40 of 1977, famously known as the "Political Parties Law." The law effectively gave the state a blank check to interfere in the affairs of opposition parties through a variety of formal and informal methods.

For example, the law mandated that each party report all of its financial activities and donations to the Central Auditing Agency, which in turn was obligated to report them to the state-controlled Political Parties Committee (PPC) each year. In effect, that allowed the regime to monitor the financial activities of their rivals, and to intimidate opposition party financiers through informal tactics and politically motivated investigations.

The Muslim Brotherhood was never subjected to that law, because it participated in elections and parliamentary life without an official political party license, and thus did not have to experience the same type of state

---

[79] For more on the history of Al-Tagammu', see Iman Hassan, *Wadha'ef al-ahzab al-siyasiyya fi nudhm al-ta'adudiyya al-muqayada: dirasat halat hizb al-tagammu' fi misr 1976–1991* (Al-Qahirah: Al-Ahaly 1995); and Al-Said, *Mujarad dhikrayat al-juzuu al-taleth*.

oversight as its legal counterparts. This is not to deny that the Brotherhood suffered from chronic state repression, arrests, and politically motivated trials. Rather, this is to say that state repression of the Brotherhood did not encompass the same interventionist strategies that were exercised against legal parties such as Al-Tagammu' and that tended to disrupt institutional development. Intuitively speaking, a political group that participates in politics without a license is at a huge disadvantage, because it is deprived of the privileges that come with legal status, such as constitutional protections and public financing. In reality, however, the lack of legal status meant the absence of heavy-handed state oversight, especially as it relates to financial transparency. Thus, as a political group that was permitted to participate in politics, albeit in varying degrees across time, the Muslim Brotherhood did not have to deal with the same financial reporting requirements as their rivals. As a result, the state had no clear mechanism by which it could check and curb the fundraising activities of the Brotherhood.

An additional instrument through which the state-dominated PPC exerted influence over the legal opposition – as opposed to the Muslim Brotherhood – is Article 13 of the Political Parties Law. The article granted the head of the PPC the power to dissolve a given party under extremely subjective circumstances, such as carrying out activities that violate the constitution, or threaten national security or social peace. That flawed legal framework afforded the regime the authority to freeze even the most law-abiding party, which stood as a powerful deterrent against legal opposition parties that contemplated whether or not to challenge the political status quo.

An additional constraint imposed on licensed political parties pertains to the fact that they were required by law to maintain open membership. At first glance, these requirements seem rather harmless and uncontroversial. Yet upon closer examination of the political context in which these opposition parties operated under Mubarak, open membership seems more of a ticking time bomb. It is this open membership requirement that has allowed security agencies to infiltrate opposition political parties through informant networks. Not bound by these same legal instruments, the Muslim Brotherhood has structured its membership requirements and procedures in very rigid ways, which has made the task of infiltration an onerous one.

Finally, the state was able to tacitly exert pressure over opposition parties through the various strings it attached to their newspapers and publications. Almost every party produced a daily or weekly newspaper, which is one of the main channels through which it was able to convey its ideas and principles, voice its critiques of the government's performance, and enhance its outreach to members and potential supporters. These publications, however, were normally printed at state-owned printing houses, which means the state was at liberty to block the printing of opposition newspapers without having to resort to direct censorship or without obtaining a court order to recall the publication from newsstands. Another channel through which the state was able to influence opposition party newspapers is their advertising departments. By being the major buyers of advertising space in opposition newspapers, government ministries had effectively become the subsidizers of opposition parties. The threat of withholding advertisement requests from these newspapers provided various government officials with a fair amount of tacit influence over opposition parties throughout the Mubarak era.

In short, in agreeing to operate under a legal status, Al-Tagammu' was effectively embracing a variety of institutional mechanisms through which the state could systematically interfere in its own affairs. Thus, chronic state interference and the absence of autonomy became one of the major hall-marks of the left's developmental trajectory in Egypt. On the other hand, Islamist incorporation policies provided a valuable balance between state support and organizational autonomy, such that the Muslim Brotherhood was able to benefit from the state's receptive policies without submitting entirely to the regime. The communist movement and its successors, on the other hand, received only limited support from Nasser during the 1960s, and, under Sadat, neither support nor autonomy.

As explained earlier, the implications of these divergences in institutional development to the contemporary context of Egyptian politics are extremely significant. It is within these divergences that one could understand why is it that the post-Mubarak political arena was inhospitable to the emergence of consensus around the democratic rules of the political game. The organizational asymmetries that these legacies generated made the production of contingent consent a difficult endeavor, paving the way to the downfall of the Second Egyptian Republic.

CONCLUSION

The purpose of this chapter is to add historical depth to discussions of the downfall of Egypt's Second Republic by analyzing the role of institutional legacies in contributing to that outcome. It makes the argument that the failure of Egypt's post-Mubarak transition cannot be understood in isolation of the main features of the political field that was inherited from the Mubarak era. Among those features are the organizational disparities across the Islamist and non-Islamist divide, which has generated an environment not conducive for a pacted transition that could have produced some consensus around the democratic process. These disparities are the product of a set of important state interventions that occurred in the 1960s and 70s and that have shaped the institutional developmental trajectories of leftist and Islamist movements in uneven and divergent ways. It is within that historical context that one must understand the failure of Egypt's post-Mubarak transition.

The aftermath of the July 3 coup underscores the enduring character of the legacies examined in this chapter. Leftist and liberal actors played a visible role in endorsing, whether explicitly or tacitly, the military's ouster of President Morsi, along with the subsequent repression and deadly violence the state employed against Muslim Brotherhood affiliates and supporters. Interestingly, these actors were not limited to political forces that historically rejected Islamist currents and consistently endorsed the repression Islamists endured at the hands of successive governments under Mubarak. Rather, supporters of the post-July 3 political order included former interlocutors who coordinated and justified strategic cooperation between Islamist and non-Islamist opposition currents under the banner of advancing democratic change during the Mubarak era.[80] Specifically, individuals who had once crossed the Islamist/non-Islamist divide to launch serious democratic reform initiatives such as Kifaya and the National Association for Change found themselves at opposite sides of political warfare in July 2013. That trend perhaps suggests that even political leaders and activists who are evidently inclined to uphold cooperation for the sake of democratic change confronted conditions that trumped their predisposition to collaborate and compromise with their rivals. At the heart of these permeating, unfavorable conditions was the uneven political field they inherited from the Mubarak era and that limited the prospects for credible, stable pacts between the country's warring political forces.

---

[80] For more on the history of cooperation between Egypt's Islamists and non-Islamists under Mubarak, see Dina Shehata, *Islamists and Secularists in Egypt: Opposition, Conflict, and Cooperation* (London: Routledge, 2010).

4

(De)liberalizing judicial independence in Egypt

SAHAR F. AZIZ[1]

The January 25th Egyptian revolution was initiated in the public square and defeated in the courts.[2] In the months following the forced resignation of longtime president Hosni Mubarak, a protracted power struggle ensued between a people demanding self-governance and a chronically authoritarian regime. As the various stakeholders within the "deep state"[3] realized their political disadvantage

[1] Associate professor at Texas A&M University School of Law and president of the Egyptian American Rule of Law Association (www.earla.org). Professor Aziz thanks Dr. Dalia Fahmy and Daanish Faruqi for their feedback on earlier drafts. She also thanks Ben Nystrom for his diligent research assistance.

[2] "Timeline: Egypt's revolution," Al Jazeera, February 14, 2011, http://www.aljazeera.com/news/middleeast/2011/01/201112515334871490.html; Amir Ahmed, "Thousands protest in Egypt," CNN, January 26, 2011, http://edition.cnn.com/2011/WORLD/meast/01/25/egypt.protests/
[3] The idea of the "deep state" was first used to describe the political structure of Turkey, which has a democratic government, but also a powerful military that steps in to intervene when the leadership veers too far, in its view, toward Islamism. Sarah Childress, "The deep state: How Egypt's shadow state won out," *Frontline*, September 17, 2013, http://www.pbs.org/wgbh/pages/frontline/foreign-affairs-defense/egypt-in-crisis/the-deep-state-how-egypts-shadow-state-won-out/ (quoting Nathan Brown, Professor of Political Science and International Affairs at George Washington University); Stephen R. Grand, *Understanding Tahrir Square – What Transitions Elsewhere Can Teach Us About the Prospects for Arab Democracy* (New York: Brookings Institution, 2014), 198. (They have created "deep states" or "states within a state" – extensive domestic intelligence services and vast military

in mass street mobilizations by youth activists and opposition groups, they strategically transferred the conflict to the courts. Cognizant of Mubarak's success in coopting significant portions of the judiciary, the military-led interim government trusted the judges to deploy thin notions of rule of law to quash Egyptians' demands for substantive justice and populist democracy. Thus, assessing the implications of Egypt's so-called January 25th revolution warrants an inquiry into the role that courts played in the retrenchment of a centralized, authoritarian state and what ultimately became a stillborn revolution.[4]

In the heady days following Mubarak's forced resignation, youth activists and the Muslim Brotherhood had few qualms about litigating the revolution. In the two decades preceding the 2011 mass uprisings, the judiciary was the only state institution that dared to check executive powers through rights-protective rulings and public condemnations of electoral fraud.[5] Indeed, the Egyptian judiciary had a long history of fighting for its independence from executive branch interference such that both secular activists and Muslim Brotherhood supporters viewed it as a liberal institution poised to support their calls for social justice.[6] What transpired since 2011, however, has exposed the fallacy of these assumptions and called into question the liberal underpinnings of Egypt's judiciary. In the end, the judges' self-ascribed roles as the guardians of

---

establishments – that are kept out of public view, cloaked in secrecy, and that often operate beyond the control of political leaders.)

[4] See, e.g., Sahar F. Aziz, "Bringing down an uprising: Egypt's stillborn revolution," *Connecticut Journal of International Law* 30 (2014) (provides a descriptive analysis of the key factors that caused Egypt's January 25th revolution to be coopted into a mere mass uprising).

[5] Tamir Moustafa, "Law versus the state: The judicialization of politics in Egypt," *Law & Social Inquiry* 28, no. 4 (2003): 883, 895–6. (The SCC even ruled national election laws unconstitutional in 1987 and 1990, forcing the dissolution of the People's Assembly, a new electoral system, and early elections. Two similar rulings forced comparable reforms to the system of elections for both the upper house, Majlis al-Shura, and local council elections nationwide. Although the rulings on election laws hardly undermined the regime's grip on power, they did significantly undermine the regime's corporatist system of opposition control. Simultaneously, judicial activism in both the SCC and the administrative courts allowed opposition activists to successfully challenge decisions of the regime-dominated Political Parties Committee and to gain formal opposition party status. By 1995, ten of Egypt's thirteen opposition parties owed their very existence to court rulings.)

[6] Sahar F. Aziz, "Independence without accountability: The judicial paradox of Egypt's failed transition," *Penn State Law Review* (forthcoming 2015).

social order and political stability has proven to be more rhetorical than substantive.[7]

Accordingly, this chapter examines how a critical mass of Egyptian judges have strayed from the judiciary's liberal roots dating back to the nineteenth century, resulting in the legitimation of the same authoritarian regime but for a new military elite coalition at the helm. Through mass death sentences of Muslim Brotherhood (MB) leaders and alleged supporters, convictions of dissident journalists, and punitive sentences for youth activists for protesting, the judiciary has signaled support for illiberal authoritarian practices that systematically quash personal, political, and legal liberty.

As such, I challenge the predominant narrative in American legal scholarship that depicts the Egyptian judiciary as a relatively liberal institution within an otherwise illiberal political context.[8] I argue that both exogenous and endogenous factors caused a critical mass of judges to incorporate illiberal (and elitist) values that consider populist political mobilizations a larger threat to social order and (thin) rule of law than an over-reaching, authoritarian executive branch. My critique brings to the forefront the Egyptian judiciary's flawed definition of judicial independence as restricted to horizontal accountability against executive interference into

---

[7] See, e.g., Boursou Daragahi, "Egypt's 'Hanging Judge' accused of politicized verdicts," *Financial Times*, April 24, 2015, http://www.ft.com/intl/cms/s/0/18898000-e297-11e4-aa1d-00144feab7de.html#axzz3ZAZ4uA9q (reporting that Judge Nagi Shehata presiding over high-profile cases against journalists and Muslim Brotherhood defendants stated: "Judges are the shadow of God on earth, and we are designated by Him to maintain justice," to *el-Watan*, a pro-regime newspaper, in February [2015]."A judge has no fear but from God.").

[8] Tamir Moustafa, "The Political Role of the Supreme Constitutional Court: Between Principles and Practice," in *Judges and Political Reform in Egypt*, ed. Nathalie Bernard-Maugiron (Cairo: The American University in Cairo Press, 2008), 94; Moustafa, "Law versus the state," 883, 885; see Nathan Brown, "Reining in the Executive: What Can the Judiciary Do?" in Bernard-Maugiron, *Judges and Political Reform in Egypt*, 111, 141 (discussing the impact of the independent nature of the courts in Egypt); Steven A. Cook, *Ruling But Not Governing: The Military and Political Development in Egypt, Algeria, and Turkey* (Baltimore: Johns Hopkins University Press, 2007), 65; Clark B. Lombardi, "The Constitution as Agreement to Agree: The Social and Political Foundations (and Effects) of the 1971 Egyptian Constitution," in *Social and Political Foundations of Constitutions*, ed. Denis Galligan and Mila Versteeg (New York: Cambridge University Press, 2013); Clark B. Lombardi, *State Law as Islamic Law in Modern Egypt: The Incorporation of the Shari'a into Egyptian Constitutional Law* (Leiden: E.J. Brill, 2006); but see Bruce Rutherford, *Egypt after Mubarak: Liberalism, Islam, and Democracy in the Arab World* (Princeton, NJ: Princeton University Press, 2013).

judicial affairs with minimal regard for vertical accountability between the state and the people.[9]

This outcome is due in large part to Egyptian judges' significant material and status interests in the status quo. For example, pervasive nepotism benefits sitting judges' sons and male relatives; lucrative secondments are distributed based on opaque political criteria rather than transparently by merit; and minimal accountability to the public exists for judicial spending or governance. Had the public's demands for systemic political reform been met, the judiciary would have undergone a transformative change in governance.[10] Thus, Egypt's judiciary fought to obtain increased autonomy from executive interference while avoiding accountability to the people. The consequence is a judiciary that has failed in its role to protect and enforce private and political liberty.[11] In the long run, the judiciary is likely to pay a high price in terms of its legitimacy before the public.[12]

While a full explication of liberalism is beyond the scope of this chapter, I begin with a brief description of liberalism to highlight the contradiction between the judiciary's liberal rhetoric and illiberal behavior. Section II proceeds to summarize the liberal roots of the Egyptian judiciary arising from its interaction with European judges in the late nineteenth century through the formation of the Mixed Courts and participation in the anti-colonialist independence movement of the early twentieth century. It also describes the various methods employed by the Nasser and Sadat regimes to quash or coopt a judiciary committed to political and legal liberalism from engaging in meaningful horizontal accountability vis-à-vis

---

[9] Siri Gloppen et al., *Courts and Power in Latin America and Africa* (New York: Palgrave Macmillan, 2010), 13.

[10] International Bar Association, "Separating Law and Politics: Challenges to the Independence of Judges and Prosecutors in Egypt," Report of the International Bar Association Human Rights Institute, February, 2014, 54.

[11] Marcela Rodriguez, "Some Thoughts on Institutional Structures in the Judicial Process," in *Transition to Democracy in Latin America: The Role of the Judiciary*, ed. Irwin P. Stotzky (Boulder, CO: Westview Press, 1993) 167.

[12] "The worst culprits in the erosion of justice, of civil society, of everything that makes life livable in Egypt are the judiciary," the renowned writer and activist Ahdah Soueif told me moments after her nephew, the prominent activist Alaa Abdel Fattah, was sentenced to five years in prison for a peaceful protest. "It's been such a bitter disappointment and knowledge that they could destroy a basic belief in justice that people have because they've decided that their interests lie with this regime. It's unbelievable." Sharif Abdel Kouddous, "Egypt's judiciary: A willing participant in repression," *LA Times*, April 23, 2015, http://www.latimes.com/opinion/op-ed/la-oe-kouddous-egypt-20150423-story.html

a nationalist authoritarian executive branch. Section III explains how Mubarak manipulated incentives and preferences to produce a fractured judiciary between loyalist judges ideologically supportive of a strong executive and distrustful of populist democracy; opportunist judges who place their individual material interests above judicial reforms they support; and reformist judges who engage the public to pressure the executive to act on its stated commitment to judicial independence. Finally, Section IV contextualizes the current judiciary's illiberal and counterrevolutionary rulings. I argue that, notwithstanding the judiciary's liberal roots and historical struggles for judicial independence from executive interference, a majority of Egyptian judges hold elitist, anti-populist, and thin notions of rule of law that emphasize formalist legal liberty while disregarding political and private liberty. That judges have been successful in doing so and still remain on the bench exposes the limitations of liberalism in serving as an ideological framework for the Egyptian people's revolutionary demands for "bread, freedom, and social justice."

THE THREE PRONGS OF LIBERALISM: PRIVATE, POLITICAL, AND LEGAL LIBERTY

Liberalism is animated by the principle that personal freedom is the only good worth pursuing so long as it does not deprive others of their freedom.[13] Toward that end, classical liberalism is comprised of private liberty, political liberty, and legal liberty.[14] Private liberty, commonly referred to as individual rights, is rooted in natural law. Private liberty grants human beings a minimum level of integrity of body and mind that in its fullest produces personal privacy. As such, the right against torture, unjustified imprisonment, constraints on movement, and forced labor are negative rights protected by private liberty.[15] Some theorists argue that economic liberties such as the right to private property and freedom of

---

[13] Brian Z. Tamanaha, "Rule of Law in the United States," in *Asian Discourses of Rule of Law: Theories and implementation of Rule of Law in Twelve Asian Countries, France and the U.S.*, ed. Randall Peerenboom (New York: RoutledgeCurzon, 2004), 56.

[14] Ibid., 58 (noting, however, that early liberals opposed popular democracy because they distrusted rule by the ignorant masses susceptible to demagoguery).

[15] Cass R. Sunstein, "The Negative Constitution: Transition in Latin America," in Stotzky, *Transition to Democracy in Latin America*, 368.

contract are also part of private liberty.[16] Any government actions that violate private liberty are thus prohibited unless they are necessary to prevent harming others.

To avoid strife and insecurity, the liberal social contract presumes that autonomous, rights-bearing individuals consensually enter a covenant to form a government authorized to create and enforce law in the interest of preserving order.[17] This covenant between the government and the governed produces political liberty. Some liberal theorists argue that democracy is integral to preserving political liberty.[18] That is, political liberty can only be realized through the right to vote and freedom of speech, assembly and association.[19] As a result, government legitimacy arises from individuals' consent to be subjected to the dictates of law that treats each person equally bound by law. This in turn establishes rule of law. Notably, some scholars argue that the consent required to produce political liberty need not be granted through elections, but rather may arise from religious, tribal, or other traditional grounds.[20]

Due to political elites' distrust of the masses to elect a competent government, representative democracy is often preferred over direct democratic governance.[21] This allows purportedly reasoned elites to govern who can prevent the government from being captured by an oppressive and passionate majority. Moreover, government powers are divided into compartments to prevent the accumulation and abuse of power. By setting up a legislative, executive, and judicial branch, a competitive interdependence among the three branches produces horizontal accountability.[22] The application of law is entrusted to an independent judiciary whose work institutionalizes the preservation of private, political, and legal liberties.[23]

---

[16] Ibid., 369.

[17] Tamanaha, "Rule of Law in the United States," 56–7.

[18] Hannah Franzki and Maria Carolina Olarte, "Understanding the Political Economy of Transitional Justice: A Critical Theory Perspective," in *Transitional Justice Theories*, ed. Susanne Buckley-Zistel, Teresa Koloma Beck, Christian Braun, and Friederike Mieth (New York: Routledge, 2014), 207.

[19] Tamanaha, "Rule of Law in the United States," 57.

[20] Ibid.

[21] Brian Z. Tamanaha, *On the Rule of Law: History, Politics, Theory* (New York: Cambridge, 2004), 120.

[22] Ibid., 35.

[23] Ibid.

Liberalism claims to be neutral in how it treats alternative visions of the good.[24] As such, the state cannot adopt or promote one vision over another unless it threatens others or the state.[25] In the face of diverse moral values, liberalism posits that the position of neutrality is the right principle on which to construct a pluralistic society that grants each individual the autonomy to pursue her or his self-defined freedom. To preserve legal liberty, therefore, judges are obligated to remain neutral in legal disputes, as well as eschew involvement in political disputes.[26]

Western liberalism adopts legal formalism as a means of protecting individual freedom. That is, so long as laws are prospective, general, clear, public, predictable, and relatively stable, they are legitimate.[27] Formalist notions of liberalism place little value on how the law is made or the substantive consequences of such laws.[28] For instance, legal liberalism has legitimated slavery, apartheid, and other oppressive legal regimes that met formal legalist criteria.[29] As a result, (thin) rule of law – often used interchangeably with formalist legal liberalism – is a highly contested term that can simultaneously legalize oppression and legitimate populist revolution against the state.

Proponents of thin rule of law emphasize neutrality as the main-stay of legal liberalism. So long as a government meets its obligation to act according to the law and treat similarly situated persons equally, regardless of the substance of the law, there is rule of law.[30] Whether the government is democratically elected or authoritarian is also irrelevant as long as the law is the means by which the state conducts it affairs.[31] Likewise, the abrogation of individual rights is acceptable if the state follows the appropriate legal measures, even if such measures are promulgated by an authoritarian state.[32] Thin rule of law is attainable without

---

[24] Ibid., 51.

[25] Ibid., 41.

[26] Ibid., 32 (keeping the peace requires laws, and unbiased law enforcers and judges).

[27] Tamanaha, "Rule of Law in the United States," 71; Randall Peerenboom, "Varieties of Rule of Law: An Introduction and Provisional Conclusion," in Peerenboom, *Asian Discourses of Rule of Law*, 2–3.

[28] Tamanaha, "Rule of Law in the United States," 57.

[29] Ibid., 72.

[30] Peerenboom, "Varieties of Rule of Law," 13.

[31] Tamanaha, "On the rule of law," 92.

[32] Rachel Kleinfeld, "Competing Definitions of the Rule of Law," in *Promoting the Rule of Law Abroad*, ed. Thomas Carothers (Washington, DC: Carnegie Endowment for International Peace, 2006), 37.

democracy.[33] For these reasons, among others, legal scholarship is replete with critiques of liberalism and (thin) rule of law.[34]

While a full explication of these theoretical debates is beyond the scope of this chapter, it is worth noting three critiques applicable to the Egyptian context. First, liberalism disconnects substantive justice from law such that rule of law perpetuates systems of domination and social hierarchies based on the unequal distribution of wealth and talent.[35] As a result, critics argue that liberalism creates liberty for the economic elite to dominate while falsely claiming to be neutral.[36] Second, law is indeterminate such that a body of legal rules does not produce a single right answer and may even allow for contradictory outcomes. Judges may manipulate rules to achieve a predetermined outcome animated by political motives. Whatever predictability of law exists, thus, may not lie in the law itself but rather in the shared social and economic background of judges.[37] Third, liberalism's emphasis on individual autonomy over-looks the role of community norms in preserving order and promoting justice, particularly in communitarian societies.[38] In Egypt, for example, liberalism has been adopted piecemeal by the economic and political elite only when it serves their interests.[39] Similarly, post-January 25 Egypt's judicial elite have deployed rule of law to justify quashing civil liberties of youth activists and political Islamists whom the judges deemed a threat to social order and, in turn, the judiciary's institutional interests. In doing so, judges have made the values of liberty, equality, and freedom devoid of meaning for many average Egyptians.[40] But the Egyptian judiciary has not always been an illiberal institution.

---

[33] Tamanaha, "On the rule of law," 92.

[34] Franzki and Olarte, "Understanding the Political Economy of Transitional Justice," 217; Tamanaha, "Rule of Law in the United States," 65.

[35] David Mednicoff, "Middle East Dilemmas," in Carothers, *Promoting the Rule of Law Abroad*, 258.

[36] Tamanaha, "Rule of Law in the United States," 65, 75.

[37] Ibid., 74.

[38] Mednicoff, "Middle East Dilemmas," 258.

[39] Nabil Abdel Fattah, "The Political Role of the Egyptian Judiciary, Judges and Political Reform," in Bernard-Maugiron, *Judges and Political Reform in Egypt*, 71.

[40] Irwin P. Stotzky, "The Tradition of Constitutional Adjudication," in Stotzky, *Transition to Democracy in Latin America*, 350; Kouddous, "Egypt's judiciary."

THE LIBERAL ROOTS OF EGYPT'S JUDICIARY

The importation of Western liberalism into the Egyptian judiciary dates back to the late nineteenth century when Egyptian judges worked along-side European judges in the Mixed Courts. Three key historical developments, in particular, exemplify the influence of liberalism on the Egyptian legal system. First, constitutionalism and rule of law were part of the nationalist rhetoric of the early 1900s as Egyptians called for self-determination from the British-controlled Crown.[41] Second, judges were on the frontlines of the Egyptian nationalist movement, culminating in the passage of the 1923 constitution – arguably the most liberal vision of state–society relations compared to subsequent constitutions. Third, the executive's pressures to circumscribe judicial independence initiated under Nasser, which continues until the present day, have fragmented the judiciary into loyalists, opportunists, and reformists. As a result, judges are left vulnerable to executive cooptation and coercion, resulting in a slow process of deliberalization of a once liberal institution.[42] Post-January 25, the dominant loyalist camp has not only issued increasingly illiberal rulings, particularly with regard to private liberty, but also abused their power by purging reformists from the judiciary.

At the turn of the twentieth century, Egypt's brightest judges were trained in France where they were exposed to French philosophy and culture. Their training was grounded in liberalism's emphasis on rights, duties, authority, sovereignty, and personal freedoms protected within a constitutional framework.[43] The constitutional foundations of Western law and civil liberties eventually became the foundation of the Egyptian nationalist movement.[44] This led to the passage of the 1923 Egyptian constitution wherein the National Courts were granted independence from the Crown.[45] Worth noting is that Egyptian liberal constitutionalism never shared the same emphasis on personal liberty found in classical liberalism. The well-being of the community, rather than the

---

[41] Rutherford, *Egypt after Mubarak*, 34 (the 1900s saw the elite of Egypt seeking more autonomy and this was heavily influenced by constitutionalism in Istanbul).

[42] Gloppen et al., *Courts and Power in Latin America and Africa*, 24.

[43] Rutherford, *Egypt after Mubarak*, 37.

[44] Mahmoud Hamad, *When the Gavel Speaks: Judicial Politics in Modern Egypt* (August 2008 – unpublished Ph.D. dissertation, The University of Utah, on file with author), 59.

[45] Ibid., 67.

individual, animates protection of personal liberty.[46] Thus, the judiciary has tolerated a more powerful and invasive state than found in Western liberal states, and views populist participation in political life as a source of disorder.[47]

Nevertheless, Egypt's judges supported a clear and impartial legal code, checks and balances between the different state branches, an independent judiciary, and property rights – all basic components of liberalism. As such, the Court of Cassation became a guardian of civil and political rights in its seminal 1925 ruling that Egyptians had the right to form political parties as an integral aspect of the right to association and the right to criticize the Crown within their freedom of speech guaranteed under the 1923 constitution.[48] During this liberal era from 1923 to 1952, the Egyptian judiciary established liberal legal precedents and legal traditions protective of citizens' and groups' rights and liberties. Judicial independence became intertwined with liberal judicialization,[49] which culminated in 1943 when judicial independence was codified in the Judicial Independence Act.[50] The public's engagement at the time with judicial matters coupled with a liberal cultural, social, and political environment buttressed the judiciary's identity as a liberal institution.[51]

But these circumstances turned out to be short-lived. Although Gamal Abdel Nasser and his Free Officers Movement had welcomed the judges' role in defeating the Crown in 1952, they expected the judiciary unquestioningly to legitimize Nasser's nationalist policies. The judges, however, did not cooperate, particularly after the devastating military defeat in 1967 that led to Israel occupying the Sinai Peninsula. The judges increasingly questioned Nasser's revolutionary legislation and issued verdicts against the regime. The consequences were devastating.[52] In 1969, Nasser issued four presidential decrees that figuratively massacred the judiciary.[53] Over two hundred judges were categorically dismissed, including the most liberal and respected reformist judges. A Supreme Council of Judicial

---

[46] Rutherford, *Egypt after Mubarak*, 67.
[47] Ibid., 75.
[48] Hamad, *When the Gavel Speaks*, 74.
[49] Ibid., 90.
[50] Ibid., 72.
[51] Ibid.
[52] Ibid., 139.
[53] Ibid., 142–3.

Organizations was created to grant the regime control over judicial appointments, promotions, and disciplinary actions.[54]

Nasser also created exceptional security courts presided over by military and security personnel who produced predetermined outcomes set by the executive branch. The ordinary courts' jurisdiction, thus, was narrowed to prevent judges from invalidating the regime's policies. And the regime appointed loyalist judges to powerful judicial positions to discipline reformist judges.[55] Over time, what was once a staunchly independent institution became increasingly comprised of loyalist and opportunist judges who no longer viewed liberalism as a component of their self-appointed role as guardians of social order.

Despite Nasser's best efforts, he was unable to completely change the liberal institutional culture within the judicial corps. After Nasser's death in 1970, reformist judges resumed defending judicial independence.[56] A new constitution in 1971, passed under Sadat's reign, established a Supreme Constitutional Court which explicitly stated that the regime was based on the rule of law, and guaranteed Egyptians nearly all internationally recognized political liberties and human rights consistent with liberal principles.[57] Over thirty percent of the constitution either directly pertained to the judiciary or linked citizens' rights and liberties with the courts as guarantors of such rights.[58] The reversion to a constitutional democracy, at least on paper, provided a legal and political basis for the judges to defend civil liberties and seek more meaningful judicial independence. Indeed, Sadat's primary motive for granting the judiciary more independence and citizens more (limited) rights was to bolster his credibility in front of the international community, and more specifically foreign investors.[59] However, Sadat's reforms were circumscribed. He manipulated fringe benefits and financial incentives to coopt the judges if their calls for judicial independence or defense of civil liberties went so far as to threaten the regime's legitimacy.

---

[54] Tamir Moustafa, "Law and Resistance in Authoritarian States: The Judicialization of Politics in Egypt," in *Rule by Law: The Politics of Courts in Authoritarian Regimes*, ed. Tamir Moustafa and Tom Ginsburg (New York: Cambridge University Press, 2008), 134.

[55] Hamad, *When the Gavel Speaks*, 118.

[56] Ibid., 146.

[57] Ibid., 166.

[58] Ibid., 176.

[59] Ibid., 31.

Although Egypt's judges were again at the forefront of liberalizing the political system after twenty years of political repression, the previous two decades under Nasser fundamentally changed the composition of the legal profession. Law schools opened up to any applicant that met a low high-school exit exam score, and thus transformed law schools from the highest-achieving students to a dumping ground for low-performing students not accepted by other colleges. The consequent deterioration in legal education with bulging class sizes left little opportunity for teaching Western political and legal thought rooted in liberal values. Instead, the Bar, and to a lesser extent the judiciary, transformed into a predominantly middle- and lower-middle-class institution whose younger members had little exposure or commitment to liberal principles.[60] Thus, in contrast to the early 1900s when the judiciary could rely on the Bar to buttress its liberal agenda, the judges became the sole proponent of liberal constitutionalism within the legal profession.[61] This made the judges more vulnerable to the Mubarak regime's intensified cooptation strategy that offered fringe benefits to reward loyalists and opportunists while penalizing reformist judges.

INCREMENTAL DELIBERALIZATION IN THE MUBARAK ERA

Like Sadat, Mubarak began his presidency touting the importance of rule of law and judicial independence as the cornerstone of his regime.[62] Lacking charisma and inheriting a bankrupt state unable to distribute social goods to the people, Mubarak was left with rule of law as the primary basis for his political legitimacy.[63] At the same time, Mubarak sought to retain a centralized and powerful executive branch that circumscribed rule of law to formalistic procedural notions. Thus, Mubarak envisioned the judiciary's role as rotely enforcing laws promulgated by an executive-controlled parliament.

Not all of the judges were willing to adhere to such thin notions of rule of law or accept their relegation to a mere rubber stamp of

---

[60] Rutherford, *Egypt after Mubarak*, 47.
[61] Ibid., 50; Mona El-Ghobashy, "The Dynamics of Elections Under Mubarak," in *The Journey to Tahrir: Revolution, Protest and Social Change in Egypt*, ed. Jeannie Sowers and Chris Toensing (London: Verso, 2012), 139.
[62] Hamad, *When the Gavel Speaks*, 235.
[63] Ibid.

authoritarian policies arising from rigged elections. In the first and only Justice Conference held in 1986, the judiciary stipulated a roadmap for comprehensive judicial reform that would provide it with meaningful independence from an over-reaching executive. Specifically, judges called for: (1) complete budgetary autonomy; (2) removing the role of the Ministry of Justice from judicial affairs; (3) rescinding all exceptional courts; (4) restructuring judicial supervision to grant full judicial control over the electoral processes; (5) granting the Court of Cassation the jurisdiction to rule on the merits of a case if it overturns a lower court ruling; (6) prohibiting trials of civilians in military courts; (7) separating prosecution and indictment powers; and (8) establishing a judicial police in the Ministry of Justice to enforce judicial rulings.[64] Unsurprisingly, none of these demands was granted. For the next twenty years, leading reformist judges made multiple attempts to amend the Judicial Authority Law to no avail.

Arising from these reform efforts was a judicial independence movement led by reformist judges who engaged the public in confronting the regime on its illiberal policies and practices. Another group of judges agreed with the need for reform but disagreed with the prominent public role of reformist judges. These judges, which I place in the opportunist camp, worried that public advocacy, rather than private consultation with the executive branch, eroded the public's respect for the state and undermined public order – and more importantly jeopardized their fringe benefits.[65] They sought to avoid the executive's collective retaliation against all judges for the reformist judges' campaign for more judicial independence. Indeed, many judges had few qualms about a strong state so long as it was not arbitrary or corrupt.[66] While agreeing that judges have an obligation to maintain public order, reformist judges believed they had a duty to draw attention to infringements of law that repress personal liberty. As such, the judiciary should be vigilant and aggressive in reining in the state and ensuring it serves the public interest.[67]

From 1986 to 2007, the reformist and loyalist camps struggled for control of the Judges Club – the vehicle through which judges defended their institutional and personal interests vis-à-vis the executive branch.[68]

---

64 Ibid.
65 Rutherford, *Egypt after Mubarak*, 146–7.
66 Ibid., 60.
67 Ibid., 146.
68 Mustapha Kamel Al-Sayyed, "The Judicial Authority and Civil Society," in Bernard-

With over ninety percent of judicial personnel as members, the Judges Club is a powerful institution capable of flexing its political muscle to fight for judicial independence.[69] During the 1980s, Judge Yahia Al-Rifai, a highly respected judge, was president of the Judges Club. His principled commitment to judicial independence breathed life into the judicial independence movement as judges became more vocal in their demands against legalized executive interference. Although Mubarak initially welcomed the judges' input, he soon grew frustrated with their insistence on substantial changes in the Judicial Authority Law. As a result, the growing tension between the executive and the vocal judicial reformists bore little fruit.

In 1992, reformist Judge Yahia Al-Rifai was defeated by Judge Muqbil Shakir as president of the Judges Club.[70] Shakir's quietist approach led to substantial increases in resources to the judiciary including remodeling of court facilities, salary increases, and substantial annual bonuses to judges.[71] These successes on bread and butter issues bolstered a quietist approach among judges in compliance with the executive branch's strategy of offering benefits to incentivize judges against confronting the regime on rule of law infringements. Indeed, many judges opposed the reformist judges more for their confrontational style that they deemed futile than on the content of the requested reforms. The executive's manipulation of benefits continues until the present day as a means of fracturing the judiciary and marginalizing vocal opposition to the regime's practices, particularly with regard to economic policies and individual rights.

In 2002, a group of reformist judges under the "Change and Renewal" list won the Judges Club elections under the leadership of Judge Zakaria Abdel Aziz.[72] Besides mobilizing judges to demand electoral reforms, the Judges Club again pressured the executive to amend the Judicial Authority Law to give the judiciary more autonomy and eliminate the

---

Maugiron, *Judges and Political Reform in Egypt*, 230; Atef Shahat Said, "The Role of the Judges' Club in Enhancing the Independence of the Judiciary and Spurring Political Reform," in Bernard-Maugiron, *Judges and Political Reform in Egypt*, 112.

[69] Ibid., 113; Fattah, "The Political Role of the Egyptian Judiciary," in Bernard-Maugiron, *Judges and Political Reform in Egypt*, 88.

[70] Rutherford, *Egypt after Mubarak*, 147.

[71] Ibid.

[72] Omar Mekky, "Evolution of the Rafaiest in Egyptian Politics," *Kuwait Times*, September 17, 2012, http://news.kuwaittimes.net/evolution-of-the-refaiest-in-egyptian-politics/; see Hamad, *When the Gavel Speaks*, 265–6 (discussing how "in 2001, reformer Zakaria Abdel Aziz surprisingly defeated the three term president of the Judges Club, Moqbel Shaker").

manipulation of benefits to indirectly influence judges.[73] After witnessing pervasive electoral fraud in the 2005 parliamentary elections, the reformist judges controlling the Judges Club formed an investigative committee. Following the lead of a young female judge in the Office of Administrative Prosecution, Noha Al-Zini, who publicly disclosed the election violations, judges collected testimony from other judges who witnessed similar fraud. The self-described judicial independence movement convened three general assembly meetings in 2005 and 2006, culminating in the publication of a report denouncing the election abuses and citing various cases of election fraud witnessed by judges.[74] Civil society, in tandem with reformist judges and Judges Club leaders, exposed the electoral fraud and security forces' interference. The Bar went even farther to create a list of thirteen judges allegedly engaged in electoral fraud and published it in independent newspapers.[75]

The executive swiftly retaliated. The Supreme Judicial Council threatened to investigate any judges who spoke to the press about election fraud.[76] Any such speeches or interviews with the press were labeled political activity that could lead to disciplinary charges of violating the Judicial Authority Law.[77] The Ministry of Justice also suspended the annual subsidies it gave to Judges Clubs, which was a primary source of funding for judges' fringe benefits.[78] And the parliament passed a law that transferred authority to distribute judicial fringe benefits from the Judges Club to the Ministry of Justice. The government also amended the constitution in 2007 to substantially weaken the role of judges in overseeing future elections by allowing non-judicial officials to serve as election monitors.[79]

---

[73] See Martin Shapiro, "Courts in Authoritarian Regimes," in Moustafa and Ginsburg, *Rule by Law*, 332 (discussing the need for judges to persuade their colleagues to create winning coalitions that produce rights-oriented judicial leadership).

[74] Ibid., 122.

[75] Hamad, *When the Gavel Speaks*, 276.

[76] Bjorn Bentlage, "Strife for Independence in an Autocratic Regime: The Egyptian Judges' Club 2000–2007," *Die Welt des Islams* 50, no. 2 (2010): 264.

[77] Article 73, Judicial Authority Law.

[78] Nathalie Bernard-Maugiron, "Introduction," in *Judges and Political Reform in Egypt*, 2; Bentlage, "Strife for Independence in an Autocratic Regime," 265.

[79] Tamir Moustafa, "*Law in the Egyptian Revolt*," Middle East Law and Governance 3 (2011): 181, 184; Clark B. Lombardi, "The Constitution as Agreement to Agree: The Social and Political Foundations (and Effects) of the 1971 Egyptian Constitution," in *Social and Political Foundations of Constitutions*, ed. Denis Galligan and Mila Versteeg (Cambridge: Cambridge University Press, 2013), 423.

The message was clear – judges would be collectively punished for the judicial independence movement's activities.

Mubarak felt sufficiently threatened to take the unprecedented act of using force against the judges. When judges protested in 2006 in front of the Judges Club in Cairo near another protest by the Muslim Brotherhood, Egyptian police attacked both the MB protesters and the judges.[80] Nearly 150 protesters were arrested on charges of supporting the judges.[81] Among those arrested was Dr. Mohammad Morsi, who was portentously to become Egypt's first democratically elected president after the January 25 uprisings.[82] The following month, Mubarak instructed the minister of justice to refer two leading judges from the Judges Club, Ahmad Mekki and Hisham Al-Bastawisi, to disciplinary proceedings on pretextual charges of "insulting the judiciary" for allegedly defaming a fellow judge.[83] As the hearings were taking place, massive and well-equipped security forces surrounded the Judges Club, the Court of Cassation, the journalists' syndicate, and the lawyers' syndicate.[84] The unprecedented use of force against judges was a clear warning of the government's intent to crack down hard on anyone planning to challenge the regime's centralized grip on power.[85] And their status as judicial elites would not protect them.

The confrontation between the Mubarak regime and the Judges Club culminated in a retaking of the Cairo Judges Club by regime loyalist Judge Ahmad al-Zind in 2009. Meanwhile, some of the leading dissident judges were "encouraged" to work outside the country or retire.[86] Taking from Sadat's playbook, the Mubarak regime appealed to judges' material interests by promising financial benefits if government loyalists were elected to the Judges Club board. Upon his election to president of the Judges Club, al-Zind and his faction got to work in undermining the credibility of the reformist movement by accusing them of inflating the number of participants in the general assembly meetings that issued resolutions condemning executive action. The loyalist camp alleged that Justices Ahmad

---

[80] Bernard-Maugiron, "Introduction," 3.
[81] Mekky, "Evolution of the Rafaiest in Egyptian Politics"; Bentlage, "Strife for Independence in an Autocratic Regime," 266.
[82] Mekky, "Evolution of the Rafaiest in Egyptian Politics."
[83] Ibid.; Bernard-Maugiron, "Introduction," 3.
[84] Bentlage, "Strife for Independence in an Autocratic Regime," 266.
[85] Hamad, *When the Gavel Speaks*, 286.
[86] Mekky, "Evolution of the Rafaiest in Egyptian Politics."

Mekki, Zakaria Abdel Aziz, and Hossam al-Ghiryani were pursuing their own personal interests, allied with the political Islamist opposition, and went as far as implying national treason.[87] Government-controlled media also defamed the judicial independence movement by accusing reformist judges of violating the Judicial Authority Law by engaging in politics and alluded to their loyalties to the Muslim Brotherhood.[88] Mubarak loyalist judges also accused reformist judges of being secretly affiliated with the Muslim Brotherhood.[89] However, these allegations were never substantiated with credible evidence.

As the ordinary judiciary struggled for more autonomy from the state, the Supreme Constitutional Court (SCC) issued monumental rulings in the 1990s that legitimated Mubarak's economic liberalization project in exchange for limited expansion of personal liberty. For instance, in 1992, the SCC ruled that the Egyptian government was constitutionally required to respect international human rights norms.[90] The SCC struck down laws that restricted citizens' rights to establish political parties, stripped prominent opposition leaders of their political rights, and denied independent candidates the right to run in parliamentary elections.[91] It also struck down a law banning any political party opposed to peace with Israel; overturned laws that interfered with governance of workers' syndicates;[92] and struck down laws that prohibited criticism of public servants on grounds that it violated constitutional rights of free speech.[93]

The SCC's liberal rulings extended to noncitizens when it ruled that denying noncitizens deprived of their property rights access to the national courts was unconstitutional.[94] In 1995, the Labor Party successfully challenged the constitutionality of criminal provisions that imposed joint

---

[87] Said, "The Role of the Judges' Club," 127.

[88] Hamad, *When the Gavel Speaks*, 197–8, 273; Mekky, "Evolution of the Rafaiest in Egyptian Politics."

[89] Hamad, *When the Gavel Speaks*, 299.

[90] Lombardi, "The Constitution as Agreement to Agree," 420.

[91] Abdel Omar Sherif, "The Rule of Law in Egypt from a Judicial Perspective: A Digest of the Landmark Decisions of the Supreme Constitutional Court," in *The Rule of Law in the Middle East and the Islamic World: Human Rights and the Judicial Process*, ed. Eugene Cotran and Mai Yamani (London: I.B. Tauris, 2000), 7.

[92] Lombardi, *State Law as Islamic Law in Modern Egypt* (citing Case No. 44, Judicial Year 7 (May 7, 1998) and Case No. 6, Judicial Year 15 (April 15, 1995)).

[93] Ibid., 20.

[94] Ibid., 14.

liability on heads of political parties, reporters, and editors-in-chief for alleged libel of public officials in party newspapers.[95] By the late 1990s, public interest litigation became the primary forum through which civil society promoted legal reform.[96] Notwithstanding these liberal rulings, the SCC did not dare strike down the emergency laws or military trials of civilians lest it invite executive retaliation.[97] Nor did the SCC grant citizens the right to appeal emergency or military court rulings to the regular courts.[98]

Although the justices delivered rulings that assisted the regime's economic liberalization project,[99] the SCC's seminal 2000 ruling mandating judicial oversight of elections went too far for the regime.[100] To rein in the SCC, Mubarak appointed Fathi Naguib in 2002 as the Chair. Naguib had been second in command at the Ministry of Justice prior to serving as the President of the Court of Cassation.[101] With this unprecedented move of appointing a Chief Justice from outside the SCC, Mubarak took control of the Court.[102] Soon after taking office, Naguib increased the number of justices from nine to fifteen.[103] Breaking the tradition of selecting new justices from the Council of State, Naguib packed the Court with justices from the ordinary courts whose jurisprudence was deferential to executive's power.[104] Within a short period, the SCC's liberal majority was eliminated

---

[95] Lombardi, *State Law as Islamic Law in Modern Egypt* 93; Eugene Cotran et al., *The Rule of Law in the Middle East and the Islamic World: Human Rights and the Judicial Process*, ed. Eugene Cotran and Mai Yamani (London: I.B. Tauris, 2000).

[96] Moustafa, "The Political Role of the Supreme Constitutional Court"; Samer Soliman, *The Autumn of Dictatorship: Fiscal Crisis and Political Change in Egypt Under Mubarak* (Stanford: Stanford University Press, 2011), 137.

[97] Tamir Moustafa and Tom Ginsburg, "Introduction," Moustafa and Ginsburg, *Rule by Law*, 16; Moustafa, "Law and Resistance in Authoritarian States," 151.

[98] Ibid., 151.

[99] Lombardi, *State Law as Islamic Law in Modern Egypt*, 153 (noting the SCC's support for the ruling party's free market economic policies).

[100] Clark B. Lombardi, "Constitutions of Arab countries in transition: Constitutional review and separation of powers," *Mediterranean Yearbook* (2014): 129.

[101] Bentlage, "Strife for Independence in an Autocratic Regime," 248.

[102] Moustafa, "Law and Resistance in Authoritarian States," 138–9 (noting the tradition of the president selecting the most senior justice on the SCC to serve as Chief Justice); Moustafa, "Law versus the state," 924.

[103] Hamad, *When the Gavel Speaks*, 263; Lombardi, *State Law as Islamic Law in Modern Egypt*, 146 (noting that, prior to the expansion of the SCC, a judgment was final after seven justices signed it and the justices' votes are secret).

[104] Moustafa, "Law versus the state," 924.

and the judicial independence movement weakened, thereby producing a judiciary poised to support the military-security state apparatus in its counterrevolutionary measures.[105]

When the 2011 mass protests erupted, the SCC was comprised mostly of loyalist judges who viewed populist democracy with suspicion and deeply distrusted the Muslim Brotherhood. The Judges Club was firmly under the control of loyalist judges led by Judge Ahmad al-Zind who had successfully marginalized the reformist camp.[106] Neither the SCC nor the ordinary courts were prepared for the revolution that would put to the test whether their proclaimed commitments to liberalism were deeply rooted values or merely rhetoric to shore up legitimacy. Based on judicial behavior thus far, the latter appears to be closer to the truth.

A COUNTERREVOLUTION IN THE COURTS

In hindsight, the counterrevolution started the day Hosni Mubarak stepped down from power on February 11, 2011.[107] Although most Egyptians agreed to allow the Supreme Council of the Armed Forces (SCAF) to serve merely as an interim government until new presidential and parliamentary elections could be conducted, SCAF maneuvered to grant itself extraordinary legislative and executive powers. SCAF postponed elections under various pretexts – ranging from the need to draft a new constitution first or amend the election law, to claims that Egyptians needed more time to determine for whom to vote. The loyalist judges cooperated with the military-security apparatus to ensure neither the military nor the judiciary's institutional interests would be threatened by revolutionary reforms. But to do so, the revolutionary disputes had to be moved to the judges' home territory – the courts.

---

[105] Ibid.; Javed Maswood and Usha Natarajan, "Democratization and Constitutional Reform in Egypt and Indonesia: Evaluating the Role of the Military," in *Arab Spring in Egypt: Revolution and Beyond*, ed. Bahgat Korany and Rabab El-Mahdi (Cairo: The American University in Cairo Press, 2012), 231; Lombardi, "The Constitution as Agreement to Agree," 421.

[106] Heba Afify, "The judges behind the verdicts," *Mada Masr*, April 29, 2014, http://www.madamasr.com/sections/politics/judges-behind-verdicts (noting that the Judges Club, led by al-Zind, largely rejected Egyptian judges that favored groups such as the Muslim Brotherhood).

[107] Aziz, "Bringing down an uprising."

During SCAF's rule, the streets and public squares were the locus of what became a protracted revolutionary process. Youth activists, and the MB when it served their interests, mobilized multiple mass protests across the country demanding a new government, accountability of the Mubarak regime, and substantive reforms to Egypt's legal and political system.[108] Their success in leveraging the streets to air three decades of populist grievances made it all the more necessary for the military and other deep state stakeholders to shift the disputes to the courts – a forum friendlier to their interests, while still claiming to take the people's complaints seriously. The secular youth and MB underestimated the extent to which a critical mass of Egyptian judges had been endogenously politicized. Thus, SCAF had little trouble litigating the counterrevolution.

From the beginning, prosecutions against former Mubarak regime officials were doomed to fail. Lackluster investigations by prosecutors, destruction of evidence by the police, and handpicked judges ensured convictions would be rare. The loyalist judges, along with the significant number of opportunist judges, perceived a democratically elected Islamist president coupled with a politically mobilized public as a threat to social order, the security of the state, and most importantly the judiciary's material interests. Such values aligned the judiciary squarely with a military-led authoritarian regime seeking to eliminate any viable political opposition that could threaten the permanency of its rule.

What transpired during the four years since January 25 exposes the extent to which a portion of the judiciary has become further deliberalized during the last decade of Mubarak's rule. While a full rendition of this deliberalization process starting in 2000 is addressed in another article,[109] here I highlight five categories of cases post-January 25 that evince continued and accelerated deliberalization of the judiciary.

The first involves the SCC's dissolution of Egypt's first parliament elected without systemic fraud and the SCC's subsequent rejections of proposed amendments to election laws. As a result, Egypt did not have

---

[108] Ben Hubbard, "Egyptians protest against new powers for military council," *Independent*, November 18, 2011, http://www.independent.co.uk/news/world/africa/egyptians-protest-against-more-powers-for-military-rulers-6264259.html; "Thousands flock to Cairo's Tahrir Square to slam emergency law," *Al Arabiya*, September 16, 2011, http://english.alarabiya.net/articles/2011/09/16/167184.html (Thousands of people protest against SCAF and its recent decision to expand emergency law.)

[109] See Aziz, "Independence without accountability."

a parliament for nearly four years from June 2012 to January 2016.[110] The second category of cases is the prosecutions of security personnel and former Mubarak officials, including Mubarak and his sons, that have resulted in under-charging defendants, acquittals, or nominal sentences.[111] The third is the prosecutions of Morsi regime officials, including former president Mohammad Morsi, and alleged Muslim Brotherhood members and supporters, leading to harsh sentences with minimal due process.[112] The fourth category of cases encompasses the prosecution of leading revolutionary youth activists for violating an anti-protest law passed specifically to stop further street protests and legalize detaining and silencing activists.[113] The final category involves the judiciary's ongoing purge of reformist judges who were either notable leaders in the judicial independence movement in 2005–6 or young reformist judges who declared the ouster of Morsi as illegal.[114]

Each group of cases evinces three trends. First, the executive branch no longer needs to exert as much pressure on judges in order to preserve the regime's interests in high-profile cases. Second, endogenous politicization among a faction of judges has compromised the independence of the judiciary from the executive. Third, judicial politicization exists at the case level and the broader political level wherein judges are ideologically biased against political Islamists and youth activists who lead the revolutionary process. These trends call into question the judiciary's commitment to the fundamental components of liberalism including judicial independence,

---

[110] David D. Kirkpatrick, "Blow to transition as court dissolves Egypt's parliament," *New York Times*, June 14, 2012, http://www.nytimes.com/2012/06/15/world/middleeast/new-political-showdown-in-egypt-as-court-invalidates-parliament.html

[111] "Hosni Mubarak sentenced to three years in prison for corruption," *Telegraph*, May 9, 2015, http://www.telegraph.co.uk/news/worldnews/africaandindianocean/egypt/11594495/Hosni-Mubarak-sentenced-to-three-years-in-prison-for-corruption.html

[112] "What's become of Egypt's Morsi," *BBC News*, June 16, 2015, http://www.bbc.com/news/world-middle-east-24772806

[113] "Egypt's Maher, Adel and Douma Sentenced to 3 years in jail," *Al-Ahram Online*, December 22, 2013, http://english.ahram.org.eg/News/89748.aspx; "Alaa Abdel Fattah: Egypt jails activist-blogger for five years," *BBC News*, February 23, 2015, http://www.bbc.com/news/world-middle-east-31583404

[114] Hamad, *When the Gavel Speaks*, 145 (describing the history in Egypt of purging outspoken judges under various leaders); "7 judges sent to retirement for MB affiliation," *Mada Masr*, January 27, 2014, http://www.madamasr.com/content/7-judges-sent-retirement-mb-affiliation; "Egypt refers 60 'pro-Brotherhood' judges to disciplinary board," *Al-Ahram Online*, October 20, 2014, http://english.ahram.org.eg/NewsContent/1/64/113517/Egypt/Politics-/Egypt-refers--proBrotherhood-judges-to-disciplinar.aspx

preservation of civil liberties, and the judges' obligation to serve as an impartial check on executive over-reaching.

Dissolving Egypt's democratically elected parliament

Soon after Mubarak was deposed, some MB members accused the SCC of being Mubarak loyalists keen on undermining the revolution.[115] Indeed, some parliamentarians affiliated with the MB went as far as calling for dissolution of the SCC. Others sought to transfer the SCC's jurisdiction to the Court of Cassation.[116] Coupled with Morsi's public criticism of the SCC, this inflammatory rhetoric triggered a war of attrition between the SCC and the Morsi regime that eventually expanded to the rest of the judiciary.

Some SCC justices responded by vocally criticizing Morsi and the Muslim Brotherhood on television and in newspaper interviews. In particular, then SCC Justice Tehanny El Gibally, expressed her disdain for the Muslim Brotherhood and outright opposition to then President Morsi as she accused them of loyalty to the international Muslim Brotherhood rather than Egypt.[117] In contrast to the judges currently under investigation for challenging the legality of Morsi's ouster in July 2013, El Gibally and other judges vocally critical of Morsi were not disciplined by the Judicial Inspection Office for violating the provisions of the Judicial Authority Law (JAL) that prohibit judges from engaging in politics. As discussed below, such selective enforcement is further evidence that the judiciary has become politicized.

The SCC went beyond rhetorical responses when it issued a ruling in June 2012 declaring unconstitutional the election law by which the sitting parliament was elected.[118] Election officials were found to have

---

[115] Daniel Nisman, "Showdown in Egypt's halls of justice," *Huffington Post*, July 8, 2013, http://www.huffingtonpost.com/daniel-nisman/showdown-in-egypts-halls-_b_3239213. html

[116] David Kirkpatrick, "Egyptian leaders meet in defiance of court and military," *New York Times*, July 10, 2012, http://www.nytimes.com/2012/07/11/world/middleeast/egyptian-parliamentary-deputies-defy-court-and-military.html?_r=0 (Some members of the MB even tried to have the Court of Cassation look at the decision to dissolve the parliament, something outside of their jurisdiction.)

[117] Sarah El Deeb, "Former judge challenges Egypt's constitution," *The Times of Israel*, January 8, 2013, http://www.timesofisrael.com/former-judge-challenges-egypts-constitution/

[118] "Q&A: Egypt's Supreme Court rulings," *BBC News*, June 17, 2012, http://www.bbc.com/news/world-middle-east-18463887 (review of what was deemed unconstitutional by the court's ruling)

violated the constitution in allowing political parties to compete for the seats designated for independents.[119] The Court-ordered remedy was to dissolve the entire parliament, as opposed to the one-third allotted to independent candidates, just weeks before Morsi became president.[120] That the parliament was controlled by the Muslim Brotherhood and Salafi political groups caused their supporters to call into question the SCC's motives.[121] In contrast to similar rulings in 1987 and 1990 when the SCC took months to make its decision, this ruling was issued within a matter of weeks. To political Islamists, this was further proof of the politicization of the SCC justices.[122] Moreover, each subsequent attempt Morsi's regime made to amend the election law in order to proceed with new parliamentary elections was rejected by the SCC. Morsi did not have a parliament during his year in office, thereby forcing him to govern by presidential decree and making him more vulnerable to accusations of authoritarianism.

The SCC's ruling that dissolved the parliament was just one among many rulings that effectively paralyzed Morsi's reform efforts. For instance, both of Morsi's parliamentary committees that he established to draft a new constitution were struck down as unconstitutionally created, and his appointment of Talaat Abdullah to replace Abdel Meguid Mahmoud as prosecutor general was reversed.[123]

But Morsi did not lose the war of attrition for lack of trying. He attempted to rein in the SCC by placing a constitutional limit on the number of justices to ten in addition to the chief justice, resulting in the removal of six justices including Tehanny El Gibally. Morsi also limited the SCC's judicial review to ex ante as opposed to post facto and proposed to decrease mandatory retirement for all judges from seventy to sixty years old.[124] These decisions proved fatal as the judiciary concluded Morsi's

---

[119] Kirkpatrick, "Blow to transition as court dissolves Egypt's parliament."

[120] Ibid.

[121] David Hearst and Abdel Rahman Hussein, "Egypt's Supreme Court dissolves parliament and outrages Islamists," *Guardian*, June 14, 2012, http://www.theguardian.com/world/2012/jun/14/egypt-parliament-dissolved-supreme-court

[122] Ibid.

[123] International Bar Association, "Separating Law and Politics," 6.

[124] Deeb, "Former judge challenges Egypt's constitution" (reduced the size of the court from eighteen to eleven); Chibli Mallat, "Reading the draft constitution of Egypt: Setbacks in substance, process, and legitimacy," *Al-Ahram Online*, December 2, 2012, http://english.ahram.org.eg/NewsContentP/4/59606/Opinion/Reading-the-Draft-Constitution-of-Egypt-Setbacks-i.aspx (limits court's review to before the fact instead of post facto review)

regime was a threat to its institutional interests.[125] Further angering the judges, Morsi took the unprecedented action in a nationally televised speech in June 2013 (just days before he was deposed) of accusing judges by name of corruption and participating in falsifying election results under Mubarak.[126] Tellingly, the names were taken from reports of election fraud issued by the judicial independence movement during the 2005 parliamentary elections.

Despite official denials, the political underpinnings of court rulings became clear once Morsi was deposed. Sitting judges openly expressed in court their disdain for the Muslim Brotherhood and the "black night" of Morsi's rule.[127] Such strong sentiments against the Muslim Brotherhood as a political opposition and specific defendants in legal proceedings are a troubling new development that signals a loss of judicial independence, due not only to external executive branch pressures, but also to endogenous politicization.

No accountability of Mubarak officials

Dubious prosecutions of former Mubarak officials are perhaps the most obvious examples of judicial bias against the revolutionary process. Because the public's demand for the criminal prosecutions of Mubarak-era officials was too great to ignore,[128] the SCAF had no choice but to charge them. However, the Mubarak-appointed prosecutor general, Abdel Meguid Mahmoud, sabotaged the trials by assigning junior prosecutors to complex corruption cases, conducting poor investigations that led to an incomplete evidentiary record, and declining to prosecute police and security personnel accused of killing protesters.[129] Rather than appoint investigating judges to conduct an impartial investigation,[130] the judges presiding over alleged police violence cases dismissed the cases. As a

---

[125] See Kleinfeld, "Competing Definitions of the Rule of Law," 264 (noting judges having little stake in broad political change).

[126] International Bar Association, "Separating Law and Politics," 14.

[127] David Kirkpatrick, "Egyptian court confirms death sentence for Morsi," *New York Times*, June 16, 2015, http://www.nytimes.com/2015/06/17/world/middleeast/egyptian-court-confirms-death-sentence-for-ousted-president-morsi.html

[128] Jeannie Sowers, "Egypt in Transformation," in Sowers and Toensing, *The Journey to Tahrir*, 13.

[129] International Bar Association, "Separating Law and Politics," 46, 48.

[130] Ibid., 43.

result, only one police officer is serving a three-year sentence for shooting protesters during the bloody Mohamed Mahmoud protests in November 2011 wherein over fifty-one protesters were killed in five days.[131] And only two police officers are serving time for killing at least 846 protesters in the January 2011 mass uprising.[132] Likewise, only one Egyptian policeman has been convicted of killing a protester after the July 2013 military coup that deposed Morsi, notwithstanding the hundreds killed in the Rabaa and al-Nahda squares sit-ins.[133]

In contrast, judges presiding over prosecutions of Muslim Brotherhood membership and leadership have convicted defendants with minimal evidence often limited to a security officer's testimony.[134] Cases that should have taken months to prosecute produced convictions in a matter of weeks. To a large extent, the judges' approach to police brutality cases and the politicization of the prosecutor general's office is a continuation of the Mubarak era.[135] But the judges' collective antagonism toward the revolution and its proponents as a threat to social order makes them even more partial to police and former Mubarak officials.

The same judicial leniency and flawed investigations infected the prosecutions of Hosni Mubarak, his sons, and his cronies. The former dictator has been cleared of corruption charges, and only faces a retrial on charges of the killings of protesters after his life sentence was remanded by the appellate court.[136] The few Mubarak-era officials charged with corruption are now free after their verdicts were overturned, while journalists and other political prisoners are denied bail on trumped-up charges.[137] Others such as Safwat al-Sherif and ex-Prime Minister

---

[131] Ibid., 48.

[132] Ibid.

[133] Laura King, "In a rare conviction, Egyptian policeman gets 15 years in protestor's death," *LA Times*, September 5, 2015, http://www.latimes.com/world/middleeast/la-fg-egypt-protester-slain-20150611-story.html

[134] "Egypt: Scant evidence for mass convictions," HRW, April 19, 2015, https://www.hrw.org/news/2015/04/19/egypt-scant-evidence-mass-convictions; "Egypt: Rab'a killings likely crimes against humanity," HRW, August 12, 2014, https://www.hrw.org/news/2014/08/12/egypt-raba-killings-likely-crimes-against-humanity

[135] International Bar Association, "Separating Law and Politics," 45.

[136] "Egypt court confirms ousted President Morsi's death sentence," Associated Press, *Boston Herald*, June 16, 2015, http://www.bostonherald.com/news_opinion/international/middle_east/2015/06/egypt_court_confirms_ousted_president_morsis_death

[137] "Egypt: Free illegally jailed journalist Al Jazeera correspondent held 9 months without charge," HRW, https://www.hrw.org/news/2014/05/15/egypt-free-illegally-jailed-journalist (At least 15 journalist are imprisoned while being denied bail for "assisting terrorism.")

Ahmed Nazif have been freed on bail despite serious corruption charges involving millions of Egyptian pounds.[138] That judges have been so lenient despite three decades of corruption and human rights violations against former senior Mubarak officials, while simultaneously denying bail, refraining from requiring proper investigations, and issuing the most severe sentences to Muslim Brotherhood defendants, is further evidence of endogenous politicization.

Deposing a democratically elected president

Of all the events that occurred after the January 25 revolution, the most surprising was the rapid political rise of the Muslim Brotherhood. Not only did they control nearly fifty percent of parliament, but they also won the presidency. Perhaps even more remarkably is the relatively free and fair elections under which the MB rose to power. After decades of rigged elections fraught with violence and fraud, the five elections that took place between 2011 and 2012 were not challenged even by the MB's most adamant detractors. Hence, the forced deposal of Morsi led by then Field Marshal Abd al-Fattah al-Sisi on July 3, 2013 was a direct affront to Egypt's slow progress toward granting its citizens political liberty through democratic elections. Notwithstanding Morsi's myriad political mistakes including a constitutional declaration that made his decrees immune from judicial review, the military's intervention moved the country further away from liberalism and firmly into the arms of authoritarianism.

Not only was Morsi deposed by the military, but he was also held incommunicado for four months without charges and outside the purview of law.[139] When the military finally disclosed his location, he

---

[138] Marwa al-Asar, "Egyptian rights group accuses justice system of double standards," *Middle East Eye*, June 2, 2015, http://www.middleeasteye.net/news/egyptian-rights-group-accuses-justice-system-double-standards-525727160 (Several former officials – including head of the dissolved ruling National Democratic Party (NDP) Safwat al-Sherif and ex-Prime Minister Ahmed Nazif – have also been freed, despite currently facing a raft of serious charges including profiteering and the illicit gain of millions of Egyptian pounds.)

[139] Maggie Michael, "Court sentences ousted Egyptian President Mohammed Morsi to 20 years in prison for protesters' deaths," *The World Post*, April 21, 2015, http://www.huffingtonpost.com/2015/04/21/mohammed-morsi-sentenced_n_7105972.htmltr

was immediately charged with terrorism, treason, and other serious crimes subject to the death penalty. Specifically, Morsi was accused of collaborating with Hamas to break out of prison during the eighteen-day revolution in 2011. Strangely, the alleged crimes were committed a year prior to Morsi's candidacy for president during which the High Elections Committee had disqualified multiple candidates on various grounds. That the military had this information as far back as January 2011 and yet did not disqualify Morsi raises serious questions as to both the veracity of the claims and the manipulation of law for political reprisal.[140]

Morsi was also charged with killing three protesters and torturing fifty-four others during the December 2012 protests at the presidential palace. These charges mirrored those facing Mubarak for the killing of protesters during the January 25 revolution. While Mubarak's trial has slowly gone through the courts with little evidence of judicial bias against him and his conviction was ultimately reversed on appeal, Morsi's legal team reportedly could not access his case files until after the trial began.[141] Moreover, Morsi's trial sped through the courts resulting in his being sentenced to death among a hundred others in two sweeping mass trials.

The Sisi regime also charged Morsi with illegally obtaining copies of intelligence reports and military plans while he was president. Although it remains unclear how having possession of such documents while president of the nation is illegal, the charges corroborate the extent to which the Sisi regime has gone to manipulate the law to settle political scores. But none of it would be possible without the cooperation of the judges. Those appointed to preside over the cases have not concealed their disdain for Morsi and other MB defendants. For instance, the judge presiding over the alleged jailbreak case condemned Morsi's rule as a "black night" and the Muslim Brotherhood as "satanic" and "diabolical."[142] Such overt partiality is far from what the founders of Egypt's judiciary envisioned when establishing a liberal institution. The rulings against Morsi signified a retraction of legal and political liberty as a new authoritarian military regime has replaced the Mubarak regime indefinitely.

---

[140] Ibid.
[141] Ibid.
[142] Kirkpatrick, "Egyptian court confirms death sentence for Morsi."

Silencing the revolutionary youth

The politicization of the judiciary also facilitated the regime's crackdown on youth activists and civil society groups that led and supported the January 25 uprisings.[143] Youth leaders who played an instrumental role in mobilizing Egyptians to stand up to Mubarak's repressive security forces in the heady days following January 25 are serving two- or three-year sentences for minor infractions of an anti-protest law hastily passed by interim president Adly Mansour without a parliament.[144] The protest law provided the legal pretext the executive needed to silence youth activists after they realized they had been duped into supporting the military's ouster of Morsi in July 2013. Despite international organizations' and human rights lawyers' condemnations of the prosecutions as violations of the right to assembly and expression, the Sisi regime continued using the draconian anti-protest law to silence dissenters of myriad ideological persuasions.[145]

While the number of youth activists jailed in the past two years is too large to address in detail, a few cases are worth highlighting as exemplars. Yara Sallam, a human rights lawyer, prominent Egyptian feminist, and a twenty-eight-year-old graduate of the elite American University in Cairo, was arrested on June 21, 2014 for allegedly violating the protest law.[146] As she was purchasing water with her cousin near the protest, security forces in civilian clothing arrested Sallam and twenty-two others accused of demonstrating in violation of the controversial protest law near the presidential

---

[143] See Nuno Garoupa and Tom Ginsburg, "The comparative law and economics of judicial councils," *Berkeley Journal of International Law* 27, no. 1 (2009): 60–1 (highlighting the tension between judicial independence and accountability and how more accountability may result in less independence and vice versa).

[144] "Egypt: Three prominent activists unlawfully detained under new assembly law," *Alkarama*, April 17, 2014, http://en.alkarama.org/egypt/1216-egypt-three-prominent-activists-unlawfully-detained-under-new-assembly-law; "Egypt's Maher, Adel and Douma sentenced to 3 years in jail," *Al-Ahram Online*, December 22, 2013, http://english.ahram.org.eg/News/89748.aspx; "Alaa Abdel Fattah: Egypt jails activist-blogger for five years," *BBC News*, February 23, 2015, http://www.bbc.com/news/world-middle-east-31583404

[145] "Egypt: Systematic abuses in the name of security," Amnesty International, April 5, 2007, http://www.amnesty.ie/sites/default/files/report/2010/04/Egypt%20Systematic%20abuses%20in%20the%20name%20of%20security.pdf

[146] Brian Dooley, "The exceptional Egyptian human rights defender Yara Sallam," *Huffington Post*, August 14, 2014, http://www.huffingtonpost.com/brian-dooley/the-exceptional-egyptian_b_5679301.html

palace.[147] Although her cousin was released a few hours later, security forces held Sallam and referred her to the prosecutor because she worked with the outspoken human rights organization the Egyptian Initiative for Human Rights (EIHR).[148] The judge in the misdemeanor court sentenced Sallam to three years later reduced to two years after appeal.[149] After significant international pressures, President Sisi issued a pardon that included Yara Sallam, Sanaa Seif, and Al Jazeera journalists, among others, a few days before he addressed the United Nations General Assembly in October 2015.[150]

Ahmed Douma, another prominent youth activist, was charged with organizing illegal protests and assaulting police officers during a protest. Judge Mohamed Nagi Shehata, who has been assigned to many post-July 3, 2013 cases involving the MB and youth activists, presided over Douma's case.[151] Douma was initially sentenced to three years in prison and fined 50,000 Egyptian pounds, but was later retried and sentenced to life in prison by Judge Shehata.[152]

In what appeared to be a systematic campaign to silence – through detention – the leading revolutionary youth, the government also targeted Ahmed Maher.[153] A cofounder of the April 6th Youth Movement grassroots movement that mobilized young Egyptians through social media and other new technologies, Maher was highly influential among

---

[147] Nourhan Fahmy, "One year behind bars due to controversial protest law," *Daily News Egypt*, June 21, 2015.

[148] Joe Stork, "Egypt's political prisoners," HRW, March 6, 2015, https://www.hrw.org/news/2015/03/06/egypts-political-prisoners

[149] "Egypt court reduces protestor sentences to 2 years," Associated Press, December 28, 2014, http://news.yahoo.com/egypt-court-reduces-protester-sentences-2-years-135448189.html

[150] Emma Graham-Harrison, "Egypt pardons and releases jailed al-Jazeera journalists," *Guardian*, September 23, 2015, http://www.theguardian.com/world/2015/sep/23/egypt-pardons-jailed-al-jazeera-journalists; "Update: Activists Yara Sallam and Sanaa Seif released from jail," *Mada Masr*, September 23, 2015, http://www.madamasr.com/news/update-activists-yara-sallam-sanaa-seif-released-prison

[151] Daragahi, "Egypt's 'Hanging Judge' accused of politicized verdicts"; Aya Nader, "The 'Executions' Judge Nagy Shehata," *Daily News Egypt*, February 16, 2015, http://www.dailynewsegypt.com/2015/02/16/executions-judge-nagy-shehata/

[152] "Egypt's Maher, Adel and Douma sentenced to 3 years in jail," *Al-Ahram Online*, December 22, 2013, http://english.ahram.org.eg/News/89748.aspx; Kouddous, "Egypt's judiciary."

[153] Shahira Amin, "Egypt: Law will 'severely erode civil liberties,'" Index on Censorship, April 14, 2014, https://www.indexoncensorship.org/2014/04/egypt-law-will-severely-erode-civil-liberties/

youth groups who suspected the military had sabotaged the revolution.[154] Maher accused the military and police of pushing Egypt backwards with regard to civil and political rights to levels worse than the last years of Mubarak's rule.[155] He also accused the Muslim Brotherhood of political ineptness and a power grab that ultimately led to a military coup in July 2013.[156] In the same trial as Douma's, Maher was sentenced to three years in prison for protesting against the anti-protest law passed in the fall of 2013. Maher's sentences were upheld on appeal.[157]

Other prominent youth activist leaders prosecuted for protesting illiberal government practices include blogger Alaa Abdel Fattah and his sister Sanaa Seif.[158] By prosecuting the activists and raising the liberty stakes, the regime effectively quashed the youth revolutionary movement through fear and deterrence. Rather than serve as a neutral check on executive over-reaching, the judiciary facilitated the regime's agenda, so much so that the use of special courts to try the political opposition has been unnecessary.

Equally troubling as the executive branch's aggressive political crackdown is the judiciary's cooperation. Rather than express concern with the threat that anti-protest laws may pose to freedom of speech, assembly, and other political rights, the judges sided with the state's narrative that protests threaten national security and social order. That then interim President Adly Mansour had been the chair of the SCC, to which he returned after Abd al-Fattah al-Sisi was elected president, further calls into question the SCC's commitment to freedom of speech and assembly, notwithstanding their rhetorical support for constitutional rights.[159] Thus, it is no surprise that youth activists, bloggers, and journalists hauled into

---

[154] Marwan Muasher, *The Second Arab Awakening and the Battle for Pluralism* (Yale: Yale University Press, 2014), 161–85.

[155] Stork, "Egypt's political prisoners."

[156] Ibid.

[157] Mai El Sadany, "Life sentence for Douma: The latest story of justice denied," Tahrir Institute for Middle East Policy, February 5, 2015, http://timep.org/commentary/life-sentence-for-douma/

[158] Dalia Rabie, "A year at the courts: Dissidents sentenced, old regime figures acquitted," *Mada Masr*, December 29, 2014, http://www.madamasr.com/sections/politics/year-courts

[159] Ryan J. Suto, "Proven guilty: Egypt's judiciary and the undermining of democracy," Atlantic Council, April 28, 2014, http://www.atlanticcouncil.org/blogs/egyptsource/proven-guilty-egypt-s-judiciary-and-the-undermining-of-democracy#.U16VlSR1W4U. twitter

criminal court find judges overtly partial to the prosecution at worst or complacent at best.[160]

One explanation for this troubling phenomenon may be that only a select number of handpicked loyalist judges (among a growing number of loyalist judges) are willing to do the executive's bidding. Prior to January 25, 2011 this explanation was plausible. However, I argue that in the past four years the judiciary's shift away from liberalism has accelerated. Although this is largely due to the threats to their material interests that the revolution posed, the explanation is more complex and nuanced. That is, Mubarak's concerted cooptation strategies were effective in shaping the culture of the judiciary to favor a strong central state particularly if that quashed the development of a populist democracy. And because the judges have always viewed themselves as the guardians of social order,[161] their increasingly illiberal notions of what it takes to produce social order is manifested in their rulings against youth activists, dissident journalists, and the Muslim Brotherhood. The judges' illiberal rulings extended to their colleagues in the reformist camp.

Expelling reformist judges

The Sisi and Mansour regimes also targeted reformist judges whose judicial independence campaigns over the past decade emboldened civil society to expand their activism from the courtrooms into the streets. Judges Club president Ahmad al-Zind actively called for aggressive prosecutions of judges who participated in the independence movement of 2005–6.[162] Al-Zind, who was later appointed minister of justice under Sisi, led the charge to discipline and expel seventy-five judges who publicly condemned the ouster of Morsi as an illegal coup.[163] Judges who openly

---

[160] Daragahi, "Egypt's 'Hanging Judge' accused of politicized verdicts."

[161] Rutherford, *Egypt after Mubarak*, 38.

[162] Tom Perry, "Egypt's Mursi faces judicial revolt over decree," Reuters, November 24, 2012, http://www.reuters.com/article/2012/11/24/us-egypt-president-idUSBRE8AM0DO 20121124; "Egypt judges call for national strike over Mursi decree," *BBC News*, November 24, 2012, http://www.bbc.com/news/world-middle-east-20476693

[163] Mara Revkin, "Egypt's injudicious judges," *The Middle East Channel*, June 11, 2012, http://mideastafrica.foreignpolicy.com/posts/2012/06/11/egypts_injudicious_judges; "Egypt: Behind Mursi's decisions, II," *Daily Kos*, November 29, 2012, http://www.dailykos.com/story/2012/11/29/1165273/-Egypt-Behind-Mursi-s-Decisions-II#

aligned themselves with the Morsi regime, whether by supporting his legal decrees or condemning the events of July 3, 2013 as a military coup, became targets of internal disciplinary investigations with minimal due process rights.[164] Politically motivated disciplinary hearings resulted in their expulsion from the judiciary, sending a chilling message to other judges.[165]

Ironically, al-Zind and his followers who openly condemned Morsi as an incompetent president, an arguably political activity, are now accusing reformist judges of violating the JAL provision prohibiting judges from engaging in politics.[166] And yet, disciplinary proceedings have not been opened against judges who vocally opposed Morsi and expressed their support for Sisi. Thus, enforcement of the JAL's prohibition against political activity was more about a judge's non-alignment with the military-security apparatus than an objective determination that a particular judge violated the JAL.

As of the fall of 2015, it is clear that key members of the judicial leadership actively supported the deep state in ousting Morsi and the MB from power. Many judges initially kept quiet as they were all too familiar with the high price of betting on the losing side of a high-stakes political game. And justifiably so, as the reformist judges that spoke out against the military's takeover of the state are now being purged from the judiciary.[167] More than three years after Egypt's uprising, the judiciary has

---

[164] Adham Youssef, "Pro-Morsi judges forced into retirement," *Daily News Egypt*, March 14, 2015, http://www.dailynewsegypt.com/2015/03/14/pro-morsi-judges-forced-into-retirement/

[165] Egyptian Initiative for Personal Rights, "Rights groups condemn forced retirement of 41 judges for expressing their opinions," March 18, 2015, http://eipr.org/en/pressrelease/2015/03/18/2344

[166] Rana Allam, "Justice Minister Al-Zind: A perfect representation of the times," *Daily News Egypt*, May 20, 2015, http://www.dailynewsegypt.com/2015/05/20/justice-minister-al-zend-a-perfect-representation-of-the-times/ (His allegiance to the Mubarak regime and to the armed forces rule is non-questionable of course. During the January 25 revolution, al-Zind attacked judges who joined in the protests, saying that "these judges do not represent the judiciary. Judges should not join the commons and the mob." Later, in the months when the Supreme Council of Armed Forces ruled post-Mubarak, al-Zind said that anyone who opposes SCAF is a "traitor." Without a doubt, one of the fiercest opponents of the January revolution and everything it stands for.) For a summary of similar events in Chile under Pinochet, see Lisa Hilbink, *Judges Beyond Politics in Democracy and Dictatorship: Lessons from Chile* (New York: Cambridge University Press, 2007), 39.

[167] Hamad, *When the Gavel Speaks*, 145 (describing the history in Egypt of purging outspoken judges under various leaders); "7 judges sent to retirement for MB affiliation," *Mada Masr*,

proven to be an endogenously politicized institution guarding its material interests in the status quo even if it means betraying its liberal origins.[168]

CONCLUSION

The events that have transpired since the mass uprisings of 2011 signify not only a court-centered counterrevolution but also a deliberalization of the Egyptian judiciary. Dating as far back as the Nasser era, Egypt's judges have been under inordinate pressure to cede their independence to the executive. Notwithstanding courageous efforts by reformist judges over the past sixty years, the executive masterfully manipulated judges' material interests to incentivize cooperation and punish independence. In the decade preceding the January 25 uprisings, the perennial power struggle between these two government branches left the judicial independence movement in tatters. As loyalist judges worked behind the scenes with the Mubarak regime to garner the support of the opportunist judges, the reformist judges' influence waned. The result is a group of judges who no longer feel obliged to remain impartial in disputes between political actors as they issue rulings directly infringing on private, political, and legal liberty.

Despite this, the post-January 25 judiciary views itself as the guardian of social order and political stability against proclaimed transgressions of political Islamists and youth revolutionaries. Formalistic and thin rule of law have become the centerpiece of a highly circumscribed definition of liberalism that discounts political liberty and dismisses personal liberty altogether. While some judges are coerced into cooperating with, or at least not challenging, the Sisi regime's authoritarian laws, that does not fully explain the judiciary's recent rulings sentencing hundreds of political Islamists to death, convicting thousands more to life in prison, and failing to hold Mubarak-era officials accountable for past crimes. Rather,

---

January 27, 2014, http://www.madamasr.com/content/7-judges-sent-retirement-mb-affiliation; "Egypt refers 60 'pro-Brotherhood' judges to disciplinary board," *Al-Ahram Online*, October 20, 2014, http://english.ahram.org.eg/NewsContent/1/64/113517/Egypt/Politics-/Egypt-refers--proBrotherhood-judges-to-disciplinar.aspx
[168] Daragahi, "Egypt's 'Hanging Judge' accused of politicized verdicts"; "Egypt using courts and jail to intimidate journalists, Amnesty International says," Reuters, May 2, 2015, http://www.theglobeandmail.com/news/world/egypt-using-courts-and-jail-to-intimidate-journalists-amnesty-international-says/article24231411/; Kouddous, "Egypt's judiciary."

a powerful faction of loyalist judges appears to be wholeheartedly in support of the Sisi regime and its nationalistic fervor promoting security over all else. In exchange for more, though not complete, autonomy from executive interference that translates into preserving their material interests, the judiciary has acquitted police accused of human rights abuses, released Mubarak-era officials with minimal sentences, and punished political dissidents of various ideological affiliations.[169] The end result is the deliberalization of an institution once considered a bastion of anti-colonial national sovereignty and liberal constitutionalism in the early twentieth century.[170]

---

[169] "Egypt court acquits police of 2011 killings," Al Jazeera America, February 22, 2014, http://america.aljazeera.com/articles/2014/2/22/egyptian-police-morsi.html (reporting that six officers were acquitted on charges of killing eighty-three protesters); "Prominent Egyptian activist among 230 sentenced to life," Al Jazeera, February 4, 2014, http://www.aljazeera.com/news/2015/02/prominent-egyptian-activist-230-sentenced-life-150204125859073.html; "We will not be silenced: April 6, after court order banning group," Al-Ahram Online, April 28, 2014, http://english.ahram.org.eg/NewsContent/1/64/100015/Egypt/Politics-/We-will-not-be-silenced-April-,-after-court-order-.aspx

[170] Jothie Rajah, "Punishing bodies, securing the nation: How rule of law can legitimate the urbane authoritarian state," Law & Social Inquiry 36, no. 4 (2011): 948.

SECTION II
Liberalism and Egyptian civil society

5

The authoritarian state's power over civil society

ANN M. LESCH

Non-governmental organizations (NGOs) operate in Egypt under severe constraints. The government monitors groups that provide charitable assistance and confronts those that seek to advance human rights. NGOs search for small openings or weakened resolve by the security system. Under President Hosni Mubarak, NGOs carved out spaces for autonomous action – and then burst forth in January 2011, anticipating significant opportunities once the ossified regime was overthrown. Expectations were upended when the military seized power, followed by the polarized year of electoral democracy and then the powerful reassertion of state control in July 2013. NGOs – and particularly advocacy organizations – came under attack. Although they have barely survived, they still attempt to hold the state system to account.

This chapter addresses the political and legal developments under Mubarak, the Supreme Council of the Armed Forces (SCAF), the Muslim Brotherhood, and now Abd al-Fattah al-Sisi. It emphasizes NGOs' efforts to address social justice concerns, in the context of regimes' actions to limit public space.

THE STRUCTURES OF AUTHORITARIANISM

The authoritarian state imposes severe constraints on autonomous organizations, given its determination to monopolize power and discourse.[1] The 1971 constitution concentrated power in the president, who appointed the prime minister, council of ministers, and governors, and dissolved the People's Assembly. The state of emergency reinforced those powers, as the president (or the interior minister, to whom he could delegate this authority) could ban publications, forbid meetings, search persons and places, and detain suspects at will. Independent bodies were nationalized: private religious charities and foundations (*awqaf*), trade unions, professional syndicates, the media, private schools, and NGOs. There was no competitive political party system until the mid-1970s, when the regime licensed a few parties that operated under severe constraints. The president headed the party that dominated the legislature.

The judiciary disciplined citizens. Under the state of emergency, civilians were charged before state security and military courts, and held in detention facilities outside the Ministry of Justice's prison system. Military court judges, appointed by the armed forces, determined what cases fell under their jurisdiction and held trials behind closed doors.[2] Those convicted in a military court cannot appeal to the Court of Cassation; only the president reviews verdicts.

Moreover, the president and the minister of justice wielded significant power over the regular judiciary. The president appointed the chief justice of the Supreme Constitutional Court (SCC) and the prosecutor general. The minister of justice appointed the presidents of the high courts. Even today, the minister assigns investigating judges to specific cases, seconds judges to administrative positions or to international organizations, and initiates disciplinary proceedings against them. The public prosecutor decides if there is enough evidence, formulates charges, and presents them to the court. The prosecutor relies heavily on evidence provided (or withheld) by the security and police forces. Judges and prosecutors seek to please the minister so that they will not be banished to the hinterland

---

[1] Ann Mosely Lesch, "Politics in Egypt," in *Comparative Politics Today*, ed. Gabriel A. Almond et al (Pearson Longman, 8th edition, 2006), 587–96; Maye Kassem, *Egyptian Politics: The Dynamics of Authoritarian Rule* (Boulder: Lynne Rienner, 2004), 87–117.

[2] International Bar Association, "Separating Law and Politics: Challenges to the Independence of Judges and Prosecutors in Egypt," International Bar Association Human Rights Institute, February 2014, 22–9, 33–5; Kassem, *Egyptian Politics*, 36–9.

or bypassed for a lucrative secondment. Moreover, state security often decides whether to prosecute a case, what evidence to present, and how to treat prisoners.

Constraints on NGOs

Prior to the 1952 revolution, the Ministry of Social Affairs (formed in 1939) licensed and audited NGOs, examined their membership lists and board minutes, and dissolved them, although NGOs could contest that in court. Under the military regime's Law 348/1956 and Law 32/1964, NGOs became adjuncts to the state. The minister of social affairs (now the minister of social solidarity, MOSS) approved or annulled the NGO, appointed (or rejected) board members, approved (or rejected or altered) budgets and fundraising programs, and served criminal charges against organizations that engaged in activities outside the approved arena.[3]

These constraints weighed heavily on advocacy groups that highlighted social and labor problems, struggled to expand public space, pressed for fair elections, opposed corruption, and/or sought academic freedom and the end to censorship. For example, in 1991, MOSS closed the Arab Women's Solidarity Association (AWSA), founded by feminist Nawal al-Saadawi, and transferred its assets to a semi-official NGO directed by a male MOSS official.[4]

In the late 1980s, advocacy groups were limited to the Egyptian Organization for Human Rights (EOHR, formed in 1985), Ibn Khaldun Center for Development Studies (1988), and the Center for Trade Union and Workers' Service (CTUWS, 1990).[5] A decade later, approximately twenty advocacy groups included the Cairo Institute for Human Rights Studies (CIHRS, 1993), El Nadeem Center for the Rehabilitation of Victims of Violence (1993), the Egyptian Center for Women's Rights (ECWR, 1996), and Hisham Mubarak Law Center (HMLC, 1999).

---

[3] Although the name of the ministry changed over time, I use MOSS throughout the chapter. Maha M. Abdelrahman, *Civil Society Exposed* (I.B. Tauris/The American University in Cairo Press, 2004), 120, 124–9; Kassem, *Egyptian Politics*, 88–9.
[4] AWSA had held a symposium criticizing the government's policy during the Gulf crisis. This violated the NGO law as it was overtly political and addressed an issue not related to gender. Abdelrahman, *Civil Society Exposed*, 137–8.
[5] "Egypt: Margins of repression: State limits on NGOs," Human Rights Watch (HRW), July 3, 2005, 23.

Most were unable to register under the NGO law or did not attempt registration. EOHR was rejected multiple times,[6] and HMLC became a law firm, registered via the Bar Association. El Nadeem's clinic registered under the health ministry, and the Ibn Khaldun Center and CTUWS registered as limited liability civil companies. A company registers under the civil code, maintains a tax record, and receives funds through a services contract or on a consulting basis. As that avoided MOSS's restrictions, many groups preferred to register as companies.

The government had scant tolerance for criticism. Having built up the security forces to fight Islamist militants in the 1990s, the regime then turned against civil society advocates. Under the cloak of suppressing Islamists, the government took control over most professional associations (e.g. medical, engineering, and teacher syndicates), abolished elections for village mayors and university deans, controlled student unions, restricted academic life, and emasculated political parties. The government encouraged the media to smear political and human rights activists. An especially fierce attack was launched by Mustafa Bakri, who had (and still has) close ties to security institutions. His *Al-Usbua* newspaper published a special eight-page supplement on Egyptian human rights organizations on November 23, 1998, which blasted them as agents of hostile foreign countries.[7] Bakri particularly targeted Hafez Abu Saeda, general secretary of EOHR. Arrested on December 1, 1998, state security charged Abu Saeda under Military Decree No. 4 (1992) with illegally accepting a check from the British Embassy to fund EOHR's report on police attacks on Copts in el-Kosheh village in order to claim that Egypt persecuted Christians.[8] The state security prosecutor used the same military decree

---

[6] Kassem, *Egyptian Politics*, 119–20; Abdelrahman, *Civil Society Exposed*, 137, 149.

[7] Statement by the Center for Human Rights Legal Aid (founded in 1994), November 26, 1998, signed by seven additional organizations, http://www.arabwestreport.info/year-1998/week-47/24-egyptian-organization-human-rights-under-attack; HRW, "Egypt: Margins of repression," 10–12, 18–19, 26–7.

[8] *Al-Usbua* alleged that a "hostile foreign country" ordered EOHR to write the September 1998 report on police brutality against Copts in el-Kosheh. The state security prosecutor charged EOHR with providing foreign countries with information harmful to the national interest and accepting foreign funds without prior state approval. EOHR proved that it funded the report itself for LE 323. The British embassy check was intended to support EOHR's Women's Legal Aid Project, which the embassy had funded for two years without governmental objection. EOHR returned the check to the embassy. "The Egyptian Organization for Human Rights under attack," Center for Human Rights Legal Aid report, November 26, 1998, http://www.arabwestreport.info/year-1998/week-47/24-

to close the Ibn Khaldun Center and arrest director Saad Eddin Ibrahim and his staff on June 30, 2000, charging that its European Commission-funded voter awareness campaign harmed Egypt's national interests.[9]

Although Abu Saeda was only held for one week and the case never went to court, the attack caused EOHR to consider disbanding. Ibrahim was detained for many months and sentenced to seven years' jail for receiving foreign funding without approval. After an appeals court quashed the verdict, the center lowered its profile and Ibrahim spent most of the 2000s abroad.[10]

Control via the NGO law

Meanwhile, parliament debated a new NGO law, against which several organizations submitted a counter-draft. Although the government's version was adopted in 1999, the Constitutional Court annulled it. A new Law 84/2002 (implemented in June 2003) retained top-down control but permitted advocacy programs and let NGOs operate in multiple fields, with MOSS permission. In practice, MOSS tried to limit NGOs to one uncontroversial activity.[11] MOSS had to approve activities that took place

egyptian-organization-human-rights-under-attack; Simon Apiku, "Government jails human rights leader over cash," *Middle East Times*, http://www.arabwestreport.info/year-1998/week-49/19-government-jails-human-rights-leader-over-cash, reprinted December 7, 1998; Simon Apiku, "EOHR braces itself for legal battle with the state," *Middle East Times*, http://www.arabwestreport.info/year-1998/week-52/16-eohr-braces-itself-legal-battle-state, reprinted December 27, 1998; Christina Lamb, "Egyptian police 'crucify' and rape Christians," *Daily Telegraph*, October 25, 1998.

[9] Saad Eddin Ibrahim investigated police brutality in el-Kosheh in August 1998, December 1999, and January 2000. Although threatened by state security, he was protected by Suzanne Mubarak, whom he had taught at the American University in Cairo. She turned against him in June 2000 when he compared the succession of Hafez Assad's son to the potential succession of Gamal Mubarak. http://www.euromedrights.org/eng/2000/07/11/open-letter-concerning-the-arrest-of-dr-saad-el-din-ibrahim, accessed June 4, 2014; Kassem, *Egyptian Politics*, 170–4; Nadia Abou El-Magd, "The meanings of Al-Kosheh," *Al-Ahram Online*, February 3, 2000, http://weekly.ahram.org.eg/2000/467/eg7.htm

[10] Sentenced *in absentia* in 2008 to two years' prison for "defaming Egypt" after he called on the US government to cut military aid, Ibrahim returned during the 2011 uprising. Profile, 2008, http://www.cartercenter.org/peace/human-rights/defenders/defenders/Egypt_saad-eddin_ibrahim

[11] The Center for Trade Union and Workers' Services, established in 1990 as a civil company, was initially ordered to omit "trade union" and "workers" from its title. The Foundation for the Child Worker and His Local Society, founded in 1993, was told that it could not

outside the governorate in which the main office was located, thereby preventing an NGO from holding training programs or informational seminars throughout the country. Field research, media-related events, and publishing required additional licenses, and NGOs risked closure for not following MOSS's detailed regulations.[12] Hoping to reduce risk, some NGOs hired MOSS-affiliated personnel, at the NGO's expense.

The law criminalized non-registered NGOs and banned activities that "threaten national unity" or "violate public order or morals." These vague terms served "as a catch-all to control the parameters of public life and political debate."[13] MOSS dissolved NGOs simply by administrative order, for technical violations or receiving funds from or affiliating with foreign organizations without prior permission. As international networks were vital for advocacy groups, this impaired their operations.[14]

State security had (and has) the final say in approving NGOs, their personnel, and activities. "Security concerns" are frequently invoked to reject them.[15] For example, an NGO must send the names of proposed new board members to MOSS at least sixty days before their election;

---

handle issues concerning children's relations with their employers or child workers' rights. HRW, "Egypt: Margins of repression," 18–23.

[12] MOSS specifies the number of board members; the terms and procedures for annual meetings; the quorum, frequency, and procedures for executive committee meetings; and the specifics of fundraising and record keeping. NGOs must give MOSS advance notice of annual meetings and provide the minutes. MOSS can convene NGO board meetings. MOSS approves NGO staff's invitations to conferences. HRW, "Egypt: Margins of repression," 12–13.

[13] Ibid., 26.

[14] El Nadeem Center is a member of the Council of International Rehabilitation Centers against Torture (RCT), the section on Torture and Psychology of the International Society for Health and Human Rights, and the World Psychiatric Association, http://alnadeem. org/en/. Andalus Institute partners with CIHRS, Euro-Mediterranean Human Rights Network, the Goethe Institute, and such funders as USAID, NED, IRI, MEPI, and the Anna Lindh Foundation, http://andalusitas.net/Partners/Default.aspx/. MOSS refused to let the Land Center for Human Rights join an international coalition on housing rights; HRW, "Egypt: Margins of repression," 33.

[15] The Egyptian Center for Housing Rights, EIPR, the Civil Observatory for Human Rights, and the Center for Human Rights were rejected on security grounds. The New Women Foundation (NWF) was rejected by the security directorate in Giza; the State Council (majlis al-dawla) overruled that rejection. The Egyptian Association Against Torture was informed that it violated "public order" by seeking to bring Egyptian legislation into compliance with international human rights standards, campaigning against torture, and participating in anti-torture networks in the Arab world and internationally. HRW, "Egypt: Margins of repression," 3, 21–23.

MOSS and any "interested party" (a code for state security) can block those individuals. Even after MOSS approves a grant request, security can block the bank from releasing the funds. And it monitors NGOs via security personnel stationed inside MOSS. Moreover, security officers pressure hotels to not host conferences and prevent printing presses from publishing brochures or monographs.[16] NGOs are harassed by anonymous phone calls, random visits, the intrusive presence of security personnel at public meetings (who sometimes examine the IDs of attendees), and searches at the airport.

Growth of advocacy organizations

Nonetheless, advocacy organizations proliferated in the 2000s and became increasingly specialized. Some registered with MOSS as associations or foundations but many became law firms, companies, or research institutes. These organizations report on and help solve problems related to rural and urban poverty, environmental deterioration, dysfunctional public schools, street children and child labor, sexual harassment, restrictions on the press, police coercion and torture, and thuggery during elections.[17]

Some handle legal cases and advocate for legal reform. For example, the Egyptian Initiative for Personal Rights (EIPR, founded in 2002) engages in advocacy and litigation on civil liberties, economic and social rights, and criminal justice. HMLC, while deeply engaged in litigation, also publishes informational monographs on professional syndicates, political parties, workers' rights, health insurance, the right to education, and the constitutionality of emergency laws. HMLC works closely with the Egyptian Center for Economic and Social Rights (ECESR, 2010), which pursues legal cases on behalf of workers, and also with the El Nadeem Center for

---

[16] Shady Talaat, Lawyers Union for Democratic and Legal Studies, "Shadow Report, Egypt, 2010 UPR: Restrictions imposed on the non-governmental organizations," submission to the High Commissioner for Human Rights, http://www.lib.ohchr. org/HRBodies/UPR/Documents/Session7/EG/LUDLS_UPR_EGY_S07_2010_ LawyerUnionforDemocraticandLegalStudies.pdf

[17] Cf. Egyptian Center for Children's Rights (founded in 2002), New Woman Foundation (founded in 1983; registered as a foundation in 2004), Egyptian Center for Women's Rights (1996), Nazra for Feminist Studies (2005), Egyptian Center for Housing Rights (2004), Land Center for Human Rights, Egyptian Association for Developing Legal Awareness (2004), Egyptian Center for the Right to Education, Andalus Institute for Tolerance and Anti-Violence Studies, and ANHRI (2007).

the Rehabilitation of Victims of Violence on cases of police and domestic violence and torture.[18]

Heba Morayef, a leading human rights analyst, reflects that the combination of strategic litigation and calling the attention of the media to police abuse made the human rights organizations a "thorn in the side of the Mubarak regime." Although under heavy surveillance by the Ministry of Interior and under threat of closure, they used their "limited space to maneuver" increasingly effectively.[19]

Moreover, as their publications became available online (often in both Arabic and English), their efforts became known internationally and their global networks expanded. Thus, the Arabic Network for Human Rights Information (ANHRI) republishes statements by Arab human rights organizations; hosts a blog and legal service website as a source for court verdicts, legal acts, and the texts of constitutions; publishes annual reports on freedom of opinion and expression; and issues guides to human rights concepts, taking testimony, writing legal briefs, observing trials, and conducting visits to prisons.[20]

A wide range of labor, political, and advocacy organizations set up the Egyptian Alliance for the Integrity of Civil Society, which drafted a Code of Ethics in 2009, endorsed by more than a hundred associations.[21] This underlined their concern to adopt accountability mechanisms to promote internal democracy and preclude internal corruption, in part to undermine the government's claim that controls must be punishment-based. The Alliance also monitored the highly problematic parliamentary elections in 2010. The core group of NGOs penned a

---

[18] El Nadeem Center registered as both a medical clinic and a company focused on the psychological rehabilitation of African refugees, victims of police violence, and female victims of domestic violence and rape, http://alnadeem.org/en/; HRW, "Egypt: Margins of repression," 33.

[19] Heba Morayef, former Egypt program director for Human Rights Watch, "Reexamining Human Rights Change in Egypt," Middle East Research and Information Project, n.d. (spring 2015), http://www.merip.org/mer/mer274/reexamining-human-rights-change-egypt

[20] Arabic Network for Human Rights Information (ANHRI), www.anhri.net/en

[21] "EOHR announces the establishment of the Egyptian Alliance for the integrity of civil society," EOHR, October 21, 2009, http://en.eohr.org/2009/10/21/eohr-announces-the-establishment-of-the-egyptian-alliance-for-the-integrity-of-civil-society; "Representatives of civil society organizations call for establishing a coalition for integrity," EOHR, November 19, 2009, http://en.eohr.org/2009/11/19/representatives-of-civil-society-organizations-call-for-establishing-a-coalition-for-integrity

common report on Egypt's human rights situation to the UN Human Rights Council for Egypt's first Universal Periodic Review in 2010.[22] When the government subsequently promised the UN to amend Law 84/2002, these groups proposed a new law to allow forming NGOs simply by "notification."[23]

Advocacy groups bolstered public efforts to promote democratic and labor rights. Kifaya, the Egyptian Movement for Change, protested at plans for Gamal Mubarak, the president's younger son, to inherit the presidency, and decried corruption and anti-democratic practices. During the 2000s, two million workers held sit-ins and strikes against privatization and roll-backs in laborers' rights. The Real Estate Tax Collectors (supported by HMLC and ECESR) won the right to establish the first independent trade union. Journalists and activists demonstrated against criminalizing speeches and writings, professional syndicates fought against sequestration, and professors struggled against limitations on academic freedom. Campaigns involved multiple organizations, which amplified the demands and offered some protection against government retaliation. Months before the January 25 uprising, ECESR and CTUWS won a court case to achieve an LE 1200 ($216) minimum wage. It is significant that economic and political demands merged in the workers' chants: "A

---

[22] Joint NGO submission in February 2010 by seven NGOs (including EIPR and ECESR), endorsed by additional organizations. Center for Economic and Social Rights, "Egypt: Submission to UN Human Rights Council's Universal Periodic Review," http://www.cesr.org/article.php?id=878

[23] EOHR, CIHRS, and other organizations drafted bills in 2008 and 2010 to replace Law 84/2002. Their drafts would register NGOs through simply notifying MOSS, gain the right to work in all fields, and cancel the government's monitoring of all documents, sending security forces to raid premises, and dissolving NGOs or stopping activities without judicial decision. NGOs would merely declare the source of funds and could develop financial resources via fees, donations, and activities, hold meetings without restriction, release reports and magazines without prior permission, join international coalitions and networks, and form the board of trustees by direct election by the NGO's general assembly. "EOHR submits a number of bills before human rights committee in the Parliament," EOHR, n.d., http://en.eohr.org/eohr-submits-a-new-bill-for-ngos-to-the-president-and-peoples-assembly; "EOHR calls on the government for a timetable and mechanisms for implementation" of the UPR recommendations, EOHR, February 23, 2010, http://en.eohr.org/2010/02/23/to-put-in-action-the-recommendations-of-un-human-rights-council; Justin Shore, "Human Rights Council Universal Periodic Review prompts Egypt to promise NGO reform," Human Rights Brief, March 24, 2010, http://hrbrief.org/2010/03/human-rights-council-universal-periodic-review-prompts-egypt-to-promise-ngo-reform

fair minimum wage or let this government go home" and "Down with Mubarak and all those who raise prices."[24]

THE POST-25 JANUARY MILITARY REGIME

The 2011 uprising articulated the yearning for dignity, social justice, and the end to the corrupt security state.[25] Egyptians crowded public spaces, seeking to reclaim citizenship rights. Workers utilized their extensive strike experience to sustain protests. Doctors volunteered in informal clinics, and NGO staff helped to find detainees and identify bodies in the morgues.

Advocacy groups played valuable supporting roles. The Cairo office of HMLC, for example, became a hub, where staff and volunteers manned emergency phone lines, dispatched lawyers to find detainees, and documented deaths and injuries.[26] On February 3, the day after the infamous "battle of the camel," military police raided the center, seized computers (including seven hundred case files), and detained two dozen staff, lawyers, and volunteers. They arrested members of the Front to Defend Egypt's Protesters and staff from the Egyptian Center for Housing Rights, located in the same building. That day marked the climax of government incitement against "foreign hands" for fomenting the protests: police arrested random foreigners in the street and the military expelled foreign journalists from protest areas. A police-organized mob surrounded the Center, shouting "spies" and "traitors" as the military arrested foreign journalists and representatives of Amnesty International and Human Rights Watch who were in the office. Army officers denounced the foreigners as Israeli spies who were "ruining our country." Although they released the Egyptians and foreigners from a military camp a day later, the raid portended the "foreign agent" charges that the military continued to level against critics.

---

[24] Ann M. Lesch, "Concentrated power breeds corruption, repression, and resistance," in *Arab Spring in Egypt*, ed. Bahgat Korany and Rabab El-Mahdi (Cairo: The American University in Cairo Press, 2012), 35.

[25] Ann M. Lesch, "Egypt's Spring: Causes of the revolution," *Middle East Policy* XVIII, 3 (Fall 2011): 35–48.

[26] Dan Williams (HRW), "My 36 hours in Egyptian captivity," February 7, 2011, http://www.thedailybeast.com/articles/2011/02/07/my-36-hours-in-egyptian-captivity.html; "Kidnapping rights activists from Hisham Mubarak Law Center," February 4, 2011, http://www.hmlc-egy.org/node/1656; Joe Stork, "Ahmed Seif Al Islam: In Memoriam," HRW, August 28, 2014, https://www.hrw.org/news/2014/08/28/ahmed-seif-al-islam-memoriam

When SCAF shunted President Mubarak aside on February 11, pro-testers went home, hoping for a genuine political transformation rather than the military officers' replacement of one *Mamluk* sultan with another. Nonetheless, some mistrusted SCAF chair Field Marshal Mohammad Hussein Tantawi, Mubarak's loyal minister of defense for twenty years, and worried about SCAF's constitutional roadmap, which postponed rewriting the constitution until after parliamentary and presidential elections. Many NGOs, politicians, and activists preferred a civilian council to manage the transition, curb SCAF, and ensure legal action against Mubarak's coterie for economic and political crimes.

Repression through military courts

Reform of the security establishment was high priority. Bahey al-Din Hassan of CIHRS and Hossam Bahgat of EIPR drafted proposals to reform the police and security forces, whose thuggish behavior was a major cause of the January uprising. Continued violations made reform pressing. A mere two weeks after removing Mubarak, the generals unleashed the military police and central security forces against unarmed protesters in Tahrir Square. The unceasing attacks on protesters throughout the seven-teen months of SCAF rule included the violent clearing of Tahrir Square on August 1, the attack on a peaceful Coptic procession on October 9, and running battles with demonstrators in November and December. Human rights organizations condemned the army's swift resort to live ammunition against protesters.[27]

Advocacy groups also decried SCAF's use of military courts to try civilians, based on the British-era anti-demonstration laws, the state of emergency, and SCAF's Law 34/2011, which criminalized "the dis-ruption of the work of public institutions or public or private work."[28] Nearly twelve thousand civilians were referred to military courts in the first seven months; only seven percent were acquitted. This was more

---

[27] E.g. fourteen groups criticized the use of live ammunition against protesters near the Ministry of Defense. "Abbasiya events a continuation of SCAF's systematic violations of human rights in the transitional period," May 7, 2012, http://eipr.org/en/pressrelease/2012/05/07/1410

[28] "World Report 2012: Egypt," HRW, http://www.hrw.org/world-report-2012/world-report-2012-egypt

than Mubarak had subjected to military courts in thirty years.[29] Convicts included curfew-breakers, bloggers who "insulted the military institution" and "distributed false news that disturbs public security,"[30] and Petrojet workers, whose wage-related demonstration took place in front of the ministry of petroleum, a civilian institution.[31] On June 4, 2013, just after the state of emergency expired, the justice minister empowered the military to arrest civilians if they operated unregistered associations, insulted officials, or spread false information to affect national security – proof that SCAF intended to retain its extraordinary powers after the transition to a civilian president.[32]

New groups – notably, the No Military Trials for Civilians, the Anti-Torture Task Force, and the Front to Defend Egypt's Protesters – joined long-standing advocacy groups to oppose the militarization of justice, provide legal assistance, call for retrials before civilian courts, decry the failure to arrest those who killed demonstrators, and demand a new law to regulate demonstrations rather than criminalize them. Human rights organizations issued numerous joint statements against, for example, arson attacks on churches in Imbaba in May 2011 and the armed forces' attack on Coptic marchers on October 9. They filed a suit with the administrative court (*majlis al-dawla*) against SCAF in July 2011 for invasive "virginity tests" performed on female detainees by military doctors, which Director of Military Intelligence Sisi had justified.[33]

---

[29] "Egypt: Retry or free 12,000 after unfair military trials," HRW, September 10, 2011, http://www.hrw.org/news/2011/09/10/egypt-retry-or-free-12000-after-unfair-military-trials

[30] Maikal Nabil Sanad, held in a military prison for nine months, "insulted the military" and "spread false information" in his blogs. International Bar Association, "Separating Law and Politics," 29; HRW, "World Report 2012: Egypt," 3–4.

[31] ECESR director Khaled Ali handled the lawsuit against Tantawi submitted by HMLC and the Hilali Foundation for Liberties. "In the first enforcement of the decree of prohibiting strikes the military court sentenced five workers in Petrojet Company to one year in prison with suspension," June 30, 2011, http://ecesr.org/en/2011/06/30/in-the-first-enforcement-of-the-decree-of-prohibiting-strikes-the-military-court-sentenced-five-workers-in-petrojet-company-to-one-year-in-prison-with-suspension/

[32] "Egypt: Military power grab creates conditions for abuse," HRW, June 21, 2012, https://www.hrw.org/news/2012/06/21/egypt-military-power-grab-creates-conditions-abuse

[33] Women Living under Muslim Laws, "Egypt: Challenging decision to conduct virginity tests on girls inside military prison," http://www.wluml.org/node/7437; "Egypt: Military pledges to stop forced 'virginity tests,'" Amnesty International, June 27, 2011, http://www.amnesty.org/en/for-media/press-releases/Egypt-military-pledges-stop-forced-virginity-tests-2011-06-27

NGOs promoted democratic principles and practices through frequent appearances on television and efforts to educate the newly emerging political parties. Some of their efforts were wide-ranging. CIHRS organized training workshops on how to enhance problem solving and planning within NGOs, ensure that municipalities will serve their constituents, apply international human rights standards, and promote human rights for women, children, work, education, health, and housing. The Andalus Institute for Tolerance and Anti-Violence Studies campaigned alongside the United Group law firm to raise awareness in villages about the electoral system and explain the role of civil society organizations in a democracy.[34] Nazra for Feminist Studies reported on violations against female human rights defenders, and the new HarassMap (later reinforced by I Saw Harassment and Tahrir Bodyguard) trained people to protect women and coordinated SMS reports on harassment. NGOs reinvigorated their efforts to observe and report on the elections for the People's Assembly (Majlis al-Sha'b), Consultative Council (Majlis al-Shura), and presidency.

Crackdown on foreign funding

Some NGOs offered training to staff in political parties on how to structure a party, organize an election campaign, and monitor elections. This required significant funding, which European governments and USAID were eager to provide. Although some organizations avoided foreign (and particularly US) funds, others welcomed USAID's offer of $45 million through a new Transition Support grants program to encourage democracy.[35] USAID signed grant- and cooperative- agreements in April with eight US organizations (notably, the National Democratic Institute, NDI, and the International Republican Institute, IRI), seven Egyptian civil companies, and nine Egyptian NGOs. Egyptian organizations obtained a mere sixteen percent ($7.4 million). By December 2011, USAID had disbursed only $9 million of the $45 million. According to the US auditors' report, civil companies' activities were on track as of March 2012, whereas

---

[34] http://andalusitas.net; http://www.ug-law.com/ug/
[35] Part of the $65 million USAID redistributed from the annual $250 million Economic Support Fund. Office of Inspector General, *Audit of USAID/Egypt's Transition Support Grants Program*, October 22, 2012, 1, 2, 4, 11, 21–25.

MOSS had approved just two of the nine NGO applications. Thus, seven NGOs' activities had halted or not yet started. Therefore, although the government subsequently criticized USAID for by-passing the Ministry of International Cooperation (MIC), USAID did not by-pass MOSS, which simply vetoed programs.[36]

MIC Minister Fayza Aboul Naga was the gate-keeper for foreign aid from governments, international organizations, and private sources.[37] Under Mubarak, she argued that US aid interfered in Egypt's internal affairs and violated its national security. She tried to shift that aid into an endowment fund controlled by the Egyptian government. She viewed the US as an enemy, not an ally: The US sought to "abort any chance for Egypt to rise…with a strong economy, since that will pose the biggest threat to American and Israeli interests."[38] Furious that the Transition Support grants by-passed her, Aboul Naga ordered the supreme state security prosecution to find out which Egyptian groups received those grants and which US organizations promoted democratization. The government also requested the Central Bank of Egypt to order banks to provide MOSS with information about all transactions by charities and civil society organizations in order to match their bank statements to financial statements the NGOs provided to MOSS.[39]

SCAF and the cabinet fully supported Aboul Naga. Senior generals criticized the US embassy for (allegedly) making grants that were not supervised by the Egyptian government and accused activist groups of

---

[36] Mohamed Elagati, "Foreign funding in Egypt after the revolution," Foundation for International Relations and Development (Madrid), 2013, 14.

[37] POMED, "Backgrounder: The campaign against NGOs in Egypt," Project on Middle East Democracy (POMED), February 10, 2012; "Egypt: Stop holding NGOs hostage," Amnesty International, February 7, 2012, http://www.amnesty.org/en/news/egypt-stop-holding-ngos-hostage-2012-02-07; "Egypt must end attacks on civil society," Amnesty International, March 1, 2012, http://www.amnesty.org/en/news/egypt-must-end-attacks-civil-society-2012-03-01

[38] "Egypt elevates official hostile to U.S., civil society," Democracy Digest, November 6, 2014, http://demdigest.net/blog/egypt-elevates-official-hostile-u-s-civil-society/; Fayza Aboulnaga, "Why Egypt moved against unregistered NGOs," Washington Post, March 9, 2012, https://www.washingtonpost.com/opinions/why-egypt-moved-against-unregistered-ngos/2012/03/05/gIQAEHrf1R_story.html

[39] IRIN, "Egypt's NGOs face tough post-revolution reality," Guardian, October 27, 2011, https://www.theguardian.com/global-development/2011/oct/27/egypt-ngos-clampdown-military-rulers

following a "foreign agenda" rather than serving Egypt's interests.[40] SCAF's Tantawi warned:

> There are foreign players who fund and set up specific projects that some individuals carry out domestically...It is possible...that foreign players are pushing the people in inappropriate directions... [as they] do not want stability for Egypt.[41]

The state security prosecutor and the minister of justice leaked serious accusations, and hinted that Egyptian NGOs could face emergency state security courts for "grand treason, conspiracy against Egypt and carrying out foreign agendas to harm Egyptian national security."[42] They leaked alleged amounts received by NGOs and claimed that thirty-nine Egyptian and foreign organizations operated "illegally," twenty-eight Egyptian organizations illegally received foreign funds, and several foreign organizations engaged in political activities.[43]

---

[40] SCAF's Major General Mohammad al-Assar spoke at the US Institute of Peace in Washington, DC, on July 25: "It is inconceivable that $40 million should go towards human rights when we have much bigger problems than this." Foreign funding to NGOs without government approval "represents a danger, in light of the recent incidents where many police weaponry was lost and about 20,000 prisoners escaped from the prisons of Egypt following the events experienced by the country." SCAF's General Hassan el-Roweini denounced the April 6th Youth Movement and Kifaya for (alleged) foreign funding. Mohannad Sabry, "Egyptian protesters sue military, raising tensions," McClatchyDC, July 25, 2011, http://www.mcclatchydc.com/2011/07/25/118202/egyptian-protesters-sue-military.html; Lauren Unger-Geoffroy, "Dispatches from Cairo: Egypt's war on NGOs," December 30, 2011, http://www.truthdig.com/report/egypts_war_on_ngos_20111230

[41] William Fisher, "Egypt: The Army's chess match?" February 14, 2012, http://pubrecord.org/world/10081/egypt-armys-chess-match; Unger-Geoffroy, "Dispatches from Cairo". USAID director Jim Bever, who approved the grants, abruptly left in August, just as Ambassador Anne Patterson arrived. "USAID director in Egypt quits over funding for pro-democracy groups," Associated Press, http://www.alarabiya.net/articles/2011/08/12/161903.html

[42] IRIN, "Egypt's NGOs face tough post-revolution reality"; Robert M. Danin, "Egypt's troubling road to the ballot box," Council on Foreign Relations, October 27, 2011, http://blogs.cfr.org/danin/2011/10/27/egypts-troubling-road-to-the-ballot-box/

[43] *Al-Fagr* on September 26 listed NGOs, including CIHRS, El Nadeem Center for the Rehabilitation of Victims of Violence, EIPR, and HMLC: none of them accepts US government funds. None could register as an NGO and therefore registered under other rubrics. Fisher, "Egypt"; Stephen McInerney, "SCAF's assault on Egypt's civil society," September 28, 2011, http://foreignpolicy.com/2011/09/28/scafs-assault-on-egypts-civil-society/

Prosecutors questioned staff at Egyptian and foreign NGOs about their licenses and funding. When SCAF installed a new cabinet in December, the new minister of justice requested detailed information on seventy-three registered NGOs.[44] On December 21, that minister ominously claimed that human rights organizations were the "third party" responsible for the Coptic march on October 9 and the months-long protests near Tahrir Square.[45] SCAF's Facebook page proclaimed: "The enemy awaits us!" "Honorable Egyptians" must support SCAF against the "barefaced interventions" by foreigners who seek to destabilize and divide Egypt.[46]

Alarmed at the government-orchestrated media campaign against "foreign hands," ANHRI called this worse than the Mubarak era. EIPR director Bahgat criticized the government for singling out "human rights organizations that played a role in exposing the authorities' violations" and treating "advocacy groups as enemies rather than partners." Attorney Negad al-Borai claimed that this fit "the military's strategy to limit the reach and resources available to civil society groups." And No Military Trials for Civilians' Mona Seif concluded: "The [military] council is trying to build a reputation for itself as the sole protector of the revolution and the ultimate source of patriotism."[47]

As tensions peaked in late December, thirty-nine NGOs appealed to the UN Human Rights Council's Special Rapporteurs[48] against the government's incitement and investigations:

> [We] hoped that civil society would be freed from the bureaucratic grasp of the state and its security apparatus and that it would be given the opportunity to perform its patriotic role by entrenching

---

[44] The new minister of justice requested from MOSS registration papers, dates of registration, names of the managers, audit reports, and inspection reports for the past five years. "Egypt: Justice Minister requests information on civil society groups," *Egypt Independent*, January 3, 2012, http://www.imra.org.il/story.php3?id=55177

[45] Sohair Reyad, "Raiding NGOs: The new way forward," CIHRS, January 4, 2012, http://www.cihrs.org/?p=757&lang=en

[46] Leila Fadel and Jody Warrick, "Egyptian security forces raid offices of U.S., other democracy groups," *Washington Post*, December 29, 2011, http://www.washingtonpost.com/world/middle_east/egyptian-security-forces-raid-offices

[47] "USAID director quits," AP, http://www.alarabiya.net/articles/2011/08/12/161903.html

[48] Text of NGOs' appeal to the UN, CIHRS, December 29, 2011, http://www.cihrs.org/?p=688&lang=en

democratic norms, respect for human rights, and social justice in post-revolutionary Egypt....[But] this hope soon faded in light of the unchanged mindset of the regime...In fact, the investigating authorities...are relying on reports prepared by the dissolved State Security Investigations Service [SSIS, *mabahith amn al-dawla*] of the Mubarak era – the very apparatus whose practices were one of the main reasons Egyptians revolted to bring down the regime.... [T]he interim government and the SCAF...[use the pretext of protecting national security] in their current assault on human rights groups...[who] decry its practices, such as the use of excessive force against unarmed demonstrators, the referral of civilians to military trials, torture by the military police, the Maspero massacre of Copts [on October 9], and other crimes.

NGOs' anguished appeal came just after the justice minister ordered prosecutors – accompanied by ministry inspection teams and heavily armed military and police officers – to storm seven institutions, seize all their documents and computers, and seal the offices.[49] EOHR's Abu Saeda then hosted a press conference at which NGOs denounced "the ferocious attack against many human rights and development NGOs."[50]

Those raids on December 29 targeted four US organizations, one German foundation, and two Egyptian NGOs: the Arab Center for the Independence of the Judiciary and the Legal Profession (ACIJLP) and the Budgetary and Human Rights Observatory (BAHRO). The Konrad Adenauer Foundation, affiliated with German Chancellor Angela Merkel's Christian Democratic Party, had quietly supported seminars and training programs for thirty years. The four US organizations were the central targets: IRI, NDI, Freedom House, and International Center for

---

[49] Peter Beaumont and Paul Harris, "US 'deeply concerned' after Egyptian forces raid NGO offices in Cairo," *Guardian*, December 29, 2011, http://www.theguardian.com/world/2011/dec/29/us-egyptian-forces-raid-cairo

[50] Quoted in Mohannad Sabry and Jonathan S. Landay, "Egypt crackdown escalates, with raids on 17 rights groups," McClatchyDC, December 29, 2011, http://www.mcclatchydc.com/2011/12/29/134420/egypt-crackdown-escalates-with.html; William Fisher, "Egypt security raids US, German and Egyptian NGOs," *The Public Record*, December 29, 2011, http://pubrecord.org/world/9964/egypt-security-raids-german-egypt-ngos; "Egypt rights groups blast raids on NGO offices," AP, December 30, 2011, http://www.wbur.org/2011/12/30/egypt-ngo-raids; Abdel-Rahman Hussein, "Egyptian activists react with fury to criminal trial for NGO workers," *Guardian*, February 6, 2012, http://www.theguardian.com/world/2012/feb/06/egyptian-activists-trials-ngo-workers

Journalists (ICFJ). Their staff were charged on February 5, 2012 with operating without a license, receiving unauthorized foreign funding, operating premises as branches of international organizations, violating tax codes, and engaging in activities "prohibited by law," including "political training programs." The ministers of justice and international cooperation lashed out at them,[51] and the prime minister proclaimed that "Egypt won't kneel."[52] Nonetheless, the government caved in to US pressure and let the foreigners flee Egypt in return for pocketing the $4.6 million bail bond.[53]

The judge issued his verdict on June 4, 2013, a year and a half later. He found all forty-three employees of the foreign NGOs guilty of "political

---

[51] Amnesty International, "Egypt: Stop holding NGOs hostage"; POMED, "Backgrounder: The campaign against NGOs in Egypt." NDI, IRI, and Freedom House had applied for registration with the Foreign Ministry in 2005, 2006, and December 2011, respectively. They were told to rent offices and recruit staff for their programs that trained Egyptian NGOs and political parties in election observation, administration, and civic engagement. NDI and IRI were accredited by the High Elections Committee to observe the November 2011–January 2012 parliamentary elections. Freedom House staff expressed concern about "pressure and harassment" from the government. ICFJ had just started and was planning a program to upgrade journalists' skills. The Konrad Adenauer Foundation supported seminars and training programs for thirty years under the Egyptian-German bilateral cultural framework. Danin, "Egypt's troubling road to the ballot box"; Nourhan Dakroury, "Convictions in NGO trial 'a disgrace,'" *Daily News Egypt*, June 4, 2013, http://www.dailynewsegypt.com/2013/06/04/convictions-in-ngo-trial-a-disgrace/; "Freedom House condemns raids of NGOs in Egypt," Freedom House, December 29, 2011, https://freedomhouse.org/article/freedom-house-condemns-raids-ngos-egypt, December 29, 2011; interview with Adenauer Foundation chair Hans-Gert Pottering, former president of the European Parliament, "'Absurd' sentences in Cairo for Germans," Deutsche Welle, June 5, 2013, http://www.dw.de/absurd-sentences-in-cairo-for-germans/a-16858963

[52] Fisher, "Egypt"; Ahmed Morsy, "Egypt's NGO crisis: Political theater preventing democratic progress," Atlantic Council, March 8, 2012, http://www.atlanticcouncil.org/blogs/egyptsource/egypt-s-ngo-crisis-political-theater-preventing-democratic-progress

[53] Ben Quinn, "Americans barred from leaving Egypt seek refuge at US embassy in Cairo," *Guardian*, http://www.theguardian.com/world/2012/jan/30/americans-barred-egypt-cairo-embassy; David Kenner, "Egypt's left behind," June 4, 2013, http://foreignpolicy.com/2013/06/04/egypts-left-behind/. The Court of Appeals set the bail at LE 2 million ($332,000) per defendant. USAID used local-currency Economic Support Funds earmarked for transitional support grants to cover the bail. NDI and IRI reimbursed USAID nearly $2.5 million each out of their $10 million grants to cover bail for the sixteen Americans and legal fees for all the employees. *Audit of USAID/Egypt's Transition Support Grants*, 2, 7; "Report: USAID tamped down internal criticism over Egypt work," Reuters, October 24, 2014, http://www.egyptindependent.com/node/2439163; Scott Higham and Steven Rich, "Whistleblowers say USAID's IG removed critical details from public reports," *Washington Post*, October 22, 2014, http://www.washingtonpost.com/investigations/whistleblowers-say-usaids-ig-removed-critical

activity" and "political training programs" through unlicensed entities; none served time in prison. The judge upheld Aboul Naga and SCAF's nationalist trope, asserting that the Mubarak regime, which "prostrated before America's will to normalize relations between Egypt and Israel," used "foreign funding for civil society organizations" to promote normalization:

> Democracy promotion, governance, [and] human rights…[sought] to breach Egypt's national security. They aimed to undermine and dismantle state institutions, leading to the division and disintegration of society…to serve American and Israeli interests.

The judge bizarrely re-conceptualized the January uprising as breaking "the chains of domination" by Israel. He claimed that the US government used NGO funding to "contain the revolution…and direct it to serving its own interests and the interests of Israel."[54]

Pressure on Egyptian NGOs

The uproar over the registration status and political intentions of the foreign organizations ignored that USAID made grants only to registered Egyptian companies or NGOs. Moreover, little attention was paid to the two Egyptian organizations raided on December 29. At the time, there was fear that their closure portended a crackdown on advocacy NGOs. Lawyer Nasser Amin, who founded the ACIJLP in 1997, was a high-profile member of the government's National Council for Human Rights. Amin was interrogated concerning charges that ACIJLP was the branch of a foreign NGO and received foreign funds without permission. BAHRO, in contrast, was a little-known organization that analyzed government

---

[54] Egyptian defendants received one-year sentences, suspended. Verdict at http://genius. com/Judge-makram-awad-excerpt-from-verdict-regarding-the-trial-of-ngos; International Bar Association, "Separating Law and Politics," 43; Zenobia Azeem, "NGO workers sentenced by Egyptian court," Al-Monitor, June 10, 2013, http://www.al-monitor.com/ pulse/originals/2013/06/ngo-workers-sentenced-egyptian-court.html; Hamza Hendawi, "Egypt convicts NGO workers, including 16 Americans," AP, June 4, 2013, http://bigstory. ap.org/article/egypt-court-convicts-nonprofit-workers; Nancy A. Youssef, "Egypt court sentences NGO workers; U.S. denounces verdict," McClatchyDC, June 4, 2013, http:// www.mcclatchydc.com/2013/06/04/192965/egypt-court-sentences-ngo-workers.html. Defendant Robert Becker earlier tweeted that the judge spewed "xenophobic anti-Israel rubbish": https://rbecker51.wordpress.com/tag/judge-makram-awad

budgets and expenditures, seeking transparency and accountability from ministries and agencies. Executive director Helmy Elrawy assumed that BAHRO was targeted because he called on the armed forces to publish its budget and "revealed the military council's violations."[55] The US's National Endowment for Democracy funded both groups.

However, the government did not close BAHRO and ACIJLP and did not indict their staff. They resumed operations quickly.[56] ACIJLP, for example, continued to hold conferences on the state of justice in the Arab region and training courses for lawyers and activists as well as monitor investigations and trials, handle cases related to public freedoms, and maintain a legal library.[57] The lockdown of Egyptian NGOs did not materialize, but fear of closure deepened.

Indeed, the raids signaled the policy change toward NGOs. SCAF's initial government, under Prime Minister Essam Sharaf, was relatively attuned to civil society and welcomed NGO-proposed revisions to the NGO law, including making NGOs autonomous, established simply by notification to a court, and having the Ministry of Justice – not MOSS – as NGOs' administrative liaison. NGOs could be free to join local and international partnerships.[58] In return, NGOs would be transparent in their operations and sources of funding, per their 2009 Code of Ethics.

---

[55] Elrawy said four vehicles with police officers and military commandos pulled up, posted men with AK-47 assault rifles outside, confiscated all documents, computers, and personal belongings, and sealed the entrance with red wax. Economics researcher Ahmed Ali, the only person present, was detained for twenty-four hours. Sabry and Landay, "Egypt crackdown escalates."

[56] Elrawy spent spring 2012 at the Center for Applied Human Rights, University of York (UK), developing indicators to help policymakers promote economic, social, and cultural rights, and he participated in a World Bank "MENA regional procurement policy review" conference in Amman in June 2012, http://www.york.ac.uk/cahr/defenders/past/helmy. BAHRO received US government funding, including $23,000 from NED to promote accountability and transparency by examining the budget allocations in the five-year development plan (2002–7) as contrasted to the actual spending, http://www.ned.org/publications/annual-reports/2008-annual-report/middle-east-and-north-africa. Elrawy's concern for human rights began with his arrest in 1992 (age twenty) for demonstrating against Mubarak. Stephen Lewis, "How one man's arrest began a nightmare of 45 days," *The Press* (York), June 11, 2012, http://www.yorkpress.co.uk/features/features/9753986

[57] Arab Center for the Independence of the Judiciary and the Legal Profession (ACIJLP), accessed June 7, 2014, http://www.acijlp.org/main/en/art.php

[58] "39 human rights and development organizations propose alternative NGO law," CIHRS, November 16, 2011, http://www.cihrs.org/?p=242&lang=en

However, SCAF installed the Kamal al-Ganzouri government in December, which not only raided the international NGOs but also reverted to the highly restrictive draft law of 2010 that banned advocacy organizations from registering as civil companies or law firms.[59] Members of the human rights committee of the People's Assembly sharply criticized the draft and continued to debate that text as well as a less restrictive alternative proposed by the Muslim Brotherhood until the SCC closed the assembly in June.

MOHAMMAD MORSI'S CONTRADICTORY POLICIES

SCAF reluctantly relinquished authority to the elected president on June 30, 2012. A long-term apparatchik in the Brotherhood, Mohammad Morsi was Egypt's first democratically elected and civilian president. Military and security officers feared – and were angry at – turning over authority to a leader of the organization that they had repressed for decades.[60]

Morsi's initial actions were relatively promising. He appointed the respected judges Mahmoud and Ahmad Mekki vice president and minister of justice, respectively, and formed commissions to review the status of persons detained and convicted during the January uprising. Morsi accepted the commissions' recommendations to drop charges against those not yet brought to trial, release many political prisoners, and amnesty those convicted for actions "committed to advocate the revolution and achieve its goals."[61] He amended the press law to abolish preventive custody for insulting the president.

The Forum of Independent Egyptian Human Rights Organizations launched a "Human Rights in 100 Days" campaign to evaluate Morsi's performance, foster accountability, and seek the release of political prisoners.[62]

---

[59] POMED, "Backgrounder: The campaign against NGOs."

[60] Ann M. Lesch, "Playing with fire: The showdown in Egypt between the General and the Islamist President," FPRI, http://www.fpri.org/2014/03/playing-fire-showdown-egypt-between-general-and-islamist-president

[61] "Morsy issues general amnesty for revolution-related crimes," *Egypt Independent*, October 8, 2012, http://www.egyptindependent.com/news/morsy-issues-general-amnesty-revolution-related-crimes; Stork, "Ahmed Seif Al Islam" (a member of the commission), HRW.

[62] Seventeen "Egyptian NGOs launch campaign to monitor new government's first 100 days," Social Watch, July 5, 2012, http://www.socialwatch.org/node/15102

When the hundred days ended, the Forum praised the prisoner releases and the amended press law, but decried the government's interventions in the judiciary, hostility to independent trade unions, intimidation of Christians, and assaults on opposition demonstrators.[63]

Morsi quickly alienated liberal political forces by reneging on promises to govern inclusively that he had made during the campaign. He clashed with the prosecutor general and the powerful head of the Judges Club. Morsi feared that the SCC would annul the Shura Council and the Constituent Assembly – recalling that the SCC had closed the People's Assembly two weeks before he took office. Meanwhile, Islamists inserted provisions in the draft constitution that steered Egypt toward a Shari'ah-based state. Liberals resigned from the Constituent Assembly in protest.

Renewed authoritarianism

Morsi issued a startling decree on November 22 that fired the prosecutor general, made the president immune from judicial oversight, and immunized the Shura Council and the Constituent Assembly from dissolution by court order. By asserting dictatorial powers, Morsi abruptly canceled his electoral legitimacy.[64] Muslim Brothers massed at the SCC, blocking judges from reaching their chambers. The president rushed the draft constitution through a referendum in December. When protesters camped outside the presidential palace, Brotherhood activists attacked the protest camp, heightening fears of civil strife.

Rights groups responded sharply to Morsi's decree, filed a lawsuit before the administrative court (*majlis al-dawla*) to annul the decree, and later rejected the draft constitution.[65] NGOs reacted not only to

---

[63] "After President Mohamed Morsy's first 100 days: Worrying indications for the future of human rights," CIHRS, October 15, 2012, http://www.cihrs.org/?p=4547&lang=en
[64] Ann M. Lesch, "A second, corrective revolution?" Foreign Policy Research Institute E-Notes, http://www.fpri.org/articles/2013/07/second-corrective-revolution
[65] Twenty-five "Rights groups file urgent lawsuit against presidential decree," CIHRS, November 24, 2012, http://www.cihrs.org/?p=5096&lang=en; joint press statement by 23 rights organizations rejecting the president's declaration, "New constitutional declaration gives Morsi sweeping powers and deals lethal blow to judicial independence," EOHR, November 26, 2012, http://en.eohr.org/2012/11/26/new-constitutional-declaration-gives-morsi-sweeping-powers-and-deals-lethal-blow-to-judicial-independence/; "President must take urgent steps to prevent Egypt from sliding into civil war," CIHRS, December 6, 2012, http://www.cihrs.org/?p=5190&lang=en; "On International Human Rights

constitutional issues but also to arrests on political grounds and violations of freedom of speech, including arrests for blasphemy.[66] For example, ACIJLP (raided in December 2011) asserted that violations of the independence of the judiciary were so numerous that the rule of law risked collapsing.[67] And BAHRO, the other NGO raided by SCAF, joined fifteen NGOs and political parties to condemn Morsi's finance minister for not releasing the draft budget to the public. BAHRO later submitted detailed comments on that budget.[68]

Debate over the NGO law

The NGO law was debated, again. During SCAF's rule, the Brotherhood presented a draft law, which the People's Assembly's human rights committee discussed alongside MOSS's draft.[69] That draft proposed a system of notification – not prior authorization – for Egyptian NGOs. The judiciary (not MOSS) would dissolve NGOs. Advocacy groups still feared that the draft was "captive to the philosophy of control, restriction and administrative tutelage" as it retained burdensome record-keeping requirements and subjected violators to the criminal code. The draft also

Day: Egyptians to vote on a constitution that undermines human rights and liberties," press statement by 23 organizations, CIHRS, December 10, 2012, http://www.cihrs.org/?p=5249&lang=en

[66] The criminal code criminalizes defamation. "Egypt: 'Outrageous' guilty verdict in blasphemy case an assault on free expression," Amnesty International, December 12, 2012, http://www.amnesty.org/en/news/egypt-outrageous-guilty-verdict-blasphemy-case-assault; "Egypt's worrying rise in criminal blasphemy cases," Amnesty International, June 11, 2013, http://www.amnestyusa.org/news/news-item/egypt-s-worrying-rise-in-criminal-blasphemy-cases, June 11, 2013; Mahmoud Salem, "Blasphemy in New and Old Egypt," Middle East Institute, June 12, 2013, http://www.mei.edu/content/blasphemy-new-and-old-egypt

[67] "The ACIJLP holds press conference to announce its annual report on 2012, entitled 'An Attack on Justice in Egypt,'" March 3, 2013, accessed June 7, 2014, http://www.acijlp.org/main/en/art.php?id=27&art=129

[68] "Release the Public Budget to the People...Now!" EIPR, April 21, 2013, http://eipr.org/en/print/pressrelease/2013/04/21/1694; Alrawi on the draft budget in "Healthcare struggles to keep up with rising costs, medicine shortages," Daily News Egypt, June 22, 2013, http://www.dailynewsegypt.com/2013/06/22/healthcare-struggles-to-keep-up-with-rising-costs

[69] "New draft law to regulate NGOs and civil society: Tangible progress along with flaws of the past," CIHRS, May 28, 2012, http://www.cihrs.org/?p=2291&lang=en

retained the vague "national unity, public order and public morals" language that MOSS and the Interior Ministry used to discipline NGOs. Foreign organizations would still need permission from the Foreign Ministry and MOSS, and MOSS could block foreign grants. The SCC dissolved the People's Assembly before it could finalize the text.

In February 2013, Morsi's cabinet submitted to the Shura Council bills drafted by the Interior Ministry that restricted protests and repressed NGOs by formalizing "direct intervention by the security services."[70] The protest law required notification three days in advance of a demonstration or public lecture, including details on the organizers, topic, duration, and location, and placed limitations on permissible slogans and chants. Security forces would wield sweeping power to disperse protests.[71] (In fall 2013, the Mansour/Sisi government promulgated this same law.)

The draft NGO law gave the "government unlimited power to object to any group's domestic fundraising or [to] its right to obtain foreign funds," decreed MOSS inspection of NGO accounts on a bimonthly basis, compelled companies and law firms to register with MOSS, viewed NGO staff as potential "foreign agents,"[72] and required permission before joining an international network. Indeed, even while the law was in draft form, MOSS informed EOHR that "security bodies" must approve any

---

[70] Elagati, "Foreign Funding in Egypt after the Revolution," 4–5; Cam McGrath, "Egyptian NGOs fear law that would cripple civil society," Inter Press Service, http://www.ipsnews. net/2013/05/egyptian-ngos-fear-law-that-would-cripple-civil-society. Vice President Mekki resigned in December 2012 and justice minister Mekki resigned in April 2013, during Islamist efforts to "purge" the judiciary. Sayed Gamaleddine, "Egypt's justice minister Ahmed Mekki resigns: Judicial sources," Al-Ahram Online, April 21, 2013, http://english. ahram.org.eg/News/69781.aspx; Basil el-Dabh, "Suleiman criticises lowered age limit of judges," Daily News Egypt, May 19, 2013, http://www.dailynewsegypt.com/2013/05/19/ suleiman-criticises-lowered-age-limit-of-judges

[71] "Rights Group: New draft laws restrict freedoms as under Mubarak," Egypt Independent, October 21, 2012, http://www.egyptindependent.com/node/1192326; "Justice minister outlines new articles for draft protest law," Egypt Independent, January 3, 2013, http://www. egyptindependent.com/node/1360651; "Protesting legally: Demonstration bill decreed highly restrictive," Egypt Independent, February 13, 2013, http://www.egyptindependent. com/node/1469106

[72] Heba Morayef, Egypt director, HRW, "Uncivil society: Why Egypt's new law regulating NGOs is still criminal," Foreign Policy, June 11, 2013, http://foreignpolicy. com/2013/06/11/uncivil-society; Kenneth Roth, executive director, HRW, "Egypt's NGO funding crackdown," April 9, 2013, Foreign Policy, http://www.hrw.org/news/2013/04/09/ egypt-s-ngo-funding-crackdown

cooperation with "international entities."[73] A Brotherhood MP claimed that restrictions would foil plots by enemies such as Israel.[74] The draft banned foreign organizations funded by their home government. The only improvement was the provision that NGOs simply notify the government when they are formed, with objection only on two grounds: "if the group is involved in military [or paramilitary] activities or if its activities are for profit."[75]

The draft created a nine-member coordinating committee, including the Interior Ministry and 'homeland security' (the renamed state security), to "decide on all matters related to the activities [including licensing, operations, and funding] of non-governmental foreign organizations and foreign funding."[76] Previously, security officers operated behind the scenes, not as formal decision-makers. The draft permitted security officers to inspect NGOs' visitor logs and records of private meetings. EOHR's Abu Saeda claimed that this would turn NGOs into agents of the state.[77] Already, "every funding request [since the January uprising] has been refused" and EOHR has closed many projects and reduced its staff from thirty to twelve. Attorney El-Borai added that state security would find many pretexts to deny funding or close NGOs, which have to cease their programs while they battle in court.

[73] "Amnesty International report criticizes Egypt's NGO restrictions," *Egypt Independent*, February 21, 2013, http://www.egyptindependent.com/node/1489821; "Shura Council discusses draft law on NGOs," *Egypt Independent*, February 25, 2013, http://www.egyptindependent.com/node/1524006; "Freedom House: Draft NGO law more restrictive than previous one," *Egypt Independent*, March 26, 2013, http://www.egyptindependent.com/node/1596226

[74] Head of the party's legal committee Mokhtar al-Ashry, "Egyptian civil society sees echoes of past in new law," Reuters, *Egypt Independent*, February 26, 2013, http://www.egyptindependent.com/node/1525556

[75] Morayef, "Uncivil society."

[76] Elagati, "Foreign Funding in Egypt after the Revolution," 15. The president's coordinating committee included the Foreign, Judicial, International Cooperation, and Social Solidarity ministries, State Council, and Central Bank, but no NGOs.

[77] McGrath, "Egyptian NGOs fear law that would cripple civil society"; Alexander Dziadosz, "Egypt NGO law could betray revolt's ideals: U.N. rights chief," Reuters, May 8, 2013, http://www.reuters.com/article/2013/05/08/US-egypt-un-ideals-idUSBRE9470WQ20130508; Dina Guirguis, "Morsi government seeks to institutionalize authoritarian relapse with NGO law," Atlantic Council, June 1, 2013, http://www.atlanticcouncil.org/blogs/egyptsource/morsi-government-seeks-to-institutionalize

Morsi's aides tried to mollify NGOs by submitting a revised bill in May.[78] First, the Interior Ministry and security agencies would not serve on the coordinating committee. Second, half of the committee would be selected by the elected National Federation for Civil Society and half would come from government ministries. Third, the committee would facilitate registration for international NGOs, not control them, and would not block funding or dissolve NGOs. Once foreign-funded NGOs registered, they would operate freely on the basis of notifying the coordinating committee, rather than waiting for approval. Fourth, fundraising would not require approval; rather, donations would be collected freely from Egyptians inside and outside Egypt and from foreign residents in Egypt. But the government would retain considerable power to restrict activities and funding, viewed as necessary "to avoid the possibility of laundering terrorist money."

Neither the protest law nor the NGO law were finalized. We will never know if a new NGO law would have reduced the government's grip, as Morsi's regime was swept aside in massive protests. When defense minister Sisi removed the president on July 3, established an interim government with a new roadmap, reinstated the state of emergency, and suppressed the Brotherhood, Egypt shifted into a dramatically new phase.

GENERAL SISI'S CONSTRICTION OF THE PUBLIC SPACE

While General Sisi was Morsi's defense minister, he warned: "No one should think that the solution is with the army...This army is a fire. Do not play against it and do not play with it."[79] Just as the Brotherhood should not toy with the army, the public must realize that, should the generals return to power, they might remain in control for thirty or even forty years. And yet Sisi claimed to have learned from SCAF's mistakes

---

[78] Khaled al-Qazzaz, President Morsi's secretary for foreign relations, "We're not building a 'police state': Why Egypt's draft NGO law is transparent, fair, and a big step forward to democracy," *Foreign Policy*, June 11, 2013, http://foreignpolicy.com/2013/06/11/ were-not-building-a-police-state/; "Egyptian presidency tries to ease concerns over NGO law," Reuters, *Egypt Independent*, May 28, 2013, http://www.egyptindependent.com/ node/1788281

[79] Bassem Sabry, "Why only democracy can save Egypt," Al-Monitor, May 19, 2013, http:// www.al-monitor.com/pulse/originals/2013/05/democracy-egypt-future.html

in 2011–12: First, "the armed forces should not be at the forefront and power has to remain in the hands of a civil government and president" and, second, parliamentary and presidential elections should be held *after* the constitution is amended, not before.[80]

Sisi therefore appointed the head of the SCC interim president and prioritized redrafting the constitution. But the new constitution consolidated the power of "sovereign institutions" – the armed forces, Interior Ministry, and judiciary – and reinforced the president's authority over the cabinet and the legislature.[81] Sisi won the presidential election in May 2014 with ninety-seven percent of the votes after SCAF explicitly authorized his candidacy – an endorsement of questionable constitutionality, as the armed forces are supposed to uphold the nation, not particular politicians.[82]

The long-delayed parliamentary elections were held at the end of 2015 according to a president-approved election law that minimized the role of political parties and maximized the presence of former NDPers, retired police and military officers, and businessmen.[83] Its first act was to ratify all but 2 of the 341 presidential decrees issued since January 2014. With the parliament dominated by the pro-regime Support Egypt bloc, MPs may complain about the cabinet's weaknesses and carp about specific economic policies, but they are unlikely to offer alternative programs or check the regime's excesses.

Tightened restrictions on protests

Military and security forces launched a massive crackdown on the Brotherhood – quickly extended to activists associated with the January 25 uprising. When the state of emergency expired, the president decreed

---

[80] Lesch, "Playing with fire."

[81] Ann M. Lesch, "Egypt: Resurgence of the security state," Foreign Policy Research Institute E-Notes, http://www.fpri.org/articles/2014/03/egypt-resurgence-security-state

[82] General Ahmad Shafiq, runner-up for president in 2012, declared SCAF's endorsement "unimaginable and unacceptable...[It] contradicts all the rules and the traditions that stipulate the armed forces' complete distance from the electoral process.'" "Sisi gets Ahmed Shafiq's support for Egypt top post," *Middle East Online*, March 3, 2014, http://www.middle-east-online.com/english/?id=4817

[83] For details on the elections and parliament's initial actions, see Ann M. Lesch, "Parliament without politics: The effort to consolidate authoritarian rule," *The Philadelphia Papers*, no. 12, Foreign Policy Research Institute, http://www.fpri.org/articles/2016/02/parliament-without-politics-effort-consolidate-authoritarian-rule

a draconian protest law on November 24 (Law 107/2013) that empowers the Interior Ministry to (dis)approve demonstrations and public gatherings, permits the police to use lethal force, and imprisons demonstrators for up to seven years for illegal gatherings.[84] The next day, security forces detained activists who objected to this law and later sentenced them to lengthy jail terms, claiming that they sought to destroy Egypt.[85] Not all democracy activists criticized the law, at least at first. Ibn Khaldun Center chair Saad Eddin Ibrahim, for example, initially believed it would only be used against the Brotherhood.[86] Nonetheless, the protest law became a key mechanism for repression. More than forty thousand have been arrested, crammed into cells, beaten, and held for extended periods without trial.[87] Some launched hunger strikes to call attention to their plight.

A year later, with no diminution in student protests or jihadist attacks, Sisi deepened the military's reach. Law 136/2014 (October 27, 2014) placed most civilian public buildings under the "security and protection" of the military judiciary.[88] The prosecutor general ordered prosecutors to "compile and send any cases related to aforementioned crimes, at any stage [of investigation], to military prosecutors."[89] He shifted to military

---

[84] Text at http://tahrirsquared/com/node/5828."Egypt: Deeply restrictive new assembly law," HRW, November 26, 2013, http://www.hrw.org/news/2013/11/26/egypt-deeply-restrictive-new-assembly-law

[85] Including activists Alaa Abdel Fattah, Ahmed Douma, and Mohamed Adel. "Egypt's prosecution argues Alaa Abdel-Fattah and co-defendants not 'true revolutionaries,'" *Al-Ahram Online*, December 20, 2014, http://english.ahram.org.eg/News/118405.aspx

[86] Reham Ibrahim, "Saad Eddin Ibrahim: Egyptians should not fear demonstration law," *Cairo Post*, November 8, 2013, http://www.thecairopost.com/news/32348/news/saad-eddin-ibrahim-egyptians-fear-demonstration-law

[87] International Development Center (Cairo), "Democracy Index: protests surged by 10 percent in November," *Egypt Independent*, December 16, 2014, http://www.egyptindependent.com/node/2441409

[88] The military judiciary acquired jurisdiction over "electricity networks and stations, gas pipes, oil fields, railways, road and bridge networks as well as other buildings, utilities and public property and anything that is considered as such." "15 independent rights groups condemn the expansion in the jurisdiction of military courts," AFTE, October 30, 2014, http://afteegypt.org/breaking-news-2/2014/10/30/8616-afteegypt.html?lang=en; Jihad Abaza, EIPR, "Dramatic deterioration of human rights: EIPR," *Daily News Egypt*, October 30, 2014, http://www.dailynewsegypt.com/2014/10/30/dramatic-deterioration-human-rights-eipr/; Patrick Kingsley, "Egypt places civilian infrastructure under army jurisdiction," *Guardian*, October 28, 2014, http://www.theguardian.com/world/2014/oct/28/egypt-civilian-infrastructure-army-jurisdiction

[89] The prosecutor shifted the cases of batches of 300, 40, and 439 Muslim Brothers to military prosecution as soon as the order was issued. "HRW: Over 800 civilians sent to

judges seven hundred cases that dated back to August 2013. Protesters at factories and government offices on public roads face military trial, along with hundreds of university students.[90] Retroactive application violates the constitutional principle that a person cannot be punished for acts that occurred before the law was issued.

Moreover, in February 2015, Sisi signed a law on "terrorist entities," including groups that "intend to advocate *by any means* to...harm national unity."[91] The prosecutor general compiles a list of entities that the Court of Appeals then vets. They are barred, their assets frozen, and their members arrested. The list includes secular activist groups, notably the April 6th Youth Movement, which supported worker strikes under Mubarak and was active throughout 2011.[92] After the prosecutor general was assassinated in Cairo on June 29, 2015, Sisi demanded "swift justice" both against "terrorist entities" and against persons already judged guilty of terrorism:

---

military court since October," *Mada Masr*, December 19, 2014, http://www.madamasr. com/news/hrw-over-800-civilians-sent-military-court-october

[90] Amira El-Fekki, "3 Al-Azhar students referred to military trial," *Daily News Egypt*, December 27, 2014, http://www.dailynewsegypt.com/2014/12/27/three-al-azhar-students-referred-military-trial; "7 Mansoura University students referred to military trial," *Daily News Egypt*, January 3, 2015, http://www.dailynewsegypt.com/2015/01/03/7-mansoura-university-students-referred-military-trial; "Military court sentences 21 student protesters to 15 years in prison," *Mada Masr*, February 11, 2015, http://www.madamasr. com/news/military-court-sentences-21-student-protesters-15-years-prison; Omar Said, "3000 civilians tried in military courts in 5 months: No to Military Trials campaign," *Mada Masr*, March 24, 2015, http://www.madamasr.com/news/politics/3000-civilians-tried-military-courts-5-months-no-military-trials-campaign

[91] A terrorist group is defined as a group "practicing or intending to advocate *by any means* to disturb public order or endanger the safety of the community and its interests, or risk its security, or harm national unity," including to harm the environment, communications, transport, places of worship, hospitals, educational institutions, diplomatic missions, and regional and international organizations in Egypt." UN, Egyptian rights groups link counter-terrorism to human rights," *Daily News Egypt*, December 14, 2014, http://www. dailynewsegypt.com/2014/12/14/un-egyptian-rights-groups-link-counter-terrorism-human-rights/; "Egypt's Sisi signs law defining 'terrorist entities,'" *Al-Ahram Online*, February 24, 2015, http://english.ahram.org.eg/News/123810.aspx; protest by 21 NGOs, "Law on terrorist entities allows rights groups and political parties to be designated terrorists," EIPR, March 1, 2015, http://eipr.org/en/pressrelease/2015/03/01/2336

[92] The April 6th Youth Movement was declared a terrorist organization. Its activists were harassed and often jailed. Leader Amr Ali, arrested from his home in September 2015, was sentenced to three years in prison; Mahmoud Mostafa, "6 April leader sentenced to 3 years in prison," *Daily News Egypt*, February 29, 2016, http://www.dailynewsegypt. com/2016/02/29/6-april-leader-sentenced-to-3-years-in-prison/

"If you [judges] issue a death sentence, the death sentence will be carried out"[93] without indulging in lengthy appeals.

An additional decree in August 2015 shielded the military and police from legal penalties when they use force against detainees and prisoners, and even fined journalists and television presenters if their writings and statements contradict the official version of a military or police action.[94] And on January 13, 2016 – the same day that Sisi addressed the new parliament – the cabinet approved the president's comprehensive decree that criminalized symbols associated with "terrorist" organizations, such as the four-fingered salute of the Brotherhood and the clenched fist of the April 6th Youth Movement.[95] That day also witnessed Sisi's issuing a presidential decree to build a new prison complex on a hundred acres in the Giza desert.[96] Already, ten new prisons have been constructed since 2011, of which nearly all were erected since July 2013.

The closure of public space

The government seeks to control all public space, whether vendors on city streets, coffee shops with chairs on sidewalks, or artists and advocacy groups reviving the spirit of January 2011. Sisi eliminated university autonomy, banned politically affiliated groups on campus, and assumed the right to appoint university presidents, who can unilaterally expel

---

[93] "President at prosecutor's funeral: Laws shackle delivery of justice," *Egypt Independent*, June 30, 2015, http://www.egyptindependent.com/node/2453341; Mohamed Hamama, "Who will pay for unleashing 'the shackled hands of justice'?" *Mada Masr*, July 1, 2015, http://madamasr.com/sections/politics/who-will-pay-unleashing-shackled-hands-justice
[94] "Egypt's parliament endorses controversial anti-terrorism law," Reuters, January 17, 2016, http://www.reuters.com/article/us-egypt-security-parliament-idUSKCN0UV0UG
[95] The new article, added to the Criminal Code, criminalized "the publication, production, promotion, importation, transfer, possession, trafficking, distribution, rent or presentation of: symbols, drawings, posters, publications, signs, photos or other objects that symbolize terrorist entities or groups who operate inside the country or abroad;…the publication of something referencing such symbols…; recording, documenting, printing or broadcasting." A specific list of symbols will be compiled in bylaws. "Cabinet approves Sisi's draft law criminalizing 'terrorist' symbols," *Mada Masr*, January 14, 2016, http://www.madamasr.com/news/cabinet-approves-sisi's-draft-law-criminalizing-'terrorist'-symbols
[96] Gamal Eid, executive director of ANHRI, was barred from traveling abroad shortly after he published this information. Albaraa Abdullah, "Egypt fills its prisons, but don't worry, it'll make more," Al-Monitor, February 3, 2016, http://www.al-monitor.com/pulse/originals/2016/02/egypt-authorities-prison-free-speech-sisi

students. He returned to the Mubarak-era policy of removing officers of professional associations and placing those syndicates under judicial guardianship, in violation of the new constitution.[97] Sisi accorded himself the power to fire the heads of regulatory agencies that audit government officials and press for corruption investigations – apparently because those agencies began to tread on powerful toes in the judiciary, Interior Ministry, and finance officers.[98] And, when the United Group drafted a law to curb police abuse and torture and submitted it to Sisi, the Supreme Judicial Council launched an investigation against the director and those judges who participated in the project.[99] Moreover, the same court that banned the Brotherhood in September 2013 banned the April 6th Youth Movement in April 2014 for defaming the state, "distort[ing] Egypt's image," and espionage,[100] even though it had backed the removal of Morsi.

Security offices closed websites and arrested individuals on the basis of blogs or tweets, despite constitutional guarantees of freedom of expression. Ramy Essam,[101] beloved for his songs in Tahrir Square, was

---

[97] Jano Charbel, "Out of the syndicates," *Mada Masr*, December 12, 2014, http://www.madamasr.com/sections/politics/out-syndicates; Adham Youssef, "Court places Pharmacists' Syndicate under judicial guardianship," *Daily News Egypt*, October 27, 2014, http://www.dailynewsegypt.com/2014/10/27/court-places-pharmacists-syndicate-judicial-guardianship

[98] This appears intended to remove the head of the Central Auditing Organization, who has reported financial violations in some state agencies and has called for a ceiling to judges' salaries. "Presidency acquires power to reshuffle corruption watchdogs," *Egypt Independent*, July 12, 2015, http://www.egyptindependent.com/node/2453983; Lesch, "Parliament without politics," 18–19.

[99] Director Negad al-Borai and a panel of legal experts worked on the draft for several years, which they reviewed at a workshop on March 11 and presented to El-Sisi on May 6. Nourhan Fahmy, "Rights groups concerned of investigations into anti-torture judges," *Daily News Egypt*, June 3, 2015, http://www.dailynewsegypt.com/2015/06/03/rights-groups-concerned-of-investigations-into-anti-torture-judges; Marwa Al-A'sar, "Egyptian lawyer interrogated for drafting anti-torture law," Al-Monitor, June 15, 2015, http://www.al-monitor.com/pulse/originals/2015/06/egypt-police-abuse-torture-jail-investigation-draft-law.html; "Press Release: United Group to host a workshop for over fifty legal experts and parliamentary candidates," March 9, 2015, http://www.ug-law.com/ug/

[100] Cairo Court of Urgent Matters. "Egypt bans secular April 6 protest movement," *Al-Akhbar*, April 28, 2014, http://english.al-akhbar.com/content/egypt-bans-secular-april-6-protest-movement

[101] Mik Aidt interview with Ramy Essam, Stockholm, Sweden, 22 November, 2011, http://freemuse.org/archives/1872; Ramy Essam, "Egypt's revolution must continue," Al Jazeera, November 14, 2014, http://www.aljazeera.com/indepth/opinion/2014/11/

banned from performing, prevented from speaking to the media, and interrogated by state security. He left in September 2014 for a fellowship in Sweden. State radio blacklisted the songs of Hamza Namira, with their hopeful calls for freedom.[102] And the artist known as Ganzeer, famous for his powerful murals of fallen martyrs and menacing soldiers, moved to Brooklyn after a TV host demanded he be sentenced to death.[103] Police blocked street-art performances, including monthly festivals by Al Fan Midan (Art in a Square)[104] and the improvisational troupe Outa Hamra (Red Tomato).[105] Moreover, al-Mawred al-Thaqafy (Culture Resource), which supported young artists and writers, froze its activities in November 2014.[106]

---

egypt-revolution-must-continue-2014; Tom Rollins, "Singer from 'The Square' in shadows of Egypt's crackdown," Al-Monitor, http://www.al-monitor.com/pulse/originals/2014/01/tahrir-movie-egypt-ramy-singer.html; Joshua Hersh, "A hero of Tahrir Square comes to New York," November 26, 2014, New Yorker, http://www.newyorker.com/news/news-desk/hero-tahrir-square-comes-new-york; Marwa Morgan, "Egyptian singer moves to Sweden seeking 'safe city residency,'" Daily News Egypt, October 29, 2014, http://www.dailynewsegypt.com/2014/10/29/egyptian-singer-moves-sweden-seeking-safe-city-residency

[102] "Egypt state radio bans singer over anti-government stances," Egypt Independent, November 19, 2014, http://www.egyptindependent.com/node/2440178

[103] Ganzeer lives in Los Angeles, as of 2015–16. His name means bicycle chain, indicating that artists are "the mechanism that pushes change forward." Patrick Kingsley, "Graffiti artists unite against Egypt's presidential hopeful Abdel Fatah al-Sisi," Guardian, May 8, 2014, http://www.theguardian.com/world/2014/may/08/graffiti-artists-united-against-abdel-fatah-al-sisi; http://www.ganzeer.com/post/85826356062/whos-afraid-of-art/, accessed May 29, 2014; Barbara Pollack, "Hieroglyphics that won't be silenced: Ganzeer takes protest art beyond Egypt," New York Times, July 13, 2014, http://www.nytimes.com/2014/07/13/arts/design/ganzeer-takes-protest-art-beyond-egypt.html; "Interview with Ganzeer," Tahrir Institute for Middle East Policy, October 31, 2014, http://timep.org/commentary/interview-ganzeer

[104] "Fighting censorship, Al-Fan Midan organisers pledge to continue performing," Daily News Egypt, September 9, 2014, http://www.dailynewsegypt.com/2014/09/24/fighting-censorship-al-fan-midan-organisers; Rowan El Shimi, "Public space negotiations: Art continues despite struggles," Al-Ahram Online, December 28, 2014, http://english.ahram.org.eg/News/118891.aspx

[105] Miriam Berger, "In tough times: Egyptian theatre troupe pushes boundaries," Al-Monitor, January 6, 2015, http://www.al-monitor.com/pulse/sites/al-monitor/contents/articles/originals/2015/01/egyptian-theatre-troupe-brings-humor.html

[106] "Al Mawred Al Thaqafy announces freeze on all activities in Egypt for the present," Al-Ahram Online, November 5, 2014, http://english.ahram.org/eg/News/114857.aspx; Shady Lewis, "My pragmatist friend surrenders," Mada Masr, December 4, 2014, http://www.madamasr.com/sections/culture/my-pragmatist-friend-surrenders

Television and newspaper moguls endorsed Sisi's demand that the media support the war against terrorism by refraining from criticizing state institutions.[107] In response, seven hundred journalists declared that "voluntarily renounc[ing] freedom of opinion and expression" was a "victory for terrorism." Sisi went even further in July 2015 when he supporting criminalizing news reports that contradict official statements, an action that ANHRI's Eid declared would transform journalism into "Goebbels' media."[108]

The regime takes direct action when self-censorship fails. State security stopped the presses for entire newspaper runs in order to remove one article or editorial,[109] silenced TV programs that criticized the police or the government,[110] closed the sole independent radio station,[111] blocked

---

[107] Ann M. Lesch, 'Egypt's new president: "I will not sleep and neither will you. We must work night and day without rest,"' FPRI E-notes, http://www.fpri.org/articles/2014/07; Adham Youssef, "State-owned, private newspaper editors vow to support government's anti-terrorism rhetoric," Daily News Egypt, October 10, 2014, http://www.dailynewsegypt.com/2014/10/27/state-owned-private-newspaper-editors-vow; Federico Manfredi, "Gag on media freedom victory for terrorism: Egyptian journalists," Daily News Egypt, November 3, 2014, http://www.dailynewsegypt.com/2014/11/02/gag-media-freedom-victory-terrorism-say-egyptian-journalists; Mohamed Mostafa, "More than 480 journalists reject press alignment with govt," Egypt Independent, November 3, 2014, http://www.egyptindependent.com/node/2439479; Aya Nader, "Leak allegedly reveals government using media to shape public opinion," Daily News Egypt, January 20, 2015, http://www.dailynewsegypt.com/2015/01/20/leak-allegedly-reveals-government-using-media

[108] The restriction was imposed after newspapers reported a higher number of deaths among soldiers in Sinai on July 1, 2015 than were officially announced; Patrick Kingsley and Manu Abdo, "Egypt journalists face jail for reporting non-government terrorism statistics," Guardian, July 5, 2015, http://www.theguardian.com/world/2015/jul/05/egypt-journalists-face-jail-for-reporting-non-government-terrorism-statistics

[109] Adham Youssef, "Officials stop printing of newspaper, stoking new fears of censorship," Daily News Egypt, December 15, 2015, http://dailynewsegypt.com/2014/12/15/officials-stop-printing-of-newspaper-stoking; Mostafa Mohie, "Censorship of Al-Masry Al-Youm interview raises questions," Mada Masr, October 4, 2014, http://www.madamasr.com/content/censorship-al-masry-al-youm-interview-raises-questions

[110] Security stopped a talk show on Dream 2 after the anchor reported that a child died in a public school and a government hospital refused to admit a pregnant woman. The education and health ministers were furious. The interior minister even claimed that the on-air report paved the way for a revolution. Nada Deyaa', "TV show cut mid-air," October 22, 2014, Daily News Egypt, http://www.dailynewsegypt.com/2014/10/22/tv-show-cut-mid-air/

[111] Security raided and closed Andalus Institute's online Horytna, AP, "Egypt police raid radio station, detain rights advocate," Al-Ahram Online, April 4, 2015, http://english.ahram.org/eg/News/126904.aspx

political dissidents from appearing on air,[112] and placed gag orders on coverage of high-profile crimes.[113] Outspoken TV hosts were forced off air,[114] Bassem Youssef discontinued his satirical show (apparently at the request of Sisi's office head), and Belal Fadl and Alaa al-Aswany abandoned their columns.[115] Reporting became dangerous: high-profile cases, such as the Al Jazeera journalists, were spotlighted internationally, but others languish behind bars.[116] According to Reporters Without Borders,

[112] A TV producer said the channel was barred from interviewing activists Ahmed Maher, Alaa Abdel Fattah, Mona Said, Amr Hamzawy, and Mostafa al-Naggar, and all Muslim Brothers. Mai Shams El-Din, "Egypt's media four years on: lamenting the loss of truth," *Mada Masr*, February 12, 2015, http://www.madamasr.com/sections/politics/egypts-media-four-years-lament; Emad Mubarak, "Censorship in Egypt: Online and offline," *Mada Masr*, November 30, 2014, http://www.madamasr.com/opinion/politics/censorship-egypt-online-and-offline

[113] David D. Kirkpatrick, "Egypt restricts news coverage of slain activist Shaimaa el-Sabbagh," *New York Times*, February 12, 2015; "Prosecutor imposes gag order on Shaimaa al-Sabbagh's death," *Mada Masr*, February 12, 2015, http://www.madamasr.com/news/prosecutor-imposes-gag-order-shaimaa-al-sabbaghs-death

[114] Heba Afify, "Egyptian media isn't taking prisoners, state's line is only line," *Mada Masr*, October 27, 2014, http://www.madamasr.com/sections/politics/egyptian-media-isnt-taking-prisoners-states-line; "Presenter's ban painful blow to freedom of expression: ANHRI," *Daily News Egypt*, October 27, 2014, http://www.dailynewsegypt.com/2014/10/27/presenters-ban-painful-blow-freedom-expression

[115] Mahmud El Shafey, "Bassem Youssef airs first direct criticism of Sisi," *Asharq al-Awsat*, February 22, 2014, http://www.aawsat.net/2014/02/articles55329257; David D. Kirkpatrick and Mayy El Sheikh, "Citing pressures and threats, Egypt's answer to Jon Stewart calls it quits," *New York Times*, June 3, 2014; "#Sisileaks: Episode 4 'Stop that annoying boy,'" *Egyptian Chronicles*, February 13, 2015; Mayy El Sheikh interviewed Belal Fadl (former *Shorouk* columnist), "A voice of dissent in Egypt is muffled, but not silent," *New York Times*, May 2, 2014, http://www.nytimes.com/2014/05/03/world/middleeast/an-egyptian-voice-of-dissent-is-muffled-but-not-silenced.html; Fadl's "The Senile State," *Mada Masr*, December 2014, http://www.madamasr.com/opinion/senile-state-part-2; Alaa Al Aswany, "Is Egypt doomed to autocracy?" *New York Times*, September 17, 2014, http://www.nytimes.com/2014/09/18/opinion/alaa-al-aswany-is-egypt-doomed-to-autocracy.html

[116] Contrasting examples include a journalist for the *Tahya Misr* website, arrested in August 2015 on assignment to cover a protest and sentenced to three years in prison even though the website's CEO testified on his behalf, and the deputy editor-in-chief of *Al-Mesryoon*, detained on November 14, 2015, but released on February 22, 2016, after the newspaper apparently convinced the authorities that he was a specialist in political Islam but not a member of a political movement. "CPJ calls for release of Yanair Gate journalist detained by Egyptian National Security," *Daily News Egypt*, January 6, 2016, http://www.dailynewsegypt.com/2016/01/06/cpj-calls-for-release-of-yanair-gate-journalist-detained-by-egyptian-national-security; Amira El-Fekki, "Al-Mesryoon's deputy chief editor walks free," *Daily News Egypt*, February 22, 2016, http://www.dailynewsegypt.com/2016/02/22/al-mesryoons-deputy-chief-editor-walks-free/. On long-term detainees,

"at least 24 journalists and bloggers are…imprisoned in connection with their reporting" as of February 2016.[117] The Committee to Protect Journalists deems Egypt the second worst jailer of journalists – second only to China.[118]

State guardianship of religion and morality

The state seeks to monopolize the religious and moral spheres, and root out "deviant" practices that threaten national unity. It closed thousands of mosques and decreed that only al-Azhar-educated clerics could preach. They must address state-dictated topics in their Friday sermons. Security officers report violations and encourage members of congregations to turn in preachers who deviate from the specified topic. Although designed to block Brotherhood preachers, the regulations also exclude pro-regime Salafis who lack al-Azhar credentials.

Al-Azhar has charged with "contempt of religion" those who differ from its interpretation of Islamic texts, blatantly contradicting the constitution's provisions for freedom of thought and expression.[119] The Grand Imam of al-Azhar even phoned a government TV station, furious that a well-known philosopher of religion was allowed to discuss sympathetically the

---

see Hend Kortan, "Photojournalist Shawkan describes 'endless nightmare' from behind bars," *Daily News Egypt*, December 20, 2014, http://www.dailynewsegypt.com/2014/12/20/photojournalist-shawkan-describes-endless; "The state of the press through Egypt's power shifts," *Daily News Egypt*, January 22, 2015, http://www.dailynewsegypt.com/2015/01/22/state-press-egypts-power-shifts

[117] "CPJ urges Egypt to halt legal clampdown on the press," Committee to Protect Journalists, July 9, 2015, https://cpj.org/2015/07/cpj-urges-egypt-to-halt-legal-clampdown-on-the-pre.php; Reporters Without Borders, "Open letter to Sisi: The situation of journalists in Egypt is unacceptable," February 22, 2016, http://www.rsf.org/egypt-the-situation-of-journalists-in-22-02-2016,48857.html

[118] China: forty-nine; Egypt: twenty-three (twelve in 2014, zero in 2012); Iran: nineteen; Eritrea: seventeen. Of twenty-eight countries that jailed journalists, eighteen jailed more than one person. "China, Egypt imprison record numbers of journalists," Committee to Protect Journalists, December 15, 2015, https://cpj.org/reports/2015/12/china-egypt-imprison-record-numbers-of-journalists-jail.php

[119] Islam El-Beheiry, whose program "With Islam" on Al-Qahera Wal-Nas private TV channel challenged the authenticity of interpretations of certain religious texts. The court reduced his initial five-year sentence to one year. Toqa Ezzidin, "El-Beheiry to serve 1-year sentence after motion to appeal is denied," *Daily News Egypt*, February 3, 2016, http://www.dailynewsegypt.com/2016/02/03/el-beheiry-to-serve-1-year-sentence-after-motion-to-appeal-is-denied

beliefs of religious minorities and to propose that parliament revoke the "contempt of religion" law. The head of the station immediately canceled that program.[120]

That provision in the 1982 Penal Code criminalizes belittling any monotheistic religion. It was intended to protect minorities but has been used by individual citizens to file contempt-of-religion cases against Christians and independent thinkers for perceived criticism of Islamic beliefs or rituals.[121] The constitution protects Islam, Christianity, and Judaism, but not Shi'ism, whose practices are banned in virtually all mosques.[122] Moreover, the fifty-person Jewish community could not prevent an administrative court from blocking an annual celebration honoring Rabbi Jacob Abu Hasira and ordering his shrine removed from the Ministry of Culture's list of monuments.[123] And there is no protection for the 1,500 Baha'i, whom the ministry of *awqaf* (religious endowments) denounces for "deviant thoughts" that "threaten Islam and Egyptian society."[124] Although atheism is not banned, the government labels it a "disturbing phenomenon" and jails atheists for contempt of religion, pursuing them through Facebook posts or public statements.[125]

---

[120] Researcher Sayed al-Qemany appeared on Ayten el-Mogy's "Hot Files" program, with permission from the head of the TV sector. Sarah El-Sheikh, "TV show goes off air due to anger from Al-Azhar," *Daily News Egypt*, February 27, 2016, http://www.dailynewsegypt. com/2016/02/27/tv-show-goes-off-air-due-to-anger-from-al-azhar

[121] Mostafa Salem, "Sixty-three individuals tried for religious defamation since revolution: EIPR," *Daily News Egypt*, September 11, 2013, http://www.dailynewsegypt. com/2013/09/11/sixty-three-individuals-tried-for-religious-defamation; "Egypt to put critic of Muslim ritual of slaughtering sheep on trial," *Al-Ahram Online*, December 27, 2014, http://english.ahram.org/eg/News/118911.aspx

[122] Amr Ezzat (EIPR), "The state of the imam: To whom do minbars belong today?" cited in Marwan Morgan, "The Egyptian state: 'The only leader,'" *Daily News Egypt*, http://www. dailynewsegypt.com/2014/08/27/egyptian-state-leader; Mai Shams el-Din, "The state of the Imam," *Mada Masr*, August 27, 2014, http://madamasr.com/content/state-imam

[123] "Alexandria court cancels controversial Jewish Abu Hasira moulid," *Al-Ahram Online*, December 29, 2014, http://english.ahram.org/eg/News/119070.aspx; Nada Dayaa', "Does the court ruling on Jewish mouled flout the constitution?" December 30, 2014, *Daily News Egypt*, http://www.dailynewsegypt.com//2014/12/30/court-ruling-jewish-mouled-flout-constitution/

[124] "Ministry of Endowments warns against 'Baha'i threat,'" *Daily News Egypt*, December 11, 2014, http://www.dailynewsegypt.com/2014/12/11/ministry-endowments-warns-bahai-threat/

[125] Ahmed Fouad, "Egypt campaigns against atheism," Al-Monitor, July 24, 2014, http:// www.al-monitor.com/pulse/originals/2014/07/egypt-government-fears-atheism.html; Patrick Kingsley, "Religion still leads the way in post-Morsi Egypt," *Guardian*, September

The regime also guards morality. Clamping down on "indecency" and "deviance" deepens control over private life. The judiciary jailed a novelist for violating "public decency" by writing about sex acts and hashish use, even though Article 67 of the constitution guarantees freedom of artistic and literary creation.[126] Moreover, al-Azhar claims that homosexuality angers God, and labels gays and lesbians public enemies. As homosexuality is not banned, the government invokes charges of habitual debauchery under the Anti-Prostitution Law of 1961, obscene behavior, and contempt of religion. EIPR reports that more than 150 people have been arrested on debauchery charges since July 2013.[127]

Reinvigorated pressure on NGOs

Advocacy groups contest the government's control over public and private space. Lawyers and prisoners' rights organizations protest detention without trial, prison conditions, beatings, and torture, and highlight prisoners' hunger strikes. ECESR, for example, challenged the government's right

18, 2014, https://www.theguardian.com/world/2014/sep/18/religion-still-leads-the-way-in-post-morsi-gypt; "Egyptian civil servant could lose job for promoting atheist beliefs," *Al-Ahram Online*, December 17, 2014, http://english.ahram.org.eg/News/118180.aspx
[126] Ahmed Naji received a two-year sentence (the maximum allowed) for the content of a chapter of his novel *The Use of Life* that was published in state-owned *Akhbar al-Adab* literary journal in 2014. The prosecutor even threatened to charge Naji with smoking hashish, like the novel's main character! "Campaigns demand suspension of prison sentence handed to novelist Ahmed Naji," *Mada Masr*, February 21, 2016, http://www.madamasr.com/news/culture/campaigns-demand-suspension-prison-sentence-handed-novelist-ahmed-naji; "Writer Ahmed Naji's jail sentence is unconstitutional, say 7 authors of Egypt's constitution," *Al-Ahram Online*, February 24, 2016, http://english.ahram.org.eg/News/188406.aspx
[127] Karim Ahmad, "Egyptian police use dating sites to hunt down gay people," http://observers.france24.com/content/20140916-egyptian-police-dating-sites-gay; "Egypt Sentences 8 in Connection With Same-Sex Wedding," *New York Times*, November 2, 2014; Najma Kousri Labidi, "Egypt's gay community under fire from local authorities," http://www.huffingtonpost.com/2014/12/02/gays-persecuted-in-egypt_n_6256490.html; Bel Trew, "They're here, they're queer, they're arrested," *Foreign Policy*, December 12, 2014, http://foreignpolicy.com/2014/12/12/egypt-gay-bath-house-cairo-lgbt/; Emir Nader, "Over 150 arrested on charges of 'debauchery' since 30 June: EIPR," *Daily News Egypt*, December 21, 2014, http://www.dailynewsegypt.com/2014/12/21/150-arrested-charges-debauchery-since-30-june-eipr; Mariam Rizk, "Crackdown on gays continues as bathhouse trial opens," *Al-Ahram Online*, December 21, 2014, http://english.ahram.org.eg/News/118522.aspx

to refer civilians to military trial,[128] and fifteen organizations protested at the expanded definition of military facilities, which "undermines the civilian justice system" and "seriously jeopardizes citizens' right to fair trials."[129] ECESR appealed against freezing the assets of January revolution activists and challenged arrests for "liking" certain Facebook pages.[130] The Association for Freedom of Thought and Expression (AFTE) opposes university presidents' arbitrary power. EIPR and EOHR highlight the absence of fair provisions for building and repairing churches and attacks on Christians.[131] And ANHRI emphasizes the discrepancy between government actions and constitutional protection of freedom of speech and association.[132]

Meanwhile, advocacy organizations fear for their own future. The security-controlled Cairo governorate evicted an educational foundation whose programs were licensed by MOSS and supported by the Ministry of Education.[133] Other restrictions include travel bans on NGO leaders,[134]

---

[128] ECESR appeal reported by Hend Kortam, "NGO requests permission to appeal constitutionality of presidential decree on vital facilities," *Daily News Egypt*, December 22, 2014, http://www.dailynewsegypt.com/2014/12/22/ngo-requests-permission-appeal-constitutionality

[129] Jihad Abaza, "Rights groups condemn jurisdiction of military courts," *Daily News Egypt*, October 31, 2014, http://www.dailynewsegypt.com/2014/10/31/rights-groups-condemn-jurisdiction-military-courts/

[130] "Rights organization appeals freeze on activists' assets," *Egypt Independent*, January 8, 2015, http://www.egyptindependent.com/news/rights-organization-appeals-freeze-activists-assets

[131] "Rights group slams discriminatory church building regulations," *Egypt Independent*, December 25, 2014, http://www.egyptindependent.com/node/2441842

[132] Interview with ANHRI's Gamal Eid, "Human rights situation in Egypt worst in 30 years: Gamal Eid," *Daily News Egypt*, January 22, 2015, http://www.dailynewsegypt.com/2015/01/22/human-rights-situation-egypt-worst-30-years

[133] "Manshiyet Nasser NGO facing eviction," *Mada Masr*, December 28, 2014, http://www.madamasr.com/news/manshiyet-nasser-ngo-facing-eviction; Nourhan Fahmy, "Nebny Foundation ordered to evacuate premises," *Daily News Egypt*, December 29, 2014, http://www.dailynewsegypt.com/2014/12/29/nebny-foundation-ordered-evacuate-premises/; Zeinab Al-Guindy, "Nebny Foundation vs Cairo Governorate," *Al-Ahram Online*, March 13, 2014, http://english.ahram.org.eg/News/96350.aspx

[134] Egyptian Democratic Academy, a non-profit youth group opened and registered in 2009. "Non-profit youth org challenges travel ban against its top staffers," *Mada Masr*, December 29, 2014, http://www.madamasr.com/news/non-profit-youth-org-challenges-travel-ban-against-its-top-staffers; http://egyda.org/announcement-about-travel-pan-of-eda-chairman-and-his-deputy/, accessed January 4, 2015; Khaled El-Sayed, Youth for Justice and Freedom Movement, barred on July 9: "Egyptian activist released after 24-hour detention at Cairo Airport," *Al-Ahram Online*, July 10, 2015, http://english.ahram.org.eg/News/135035.aspx

blocking foreign human rights advocates from entering Egypt,[135] and detaining or banning dual nationals who are public intellectuals.[136] State security even prevented an NGO leader from flying to Germany to address the parliament on Egypt's human rights situation, concerned that the address would be delivered just before Sisi visited Berlin.[137]

Security raids on ECESR offices in December 2013 and May 2014 heightened these fears, particularly as the second raid occurred just before the presidential election.[138] Government inspectors searched the

---

[135] Ken Roth and Sarah Leah Whitson of HRW were barred on August 10, 2014, which prevented them from holding a press conference to release *All According to Plan: The Rab'a Massacre and Mass Killings of Protesters in Egypt*. Ashraf Mihael of the Danish Institute for Human Rights was unable to join a Danish government-funded youth training program with Egyptian NGOs, including the Egyptian Democratic Academy. Michele Dunne (researcher at the Carnegie Endowment for International Peace) could not join a conference at the Egyptian Council for Foreign Affairs. "Danish NGO official deported from Egypt over 'suspicious training,'" *Al-Ahram Online*, October 28, 2014, http://english.ahram.org.eg/News/114131.aspx; Emil Mikkelsen, "Danish-Egyptian HR rep denied entry into Cairo," *Mada Masr*, October 28, 2014, http://www.madamasr.com/news/danish-egyptian-hr-rep-denied-entry-cairo; David D. Kirkpatrick, "Egypt denies entry to American scholar critical of its government," *New York Times*, December 13, 2014, http://www.nytimes.com/2014/12/14/world/middleeast/egypt-denies-entry-to-american-scholar-critical-of-its-government.html

[136] These include researcher Ismail Alexandrani, detained on November 29, 2015, as he flew from Berlin into Hurghada airport for a family visit. The national security prosecutor accused him of disseminating false information about conditions in Sinai and joining a banned group (the Muslim Brotherhood). He has researched state policy in Sinai for the Paris-based Arab Reform Initiative as well as during his just completed fellowship at the Woodrow Wilson International Center for Scholars in Washington, DC. Salma Abdallah; "Prosecution renews detention of journalist Ismail Alexandrani's for fourth time," *Daily News Egypt*, January 12, 2016, http://www.dailynewsegypt.com/2016/01/12/prosecution-renews-detention-of-journalist-ismail-alexandranis-for-fourth-time/

[137] "Egypt govt takes 'revenge' on us," *Al-Ahram Online*, June 11, 2015, http://english.ahram.org/eg/News/132485.aspx; "Egypt: Executive Director of ECRF Mohamed Lotfy Banned from Travelling," ANHRI, June 2, 2015, http://anhri.net/?p=145227&lang=en

[138] Sixty armed security and police personnel raided at 11:30 pm on December 18, 2013, without a warrant, confiscated three computers (later returned), and assaulted, blindfolded, and (briefly) arrested staff and volunteers. The April 6th Youth Movement's Mohamed Adel was detained for participating in a demonstration two weeks earlier, unrelated to ECESR. ECESR staff were finalizing a documentary film about four labor protests (including the Iron and Steel Workers' Union strike) to screen at a press conference the next day. Security forces raided ECESR's Alexandria branch on May 22, 2014, briefly arrested fifteen persons, harassed two women, and confiscated several computers and documents, in the midst of a press conference supporting labor activist Mahinour al-Massry, who was serving a two-year sentence for violating the protest law. AbdelHalim H. AbdAllah, "Rights groups outraged

CIHRS office, shortly after its director reported human rights violations to the European Parliament's human rights committee.[139] And, on May 2, 2014, security raided the pioneering Belady Foundation, which provided workshops, art classes, and a safe shelter for street children, arresting the couple that founded it and their six volunteer staff.[140] Twenty-two human rights organizations claim the government uses "the cover of its war against terrorism" to reconstruct the pre-January 25 police state and intimidate organizations "with no political affiliations...but rather specializ[ing] in the defense of citizens' rights."[141]

Human rights organizations feared that the government would retaliate for their submission to the UN Human Rights Council's Universal Periodic Review. They had submitted strongly worded interventions during Egypt's first review in spring 2010. For the fourth-year appraisal on November 5, 2014, the nineteen members of the Forum of Independent Human Rights Organizations submitted a report that countered the

---

by the raid on ECESR," *Daily News Egypt*, December 19, 2013, http://www.dailynewsegypt. com/2013/12/19/rights-groups-outraged-by-the-raid-on-ecesr/; "EMHRN and Oxfam condemn raids and arrests targeting the Egyptian Center for Economic and Social Rights," Euro-Mediterranean Human Rights Network and Oxfam (EMHRN), December 20, 2013, http://euromedrights.org/publication/emhrn-and-oxfam-condemn-raids-and-arrests-targeting-the-egyptian-center-for-economic-and-social-rights; "Urgent appeal for action: Egypt security forces raid leading human right organization, human rights defenders arrested and held incommunicado," CIHRS, December 19, 2013, http://www. cihrs.org/?p=7736&lang=en; "In Solidarity with the Egyptian Center for Economic and Social Rights," Arab NGO Network for Development, December 18, 2013, http:// www.socialwatch.org/node/16336;"ECESR Raided...Again!" ECESR, http://ecesr.org/ en/?p=421886; Statement, CIHRS, http://www.cihrs.org/?p=8640&lang=en

[139] "Egypt govt takes 'revenge' on us," June 11, 2015.

[140] Founded by US citizen Aya Hegazy and her husband Mohamed Hassanein Heikal in February 2014 and still "under establishment," which enables a foundation to operate pending MOSS approval. Despite the lack of forensic evidence, they were charged with, *inter alia*, sexual abuse, human trafficking, and inciting children against the government. *Egyptian Chronicles*, December 21, 2015; Aya Nader, "Couple spend their wedding money on street children, end up in an Egyptian prison," Egyptian Streets, February 12, 2016, http://egyptianstreets.com/2016/02/12/couple-spend-their-wedding-money-on-street-children-end-up-in-an-egyptian-prison

[141] "Egyptian human rights organizations oppressed...A return to what is worse than the pre-January 25th Era," CIHRS, December 19, 2013, http://www.cihrs.org/?p=7749&lang=en. Submissions included "From Civil Society Groups to the UN: 100 Recommendations for the Egyptian Government on 12 Rights Issues Involving violations in Law and Practice," http://eipr.org/en/pressrelease/2014/11/03/2260; and "Haunted by the toppling of former regimes by popular protests, successive governments see demonstrations as a threat," http://afteegypt.org/breaking-news-2/2014/11/04/8672-afteegypt.html?lang-en

government's claim of significant improvements in human rights; rather, human rights had "dramatically deteriorated," due to the protest law, lack of impartial investigation into excessive force by the police, arbitrary trial processes, and lengthy pre-trial detentions of persons who merely expressed their political views. NGO reports had been submitted in early 2014, when the atmosphere was not so hostile. But the November review came only five days before the deadline to comply with the NGO law, discussed below. Fearing arrest, the Forum canceled its public meetings in Geneva alongside the review session and seven organizations pulled out of the NGO delegation.[142] Nonetheless, twenty democracy activists did go to Geneva. Ibn Khaldun Center director Dalia Ziada, for example, stressed principles in the new constitution that upheld women's equality and the rights of Christians, while conceding that implementation remained limited. She also emphasized the Brotherhood's violence, which she felt the international community ignored.[143]

Simultaneously with the UN review, Sisi appointed Fayza Aboul Naga as one of two national security advisors.[144] As Aboul Naga had orchestrated SCAF's attacks on foreign NGOs and called Egyptian NGOs security threats, her appointment underlined the dominant rhetoric that NGOs are agents of hostile powers. Indeed, Sisi had already amended

---

[142] AFTE, ANHRI, CIHRS, ECESR, ECWR, EIPR, ECESR, and Nazra. "As a result of a direct threat to their work Egyptian HR organizations have decided not to participate in Egypt's UPR before the UN," ECESR, November 5, 2014, http://ecesr.org/en/?p=422058; and http://www.cihrs.org/?p=9836&lang=en; "7 Egyptian rights groups back out of UNHRC summit over fears of persecution," Al-Ahram Online, November 4, 2014, http://english.ahram.org.eg/News/114765.aspx; "Egypt receives 300 recommendations in UN human rights review," Daily News Egypt, November 8, 2014, http://www.dailynewsegypt.com/2014/11/08/egypt-receives-300-recommendations-un-human-rights-review; "CIHRS director: government suppresses dissent under guise of fighting terrorism," Egypt Independent, November 9, 2014, http://www.egyptindependent/com/node/2439675

[143] Ziada resigned after Ibrahim published a column in Al-Masry al-Youm that, she felt, criticized her for participating in the non-governmental delegation and white-washing the government. However, the column – while patronizing her as the Center's "beautiful director" – actually praised the way she handled herself and documented Brotherhood violence. Saad el-Din Ibrahim, "Shall we charge Sisi with receiving funds from abroad?" Egypt Independent, November 16, 2014, http://www.egyptindependent.com/node/2440054; Ayat al-Tawy, "Egyptian rights group divided over pro-regime support," Al-Ahram Online, November 26, 2014, http://english.ahram.org.eg/News/115654.aspx

[144] David D. Kirkpatrick, "Egypt elevates an official hostile to U.S.," New York Times, November 6, 2014; "Mubarak-era minister, foreign funding crusader breaks into security sector," Mada Masr, November 7, 2014, http://www.madamasr.com/news/mubarak-era-minister-foreign-funding-crusader-breaks-security-sector

article 78 of the Penal Code to make life imprisonment the punishment for receiving foreign or local funding in order to act against state interests – and even the death sentence if the crime is committed "at wartime or for the purpose of terrorism."[145] While aimed at terrorists, the provision equally targets politicians, journalists, and NGOs. Egyptian Commission for Rights and Freedoms' Mohamed Lotfy observed: "It's a crazy amendment…Making a film about poverty or writing a report about a protest or attacks on Copts or human rights abuses in Sinai could be deemed harmful to national unity…It is a signal to prosecutors that this issue is very important and that they should look for people who violate it."[146]

New legal constraints on NGOs

When Sisi came to power in July 2013, the new government had signaled a different approach toward civil society. Prime Minister Hazem Beblawi and Deputy Prime Minister and MIC minister Ziad Bahaa el-Din (both active in the Social Democratic Party) endorsed the "right of civil society to set its own law and be supported by the government."[147] MOSS minister Ahmed Borai of the liberal *Dostour* (Constitution) party created

---

[145] Text, issued September 21, 2014: "Anyone who asks for himself or for others or accepts or takes – even through an intermediary – from a foreign state or those who work for its interests or a legal person or a local or an international organization or any other entity that is not affiliated with a foreign state and does not work for its interest, cash or transferred money or equipment or machines or weapons or ammunition or items like it or other things or was promised of any of that…with the intention of committing acts harmful to national interest or acts like it or acts that breach the country's independence or unity or territorial integrity or committing attacks that disrupt public security and safety, shall be punished…." Reem Gehad, "Egypt amends penal code to stipulate harsher punishments on foreign funding," *Al-Ahram Online*, September 23, 2014, http://english.ahram.org.eg/ News/111488.aspx; "President amends law to include life sentence for receiving funds, arms," *Mada Masr*, September 23, 2014, http://www.madamasr.com/content/president-amends-law-include-life-sentence-receiving-funds-arms; "Foreign funding law raises concern over future of human rights organisations," *Daily News Egypt*, September 24, 2014, http://www. dailynewsegypt.com/2014/09/24/foreign-funding-law-raises-concern-future-human-rights-organisations

[146] Patrick Kingsley, "Egypt's human rights groups 'targeted' by crackdown on foreign funding," *Guardian*, September 24, 2014, http://www.theguardian.com/world/2014/ sep/24/egypt-human-rights-crackdown-foreign-funding

[147] Bahaa el-Din, "CEOSS Discusses the New NGO Draft Law," CEOSS, n.d. (about September 29, 2013), http://en.ceoss-eg.org/ceoss-discusses-the-new-ngo-draft-law/

an inclusive drafting process that involved seventeen NGOs along with MOSS, MIC and the foreign ministry. Their draft law received wide support for simplifying registration procedures, narrowing the reasons for dissolving NGOs, reducing penalties, and dropping the requirement that MOSS approve NGOs' foreign funding in advance, while allowing MOSS to object afterwards.[148] The draft required all associations to register – including companies, informal networks, and short-term advocacy campaigns – and allowed the government to ban and suspend international NGOs.

By the end of 2013, the political climate hardened. The government issued the protest law, declared the Brotherhood a terrorist organization, and arrested Al Jazeera journalists. The hyper-nationalist press denounced NGOs as "illegitimate" "fifth columns" responsible for "invasion, war, and national ruin."[149] Even Borai suddenly demanded tight control over NGOs as "evil groups" threaten Egyptian security.[150] He asserted that NGOs should merely "help the government in whatever the government is incapable of doing," such as health care and education.[151]

Deputy Prime Minister Bahaa el-Din resigned on January 27, 2014,[152] alienated by the harsh policies, and Sisi soon expelled all the liberals from the cabinet. New Prime Minister Ibrahim Mehleb stressed "the battle

---

[148] Hafez Abu Saeda facilitated the committee, which included Khaled Ali (ECESR), Bahey al-Din Hassan (CIHRS), Negad al-Borai (United Group), and Ezz Eddin Farghal (Federation of Community Service Organizations). "Draft NGO law to be released tomorrow," *Mada Masr*, September 25, 2013, http://www.madamasr.com/news/draft-ngo-law-be-released-tomorrow

[149] Richard Spencer, "Egypt court disbands Muslim Brotherhood," *Telegraph*, September 23, 2013, http://www.telegraph.co.uk/news/worldnews/africaandindianocean/egypt/10329543/Egypt-court-disbands-Muslim-Brotherhood.html

[150] "Solidarity minister: Government surveillance of NGOs is temporary," *Egypt Independent*, October 15, 2013, http://www.egyptindependent.com/node/2209521; Alyaa Hamed, "Civil society at a crossroads," *Al-Ahram Online*, October 15, 2014, http://weekly.ahram.org.eg/7482.aspx; "Controversial NGO law sent to Social Solidarity Ministry this week," *Egypt Independent*, November 27, 2013, http://www.egyptindependent.com/node/234506; Amy Hawthorne and Mohamed ElGohari, "The ongoing struggle for Egyptian civil society," Atlantic Council, December 17, 2013, http://www.atlanticcouncil.org/blogs/egyptsource/the-ongoing-struggle-for-egyptian-civil-society

[151] AP, "Egypt's rights groups, civil society fear being silenced under heavier restrictions," *Fox News*, October 4, 2014, http://www.foxnews.com/world/2014/10/04/egypt-rights-groups-civil-society-fear-being-silenced

[152] "A Dialogue with Ziad Bahaa-Eldin," Arab Reform Initiative, May 2014, www.arab-reform.net/dialogue-ziad-bahaa-eldin; "Egypt's Deputy PM Ziad Bahaa El-din resigns," *Al-Ahram Online*, January 27, 2014, http://english.ahram.org.eg/News/92755.aspx

that Egypt is waging against the forces of evil and terror."[153] New MOSS minister Ghada Wali withdrew Borai's draft law. After Sisi was elected president in May, she unveiled a new NGO law on June 26, 2014.[154]

Article 75 of the January 2014 constitution states that NGOs and foundations

> shall acquire legal personality upon notification. Such associations and foundations shall have the right to practice their activities freely and administrative agencies may not interfere in their affairs or dissolve them or dissolve their boards of directors or boards of trustees, save by a court judgment.[155]

But Wali's draft law – written without consulting NGOs – revived the draconian Interior Ministry draft of February 2013 and reinstated the coordinating committee that included the Interior Ministry and state security. The government-appointed National Council on Human Rights (NCHR) joined twenty-nine NGOs to reject the draft.[156] A human rights lawyer warned: security officers will participate in every NGO board meeting and transform NGOs into state-organs.[157]

---

[153] Hamza Hendawi, "Egypt's new premier calls for protests to end," March 2, 2014, http://www.statesman.com/ap/ap/top-news/egypt-new-premier-urges-end-to-protests/nd14M2
[154] Aya Nader and Menna Zaki, "29 NGOs protest new civil society draft law," *Daily News Egypt*, July 9, 2014, http://www.dailynewsegypt.com/2014/07/09/29-ngos-protest-new-civil-society-draft-law; "NGOs demand government to stop fight against civil society," *Daily News Egypt*, July 24, 2014, http://www.dailynewsegypt.com/2014/07/24/ngos-demand-government-stop-fight-civil-society; Rana Muhammad Taha, "NCHR calls for postponing issuance of civil society draft law," *Daily News Egypt*, July 16, 2014, http://www.dailynewsegypt.com/2014/07/16/nchr-calls-postponing-issuance-civil-society-draft-law; "Egypt: Draft Law threatens independent organizations," HRW, July 14, 2014, http://www.hrw.org/news/2014/07/14/egypt-draft-law-threatens-independent-organizations
[155] "Over 45,000 NGOs register at Ministry of Social Solidarity: El-Helw," *Daily News Egypt*, December 8, 2014, http://www.dailynewsegypt.com/2014/12/08/45000-ngos-register-ministry-social-solidarity-el-helw
[156] "Egypt's rights groups object to proposed NGO draft law," *Al-Ahram Online*, July 10, 2014, http://English.ahram.org.eg/News/105954.aspx; "Egypt: NGOs demand government to stop fight against civil society," NGO News Africa, July 25, 2014, http://ngonewsafrica.org/archives/14556
[157] "United Group slams NGO draft law," *Mada Masr*, September 18, 2014, http://www.madamasr.com/content/united-group-slams-ngo-draft-law

As opposition mounted, MOSS offered to delay the changes until after parliamentary elections, while insisting that all associations must comply with the 2002 law, because Egypt "is subject to foreign interference and NGOs are fertile soil for that."[158] The minister announced that the government would immediately close all civil companies and law firms, and seize their assets. The Forum of Independent Human Rights Organizations termed this "sword to our necks" an effort to "silence us as a way of getting revenge for the role we played in the revolution."[159] CIHRS's Hasan met with Prime Minister Mehleb on July 24, but Mehleb never held a promised meeting with NGO representatives. The Forum's appeal to Sisi on August 27 did result in MOSS extending the registration deadline until November 10 – without modifying the draconian conditions.[160]

NGOs faced stark choices. The Arab Penal Reform Organization (APRO) shut itself down. Already registered as a for-profit law firm subject to Egyptian laws and scrutiny by Egyptian tax authorities, APRO refused to register under Law 84/2002.[161] Some NGOs that operated in other Arab countries closed their local offices. For example, CIHRS transferred its main office to Tunis, while keeping a limited staff in Cairo.[162] CIHRS's fears were realized when the government raided the Cairo office in June

---

[158] Mariam Rizk, "Egypt's NGOs continue struggle with restrictive draft law," *Al-Ahram Online*, September 22, 2014, http://english.ahram.org.eg/News/111294.aspx; "Egypt's NGOs under threat: Rights groups," *Daily News Egypt*, August 28, 2014, http://www.dailynewsegypt.com/2014/08/28/egypts-ngos-threat-rights-groups/; "Egypt extends deadline for NGOs to register or face investigation," *Al-Ahram Online*, August 31, 2014, http://english.ahram.org.eg/News/109643.aspx

[159] Al-Sharif Nassef, "Civil society law one more link on chain to shackle dissent in Egypt," *Mada Masr*, August 15, 2014, http://www.madamasr.com/content/civil-society-law-one-more-link-chain-shackle-dissent-egypt

[160] Tom Stevenson, "Egypt cracks down on human rights groups," Al-Monitor, August 15, 2014, http://www.al-monitor.com/pulse/originals/2014/08/stevenson-egypt-human-civil-rights.html; Sarah Lynch, "Legal sword hangs over the heads of Egyptian NGOs," August 15, 2014, http://www.al-Fanarmedia.org/2014/08/legal-sword-hangs-head-egyptian-ngos

[161] Director Mohamed Zarea sent a letter on November 3 to the Egyptian Tax Authority announcing its closure. "Rights group suspends work, cites 'unfavorable' environment," *Egypt Independent*, November 5, 2014, http://www.egyptindependent.com/node/2439576/

[162] "Egyptian rights group partially relocates abroad amid 'constant threats' against civil society," *Al-Ahram Online*, December 10, 2014, http://english.ahram.org.eg./News/117591.aspx; "Rights watchdog relocates regional hub from Cairo," World Bulletin, December 10, 2014, http://www.worldbulletin.net/servisler/haberYazdir/150381/haber

2015 in the midst of death threats against director Bahey al-Din Hassan. He didn't dare return to Egypt.[163]

Few foreign organizations remained. Human Rights Watch closed its Cairo office in early 2014, well before its report on the Rabaa massacre. The Carter Center also closed, frustrated that it could not even open a bank account to pay rent and staff or get work permits for foreign employees. Both organizations' applications for registration had been pending for years.[164] The Foreign Ministry explicitly rejected the International Crisis Group, citing a decision by the government's security-dominated coordinating committee. (As the draft law was still pending, that committee actually had no legal status.) And the respected Friedrich Naumann Foundation, affiliated with Germany's Free Democratic Party, moved its regional office to Jordan in January 2016, lamenting that "every conference that we organize with our Egyptian partners is misunderstood as a possible threat to the internal security of Egypt."[165]

Some NGOs remained defiant. Gamal Eid, executive director of the Arabic Network of Human Rights Information (ANHRI) proclaimed that ANHRI functioned as a group of lawyers who do not receive external funding; ANHRI would not register under Law 84/2002 and would not stop its activities. Eid preferred to have ANHRI shut down than to operate under state security's control. Similarly, the Human Rights Center for the Assistance of Prisoners declared, "We will keep working until either they cancel the announcement or close us down."[166] The United Group, in operation as a law firm since 1943, sought to retain that status. EIPR, registered as a company that pays income tax and social security and obtains

---

[163] "Egypt govt takes 'revenge' on us," June 11, 2015.

[164] The Carter Center "filed required documentation for registration with the Ministry of Foreign Affairs [in 2011, but] never received formal registration." Press release on October 15, 2014, http://www.cartercenter.org/news/pr/egypt-101514.html; Editorial, "From Jimmy Carter, a Rebuke to Egypt," New York Times, October 18, 2014, http://www.nytimes.com/2014/10/19/opinion/sunday/from-jimmy-carter-a-rebuke-to-egypt.html

[165] AP, "Citing security restrictions, German think-tank pulls out of Egypt," Egypt Independent, January 2, 2016, http://www.egyptindependent.com/node/2465403

[166] Alyaa Hamad, "Civil society at the crossroads," Al-Ahram Online, October 15, 2014, http://weekly.ahram.org.eg/7482.aspx; "Egypt: Some NGOs shut down to avoid abiding by 'repressive' law," Al-Akhbar, November 11, 2014, http://english.al-akhbar.com/node/22414; "Human rights situation in Egypt worst in 30 years: Gamal Eid," Daily News Egypt, January 22, 2015, http://www.dailynewsegypt.com/2015/01/22/human-rights-situation-egypt-worst-30-years-

foreign funding under that company status, initially refused to register. Later, EIPR concluded that it must register, but pledged to struggle for a law that "regulates the work of civil society associations in Egypt in a democratic, clear and transparent manner."[167]

At least nine foreign and eight Egyptian organizations met the November 10 deadline.[168] These included the year-old Egyptian Commission for Rights and Freedoms, registered as a company, which addresses a wide range of issues, from academic freedom to economic justice.[169] The decades-old Ibn Khaldun Center, which had initially resisted change to its status as a company, also decided to comply.[170] The center was a shadow of its former self, embroiled in internal tensions and almost insolvent. Founder Saad Eddin Ibrahim had campaigned for Shafiq against Morsi in June 2012, even though the Center monitored the election; the Center subsequently insisted that Shafiq had won.[171] In 2013, Ibrahim declared Sisi Egypt's "savior from darkness," and the Center praised the police's violent dispersal of the Rabaa sit-in. Ibrahim and executive director Dalia Ziada supported both the protest law and the terrorist-entities decree as necessary to quell violent attacks.[172]

---

[167] Mahmoud Mostafa, "EIPR to register under 'flawed' NGO law, will continue work to replace it," *Daily News Egypt*, December 22, 2014, http://www.dailynewsegypt.com/2014/12/22/eipr-register-flawed-ngo-law-will-continue-work; Sharif Abdel Kouddous, "Egypt escalates repression against human rights groups and NGOs," *The Nation*, November 12, 2014, http://www.thenation.com/article/190529/egypt-escalate-repression-against-human-rights-groups; Menna Zaki, "Civil society workers ask for freedom, end of threats," *Daily News Egypt*, January 3, 2015, http://www.dailynewsegypt.com/2015/01/03/year-end-2014-demands-civil-society-media

[168] "Ministry of Solidarity: 9 foreign, 8 Egyptian organizations legalized their status," *Egypt Independent*, November 10, 2014, http://www.egyptindependent.com/node/2439767

[169] Executive director Mohamed Lotfy said that, as ECRF was only a year old and had just moved into a new office, it would register in order to protect the twenty-person staff. Merrit Kennedy, "Egypt's civil society fears it will be silenced," AP, October 4, 2014, https://uk.news.yahoo.com/egypts-civil-society-fears-silenced-070101505.html

[170] "Egypt: Some NGOs shut down to avoid abiding by 'repressive' law," November 11, 2014.

[171] Raymond Ibrahim, "Did the Muslim Brotherhood really win the presidency in Egypt?" *Front Page Magazine*, http://www.frontpagemag.com/fpm/163393/did-muslim-brotherhood-really-win-presidency-egypt-raymond-ibrahim; Dalia Ziada, "It is a SECOND REVOLUTION!" June 28, 2013, http://daliaziada.blogspot.com/

[172] "Savior" quotation in Yasmine Saleh, "Egypt military officers back army chief for president," http://www.reuters.com/article/2013/10/23/us-egypt-sisi; Aaron T. Rose, "Research centre finds sit-in dispersal adhered to international standards," *Daily News Egypt*, August 24, 2013, http://www.dailynewsegypt.com/2013/08/24/research-centre-finds-sit-in-dispersal-adhered-to-international-standards; Mohamed Elsaied and Manal

However, Ziada went further than Ibrahim through her international campaign to place the Brotherhood on terrorist lists. After she resigned in November 2014, she accelerated that campaign. She even alleged that the Brotherhood (rather than the police) had attacked protesters in January 2011 and that a leading youth activist was funded by Hamas.[173]

Throughout the following year, pressure mounted on human rights organizations and autonomous actors. The government pressured independent trade unions that had emerged just before and after the overthrow of the Mubarak regime, cracked down on youth who expressed their anger through the Ultra soccer support groups, and canceled the results of university student union elections in November 2015, when the regime-backed slate failed to win a single seat. All the students who won supported the January revolution and demanded the restoration of academic freedom. This was intolerable to the security sector, the minister of higher education, and the university presidents whom Sisi had appointed.[174]

Elessawy, "Egyptians will teach the MB a lesson today, Head of Ibn Khaldun center says," *Cairo Post*, January 14, 2014, http://www.thecairopost.com/news/73231/news/egyptians-will-teach-the-mb-a-lesson-today; "Human rights in Egypt face obstacles that will soon be eliminated: Ziada," *Daily News Egypt*, February 25, 2015, http://www.dailynewsegypt.com/2015/02/25/human-rights-egypt-face-obstacles-will-soon-end

[173] Aya Samir, "Ibn Khaldun director on her resignation: NGO was a thorn in the side of Egypt," *Cairo Post*, November 16, 2014, http://www.thecairopost.com/news/129074/inside-egypt/ibn-khaldun-director-on-her-resignation;"We have human rights violations, whoever overlooks them is blind: Saad Eddin Ibrahim," *Daily News Egypt*, February 24, 2015, http://www.dailynewsegypt.com/2015/02/24/human-rights-violations-whoever-overlooks-blind; Ahmed Shehata, "Group uses democratic rhetoric to push its own agenda," The Hill, March 7, 2014, http://thehill.com/blogs/congress-blog/foreign-policy/200149-group-uses-democratic-rhetoric; Ziada speech to 2014 Geneva Summit, YouTube, March 3, 2014, www.genevasummit.org/speaker/131/dalia_ziada; David D. Kirkpatrick and Merna Thomas, "Egyptian judges drop all charges against Mubarak," New York Times, November 29, 2014, http://www.nytimes.com/2014/11/30/world/hosni-mubarak-charges-dismissed-by-egyptian-court.html; Sonia Farid, "Why was Ahmed Douma given a life sentence?" Atlantic Council, March 12, 2015, http://www.atlanticcouncil.org/blogs/menasource/why-was-ahmed-douma-given-a-life-sentence; Bishoy Ramzy, "Egyptian studies center prepares a report about MB's crimes," Al Bawaba EG, June 24, 2015, http://www.albawabaeg.com/56832

[174] Mai Shams El-Din, "Fate of student union elections unknown as conflict widens between students and state," *Mada Masr*, December 17, 2015, http://www.madamasr.com/sections/politics/fate-student-union-elections-unknown-conflict-widens-between-students-and-state; Mai Shams El-Din, "Students vow to continue fight over national students union, ministry procrastinates," *Mada Masr*, December 29, 2015, http://www.madamasr.com/sections/politics/students-vow-continue-fight-over-national-students-union

THE CONSOLIDATION OF AUTHORITARIAN CONTROL

The first two months of 2016 witnessed aggressive displays of police power and crackdowns on civil society. After Sisi opposed commemorations on the fifth anniversary of the January revolution, declaring that those who protest "want to destroy the country,"[175] the police went on a rampage. They closed downtown cultural spaces, grabbed people out of cafes and off the street, and raided five thousand apartments, from which they arrested "suspicious" occupants.[176] The Interior Ministry's Censorship Authority led the raid on the Townhouse art gallery and its companion Rawabet theatre on December 28, 2015, during which security forces confiscated computers, books, documents, and exhibition and archive material. The gallery was warned that, in order to reopen, it must obtain prior state approval for all programs, including workshops and exhibits.[177] Similarly, the security forces who raided Merit Publishing House the next day focused on the political views of its founder, its hosting of political seminars under the guise of book launches, and its events in solidarity with detained writers.[178]

Security forces stormed the Egyptian Democratic Academy (EDA) a week later and seized its general manager, who had already received threatening phone calls and circumvented several kidnap attempts by security-backed thugs.[179] As EDA monitors the performance of parliament as

---

[175] "Al-Sisi emphasises submission to Egyptian political mandate in Al-Azhar speech," *Daily News Egypt*, December 22, 2015, http://www.dailynewsegypt.com/2015/12/22/al-sisi-emphasises-submission-to-egyptian-political-mandate-in-al-azhar-speech

[176] Raids included Townhouse gallery, Rawabet theatre, Merit publishers, Studio Emad Eddin, and Masr al-Arabia. Ruth Michaelson, "Egyptian police raid Cairo homes as country prepares to mark 2011 uprising," *Guardian*, January 22, 2016, https://www.theguardian.com/world/2016/jan/21/egyptian-police-raid-cairo-homes-2011-uprising

[177] David Batty, "Cairo gallery bemoans unprecedented censorship as it prepares to reopen," *Guardian*, February 22, 2016, https://www.theguardian.com/world/2016/feb/22/egypt-cairo-art-gallery-townhouse-unprecedented-censorship

[178] Merit, a haven for protesters during the January 2011 revolution, particularly publishes the works of young experimental writers; "Update: Prosecution orders release of Merit Publishing House staff member, summons founder," *Mada Masr*, December 29, 2015, http://www.madamasr.com/news/culture/update-prosecution-orders-release-merit-publishing-house-staff-member-summons-founder

[179] EDA was raided late at night on January 5, 2016. Amira El-Fekki, "Manager of Democratic Institute detained, pending investigations," January 6, 2016, http://www.dailynewsegypt.com/2016/01/06/manager-of-democratic-institute-detained-pending-investigations

well as elections, including for the student unions and worker syndicates, these threats seemed designed to halt its efforts to uphold the rule of law.

Security agents trolled social media in order to arrest Facebook page administrators – and even people who simply 'liked' certain pages – and they blocked well-known activists from flying abroad. Security forces mobilized on the streets and the military took direct control over the prisons in the days before the anniversary. The disappearance of an Italian scholar that day, whose brutalized body was thrown onto a street nine days later, had a particularly chilling impact: even foreigners could be tortured with impunity.[180]

The arrests, closures, security mobilization, and interference in the media prompted Naguib Sawiris to state on his ONTv station that the security dragnet and sense of alienation "remind me of the atmosphere before the 25 of January revolution"[181] – an extraordinary statement for the tycoon founder of the Free Egyptians Party.

There was no let-up in the security operations after the anniversary, even though Sisi subsequently expressed concern in phone calls to TV talk-shows in which he declared that he wasn't bothered by criticism by a young cartoonist (who had just been detained) and that he sought to include Ultras in the investigation of a mass-killing of soccer fans four years earlier.[182] A lawyer took a case against former presidential candidate Hamdeen Sabbahi for inciting against the regime, reviving fears of the Mubarak-era cases against politicians who dared to run against him for president.[183] And a Cairo University doctoral student who studied

---

[180] Guilio Regeni, Ph.D. student at Cambridge University, researched independent trade unions, a topic highly sensitive to the security state. Kareem Fahim, Nour Youssef, and Declan Walsh, "Death of student, Giulio Regeni, highlights perils for Egyptians, too," *New York Times*, February 12, 2016, http://www.nytimes.com/2016/02/13/world/middleeast/giulio-regeni-egypt-killing.html; "Italian student showed signs of electrocution – Egypt forensic source," Reuters, February 13, 2016, http://www.reuters.com/article/us-egypt-italian-id; Stephanie Kirchgaessner and Ruth Michaelson, "Why was he killed? Brutal death of Italian student in Egypt confounds experts," *Guardian*, February 24, 2016, http://www.theguardian.com/world/2016/feb/24/why-was-he-killed-brutal-death-of-italian-student-in-egypt-confounds-experts

[181] "Egypt's current conditions remind me of days before 25 January revolution, says Sawiris," *Al-Ahram Online*, January 12, 2016, http://english.ahram.org.eg/News/18077.aspx

[182] "Sisi urges dialogue with Ultras on anniversary of stadium massacre" and "Sisi says not upset with [cartoonist] Gawish," *Egypt Independent*, February 2, 2016, http://www.egyptindependent.com/node/2466087 and node/2466090

[183] Sabbahi was the only candidate against Sisi in 2014. In an interview on TV on January 7, he said that Sisi's popularity was falling because he was failing to provide solutions to

Islamic movements and served as executive director of the university's Civilization Center for Political Studies was arrested from his home at midnight on February 21.[184]

Prominent public intellectuals remained on no-fly lists: ANHRI's Gamal Eid was blocked at passport control on February 4 as he headed on business to Athens.[185] Pioneering human rights activist and investigative reporter Hossam Bahgat was prevented from attending a UN meeting in Amman on Justice in the Arab World.[186] And, on February 27, CEO Hossam El-Din of EDA, which had been raided in December, was prevented from flying to Washington DC to participate in a State Department conference on combatting corruption through legislation.[187]

Meanwhile, the Health Ministry charged that the twenty-three-year-old El Nadeem Center for Rehabilitation of Victims of Violence and Torture violated its license by operating not only as a clinic to treat psychological diseases but also as a rights center reporting on torture

people's problems and called on Sisi to achieve the social justice demands of the January 25 and June 30 revolutions. Amira El-Fekki, "Former rival presidential candidate Sabahy slams Al-Sisi's regime," *Daily News Egypt,* January 7, 2016, http://www.dailynewsegypt. com/2016/01/07/former-rival-presidential-candidate-sabahy-slams-al-sisis-regime; "Former presidential candidate referred to prosecution," *Daily News Egypt,* February 16, 2016, http://www.dailynewsegypt.com/2016/02/16/former-presidential-candidate-referred-to-prosecution

[184] Medhat Maher, even though he had been acquitted of charges of membership in the Muslim Brotherhood in March 2015. See Center director Professor Nadia Mostafa's statement in "Researcher of Islamist movements arrested for alleged Brotherhood links," *Mada Masr,* February 29, 2016, http://www.madamasr.com/news/researcher-islamist-movements-arrested-alleged-brotherhood-links

[185] "Human rights lawyer Gamal Eid banned from travel," *Mada Masr,* February 4, 2016, http://www.madamasr.com/news/human-rights-lawyer-gamal-eid-banned-travel

[186] Founder of EIPR in 2002, Bahgat spent AY 2014–15 at Columbia University. When he bravely returned to Cairo to write for *Mada Masr,* he was briefly arrested in November for his article on the secret military trial of officers who had plotted a coup. He then traveled to Berlin and Amman for conferences, but was prevented from traveling to Amman on February 23. Hossam Bahgat, "A coup busted? The secret military trial of 26 officers for plotting 'regime change' with the Brotherhood," *Mada Masr,* October 14, 2015, http://www. madamasr.com/sections/politics/coup-busted; David D. Kirkpatrick, "Hossam Bahgat, journalist and advocate, is released by Egypt's military," *New York Times,* November 10, 2015, http://www.nytimes.com/2015/11/11/world/middleeast/hossam-bahgat-egypt. html; "Hossam Bahgat banned from travelling," *Daily News Egypt,* February 24, 2016, http://www.dailynewsegypt.com/2016/02/24/hossam-bahgat-banned-from-travelling/

[187] Taha Sakr, "Egypt puts travel ban on CEO of local democratic institute," *Daily News Egypt,* February 28, 2016, http://www.dailynewsegypt.com/2016/02/28/egypt-puts-travel-ban-on-ceo-of-local-democratic-institute

and rehabilitating victims of sexual assault, domestic violence, and police torture. The directors explained that the clinic and center were registered separately, the latter as an NGO that has no relation to the Health Ministry. In a meeting with ministry officials, it became evident that El Nadeem's reports on police torture and the state's human rights violations were the reasons for the closure order: the decision was made by "the highest authority which encompasses all other ministries," a reference to the prime minister or to Sisi himself.[188]

NGOs remain uncertain of their future. MOSS has retained the essence of the bill submitted in 2014, in particular the inclusion of the Ministry of Interior on the coordinating committee and government control over NGOs' funding.[189] MOSS frames the tightly constraining regulations as necessary because "we are a country under attack," like the United States after 9/11. NGOs counter that narrative by stressing that they want to tackle Egypt's serious social problems, oppose terrorism, and have nothing to hide.[190] At times, the minister seemed to want to reach a resolution, by suggesting that MOSS examine each organization separately and hinting that a way might be found to legalize their status as civil companies or law firms.[191]

In actuality, decisions are made by the Interior Ministry, not MOSS. State security provided MOSS with the names of a hundred NGOs to

[188] Quotation from "Al-Nadeem: Closure order is political and came from Egypt's Cabinet," *Mada Masr*, February 21, 2016, http://www.madamasr.com/news/al-nadeem-closure-order-political-and-came-egypts-cabinet; Rania Tarek, "Health ministry claims licence violation behind El Nadeem Centre closure," *Daily News Egypt*, February 22, 2016, http://www.dailynewsegypt.com/2016/02/22/health-ministry-claims-licence-violation-behind-el-nadeem-centre-closure; "Anti-torture NGO vows to keep working despite closure," *Egypt Independent*, February 23, 2016, http://www.egyptindependent.com/node/2467046; "Anti-torture NGO El-Nadeem rejects health ministry's reasons for shutdown," *Al-Ahram Online*, February 25, 2016, http://english.ahram.org.eg/News/188500.aspx
[189] Khaled Hassan, "NGO bill sparks controversy in Egypt," Al-Monitor, January 3, 2016, http://www.al-monitor.com/pulse/originals/2016/01/ngo-bill-controversy-freedoms-egypt-parliament.html.=
[190] "Minister sends mixed messages on NGO crackdown," *Mada Masr*, November 11, 2014, http://www.madamasr.com/news/minister-sends-mixed-messages-ngo-crackdown; "Rights groups seek dialogue with government," *Daily News Egypt*, November 18, 2014, http://www.dailynewsegypt.com/2014/11/18/rights-groups-seek-dialogue-government/
[191] Mariam Rizk, "No legal action against civil groups registered under any Egyptian law: Minister," *Al-Ahram Online*, November 11, 2014, http://english.ahram.org.eg/News/115278.aspx; "Ministry of Solidarity: 9 foreign, 8 Egyptian organizations legalized their status," *Egypt Independent*, November 10, 2014, http://www.egyptindependent.com/news/ministry-solidarity-9-foreign-8-egyptian-organizations-legalized-their-status

investigate and of leading advocates to arrest in late 2014.[192] This ambiguity – coupled with the reopening of the cases against NGO that were originally filed in 2011 – leaves NGOs on edge, not knowing when the ax might fall. Those registered as companies and law firms fear to take the installments on payments from abroad, as banks must report funds received into their accounts. Given NGOs' uncertain legal status, they could be legally liable through Sisi's draconian decree that criminalizes unauthorized payments. Some are already threatened with having their personal or institutional assets frozen. Thus, advocacy organizations not only are severely constrained in paying staff and continuing research and action projects, but also fear arrest and the complete shutdown of their operations.

The Egyptian regime views autonomous actors with deep distrust. There is a sharp discontinuity between government statements about the transition to democracy and the pervasive mindset "that civil society work is harmful to national security."[193] Indeed, Sisi dropped the pretense of democratizing when he declaimed angrily on February 24, 2016:[194]

It is too early before you start practicing democracy with its broad meaning... Do not listen to anyone's words but mine....Unjustified media attacks on the government's performance must stop....If you want to take care of [Egypt] along with me, you are welcome. If not, please be silent....I swear to God, I will make anyone who thinks to [harm] this country perish from the face of the earth.

Alaa al-Aswany wrote in his valedictory newspaper column: "Different views are no longer allowed: Only one view, one thought, and one talk... It is no longer acceptable to say the truth but to praise only."[195] At best, NGOs provide ancillary services; at worst, they are enemies to keep under surveillance and, when necessary, crush. Except for the brief

---

[192] Stephen Kalin and Lin Noueihed, "Don't prejudge Egypt's new draft NGO law, says minister," Reuters, October 23, 2014, http://www.reuters.com/article/us-egypt-ngos-idUSKCN0IC1WP20141023

[193] Mohamed Zarie, director of the Human Rights Centre for the Assistance of Prisoners, in Alyaa Hamad, "Civil society at the crossroads," Al-Ahram Online, October 15, 2014, http://weekly.ahram.org.eg/7482.aspx

[194] "Sisi's 'Egypt Vision 2030' speech garners positive, negative reactions," Egypt Independent, February 25, 2016, http://www.egyptindependent.com/node/2467112

[195] Al-Masry al-Youm, June 2014, quoted in Lesch, "Egypt's new president."

moment in 2013 when Deputy Prime Minister Bahaa el-Din endorsed the "right of civil society to set its own law and be supported by the government," rulers do not perceive NGOs, trade unions, professional syndicates, cultural associations, and the media as legitimate autonomous actors with the intrinsic right to craft their own objectives, manage their own operations, and critique and monitor the government. They certainly do not endorse Bahaa el-Din's view that security and prosperity can only be achieved through democracy.[196]

Neutering and subduing society under an all-powerful presidency weakens rather than strengthens Egypt. It weakens the rule of law, undermines the accountability and transparency of government, and silences alternative voices.[197] NGOs struggle to voice alternatives that will promote political, social and economic justice. They pay a high price for their efforts.

[196] Arab Reform Initiative, May 2014, accessed December 5, 2014, www.arab-reform.net/dialogue-ziad-bahaa-eldin
[197] Mohammed Nosseir, "Which is better for Al-Sisi: Strengthening Egyptian society or neutering it," *Daily News Egypt*, December 6, 2014, http://www.dailynewsegypt.com/2014/12/06/better-al-sisi-strengthening-egyptian-society-or-neutering-it

6

Myth or reality?

The discursive construction of the Muslim Brotherhood in Egypt

MOHAMAD ELMASRY

F
ew institutions are as central to the preservation of a liberal civil
society as a free press. Indeed, it is no accident that a preponderance of early Egyptian liberal thinkers saw the media as central to
their reform project: from Ahmad Lutfi al-Sayyid's newspaper *Al-Jarida*
in the early twentieth century to the pages of *Ruz al-Yusuf* under editor
Ihsan Abd al-Quddus in the 1950s, journalism proved one of the most
prominent vehicles for the articulation of liberal reform, and for the cultivation of a nascent Egyptian civil society. Regrettably, though, during
Egypt's brief 2011–13 democratic experiment and the concomitant rise
and fall of the Muslim Brotherhood, journalists and news outlets with
ostensibly liberal missions largely failed to live up to those ideals.

The story of the Muslim Brotherhood (MB) in Egypt following the
2011 uprising can perhaps best be described as one of a meteoric rise,
and an equally meteoric fall. Following the ouster of Hosni Mubarak,
the group went on to win five consecutive free-and-fair elections and
referendums in 2011 and 2012 – four by wide margins. After decades of
repression, it seemed the MB was now poised to rise to become among the
most important players in Egypt's emerging democratic order. Yet only a
year after the election of Brotherhood candidate Mohammad Morsi to
Egypt's presidency, those ambitions were quickly dashed; with the military
coup that brought down Morsi's rule on July 3, 2013 came a campaign of
repression hitherto unseen in the movement's history.

Indeed, in the weeks and months that followed the coup, the Brotherhood was systematically eliminated from Egyptian political and public life, both in official and unofficial channels: thousands of Brotherhood members and supporters were killed in what Human Rights Watch called "the worst mass unlawful killings" in Egypt's modern history; tens of thousands of anti-coup protesters and activists were arrested for political crimes; the Brotherhood was banned and declared a terrorist organization; MB members received the largest mass death sentences in modern world history; MB (and other Islamist) charitable organizations were shut down; and individual Muslim Brothers were prevented by new legislation from running for office as independent candidates. Egyptian state institutions willfully colluded with, and aggressively supported, the exclusion of the MB from Egyptian public life.

Without question, Brotherhood incompetence, inexperience, a general lack of transparency, and a series of miscalculations and mistakes – including an arguably problematic alliance with conservative Salafists (who later supported the coup) – contributed to both liberal fears about the future of Egypt, and, ultimately, the political downfall of the MB. But, in all likelihood, poor governance and incompetence alone would not have been sufficient, in the minds of many Brotherhood opponents, to warrant the forced removal of an elected president, much less the subsequent mass repression of his supporters. How did it become possible for the Brotherhood to be demoted – almost overnight – from dominating successive elections to public enemy #1? How could Egyptians willfully vote the MB into office, only to then celebrate the mass execution of Brotherhood members a mere year later?

I argue that the Brotherhood's dramatic fall from grace was enabled in large part by a systematic discourse demonizing the group not as simply incompetent and ineffectual, but as outright treasonous to Egyptian state and society. This discourse, moreover, was emboldened primarily through the vehicle of the Egyptian news media: both the state-run press and privately owned media, discarding journalistic principles of neutrality and balance, ultimately gave credence to a hegemonic narrative portraying the MB as enemies of the state. Rather than fulfill the role of a liberal institution tasked with protecting civil society, Egyptian news media instead ultimately contributed to Egypt's return to authoritarianism.

Accordingly, this chapter explores some of the news and political discourses that provided the necessary ammunition for a series of cataclysmic events, starting with Morsi's overthrow. I argue here that foundational myths propagated about Morsi and the Muslim Brothers – and adopted wholesale by privately owned media outlets – likely led many Egyptians to view the group as traitors and support both the military coup and the post-coup campaign of elimination launched against the MB. The Egyptian media – both state and private – constructed a series of hegemonic discourses about the Muslim Brotherhood and Morsi. This work began before June 30, 2013, and continued with greater force in the aftermath of the coup. These discourses, I argue, helped convince many Egyptians that the problems with the Muslim Brotherhood go beyond poor governance and simple incompetence. Rather, the discourses suggested that the Brotherhood is a sinister group interested in destroying much of what is good about Egyptian society.

Arguably, a lack of professionalism among Egyptian news outlets may have contributed to the discursive campaign against the Brotherhood. The next section reviews relevant literature about the Egyptian press system, with attention to scholarly literature examining Egypt's historically censorial political and press cultures, and the nation's traditional lack of journalistic professionalism.

THE EGYPTIAN PRESS SYSTEM

A good deal of scholarly work has been devoted to examining the Egyptian press. Work has focused on the historical trajectory of Egyptian journalism under former presidents Nasser, Sadat, and Mubarak;[1] Egyptian press law;[2] the structure of the Egyptian press system;[3] the differences between privately owned, government-owned, and opposition-owned Egyptian newspapers;[4] satellite television;[5] internet usage;[6] and social

[1] N. Mellor, *The Making of Arab News* (Oxford: Rowman and Littlefield, 2005).
[2] W. Rugh, *Arab Mass Media: Newspapers, Radio, and Television in Arab Politics* (Westport: Praeger, 2004); N. Sakr, "Contested blueprints for Egypt's satellite channels: Regrouping the options by redefining the debate," *International Communication Gazette* 63 (2001): 149.
[3] M. H. Elmasry, "Producing news in Mubarak's Egypt: An analysis of Egyptian newspaper production during the late Hosni Mubarak era," *Journal of Arab & Muslim Media Research* 4, no. 2&3 (2011): 121–44.
[4] K. J. Cooper, "Politics and priorities: Inside the Egyptian press," *Arab Media & Society* 6 (Fall 2008), http://www.arabmediasociety.com/?article=689
[5] L. Pintak, "Satellite TV news and Arab democracy," *Journalism Practice* 2, no. 1 (2008); Sakr, "Contested blueprints for Egypt's satellite channels."
[6] R. Abdulla, "Taking the e-train: The development of the internet in Egypt," *Global Media and Communication* 1, no. 2 (2005): 149–65.

media patterns.[7] Perhaps more important for the purposes of the present research, scholarship has also examined Egypt's traditionally censorial media environment[8] – including Egyptian journalism's historical subservience to the nation's military – and the country's standards of journalistic professionalism.[9] The dynamic between the military, government, and journalism, and Egypt's historical lack of professional journalistic standards are particularly relevant to this examination of news portrayals of Morsi and the Muslim Brotherhood.

Government censorship

In their 1954 groundbreaking work on *Four Theories of the Press*,[10] Siebert, Peterson, and Schramm famously noted that press systems naturally reflect the larger sociopolitical systems in which they are situated. Thus, democratic political systems will feature free, largely democratic press apparatuses, while authoritarian political systems will produce obsequious press outlets that serve as little more than government mouthpieces. Given this general rule, it is not surprising that successive Egyptian dictatorships have produced press systems characterized by a lack of journalistic freedom.

Like many Arab countries, for most of its history, Egypt has been plagued by a censorial press culture, with ruling regimes exerting near-complete control over the news system.[11] Following Egypt's 1952 coup against the King Faruk monarchy, new president Gamal Abdel Nasser, who was president of Egypt from 1954 until his death in 1970, spoke of his desire for an independent, free Egypt that would mold itself after the West, while preserving its essential cultural identity.[12] Nasser, though,

---

[7] S. Khamis and K. Vaughn, "We are all Khaled Said: The potentials and limitations of cyberactivism in triggering public mobilization and promoting political change," *Journal of Arab & Muslim Media Research* 4, no. 2&3 (2011): 145–63.

[8] Elmasry, "Producing news in Mubarak's Egypt"; Mellor, *The Making of Arab News*; Pintak, "Satellite TV news and Arab democracy."

[9] M. H. Elmasry, D. M. Basiony, and S. F. Elkamel, "Egyptian journalistic professionalism in the context of revolution: Comparing survey results from before and after the January 25, 2011 uprising," *International Journal of Communication* 8 (2014): 1615–37.

[10] F. S. Siebert, T. Peterson, and W. Schramm, *Four Theories of the Press* (Books for Libraries Press, 1956).

[11] Mellor, *The Making of Arab News*.

[12] P. Woodward, *Nasser* (London: Longman, 1992).

ultimately moved against a Western-style political system, opting instead for a de facto single-party system, political exclusion and marginalization, and very little press freedom. Nasser nationalized the press in 1960, putting all Egyptian news outlets under government ownership and ensuring a completely servile media apparatus.[13] The press in the Nasser period treated the president, and, importantly, the military, as "red lines" not to be crossed. These "red lines" became firmly established as journalistic norms in Egypt, with the person of the president and military continuing to remain off limits through the Anwar Sadat and Hosni Mubarak periods.[14]

Sadat took over as Egypt's president in 1970 and ruled until his assassination in 1981. He employed democratic rhetoric to a greater extent than Nasser, arguing in 1972 that press freedom was essential to both democracy in general and Egypt in particular.[15] In 1976, Sadat followed through on his rhetoric to some extent when he established a multiparty political system and gave each party the right to publish a newspaper. Although there were significant restrictions on political pluralism and press content – including the aforementioned restrictions on coverage of the president and military – Sadat's moves were thought to be a step in the right direction. A brief period of comparatively greater press freedoms would prove to be short-lived, however, as Sadat sought, in the late 1970s and early 1980s, to quell growing opposition to his economic liberalization policy (*al-Infitah*) and the Camp David peace initiative. In early 1981, Sadat declared a state of emergency, arrested thousands of people, including many journalists, and shut down news outlets.[16] Overall, while Sadat's time in office included brief periods of relative political and press freedom, the "prevailing character [of the regime] was repression."[17]

Mubarak was president of Egypt from 1981 until Egypt's 2011 uprising, and his time in power was characterized by significant ambivalence regarding political and press freedom. He exhibited some democratic tendencies – highlighted by the allowing of more political parties, and, importantly, private press licenses – but he used political and press laws

---

[13] S. Dabbous, "Egypt," *Mass Media in the Middle East: A Comprehensive Handbook*, ed. Y. Kamalipour and H. Mowlana (London: Greenwood Press, 1994), 60–73.

[14] Elmasry, "Producing news in Mubarak's Egypt."

[15] K. J. Beattie, *Egypt During the Sadat Years* (New York: Palgrave, 2000).

[16] M. K. Nasser, "Egyptian mass media under Nasser and Sadat: Two models of press management and control," *Journalism Monographs*, no. 124 (1990).

[17] M. H. Elmasry, *Producing the News in Egypt: A Press System Study of Cairo Newspapers* (Ph.D. Dissertation, University of Iowa, 2009), 9.

to maintain an essentially authoritarian system.[18] In particular, Mubarak used the Press Law of 1996, the Emergency Law, and the Penal Code to maintain control over press output.

The Press Law of 1996 allowed the government to ban publications, among other things, and the Emergency Law – which was on the books for the duration of Mubarak's presidency – gave the government the right to "order censorship on correspondence of all kinds, as well as on newspapers, publications, drawings and all means of expression...provided that the censorship is applied to matters related to public peace or national security."[19] The Penal Code ordered, among other things, "a fine not less than 10,000 pounds and not exceeding 20,000 pounds...for whomever insults a public official."[20]

Journalistic professionalism in Egypt

Egypt's authoritarian political environment has led to both institutional corruption and inefficiency, which have combined to water down the quality of Egypt's education system (including its journalism education system).[21] Scholar Joris Luyendijk argues that the difficulties associated with working in a politically repressive environment have effectively prevented the consistent, professional practice of journalism. For instance, the state's tight control over information makes it nearly impossible for journalists to collect and verify information, two prerequisites to professional journalism.[22]

Journalism scholars generally view professionalism as a series of attributes that includes education, training, licensure, salary, and journalistic ideology and ethics.[23] Empirical research into Egyptian news suggests

---

[18] A. Goldschmidt, *A Brief History of Egypt* (New York: Facts on File, 2008).

[19] International Research and Exchange Board "Media Sustainability Index 2005 – The Middle East and North Africa," 2005, 19, accessed January 31, 2009, www.irex.org

[20] Egyptian Council of Lords & Council of Representatives. *The Penal Law, number 58 of 1937 (modified by law 147 of 2006): According to its Latest Revisions* (Dar al-Haqqaaniya. Cairo, 2008), 196–8. (In Arabic.)

[21] P. J. Vatikiotis, *The History of Modern Egypt: From Muhammad Ali to Mubarak* (Baltimore: The Johns Hopkins University Press, 1991).

[22] B. Kester, "Working at the end of the assembly line: A conversation with Joris Luyendijk about the impossibility of doing Western-style journalism in Arab countries," *International Journal of Press/Politics* 13, no. 4 (2008): 500–6.

[23] D. Weaver, R. Beam, B. Brownlee, P. Voakes, and C. Wilhoit, "The American journalist in

that the nation's journalists rank low on these key attributes. For example, surveys carried out in 2008 and 2013 by Elmasry et al[24] showed that many Egyptian journalists work without journalism-related degrees, or without having gone through formal journalism training of any kind. Egyptian journalists have also complained about their formal university journalism education, which they said was largely theoretical and did not offer training on story ideation, information gathering, interviewing, or article construction.[25] Many Egyptian journalists also work without having attained their journalism licenses through the Syndicate of Journalists.[26] Additionally, journalists earn low salaries, and, in many cases, are forced to work second jobs.

Importantly, research[27] also suggests that objectivity is not dominant in Egypt, where journalists often perceive themselves as activists rather than watchdogs. Some journalists have explained the process through which news stories are intentionally biased by news editors.[28] A 2006 survey by Ramaprasad and Hamdy[29] suggests that Egyptian journalists, in the first place, are fundamentally limited in their ability to perform democratic news functions, including gathering and verifying information.

I argue in this chapter that the relative lack of journalistic professionalism in Egypt contributed to the discursive construction of the Muslim Brotherhood as a fundamentally disloyal, anti-revolutionary group. Anti-Brotherhood discourses often started as rumor or hearsay, with many beginning as political arguments by Brotherhood opponents

---

the 21st century: Key findings," *John S. and James L. Knight Foundation*, 2003, accessed June 2, 2009, http://www.knightfoundation.org/research_publications/detail.dot?id=178211

[24] Elmasry, Basiony, and Elkamel, "Egyptian journalistic professionalism in the context of revolution."

[25] Elmasry, "Producing news in Mubarak's Egypt."

[26] Elmasry, Basiony, and Elkamel, "Egyptian journalistic professionalism in the context of revolution."

[27] See Elmasry, "Producing news in Mubarak's Egypt"; M. H. Elmasry, "Unpacking Anti-Muslim Brotherhood discourses," *Jadaliyya*, June 28, 2013, http://www.jadaliyya.com/pages/index/12466/unpacking-anti-muslim-brotherhood-discourse; Elmasry, Basiony, and Elkamel, "Egyptian journalistic professionalism in the context of revolution"; A. Schleifer, "Egypt's media quagmire worsens," *Al-Arabiya*, April 3, 2013, http:///English.alarabiya.net/en/views/2013/04/03/Are-Egypt-s-journalists-all-activists-.html

[28] Elmasry, Basiony, and Elkamel, "Egyptian journalistic professionalism in the context of revolution."

[29] J. Ramaprasad and N. Hamdy, "Functions of Egyptian journalists: Perceived importance and actual performance," *International Communication Gazette* 68, no. 2 (2006): 167–85.

or as analyses written by anti-Brotherhood academics and authors. Importantly, anti-Brotherhood politicians and analysts were given prominent platforms by privately owned Egyptian news outlets bent on portraying the Brotherhood as a threat to the nation. Importantly, key discourses about the Brotherhood relied on myths, not facts, to thrive, and were uncritically echoed by these news outlets. The following pages examine two important anti-Brotherhood discourses: disloyalty, and anti-revolutionary.

DISLOYAL TO EGYPT

One important myth propagated against the Muslim Brotherhood suggested that the group is fundamentally disloyal to Egypt. This disloyalty discourse – along with a series of closely related sub-discourses – projected the Brotherhood as a group that is not truly Egyptian and which does not give priority to legitimate Egyptian national interests. The entire discursive pattern of disloyalty represents an example of a narrative – or series of narratives – that began prior to the large June 30, 2013 protests, but which was highlighted, emphasized, and driven home in the aftermath of Morsi's forced removal from office on July 3, 2013. The disloyalty discourse was used as a key justification both for the coup and the post-coup elimination of the Brotherhood from politics and public life.

The sections that follow specifically examine sub-discourses suggesting that the Morsi and the Muslim Brotherhood are a foreign group with strong ties to Egypt's foreign enemies, exclusively devoted to Islamists (and not Egypt at large), and more akin to a foreign occupier than part of "the nation." Together, these three sub-discourses projected an image of disloyalty by suggesting that Morsi was conspiring with foreign enemies against Egypt, attempting to sell off vital sections of Egypt, exclusively devoted to members of the Muslim Brotherhood (at the expense of the non-Brotherhood citizens of Egypt), and not truly part of "the nation."

Foreign group with ties to Egypt's enemies

Morsi and the Muslim Brotherhood were discursively constructed as foreign to Egypt, and as having illegitimate ties to foreign enemies. For instance, on June 21, 2013, privately owned and widely viewed news network ONTv hosted prominent novelist and political analyst Gamal El-Ghitani as a featured guest on its program *The Complete Picture*.[30] El-Ghitani argued that the Brotherhood's governance of Egypt constituted a "foreign occupation" of Egypt. El-Ghitani had also delivered this thesis in an interview published in online newspaper 24 on May 21, 2013.[31]

Mainstream news sources also fed the discursive construction of the Brotherhood as a disloyal group by presenting it as having problematic ties with foreign entities interested in destabilizing and dividing Egypt. News articles during Morsi's one-year presidency discussed the Brotherhood's allegedly close relations with Israel,[32] the Lebanese faction Hezbollah,[33] and the Palestinian faction Hamas,[34] all seen as political enemies by many Egyptians.

News stories accused the Muslim Brotherhood of wanting to establish a global caliphate,[35] conspiring with Hamas and Hezbollah to organize a mass prison break during the 2011 anti-Mubarak uprising,[36] and suggested that the Brotherhood and Hamas had combined to murder hundreds of Egyptians during the 2011 uprising against Mubarak.[37] Stories about the Brotherhood's alleged illegal collaborations with foreign entities were featured prominently on Egyptian television evening news talk shows.

---

[30] *The Complete Picture*, ONTv, June 21, 2013, https://www.youtube.com/watch?v=f8HFDJigLJM&app=desktop

[31] "Gamal Al-Ghitany: The Brotherhood is a foreign organization and their governance of Egypt constitutes a foreign occupation," 24, May 21, 2013, http://24.ae/Article.aspx?ArticleId=20861

[32] Al-Iraqi and Al-Sawi, January 8, 2013, http://www.masrawy.com/news/egypt/politics/2013/january/8/5483862.aspx; Al-Hooti and Said, "Bil Suwur, Khatib al-Tahrir: al-Ikhwan Sana'a sahyuniya hadafha taftit al-watan al-'Arabi," January 25, 2013, http://www.youm7.com/News.asp?NewsID=921174#.U8CL6_1FbS8

[33] K. Lotfy, "Prosecution: 'The Brotherhood conspired with Hamas and Hezbollah to open the prisons during the revolution,'" *Al-Ahram*, June 22, 2013, http://gate.ahram.org.eg/News/362475.aspx

[34] S. Ibrahim, "The Brotherhood, Hamas, and the Caliphate," *Al-Masry al-Youm*, November 23, 2012, http://www.almasryalyoum.com/news/details/191647

[35] Abou Al-Makarem, "The Brotherhood seeks an Islamic Caliphate in Sinai with the help of Hamas," Al-Wafd, June 9, 2013, http://www.alwafd.org/تقارير-وتحليلات/494624-الاخوان حماس-بأيدي-بسيناء-اسلامية-خلافة-لإقامة-تسعي

[36] Lotfy, "Prosecution."

[37] M. Mamdouh, "The organizer of the Sulaiman Ultras: The Brotherhood and Hamas killed the revolutionaries," June 2, 2012, http://www.alwafd.org/أخبار-وتقارير/10-محلية/219471-المتظاهرين-قتلوا-حماس-الإخوان-سليمان-ألتراس-منسق

Ongoing news stories also focused on Morsi's alleged interest in selling off the Suez Canal[38] and Sinai Peninsula[39] to foreign entities, with some stories suggesting that deals were already in place. Importantly, these alleged sales were not discussed merely in isolated reports, but, rather, constituted ongoing news stories. Popular broadcaster Tawfik Okasha also lamented the alleged sale of the Great Pyramids of Giza on his *Al-Fira'een* Network,[40] and ONTv discussed the alleged three- to five-year renting out of the Pyramids to foreign entities.[41]

These discourses were propagated in the media environment, but were not disconnected from politics. Anti-Morsi political forces played up the alleged sales and demonstrations were held in protest.[42] At the time of this writing, Morsi was on trial for espionage for allegedly conspiring with Hamas and Hezbollah.

"My family and my clan"

Importantly, news discourses suggested that Morsi was loyal to the Muslim Brotherhood, but not to all Egyptians. News figures, writers, and analysts claimed that Morsi was "not a president for all Egyptians," and that, instead, he was exclusively devoted to the MB.

News figures and politicians routinely claimed that Morsi exclusively addressed the Muslim Brotherhood – and not all Egyptians – in his speeches.

---

[38] H. Sobhi, "Human chain in Port Said protests the sale of the Suez Canal," *Al-Watan*, January 24, 2013, http://www.elwatannews.com/news/details/118661; I. Nabih, "The sale of the Suez Canal to the people of Gaza and the division of Egypt into sections is a present for those who are sleeping," Al-Wafd, May 25, 2013, http://www.alwafd.org/تقارير-هدية-لاقاليم-مصر-وتقسيم-غزة-لاهل-وسيناء-السويس-قناة-اقليم-مصر-بيع-تقسيم-مخطط-482203/وتحليلات-للنائمين; M. Mokhtar, "Israeli newspaper: The Muslim Brotherhood intends to sell the Suez Canal to foreigners," *Youm 7*, May 27, 2013, http://www.youm7.com/News. asp?NewsID=1085282#.U8Ld2_1FbS8

[39] A. Abdelmoneim, "The kidnapping of soldiers reveals the scenario of the sale of Sinai," *Youm 7*, May 21, 2013, http://www1.youm7.com/News.asp?NewsID=1075889#. U8Leo_1FbS8; A. Sorour, "The families of Sinai to Morsi: The Land of Fairuz is not for sale," *Al-Masry al-Youm*, December 31, 2013, http://www.almasryalyoum.com/news/details/268749

[40] Okasha, Show clip about sale of pyramids, 2012, https://www.youtube.com/watch?v=v3l93qQX_IA

[41] Clip from show alleging rental of Pyramids for three years, ONTv, 2013, https://www.youtube.com/watch?v=b3XkhN-mWkA

[42] Sobhi, "Human chain in Port Said protests the sale of the Suez Canal."

Specifically, it was alleged that Morsi was in the habit of beginning his public addresses with the phrase "O my people and my clan," which, news and political analysis claimed, was a clear signal that Morsi favored the MB and didn't care about the non-Brotherhood citizens of Egypt. Taken in the context of other ongoing news stories about the Brotherhood's close ties with foreign Islamist entities and attempts to sell off key parts of Egypt, this was a particularly damning sub-discourse.

The "my people and my clan" introductory line was taken as a key piece of evidence for the position that Morsi and the Brotherhood were loyal to one another, but not to Egypt or the non-Brotherhood citizens of the country. The "my family and my clan" issue became a major story in Egypt, and, in spite of a lack of substantive evidence, was discussed seriously and extensively in news media and also in some academic circles.

For example, political figures such as Amr Moussa[43] and news broadcasters Lamees al-Hadeedy[44] and Yousef al-Hoseiny[45] took turns lamenting Morsi's usage of "my family and my clan" in his speeches. Each intimated that Morsi was devoted to his group of Muslim Brothers, not Egypt as a whole.

In one episode of his ONTv news program *Respectable Gentlemen*,[46] al-Hoseiny alleged that, in his first formal address as president, Morsi was "brutally honest" and forthright about his desire to exclusively address the Muslim Brothers, and exclude the Egyptian nation at large. The program showed a small portion of a clip from Morsi's first formal televised address, during which he uses the phrase "my family and my clan."

ONTv, however, only played a small portion of Morsi's speech, cutting the speech off when the context would have made Morsi's reference clear. A review of Morsi's entire introduction clarifies that the speech defined all Egyptians – and not just the Muslim Brothers – as Morsi's "family" and "clan."[47]

---

[43] Al-Hayat, Amr Moussa clip about Morsi's alleged allegiance to his "family and clan," 2013, http://m.youtube.com/watch?v=LAYOixBoNIQ
[44] I. Al-Sharnoobi, "Al-Hadeedy: When Morsi said 'My family and my clan' I knew the country was being stolen," *Veto*, July 3, 2013, http://www.vetogate.com/440158
[45] A show clip about Morsi's "My family and my clan," reference *Respectable Gentlemen*, ONTv, 2012, https://www.youtube.com/watch?v=bYMU31GfiUM
[46] Ibid.
[47] M. Morsi, President Morsi's first televised address, June 24, 2012, https://www.youtube.com/watch?v=QZ1eVceQFl4

Morsi says: "O Great Egyptian people...you who are celebrating democracy today in Egypt...my beloved ones, my family and my clan, my brothers, my sons and daughters, you who are looking toward the future, and you who desire good, progress, growth, stability, and safety for our nation of Egypt...all of my beloved ones..."

The speech goes on to thank Egyptians for instigating the uprising against Mubarak, which, Morsi says, led directly to Egypt's first democratic presidential election. Morsi praises the sacrifices made by all Egyptians who protested against the Mubarak regime, including the martyrs and "the mothers of the martyrs." He then thanks "all my family members" who have "lost those who are valuable to them and sacrificed them for the sake of the nation." Given that the overwhelming majority of the revolution's martyrs were not members of the Muslim Brotherhood, Morsi's praise can be seen as general, and not exclusive to a specific group. Morsi then prayed for the martyrs and those injured in the anti-Mubarak uprising – those who "paved the road for us."

Later in the speech, Morsi's words make it even clearer that he is addressing all Egyptians. Morsi praises the Egyptian army and says he "loves" its members, praises the Egyptian judiciary, and refers to the Egyptian police as "my brothers and my sons." Morsi then repeats the "my family and my clan" line:

I say to everyone [in Egypt], to all sections of Egyptian society, my family and my clan, I say to all [Egyptians] on this great day, that on this day, with your will and choice...I am a president for all Egyptians, regardless of where they are, inside of Egypt and outside of Egypt, in all of the governorates..."

He then goes on to describe the Egyptian "family" as including Nubian Egyptians and other groups. Later, Morsi says, "all my family members – all Egyptians – the Muslims and the Christians, the men and the women, the old and the young...all of these family members of mine." Morsi's use of "family," then, is a general and inclusive reference.

There is no indication anywhere in the twenty-six-minute speech that Morsi intends to address only the Muslim Brotherhood. In fact, on the contrary, Morsi's speech is clear in its attempt to address all Egyptians. Nonetheless, al-Hoseiny, Moussa, al-Hadeedy, and numerous other political and media figures allowed this myth – that Morsi addressed only the MB – to take on a life of its own. Some academics also aided in propagating the myth both inside and outside of Egypt.

In an academic presentation delivered at the University of California at Berkeley, scholar Sarah El-Tantawi[48] said that Morsi's usage of "my family and my clan" was a major concern for anti-Morsi Egyptians who protested on June 30, 2013. El-Tantawi posited that Morsi's use of a particularly narrow address represented a "great departure from, let's say, Gamal Abdel Nasser, who used to say 'O my brothers and fellow citizens', and then Sadat, who modified it to say, 'O my brothers and sisters, fellow citizens'. So these kinds of things people noticed and were upset about."

But Morsi's speeches do not deviate in any meaningful way from the national citizenship discourses adopted by Nasser and Sadat. Morsi, in fact, nearly always began his speeches by addressing the entire Egyptian nation, and often made a point of addressing his "opponents." He also regularly referred to Egyptian citizens – on the whole – as his "family," and regularly addressed Egyptian "citizens."

For instance, in an informal inauguration at Tahrir Square on June 29, 2012, Morsi began his address with "O great Egyptian nation... O beloved ones. O great Egyptian people...O brothers and sisters... O sons and daughters...O Muslims in Egypt...O Christians in Egypt... O honorable citizens...O Egyptians inside of Egypt and outside of Egypt...my family and my beloved ones."[49]

On October 6, 2012, Morsi opened his speech at Cairo Stadium with: "O brothers and sisters. Ladies and gentlemen. All in attendance. All of the Egyptian people. Those attending this gathering, and those who are not in attendance...Great Egyptian people. I greet all of you."[50]

On December 6, 2012, Morsi began his televised address to the Egyptian people in this way: "O Honorable Egyptian nation, ladies and gentlemen." This trend continued through Morsi's June and July televised addresses, which also began with "O great Egyptian nation."[51]

---

[48] S. El-Tantawi, Berkeley speech, 2013, http://vimeo.com/75790556

[49] M. Morsi, President Morsi's informal inauguration speech from Tahrir Square, Cairo, Egypt, June 29, 2012, https://www.youtube.com/watch?v=N_DqkzqHTAM

[50] M. Morsi, President Morsi October 6th commemoration speech from Cairo Stadium, Cairo, Egypt, October 6, 2012, https://www.youtube.com/results?search_query=خطابات+الرئيس+مرسي+أكتوبر+2012

[51] M. Morsi, President Morsi televised address, December 6, 2012, https://www.youtube.com/watch?v=jScbDgnZBxQ

In a speech delivered on November 23, 2012 in front of Muslim Brotherhood supporters, Morsi uses the phrase *"ahli"* ("my family") to address his audience.[52] Morsi addresses his audience in this way: "O beloved ones. O all Egyptians…O honorable gathering…I am with you [in this gathering]…but I am also with all of Egypt's sons and daughters at the same time regardless of where they are…with those who oppose me and those who support me…[This is] "a speech to *my family*, to the whole of the Egyptian people, the sons and daughters of this nation…" Taken in context, Morsi's usage of "my family" in this speech is a clear reference to all Egyptians, not just members of the Muslim Brotherhood.

"The nation"

After the large anti-Morsi protests on June 30, 2013, many analysts joined a chorus of voices suggesting that the Brotherhood was foreign, unpatriotic, and not loyal to Egypt. At the same time, Egyptian state and private news outlets began referring to anti-Morsi Egyptians as "the nation," and pro-Morsi protesters as treasonous.

As evidence that "the nation" had risen up against a despised president and his unrepresentative (and very small) group, numerous news outlets reported that thirty-three million Egyptians had protested against Morsi and the Brotherhood on June 30. (According to crowd-sizing experts, the cited protest figures were off by many millions, with overall protest figures likely between one and two million in total[53])

Upon showing a video of anti-Morsi protesters during his July 3, 2013 broadcast, Al-Nahar Network's Mahmoud Saad proclaimed, "these are the people." Saad referred to pro-Morsi protesters as "them," said the pro-Morsi protests were small (standing on mere "street corners"), and claimed that the protesters there were a part of "extremist groups."[54] During her July 3,

---

[52] M. Morsi, President Morsi speech from Ittahidiyya Palace, November 23, 2012, https://www.youtube.com/watch?v=DV3-DK_-zdY

[53] Middle East Monitor, "June 30 anti-Morsi crowd figures just don't add up," *Middle East Monitor*, July 16, 2013, https://www.middleeastmonitor.com/resources/commentary-and-analysis/6574-30-june-anti-morsi-crowd-figures-just-dont-add-up

[54] Tahrir Network, Akher Al-Nahar, July 3, 2013, http://televisionmasr.blogspot.com/2013/07/3-7-2013_5463.html

2013 broadcast, al-Hadeedy referred to anti-Morsi protesters as "the nation," and argued that key Muslim Brotherhood figures were guilty of espionage.[55]

On July 26, 2013, the CBC Network's Khairy Ramadan said the Muslim Brotherhood does not "understand the meaning of nation."[56] During the same broadcast, Ramadan referred to the MB as "foreign agents" and "unpatriotic." He repeatedly referred to anti-Brotherhood protesters as "the nation" and referred to the Brotherhood as "terrorists." The CBC's al-Hadeedy proclaimed on July 3, 2013, the day of the coup, that "Egypt is coming back to us." She also said that no one can "rape" the people of Egypt, "neither the French, nor the English, nor the Israelis... nor the Muslim Brotherhood."[57]

In August 2013, Tahrir Network anchor Dina Abdelrahman encapsulated "the nation" sub-discourse in this way: "There are not two groups (in Egypt). There is the Egyptian nation (on one side) and there is a group of Muslim Brothers (on the other side)."[58]

ANTI-REVOLUTIONARY

Another powerful media and political discourse about the Muslim Brotherhood – propagated in many Egyptian media outlets, political analysts and explicitly pro-military political forces – intimated that the group is anti-democratic, and, in the first place, not a genuine part of Egypt's January 25 revolutionary movement. This discursive pattern was particularly damning given the January 25 revolution's lofty place in post-2011 Egyptian politics and society, its taken-for-granted goodness, and its stated objective of creating a democratic order.

Egypt's January 25 revolution quickly achieved hegemonic status as an unquestioned good in the struggle for democracy and against dictatorship. Egyptians who wanted political credibility extolled the praises

[55] CBC Egypt, Huna Al-Aasima, July 3, 2013, https://www.youtube.com/watch?v=huJGw6TxOuI
[56] CBC Egypt, Huna Al-Aasima, July 26, 2013, https://www.youtube.com/watch?v=z9jJUHjdHv8
[57] CBC Egypt, Huna Al-Aasima, July 3, 2013
[58] Tahrir Network, Akher Al-Nahar, August 14, 2013, http://www.dailymotion.com/video/x134rjj_a5er-alnahar-14-8-2013-p1_news?search_algo=2

of the revolution, even if they were not, apparently, on board with the revolution or its goals. The Egyptian military, Mubarak-appointed judges, Mubarak-friendly media personalities, and the police took turns exalting the "glorious January 25 revolution." To be seen as against the revolution was to be discredited as part of the despised *ancien régime*.

A consensus of western scholars and experts viewed Morsi's forced removal on July 3 as a military coup. However, inside Egypt, it was painted as a continuation of the January 25 revolution. The Egyptian military, police, and both state-owned and privately owned media suggested that the Egyptian army had moved against Morsi and the MB to restore Egypt's revolutionary path. The narrative claimed that, by ousting a fundamentally counterrevolutionary and anti-democratic force, Egyptian democracy would be re-established. This narrative was quickly embraced by most of the liberal political forces supportive of the June 30 protest movement, many of whom had already been claiming since mid-2011 that the Brotherhood was much more interested in an Islamic dictatorship than democracy. Thus, the narratives suggesting that the Brotherhood was opposed to the January 25 revolution, its goals, and democracy in general played a key role in justifying the events that transpired in Egypt between June 30 and July 3, 2013.

As evidence, anti-Morsi forces pointed to several factors: the MB's absence from Tahrir Square during the early 2011 uprising against Mubarak; the Brotherhood's "secret" February 2011 meeting with Mubarak's vice president; Morsi's November 2012 power grab; and the Brotherhood's attempt to "brotherhoodize" Egyptian politics. Each of these points was highlighted in Egyptian media and political circles, and, ultimately, did a good deal of harm to the Muslim Brotherhood's reputation as legitimate democratic actors.

The Brotherhood's January 25 presence

Brookings Institute Fellow Hesham Hellyer neatly captured the essence of the narrative that accused the Brotherhood of being fundamentally opposed to both the January 25 revolution and its democratic goals: "Some, particularly in the anti-Mubarak, but pro-military, private media, are positing the notion that the Muslim Brotherhood was essentially absent from Tahrir Square and the various squares around the country at the beginning of the uprising. It joined, according to this narrative, very late, and was essentially inconsequential."[59]

Hellyer goes on to describe a more extreme manifestation of this narrative, one that suggested that the Brotherhood was fundamentally opposed to the January 25 uprising. Hellyer notes pro-military media claimed "protesters that were killed by pro-Mubarak forces...were killed, actually, by the Brotherhood."

It is certainly fair – and, I would argue, accurate – to suggest that the Brotherhood does not deserve as much revolutionary credit as liberal Egyptian political forces who essentially instigated the uprising, or those individuals and groups who officially participated in the January 25 protests. The MB did not join the revolution in an official capacity until January 27, two days after protests began.[60] Moreover, at its core, the Brotherhood is a gradualist, reformist movement, and it was not as effective as youth revolutionaries at producing dramatic revolutionary change. However, in the end, the Brotherhood played a key role in the anti-Mubarak uprising, and, for a variety of reasons, their early official absence from Tahrir Square should not be exaggerated.

First, January 25, 2011 protests were not billed as a "revolution" to begin with. According to Google executive Wael Ghonim, credited with instigating and organizing the revolution, the January 25 protesters "had no thoughts of a revolution, we just wanted a better country."[61] Second, the Brotherhood was not the only group to officially (or unofficially) avoid January 25 protest sites. In fact, the overwhelming majority of Egyptians did not participate in January 25, 2011 demonstrations. According to Hellyer, "It was a relatively small crowd that went to the streets on the Jan. 25."[62] Third, although failing to officially sign off on January 25 protests, the Brotherhood did not prevent its members from attending protests. Muslim Brotherhood youth members attended Tahrir Square protests on January 25, and they were joined by at least a small contingent

[59] H. A. Hellyer, "Faking Egypt's past: The Brotherhood and Jan. 25," *Al-Arabiya*, January 20, 2014, http://english.alarabiya.net/en/views/news/middle-east/2014/01/20/Faking-Egypt-s-past-the-Brotherhood-and-Jan-25.html
[60] Ibid.
[61] S. Hattenstone, "Protesters' stories: Wael Ghonim and Egypt," *Guardian*, January 13, 2012, http://www.theguardian.com/world/2012/jan/13/protesters-egypt-tahrir-wael-ghonim
[62] Hellyer, "Faking Egypt's past."

of Muslim Brotherhood leaders, including Mohamed El-Beltagy[63] and Abdel Moneim Abul Fotouh.[64] Thus, the notion that the Brotherhood was completely absent from the January 25 scene is misleading. In any case, the Brotherhood protested alongside other revolutionaries from the "day of rage" (on January 28, 2011) through Mubarak's February 11, 2011 resignation.

The "secret meeting" with Omar Suleiman

In an example of a sub-discourse that took on a life of its own, it was widely claimed in the Egyptian media and political circles that the Brotherhood held a secret meeting during the heart of the revolution with Mubarak's vice president, Omar Suleiman. Political analyst Wael Eskander summarizes: "Many reports have claimed that during the turmoil of the eighteen-day uprising in February 2011, members of the MBs Guidance Bureau met secretly with then Vice President Omar Suleiman, reportedly to work out an agreement that would clear out Tahrir Square of protesters calling for the fall of the Hosni Mubarak regime."[65] Eskander, himself apparently accepting the notion, suggests that the "alleged deal eventually fell through when the MB's youth refused to evacuate the square."

However, reports of a secret meeting between the Brotherhood and Suleiman are inaccurate. First, the February 6, 2011 meeting in question was not secret: it was widely covered by major international press outlets.

Second, only two Brotherhood members – out of a total of fifty anti-Mubarak political figures – met with Suleiman. David Kirkpatrick and David Sanger of *The New York Times* reported: "They met as part of a group of about 50 prominent Egyptians and opposition figures, including officials of the small, recognized opposition parties, as well as a handful of young people who helped start the protest movement."[66]

---

[63] R. F. Worth, "Egypt's human bellweather," *New York Times*, January 19, 2012, http://www.nytimes.com/2012/01/22/magazine/mohamed-beltagy-future-of-egypt.html?pagewanted=all&_r=0

[64] Z. El Gundi, "Abdel-Moneim Abul-Fotouh," *Al-Ahram Online*, April 2, 2012, http://english.ahram.org.eg/NewsContent/36/124/36854/Presidential-elections-/Meet-the-candidates/AbdelMoneim-AbulFotouh.aspx

[65] W. Eskander, "Brothers and officers: A history of pacts," *Jadaliyya*, January 25, 2013, http://www.jadaliyya.com/pages/index/9765/brothers-and-officers_a-history-of-pacts

[66] D. Kirkpatrick and D. Sanger, "After first talks, Egypt opposition vows new protest,"

According to Reuters' coverage of the meeting, Mohamed El Baradei's National Association for Change was one of the groups represented at the meeting.[67]

Third, there is no substantive evidence – as has been widely intimated – that the Brotherhood was interested in a compromise that would have derailed a democratic transformation and witnessed Mubarak stay on as president. Immediately after the meeting, and after Suleiman announced Mubarak would not step down, one of the Brotherhood representatives who attended the meeting said, "We did not come out with results."[68] The BBC's report on the meeting indicated that the Brotherhood's representatives demanded "the immediate resignation of President Mubarak." The report quotes a senior Brotherhood official as saying, "Our demands are still the same... They didn't respond to most of our demands. They only responded to some of our demands, but in a superficial way."[69]

The Mubarak government may have initially proposed the notion that the Brotherhood was trying to subvert the revolution and work out a deal with the government. Kirkpatrick and Sanger wrote: "Leaders of the protest movement, including both its youthful members and Brotherhood officials, denounced Mr. Suleiman's portrayal of the meeting as a political ploy intended to suggest that some in their ranks were collaborating."[70]

Some of Egypt's revolutionary groups may have also advanced the notion that the Brotherhood had "betrayed" the revolution by meeting with Suleiman. Importantly, not all revolutionary groups were present at the meeting, with some, like the April 6th Youth Movement, rejecting the idea of meeting with a representative from the Mubarak government until Mubarak formally stepped down. There were legitimate disagreements among revolutionary forces about the appropriateness of dialogue with the Mubarak regime. The point, though, is that suggestions that the Brotherhood attempted to subvert the revolution are misplaced, and fundamentally lacking in substantive evidence.

New York Times, February 6, 2011, http://www.nytimes.com/2011/02/07/world/middleeast/07egypt.html?pagewanted=all

[67] M. Awad, "Egypt's Suleiman meets opposition parties," Reuters, February 6, 2011, http://www.reuters.com/article/2011/02/06/us-egypt-dialogue-idUSTRE7150K520110206

[68] Kirkpatrick and Sanger, "After first talks, Egypt opposition vows new protest."

[69] "Egypt protests: Opposition wary after Suleiman talks," *BBC News*, February 7, 2011, http://www.bbc.co.uk/news/world-middle-east-12377179

[70] Kirkpatrick and Sanger, "After first talks, Egypt opposition vows new protest."

Morsi's November 2012 decree

On November 22, 2012, Morsi issued a controversial presidential decree granting himself sweeping powers and making his decisions immune from judicial oversight. According to Morsi's spokesperson, under the decree's provisions Morsi's decisions were "final and not subject to appeal (by the judiciary)".[71] In addition, Morsi could "issue any decision or measure to protect the revolution."[72]

Privately owned and opposition-party-owned media, and the Brotherhood's political opponents portrayed the move as a dictatorial power grab, and suggested it was evidence that the MB wanted to create a dictatorship.

Political opposition figure Mohamed El Baradei tweeted, "Morsi today usurped all state powers and appointed himself Egypt's new pharaoh."[73] Ghonim said, "The revolution was not staged in search for a benign dictator, there is a difference between revolutionary decisions and dictatorial decisions. God is the only one whose decisions are not questioned."[74]

Morsi's decree was legitimately controversial, and, by its nature, was bound to generate a fair amount of rebuke, particularly from opponents. However, the decree's negative ramifications were grossly exaggerated in the Egyptian media and political circles. Disagreeing with Morsi's decree – which was mishandled on a number of levels – was politically legitimate. Claiming that Morsi had turned into a dictator, however, represented a gross exaggeration, and fed an already existing myth about the Muslim Brotherhood's alleged dictatorial, anti-democratic fantasies.

Context is important in examining the decree's implications. Morsi had been engaged in a battle with Mubarak-appointed judges arguably bent on derailing Egypt's democratic experiment. The judiciary had already disbanded Egypt's first freely elected parliament – just four months after twenty-six million Egyptians had voted them into office. The judiciary also

---

[71] R. Spencer, "Mohammed Morsi grants himself sweeping new powers in wake of Gaza," *Telegraph*, November 22, 2012, http://www.telegraph.co.uk/news/worldnews/africaandindianocean/egypt/9697347/Mohammed-Morsi-grants-himself-sweeping-new-powers-in-wake-of-Gaza.html

[72] Ibid.

[73] Ibid.

[74] H. Hendawi, "Morsi's constitutional declarations grant Egypt's president far-reaching power," *The Huffington Post*, November 22, 2012, http://www.huffingtonpost.com/2012/11/22/morsi-constitutional-declaration_n_2175651.html

disbanded the first constitutional assembly, and, importantly, reportedly threatened to disband a second constitutional assembly – even after all of Egypt's (then) twenty-two parties had agreed to its formation and specific composition. The judiciary also threatened to reverse Morsi's August 2012 decree, which effectively removed the military from politics. The reversal of that decree would have created a quasi-military dictatorship, putting the military above the elected president and giving the military veto power over every article in the new constitution. It was in this context that Morsi decided to issue his decree and place his decisions above judicial oversight. In any case, the decree lasted just over two weeks.

Another point left out of much of the discussion inside Egypt was the decree's duration. Had Morsi desired to become a long-term dictator, he would have likely offered up no indication that the terms of the decree would end. However, article 2 of the decree stated that it would become null and void upon the holding of a constitutional referendum (on the draft constitution which, at the time of the decree, was near completion) and parliamentary elections.

Moreover, the constitution that Morsi desired Egyptians to vote on, absolutely prohibited single-party dominance and would have legally and constitutionally prevented a Mubarak-style dictatorship from emerging. The 2012 constitution – mockingly referred to as the "Morsi Constitution" in Egypt's anti-Brotherhood circles – decreed regular elections and strict term limits for elected officials (including the president). The constitution also greatly reduced the president's powers by severely curtailing his right to declare a state of emergency, stipulating a powerful prime minister, who, according to some Egyptian scholars of constitutional law, would have wielded greater power than the elected president. Moreover, the constitution included an impeachment mechanism and guaranteed political inclusion by giving all Egyptians the right to establish and join political parties. In addition, all Egyptians could have owned a newspaper without government approval.

Although Morsi's decree was poorly timed, mishandled, and, given the timing, controversial, it did not provide an opportunity for dictatorship and could not have created a "new pharaoh."

Brotherhoodization of Egypt

Another anti-Brotherhood discourse claimed that the MB was actively "brotherhoodizing" the state – taking over all of the state's institution.

This discourse dovetailed nicely with already circulating claims that Morsi and the Brotherhood were anti-democratic dictators bent on eliminating all political competition.

The "Brotherhoodization" claims were ubiquitous during Morsi's one-year term. As I have written elsewhere, the Brotherhoodization discourse had become "so hegemonic that many Egyptians [took] it as a given. It [was] difficult to find an independent talk show that [did] not regularly obsess over the Brotherhood's takeover."[75]

The MB was alleged to have taken over the military, judiciary, police, media, and government. In fact, as evidence for the Brotherhoodization thesis, some media outlets claimed that Morsi's interior minister Mohamed Ibrahim and defense minister Abd al-Fattah al-Sisi – who orchestrated the military coup against Morsi – were either closet MB members or staunch supporters of the group.

There was not serious evidence for the Brotherhoodization thesis. The MB never had control over the military, police, or judiciary, and, for legal and logistical reasons, it would not have been possible for the group to gain control in the short term. Had the Muslim Brothers desired, theoretically, to take these institutions over, it would have taken many years to develop a stable of Brotherhood members or loyalists ready to be appointed.

Nor did the MB hold a monopoly over the Egyptian media. Most Egyptian media outlets took highly critical positions and engaged in an hysterical anti-Brotherhood media campaign.[76] Even the state-owned newspaper *Al-Ahram*, typically a staunch government ally, "seemed to abandon – to a considerable extent – the government mouthpiece role it maintained during the Mubarak era."[77]

The Muslim Brotherhood did hold considerable sway over the government. However, this was to be expected given the group's status as an elected government, and also their position as the largest and most organized political force in the country. Importantly, though, Egypt's anti-Brotherhood opposition and media greatly exaggerated the extent of the Brotherhood's influence in government.

---

[75] Elmasry, "Unpacking Anti-Muslim Brotherhood discourses."

[76] Ibid.

[77] M. H. Elmasry and M. El-Nawawy, "One country, two eras: How three Egyptian newspapers framed two presidents," *Global Media Journal: Mediterranean Edition* 9, no. 1 (2014): 27–39; 36.

Even after the June 2012 appointments, the Brotherhood only held thirty-four percent (twenty-one out of sixty-two) of the government's cabinet and governor positions.[78] Importantly, this percentage would likely have been much lower had non-Brotherhood politicians been willing to accept positions in the Morsi government. Numerous non-Brotherhood, liberal politicians were offered government positions, but declined. These included Ayman Nour of the al-Ghad Party, former presidential candidate Hamdeen Sabbahi, Ahmed Maher of the April 6th Youth Movement, political scientist Moataz Abdel Fattah, and multiple former members of the (2012) Kamal al-Ganzouri government (who were allowed to continue in their posts), among many others.

CONCLUSION

It is now clear that there were elements inside Egyptian society who were a priori unprepared to accept a Muslim Brotherhood government. Numerous scholars and experts have examined attempts, beginning as early as June 2012 (before Morsi was inaugurated president), to undermine Morsi's political project. Political forces associated with Egypt's 'deep state' – and also among anti-Islamist political parties – actively sought ways to bring down the Morsi government. Ultimately, they succeeded, aided in large part by a series of myths that suggested the Brotherhood was disloyal, foreign to Egypt, fundamentally at odds with the January 25 revolutionary moment, and essentially anti-democratic and dictatorial.

The widespread dissemination of those anti-Brotherhood myths, moreover, was emblematic of a categorical failure of the Egyptian news media to live up to the standards of liberal institutions – indeed, to the standards originally envisioned for the press by early Egyptian liberal reformers. In cavalierly disregarding their responsibility to encourage a vibrant civil society, prominent Egyptian news media outlets in effect allied with and emboldened the very deep state agenda civil society was designed to protect against in the first place. Many private news owners, many of whom were sympathetic to Egypt's *ancien régime*, enthusiastically embraced anti-Brotherhood politicians and analysts, and news professionals uncritically adopted anti-Brotherhood narratives. Unsurprisingly, given Egypt's lack of professional journalism standards, little attempt was

---

[78] Elmasry, "Unpacking Anti-Muslim Brotherhood discourses."

given to provide balance or critical voice. Importantly, a relative explosion of media freedom following the anti-Mubarak uprising facilitated the coverage, which was often hysterical and could, in most cases, proceed without fear of substantive consequences for news owners, editors, and journalists.

It would have been difficult to justify the Brotherhood's outright elimination on the basis of simple incompetence and poor governance theses, especially in the face of a democratic framework that would have allowed any of Egypt's other political forces to take office via elections in the event of the Brotherhood's failure. Anti-Brotherhood forces instead rode a series of myths which, at the time of writing, continue to exert a powerful sway over many Egyptians. In 2014, hundreds of Muslim Brothers were sentenced to death without due process in the largest mass death sentences in modern world history. Many Egyptians celebrated the sentences and praised the Egyptian judiciary, which did not listen to the arguments of the defense and which presided over trials that lasted just a few hours.

It is possible, of course, had the Brotherhood been allowed to continue to govern, that the group would have adopted the kind of totalitarian or extreme religious stances many Egyptians feared. As Shadi Hamid has noted, however, such fears remained purely "speculative" in nature.[79] There is little evidence, if any, for many of the claims – which I have termed "myths" – made about the MB and their short time in office.

None of this should be seen as an endorsement of the Muslim Brothers, or their performance as governors of Egypt. The MB was handed a diffi-cult set of political cards, but handled its opportunity poorly. The group failed to demonstrate sufficient transparency or to adequately separate its Islamic activism from its governance. Most of all, the MB was unable to avoid critical mistakes and miscalculations during a period that could not afford them. When Egypt needed a great government performance, it didn't get it. Now, the Muslim Brothers and the liberal revolutionaries who helped propagate myths about them are forced to reflect on how they may be able to reverse a deeply entrenched counterrevolution and eliminate an emerging military dictatorship.

---

[79] M. Al-Salih, "'Mursi was a Muslim Brotherhood enforcer': Brookings Analyst," *Asharq Al-Awsat*, July 4, 2014, http://www.aawsat.net/2014/07/article55333754

7

Student political activism in democratizing Egypt[1]

Abdel-Fattah Mady[2]

INTRODUCTION

The Egyptian university throughout the nation's modern history has been a fulcrum for generating political and civic activism. Indeed, it is not altogether surprising that the current regime is so intent on cracking down on student activism, precisely because it so astutely recognizes the potential of the university as a site of civic debate and protest.[3] Presently, there are nearly two million university students enrolled in twenty-four state universities and twenty private universities throughout Egypt.[4] Owing to a student body that has grown tremendously since the early twentieth century – the national education budget doubled between 1930 and 1953, and the student body accordingly doubled

---

[1] The author would like to express his gratitude and appreciation to Muhammad Alsayed, Radwa Darwish, and Muhammad Abdelsalam for providing various types of research assistance in support of this project. Moreover, I am highly indebted to Daanish Faruqi, who has been very helpful in editing and finalizing this chapter. All mistakes remain the responsibility of the author.
[2] Associate Professor of Political Science, Alexandria University, Egypt, and was Visiting Fellow at the Woodrow Wilson International Center for Scholars, Washington DC. Author can be reached at: www.abdelfattahmady.net
[3] Louisa Loveluck, "Egypt's universities, centers of dissent, reopen under strict new controls," *Christian Science Monitor*, October 10, 2014, http://www.csmonitor.com/World/Middle-East/2014/1010/Egypt-s-universities-centers-of-dissent-reopen-under-strict-new-controls
[4] "Supreme Council of Universities," April 18, 2015, http://www.scu.eun.eg/

from 1945 to 1951 alone[5] – the university will continue to serve as a deeply conducive site to political organizing. Accordingly, to explicate the full implications of university political organizing on the Egyptian body politic, this chapter will address the history of student activism in Egypt. By examining the role and impact of Egyptian university student activism on the promulgation of political activism and democratization, we will ultimately be able to offer a meaningful prognosis on its future role in contributing to Egyptian civic and democratic life.

Sketching the landscape of university activism across its longitudinal history in modern Egypt will prove pivotal in addressing its role and impact in Egyptian civic life, past, present, and future. I will proceed with this investigation with several key metrics in mind. How effective has student activism been in generating positive political change? What role has political affiliation of the student body – be it of leftist, liberal, or Islamist disposition – had on the direction of activist initiatives on campuses? What is the relationship between student activism and broader movements in Egyptian political and civil society? How did student activism respond to or evolve in the aftermath of the 2011 revolution culminating in the overthrow of Mubarak, or the subsequent 2013 revolution that culminated in the overthrow of Mohammad Morsi? And finally, what are the implications for future activism in the aftermath of the return of authoritarian rule under Sisi? Or more specifically, what future role does student activism stand to play in democratizing Egypt and cultivating a vibrant civil society?

Indeed, even in the context of the authoritarianism of post-coup Egypt, the university remains a pillar of Egyptian civic life – lionized as such even by figures otherwise wholly supportive of the Sisi regime's crackdown on civil society. For example, the paradoxical career of Dr. Mohammad Abol Ghar is a case in point. From a vibrant career prior to the January 2011 uprisings in support of substantive democratic reform, to his role as cofounder and interim leader of the Egyptian Social Democratic Party following the ouster of Hosni Mubarak, the Cairo University gynecology professor has since thrown his firm support behind the July 3 overthrow of Mohammad Morsi and the concomitant crackdown on Egyptian civil society. Going so far as to argue explicitly that national security interests trump individual freedoms, most recently Abol

---

[5] Ahmed Abdalla, *Alttalaba wa Al-siyaasa fi Misr* (*The Students and Politics in Egypt*), trans. Ekram Youssef (Cairo: Sina Publishers, 1991), 41.

Ghar has given his imprimatur for the democratic process to precisely limit rights and freedoms to fit the current security needs of the state.[6] Yet for all his proclivities to support the new authoritarianism in Egypt, there is one arena in Egyptian civil society he is not willing to circumscribe in the name of national interest: the Egyptian university system. Fully faithful to the project he helped inaugurate in the March 9th Movement for University Independence, Abol Ghar in one of his regular columns for *Al-Masry al-Youm* offers significant pushback to the military regime he now so strongly supports. Addressed as an open letter offering advice (*nasihah*) to Sisi, Abol Ghar firmly yet politely and respectfully chastises the Egyptian leader for attempting to politically manipulate the system of selection of university leadership. Declaring such a decree unconstitutional, Abol Ghar exhorts Sisi to reconsider the consequences of this hasty measure, arguing, "Mr. President, without an independent and free university, nations do not progress. The legislation of this law in this hasty manner is flawed and harmful, and you will go down in history for this huge mistake."[7]

Suffice to say, despite Abol Ghar's lukewarm commitments to "social justice and democratic change"[8] under the current regime, he nonetheless firmly maintains them in the context of the university system. Thus, even in tenuous times in which Egyptian civic life is otherwise under attack, it seems that leftist and liberal activists in this vein continue to covet the free and independent Egyptian university as a site for the promulgation of liberal values. The student movement within the university context, moreover, is a fundamental component of the university's role in the cultivation and preservation of Egyptian civic life. It is thus imperative

---

[6] Karima 'Abd al-Ghani, "Abol Ghar li'al-Ahram': Qalb al masriyiin jami'an ma' al-dawla," *Al-Ahram Online*, November 13, 2015, http://www.ahram.org.eg/News/131723/145/453551/%D8%A7%D9%86%D8%AA%D8%AE%D8%A7%D8%A8%D8%A7%D8%AA-%D9%85%D8%AC%D9%84%D8%B3-%D8%A7%D9%84%D9%86%D9%88%D8%A7%D8%A8/%D8%A3%D8%A8%D9%88%D8%A7%D9%84%D8%BA%D8%A7%D8%B1-%D9%84%D9%80-%C2%AB%D8%A7%D9%84%D8%A3%D9%87%D8%B1%D8%A7%D9%85%C2%BB-%D9%82%D9%84%D8%A8-%D8%A7%D9%84%D9%85%D8%B5%D8%B1%D9%8A%D9%8A%D9%86-%D8%AC%D9%85%D9%8A%D8%B9%D8%A7-%D9%85%D8%B9-%D8%A7%D9%84%D8%AF%D9%88%D9%84%D8%A9.aspx

[7] Mohammad Abol Ghar, "Min Mandela ila-l Sisi: al-Jami'ah," *Al-Masry al-Youm*, June 30, 2014, http://www.almasryalyoum.com/news/details/473745

[8] "Mohamed Abul-Ghar," *Jadaliyya*, November 18, 2011, http://www.jadaliyya.com/pages/index/3173/mohamed-abul-ghar

to better situate the student movement across its historical trajectory, to do full justice to its potential as a fulcrum of civil society.

To properly address these concerns, I will proceed in a linear chronological fashion. First, I will offer a brief history of the emergence of student movements during the colonial period. Then I will move on in the second section to analyze student activism under Nasser, with a particular focus on the 1954 crisis and the 1968 student uprisings. In the third and fourth sections, I will investigate, respectively, the uprisings of 1972–3 and 1977 under Sadat, and student activism more broadly under Mubarak. I will end by exploring student activism in the contemporary context, from the 2011 uprising to its current status in the aftermath of the crackdown on the university scene under Sisi since 2013, and the implications for future activism in this milieu.

EMERGENCE OF EGYPT'S STUDENT MOVEMENT

Nascent beginnings of the student movement in Egypt began as early as the eighteenth century, during which seminary students from al-Azhar University played a palpable role in protesting at the oppressive policies of the Ottoman rulers and their Mamluk soldiers. Azhar students continued in this tradition of protest against the French invasion of Egypt (1798–1801).[9] By the early nineteenth century, the modern state infrastructure and educational system established by Mohammed Ali Pasha (d. 1849) began to supplant the role of the Azhar system, such that students from the higher education schools established under Ali's leadership increasingly emerged in the public sphere.[10] And most Azhari sheikhs and students as well as higher education students supported Ahmed 'Urabi's revolution in 1881–2.[11]

However, it would be premature to label student political activism during this early period as a bona fide *haraka tullabiyya* (student movement), for student demands here were actually an extension of demands

---

[9] See Muhammad Afifi, *Alharaka Altollabiya wa Alwataniya Almasriya* (*Student Movement and Egyptian Nationalism*), The Arab Center for Research and Studies, April 8, 2014, accessed February 12, 2015, http://www.acrseg.org/3719

[10] Abd al-Rahman al-Rafai, *Asr Muhammad Ali's* (*Muhammad Ali's Era*), 5th ed. (Cairo: Al-Mareef Publishers, 1989), 397.

[11] Abd al-Rahman al-Rafai, *Ahmad Urabi: Al-Zaeem Al-Moftara Alei* (*Ahmed 'Urabi: The Leader Maligned*), 242.

articulated by Egyptian society more broadly during this period. With the rise of Mustafa Kamil (d. 1908) and the establishment of the Club of Higher Education schools, students played a vital role in Kamil's National Party.[12] They protested for two primary national goals: formal independence, and a modern, democratic constitution.

Students of higher education schools, particularly law school students, ignited the first flame of the 1919 revolution.[13] One of the revolution's outcomes was the rise of an inclusive, broad, national movement in which Muslims and Christians took part, demanding Egypt's independence and a democratic constitution. Students formed the backbone of this national movement, and as their number increased thanks to the development of the educational system in the mid-1930s, so did students' political power. As the political scientist and former student leader Ahmed Abdalla (d. 2006)[14] writes, during this period students were galvanized by the deteriorating economic situation and the concomitant lack of job opportunities for university graduates, as well as political instability and the constitutional relapse resulting from the abolition of the 1923 constitution – which had otherwise guaranteed a reasonable extension of parliamentary representative democracy, liberties, and political pluralism.[15]

In light of those concerns, student activists in the early twentieth century communicated two specific goals to political parties, particularly the Wafd Party. The first was specifically educational, and dealt with the paucity of meaningful post-graduation employment opportunities; in particular, students held the state responsible for low wages and for limited access to government jobs, despite its willfully employing non-Egyptians

---

[12] For more details, see Haggai Erlich, *Students and University in 20th Century Egyptian Politics* (Abingdon: Routledge, 1989), 18–22.

[13] Abd al-Rahman al-Rafai, *Thwarat 1919: Tariekh Masr Alqawmi: 1914–1921 (The 1919 Revolution: Egypt's National History from 1914 to 1921)* (Cairo: Al-Mareef Publishers, 1987), 193.

[14] Ahmed Abdalla was a student leader in the 1960s and 70s and an independent political scientist and political activist in the 1980s and 90s. He wrote considerably about student activism, and about Egyptian politics and sociology. His doctoral dissertation at Cambridge University, focusing on the Egyptian student movement, was ultimately published as his first book. See Ahmed Abdalla, *The Student Movement and National Politics in Egypt: 1923–1973* (Cairo: The American University in Cairo Press, 2008). For more on Abdalla more broadly, see this obituary: Marsha Pripstein Posusney, Michaelle Browers, "Ahmed Abdalla Rozza," *Middle East Report* 36, no. 240 (Fall 2006).

[15] Abdalla, *The Student Movement and National Politics in Egypt*, 48–9.

in industrial and commercial institutions.[16] The second goal, broader in scope, was in alignment with the national cause, seeking restoration of the 1923 constitution and formal Egyptian independence. Given its broader ambitions, the student movement in this respect gained the support of several other sectors of society, including trade syndicates, unions, teachers, judges, and journalists.[17]

And in so doing, the student movement gave rise to the 1935 uprising, which achieved several goals. All main national political parties and student groups formed a united national bloc,[18] and, in December 1935, the government restored the 1923 constitution.[19] Moreover, established political parties (such as the Wafd Party) and other political movements (like the Young Egypt Party (Misr El-Fatah) and the Muslim Brotherhood) included many students who played prominent roles, especially during elections, mobilization, and protests.[20] New communist political groups also formed student wings, and some students engaged in secret communist groups. Communists played an influential role in the 1946 uprising, yet ultimately became feeble inside the student movement after refusing to participate in the Palestine War.[21] All this is to say, the student movement officially became a political actor in the Egyptian public sphere following the 1935 uprising. Yet, at the same time, the nascent movement suffered from political fissures that eventually led to violent clashes among Wafd Party supporters and opponents in 1937. By the end of World War II, the student movement had become a subject of dispute among several political streams: Wafd Party; left-wing currents; Misr El-Fatah; and the Muslim Brotherhood. Nonetheless, despite such political divisions, common national goals (formal independence, the constitution, and the

---

[16] Ibid., 50.

[17] Ibid., 51. During this period, the student movement was supported and encouraged by several members of the Egyptian state and civil society, namely judges. Some courts went as far as issuing extenuating decrees on behalf of students after the 1935–6 uprising. Moreover, the vast majority of faculty members also supported the student movement during this phase – in contradistinction to the Republic era, at which point the government wholly dominated the university faculty.

[18] Abdalla, *The Student Movement and National Politics in Egypt*, 57.

[19] Abd al-Rahman al-Rafai, *Fi Aqab althawra almasiriya 1919* (*After the 1919 Egyptian Revolution*) (Cairo: Al-Mareef Publishers, 1988), 224.

[20] Abdalla, *The Student Movement and National Politics in Egypt*, 59–61; and Abd al-Rahman al-Rafai, *After the 1919 Egyptian Revolution*, Vol. 3, 56.

[21] Abdalla, *The Student Movement and National Politics in Egypt*, 65.

annulment of the 1936 treaty) united these factions, as they all joined protests against the British and the king.

That said, despite student protests being overwhelmingly peaceful, the response by the palace and the British to student demands were outright brutal, relying on repression, spreading misinformation about the student movement in the press, university shutdowns, and other similar repressive measures.[22] The British and Egyptian administrations alike also resorted to infiltrating the student movement to sow division and dissent among student activists, going so far as establishing pro-government organizations inside the universities to confront Wafd Party governments. Muhammad Mahmoud, prime minister of Egypt 1928–9 and 1937–9, even recommended the founding of a group of "Patriot Students" to monitor subversive student activist groups on campus – a proposition resurrected nearly a century later by regime loyalists in the aftermath of the coup of July 2013, as we shall see later in the chapter.[23]

Nonetheless, student protests and political divisions continued until a new uprising, led both by high school students and by students at Cairo University, commenced on February 9, 1946. This demonstration was an immediate response to British forces having infamously opened Abbas Bridge, during which tens of students fell into the Nile.[24] Students issued three demands: the evacuation of the British troops and raising the cause for Egyptian independence in the UN Security Council; liberation of Egypt from economic slavery; and the formation of a student general union. And despite suffering from political fissures, mismanagement, and a lack of unified leadership, the student uprising nonetheless made considerable gains here, as Britain declared it would withdraw from Egyptian cities, and settle only in the Suez Canal region. Still, facing continuing and enduring repression, both from the British and from the Egyptian monarchy, the student movement resumed its protests at the beginning of the 1946–7 academic year. In 1951, it issued a National Covenant, which called for armed resistance to obtain national independence. In effect, then, universities were being converted into military training camps, and brigades of the Muslim Brotherhood, among others, volunteered to fight the British in the Canal region. As such, alongside peasants, laborers,

---

[22] Abd al-Rahman al-Rafai, *After the 1919 Egyptian Revolution*, Vol. 2, 216.

[23] Abdalla, *The Student Movement and National Politics in Egypt*, 108.

[24] Abd al-Rahman al-Rafai, *After the 1919 Egyptian Revolution*, Vol. 3, 187.

educated citizens, and some police and army officers, students engaged in the fight for national independence.

Having sketched this landscape of the emergence of the student movement in its early years, we can more seamlessly make sense of how it came to maturity. This ultimately takes place beyond the colonial period, particularly during the reign of Nasser.

STUDENT ACTIVISM UNDER NASSER

This phase of student involvement in politics under Gamal Abdel Nasser (1952–70) began under a political context utterly distinct from the colonial period. The emerging representative democratic system was demolished, and the military became directly engaged in politics. In addition, the ruling elites changed, as the military and a single-party regime came to dominate political life. The new regime, repressing both communists and Islamists alike, also adopted a centralized, socialist economic approach. Despite having achieved formal independence, Egypt was still far from its original democratic aspirations, having regressed instead into a totalitarian police state, which invariably came to have a deleterious impact on education and on student movements.

To be fair, Egyptian education had developed decidedly during this period, as budgets doubled; indeed, the expenditure in the first thirteen years of Nasser's regime was three times that of the educational system during the seventy-year British occupation.[25] Nasser presided over a vast expansion of primary and girls' education, and in technical education, while tuition fees were completely abolished. As for religious education, under Nasser the Azhar curriculum was augmented to include non-religious subjects in 1961. Moreover, this period also saw the establishment of regional universities, as well as the expansion of Faculties of Commerce, Law, and Arts. Nonetheless, there remained a serious concern that the *quantitative* investment made in education during the Nasser period could not be accompanied easily by a similar commitment to a *qualitative* improvement in education more broadly. It is in this uneasy context that student activists proceed.

---

[25] Abdalla, *The Student Movement and National Politics in Egypt*, 127.

Students and the 1954 crisis

Immediately upon coming to power, the new regime attempted to court student groups and gain their loyalty. Yet, just as quickly, the military regime faced resistance from intellectuals and students, as well as from laborers. With respect to the latter, it faced some immediate credibility concerns with students due to the Kafr El-Dawwar incident, in which two laborers under the age of twenty were executed twenty days after the July 1952 coup.[26] Still, despite this rocky beginning, the nascent regime eventually gained student support during its early years. However, when the Revolutionary Command Council broke off into two separate wings, in which Mohammed Naguib – who sought military withdrawal and a return to democratic civilian rule – was ultimately bested by Nasser and his plans to implement one-party military rule, the students' front responded by abandoning the regime and demanding the ousting of the military dictatorship.

As for the Muslim Brotherhood, while it first supported the Free Officers Movement, following this rift in the Revolutionary Command Council, it turned its support to Mohammed Naguib's group, demanding that the military return to its barracks, as a prerequisite for the development of a properly democratic order. On the other hand, the Brotherhood engaged in a struggle for power with Nasser and his group, to the point that Brotherhood-affiliated students directly clashed with the state-led Liberation Rally organization. In March 1954, students from Cairo University formed a national front in opposition to military rule, which the Brotherhood had ultimately joined. The regime dealt with the protests using the same methods as its predecessors in the colonial period: with brute force, with duplicitous media campaigns maligning the student movement, and by ultimately closing the university. Through such tactics, the regime managed to simultaneously repress the democratic wing within the Revolutionary Command Council, the Brotherhood, and the broader student movement.[27]

During the 1954 crisis, the Alexandria University Faculty Members Club was at the forefront of the protesters who demanded the suspension

---

[26] Ahmad Hammrough, *Thawrat Thalatha wa Eshroun Yolou* (*The July 23rd Revolution*), Vol. 1 (Cairo: Egyptian General Association of Book, 1992), 291–2.

[27] For more details about the 1954 crisis, see ibid., 331–66.

of martial law and the dissolution of the Revolutionary Command Council. The regime again responded with an iron fist, compromising the academic integrity of the institution by arresting a number of professors, and outright dismissing others from their posts.[28] Thus, by the end of this crisis, the regime had managed to dominate not only politics and the university, but also civil society as a whole – of which the university was a central part, per the visions for higher education articulated by early Egyptian reformers. Jettisoning those lofty ideals of the nation's early intellectual leaders, the new military regime in Egypt had instead adopted totalitarian rule, based on a single-party system. Eventually, members of the student movement, like leftist and liberal activists in general, either supported the regime or withdrew from the public sphere altogether. Others instead chose to emigrate. This emasculated state became the status quo in Egyptian protest movements for decades, only to be resuscitated after the regime's military defeat in the 1967 Arab-Israeli war. Thereafter, the student movement formatively reemerged in Egyptian political life via two uprisings in the same year.[29]

The uprisings of February and March 1968

The 1967 military defeat was the first flame that motivated many Egyptians to emerge from their political passivity. Coupled with that defeat, expansion in education yielded a new educated middle class, which gradually opposed the regime's policies more and more intensely. Demonstrations

---

[28] Abdalla, *The Student Movement and National Politics in Egypt*, 144.

[29] It is important to briefly outline Nasser's repressive policy against university students and faculty members, which prompted student revolts in 1968. According to Ahmed Abdalla, the regime dominated the university context by several methods, including: politicizing class syllabi for the sake of garnering support for the regime; imposing a mandatory "national education" class in order to glorify the regime and instill loyalty; enacting a university bylaw in 1966 that banned any student political activism, and further restricting student activities to those practiced by regime-led organizations; appointment of a university police guard under the authority of the Interior Ministry; taking state stewardship of the university establishment by founding the Supreme Council of Universities, headed by the Ministry of Education, in 1961; selecting faculty deans by political appointment rather than by election; and creating a new class of loyalists by appointing university faculty to administrative and ministerial posts, among other repressive measures. For more details, see Abdalla, *The Student Movement and National Politics in Egypt*, 147–57; and Hisham al-Salamuni, *al-Jil alladhi wajaha Abd al-Nasir wa-al-Sadat* (*The Generation that faces Abdel Nasser and Sadat*) (Cairo: Dar Qiba', 1999), 213–16.

erupted first among the laborers in Helwan on February 21, 1968 in protest against the lenient sentences issued to Air Force officers accused of carelessness during the war.[30] Mass demonstrations soon gave way to a bona fide mass uprising, spearheaded in large part by students. The regime responded with its typical repression, and in the process killed many protesters. Regime escalation then gave rise to an escalation in the protesters' demands, which came to include releasing political detainees and prosecuting those accused of killing protesters.[31]

As the regime-controlled media subsequently reported that the pro-testors' demands were concerned only with sentencing, students at Cairo and Alexandria Universities released a series of more explicitly political demands. These demands included, among others: the discharge of political detainees, achieving a democratically elected representative government, instituting the freedom of speech and of the press, annulment of anti-freedom laws, the removal of Nasser's brother from his nepotistic post in the Socialist Union in Alexandria, investigating the murder of protesters killed in Helwan, investigating the Air Force incident, removing the Intelligence Directorate and the Investigation Service from the universities, and investigating violations of the university's independence and police brutality against students.[32]

As the demonstrations became wider, and with the police unable to continue to contain them, the regime attempted to coddle the students' rage by arranging meetings between student representatives and state officials – including with Nasser himself. The regime had also utilized members of the university administration and faculty in persuading the students to limit their protests to within the confines of university facilities. State officials and journalists constantly slandered and accused the students of betrayal, claiming that elements of the old feudal regime were the hidden hand behind student demands for democracy and freedom. State-run media even went as far as to announce that the protests were penetrated by some elements that worked for imperialist and Zionist forces in order to defeat the Arab nation.[33]

---

[30] *Mothakarat Mohamed Najib: Konto Raeesan Li Misr* (*Mohammad Najib Memoir: I was Egypt's President*) (Cairo: Modern Egyptian Bureau, 1984); and Al-Salamuni, *al-Jil alladhi wajaha Abd al-Nasir wa-al-Sadat*, 274–82.

[31] For more details, see Tarek Osman, *Egypt on the Brink from Nasser to Mubarak* (Yale: Yale University Press, 2011), 64–5.

[32] Abdalla, *The Student Movement and National Politics in Egypt*, 186.

[33] For more details, see Al-Salamuni, *al-Jil alladhi wajaha Abd al-Nasir wa-al-Sadat*, 174–6.

Nonetheless, despite the desperate attempts by the state to suppress it, this uprising generated positive outcomes: above all else, both students and the Egyptian public more broadly found a renewed interest in the public sphere. Moreover, Nasser issued a decree to appeal for the prosecution of the Air Force officers and formed a new government with mostly civilian officials. He also issued the March 30 statement that included a promise to introduce liberal reforms.[34] At the university level, the uprising paved the way for eliminating some restrictions then being placed on student activism. With active student participation, a new students' bylaw was drafted in 1968, invalidating the stewardship by faculty over student activism, and inaugurating the General Union of Egyptian Students. Though, to be clear, the bylaw also maintained the presence of university security, provided that they did not intervene in direct activities of student activists.

The November 1968 uprising

Against this backdrop earlier in the year, a new uprising erupted in the city of al-Mansoura as high school students protested against a new law regarding secondary education. The demonstrations later expanded, exacerbated by the rampant repression by the state of al-Mansoura's students, and ultimately specific demands were made regarding the universities and the political regime. The largest clashes were among the Faculty of Engineering at Alexandria University, where unrest and sit-ins dramatically increased. Subsequently, mass demonstrations extended throughout the city, resulting in the deaths of dozens and the considerable vandalizing of private property. Student activist demands, though deeply influenced by their own educational and social difficulties, were articulated in largely political terms: prosecuting the officials responsible for the al-Mansoura incidents, the resignation of the minister of interior, releasing all political detainees, enforcing the freedom of the press, reinstatement of the rule of law, and a systematic improvement in the state of the Egyptian university system.

Predictably, the government responded through force, repression, accusations of betrayal and disloyalty to the state, by attacking the reactionary

---

[34] See Erlich, *Students and University in 20th Century Egyptian Politics*, 190–4; and Al-Salamuni, *al-Jil alladhi wajaha Abd al-Nasir wa-al-Sadat*, 213–16.

forces, and by encouraging political divisions among student activist groups. At this point, the university administration – and even some university faculty – were openly advocating on behalf of the regime, and thus taking great pride in undermining student activism and serving as whistleblowers against students and faculty who protested about regime policies.[35] Needless to say, the odds were stacked against the student movement at this juncture. And even worse, the uprising ultimately had highly deleterious consequences for student activism more broadly, as it led to the regime reneging on its prior commitments to university independence, and to again dominating campus life – going so far as reinstating faculty supervision over student activism in 1969.[36] This climate of fear and massive surveillance came to define student activism for the rest of the Nasser period, only for the student movement to transform again during the Sadat era.

STUDENT ACTIVISM DURING SADAT'S ERA

The first years of Sadat's reign saw remarkable renewal of student activity. Regenerated after the setbacks dealt to the movement under the Nasser era, student groups reemerged to focus on two broad political goals: Sinai's liberation from Israel, and establishing genuinely democratic governance. Students thus formed activist groups, actively published wall magazines critical of the regime, and held public conferences and seminars. Moreover, university campuses witnessed a return of sit-ins and political unrest.[37]

On the heels of student elections of the 1971–2 academic year, Sadat capitulated to popular demands and expelled security forces from university campuses. Nevertheless, this proved insufficient to tame fully student upheaval: his speech on January 13, 1972, wherein he provided lukewarm justifications for failing to fulfill his promise that 1971 would be a year of decisiveness in liberating Sinai, prompted enraged students to stage protests, unrest, and sit-ins, starting from the Faculty of Engineering in Cairo University and spreading throughout most of the universities.

---

[35] Abdalla, *The Student Movement and National Politics in Egypt*, 201.
[36] For more details, see Al-Salamuni, *al-Jil alladhi wajaha Abd al-Nasir wa-al-Sadat*, 176.
[37] See Raymond A. Hinnebusch, *Egyptian Politics Under Sadat: The Post-Populist Development of an Authoritarian-Modernizing State* (Cambridge: Cambridge University Press, 1985), 51–2, 243–4; and Erlich, *Students and University in 20th Century Egyptian Politics*, 207.

From the inception of these protests, students focused intently on the broader political agenda of liberation of Sinai from Israeli occupation, and progress toward democratic governance. Dovetailing on those political demands, they included a distinctly economic critique, demanding progress in socio-economic development more broadly, the establishment of a minimum wage, de-linking the Egyptian economy from Western interests, decrying the economic stratification of Egyptian society and lavish lifestyle of the upper classes, and demanding the release of the detained Helwan laborers.[38]

To be clear, the most active stream during this uprising was the left-wing elements of the student movement. Building on that spark ignited by student leftist activists, and despite the antagonistic attitude of the official unions, the uprising then gained support by a number of student union leaders, in addition to the support of the masses and the professional syndicates. This stood to be an uprising of truly national proportions.

On the one hand, the government's reaction was consistent with its tactics since the days of British colonialism: brute repression and silencing of the student movement. But on the other, going even beyond the metrics of brutality employed during Nasser's reign, Sadat's regime went as far as employing national security forces to storm Cairo University campus on January 24, 1972. Moreover, the regime tried to contain the uprising by sending ministers and state officials to meet and pacify student activists. Meanwhile, echoing national media condemnations of the student movement, Sadat attacked student activists by accusing them of treason – all while continuing to maintain his resilience to fight to liberate Sinai, without being willing to declare the specifics of his plan to do so in public. Attempting to dismiss the credibility of the student movement, Sadat accused a small number of "lurking elements" (qilla mundassa) of being behind the protests, adding that some students had gone on suspicious trips abroad, and insinuating that student activists attacked each other only to falsely accuse the police of brutality and repression.[39]

In general, under Sadat, the student activist movement had become more politically mature than its predecessors, and was able to mobilize the masses more successfully in protest at the regime and its policies. In fact, in this latest spate student movements were able to make their way as far as Cairo's Tahrir Square before the police forces could finally disperse

---

[38] For more details, see Abdalla, *The Student Movement and National Politics in Egypt*, 224.
[39] Ibid., 222.

them. Following this uprising in January 1972, Sadat's government issued a decree formally banning demonstrations. At the same time, it instituted specific measures in preparation for a war economy, and allowed students to volunteer and join the war effort.[40] This climate came to inform the rest of the Sadat period. In particular, Sadat recognized the allure of leftist movements on university campuses, and made it a point to actively undermine them moving forward.

The uprisings of the 1970s: 1972–3

During the summer of 1972, three ideological blocs formed in the university sphere; the left-wing bloc that led the January 1972 uprising; the Nasserist bloc; and the Islamist bloc emerging from the Youth of Islam Group in the Faculty of Engineering of Cairo University. Recognizing a potential counterweight to the pernicious influence of leftist campus politics, Sadat's government welcomed the emerging Islamist stream as a bulwark against the left-wing bloc.[41] Consequently, university campuses at that time came to experience clashes among the leftists and the Islamists, with each offering competing political platforms via wall newspapers and conferences on campus.

That said, even as it propped up Islamist student groups to counter leftist ones, in response to the continuation of demonstrations from earlier in the academic year – despite Sadat's decree formally banning demonstrations following the January 1972 uprising – the government ultimately shifted gears and increasingly began to repress both leftist and Islamist student leaders alike. In response, student activists flared with anger and resorted to strikes and sit-ins. As a caveat, this spate of uprisings did not have complete uniformity in political platform or demands: whereas the Islamists focused narrowly on student demands (among them a revised student bylaw, and integrity in the student election process), the leftist bloc focused on broader national goals (namely democratic and economic

---

[40] For more details, see Erlich, *Students and University in 20th Century Egyptian Politics*, 211–12.

[41] For more details on the rise of Islamists in the 1970s, see John R. Bradley, *Inside Egypt: The Land of the Pharaohs on the Brink of a Revolution* (Palgrave Macmillan Trade, 2008), 56–7; Abdel Moneim Abul Fotouh, *Shahid 'ala tarikh al-harakah al-Islamiyah fi Misr, 1970–1984* (*A witness on the Student Movement in Egypt 1970–1984*), ed. Hossam Tammam (Cairo: Dar al-Shorouq, 2010).

reforms). Nonetheless, these latest protests did manage to strike a nerve by capitalizing on the national rage resulting from Egypt's humiliating defeat by Israel in June 1967, and in so doing all parties involved – including intellectuals, university faculty, and members of professional guilds – renewed broader calls for democracy, and for university reform and independence. This incident is particularly remarkable in that several faculty members broke their silence for the first time since 1954 by publicly supporting students in their political struggles – though others opposed them, some of whom were later granted ministerial posts as a reward for their loyalty to the regime.[42]

Sadat's government responded in the typical fashion, by confronting student protesters with excessive force, mass arrests, through the establishment of fact-finding committees, as well as by outright closing the universities. Sadat agitated the situation further by claiming that the left and right wings had a plan to confront "The Alliance of Popular Working Forces," the main ideology of the state. Moreover, the government also expelled dozens of professionals in the aftermath of this latest crackdown, and censored several authors and writers. Some judges responded sympathetically to the student protesters, by issuing lenient sentences and discharging them on bail; rejecting these overtures, Sadat went as far as to use his constitutional authority as president to appeal against some of these judicial orders.[43]

However, the tumultuous political climate that culminated in the October War in 1973 with Israel led Sadat to shift gears, retreating from his heavy-handedness with student activists by halting pending trials, and by reinstating hitherto alienated activists and journalists. Consequently, when the war broke out, students engaged in wartime civil defense of the state, both inside and outside the universities. In the aftermath of the war, Sadat inaugurated a policy of economic opening to private investment and political pluralism, a period known as the Opening, or *al-Infitah*. Many student movement leaders willingly followed Sadat in his posturing of openness, and joined newly established political parties. Still, others firmly opposed Sadat's new initiative, thus paving the way for renewed confrontation with the regime.[44]

---

[42] Abdalla, *The Student Movement and National Politics in Egypt*, 240–1.
[43] Ibid., 241.
[44] Ibid., 242.

That propensity for renewed conflict escalated further in 1976, when a new student bylaw was enacted that many students considered one of the most charitable in the history of the Egyptian university system. Although this bylaw banned any political activity outside the framework of student unions, it nonetheless considered political activism a form of bona fide student activity, thereby protecting it. The bylaw also endorsed the activity of the General Union of Egyptian Students, and ended the practice of faculty supervision over student union committees.[45] Thus, students were now free to pursue political activity unhindered, and accordingly they continued to engage in civil discourse with renewed passion and zeal. This all came full circle in 1977.

The 1977 uprising

For all the reasons mentioned above, clashes between students and the regime continued after the 1973 war. In particular, Sadat's decision to raise the price of basic commodities in the context of his economic liberalization of the country caused great unrest, leading to an uprising in 1977 spearheaded by factory laborers. Led by leftists, the movement came to attract students and other ordinary peoples in multiple Egyptian cities, to the extent that police stations and presidential headquarters were burned. The government's reaction was particularly repressive, to the extent that Sadat and state-run media described the protest as the "uprising of thieves" and a "communist conspiracy," and thousands of activists, writers, and intellectuals were arrested in the aftermath.[46]

Nonetheless, the uprising did force Sadat to rescind his plans to raise the price of basic commodities. In response to the renewed threat posed by the student movement, Sadat replaced the politically lenient student bylaw of 1976 with a far more restrictive one in 1979 – one that dissolved the political committee, and banned the hosting of seminars or distribution of pamphlets and publications by student activists without explicit permission by the university president or the faculty dean. This

---

[45] For more detail on the student bylaw, see *Al-hoquq wa alhuriyat al-tullabiyia* (*Student Rights and Freedoms*) (Association for Freedom of Thought and Expression, 2008), 11–14, accessed January 12, 2015, http://afteegypt.org/wp-content/uploads/2008/11/sfrstudy.pdf
[46] See Anthony Mcdermott, *Egypt from Nasser to Mubarak: A Flawed Revolution* (Abingdon: Routledge, 2012), 109–10; and Judith Tucker, "While Sadat shuffles: Economic decay, political ferment in Egypt," *MERIP*, no. 65 (March 1978), 3–5.

restrictive new bylaw also included the establishment of a new system of supervision and surveillance of student activists, comprised of professors on the student union's committees, as well as hiring security forces within university campuses as added surveillance. Moreover, this new bylaw undermined or erased some of the union goals as articulated in the 1976 bylaw, such as "providing students with the basic talents that shall support the growth of their characters and intellect," and "reinforcement of their connection with student organizations and unions throughout the Arab world." Moreover, this restrictive new bylaw also compromised student unions' financial independence.[47]

To conclude this section, it is worth reiterating that the Sadat years greatly contributed to the emergence and development of the Islamist movement in student activism, and the concomitant retreat of the leftist bloc. Sadat's administration deliberately encouraged this dissention between the two, supporting the Islamists specifically to undermine the putative threat of leftist activism – only to ultimately turn its guns on the Islamist student bloc as well, upon learning that he could not wholly contain it and make it docile to his political agenda.[48] Ultimately, though, Sadat's intransigence wound up emboldening the Islamist bloc of the student movement, beginning with his 1977 visit to Israel. Capitalizing on the anger this posturing to Israel produced among Egypt's Islamists, Islamist student blocs went on to win a landslide in 1978–9 elections. Meanwhile, Sadat's government continued with its policy of repressing dissident students, even augmenting the role of university security and surveillance in the process. Tensions increased further in 1979, when Sadat granted political sanctuary and asylum to the deposed Shah of Iran – a figure deeply reviled by Islamists. In the aftermath of that episode, Sadat conducted a now infamous raid encompassing all those who opposed the peace treaty with Israel – including writers, journalists, political party leaders, and university professors. In the process, Sadat's regime arrested nearly six hundred students, mostly Islamists, and unceremoniously closed down opposition newspapers.[49]

---

[47] Abdalla, *The Student Movement and National Politics in Egypt*, 276–7.

[48] See, for instance, Abdullah Al-Arian, *Answering the Call: Popular Islamic Activism in Sadat's Egypt* (Oxford: Oxford University Press, 2014), 172–3.

[49] For more details, see Abdalla, *The Student Movement and National Politics in Egypt*, 275; Fawaz A. Gerges, "The end of the Islamist insurgency in Egypt?: Costs and prospects," *Middle East Journal* 54, no. 4 (Autumn, 2000): 592–612. For more on Islamist activism under Sadat more broadly, see Al-Arian, *Answering the Call*.

This raid occurred on September 3, 1981, mere weeks before his assassination by extremist Islamists. Ultimately, then, Sadat's attempt to temporarily shore up the Islamist student movement to undermine the leftist one, only to betray his erstwhile Islamist student allies in the end, proved to be a Faustian bargain. Consequently, Islamism proved to gain a formative influence in the university activist scene under the Mubarak era, as we shall see in the next section.

STUDENT ACTIVISM DURING MUBARAK'S ERA

The mid-1980s witnessed a significant increase in the development of higher education: the total number of enrolled university students doubled, with more than 500,000 students now enrolled after the foundation of many regional universities. The higher education budget during this period, moreover, had reached nearly 370 million Egyptian pounds.[50] However, this quantitative development did not give rise to qualitative development in the Egyptian education system. Moreover, feeble social and economic policies, the adoption of unregulated free market economics, and the spread of corruption and patronage throughout the Egyptian public and private sectors all contributed to a growing disillusionment by students and university graduates in the possibility of a better future through the improvement of higher education. Ultimately, this malaise among the student body gave rise to political alienation among Egyptians more broadly.[51]

That said, this environment of disillusionment and alienation did not immediately translate into insurrection student activist groups as such. During Hosni Mubarak's repressive reign, Egypt did not witness large-scale student uprisings similar to those of the 1960s and 70s. Nevertheless, Mubarak's harsh administrative and security policies did not preclude some more modest direct action against the status quo by student activists. Student protests started in Al-Mansoura University in the academic year 1983–4, and then expanded to other universities. Student demands during this period focused on the reinstatement of the 1976 bylaw, lifting the restrictions imposed on their activities and unions, the restoration of the General Union of Egyptian Students, the expulsion

---

[50] Abdalla, *The Student Movement and National Politics in Egypt*, 267.
[51] See Abdel-Fattah Mady, "Popular discontent, revolution, and democratization in Egypt in a globalizing world," *Indiana Journal of Global Legal Studies* 20, no. 1 (2013): 315–25.

of the security forces from university campuses, and the elimination of the broader milieu of invasive state supervision imposed on universities.[52]

More broadly, student activism was motivated in this period by a yearning for genuine democracy and the liberal rule of law, by a refusal and rejection of Egypt's normalizing ties with Israel, and by solidarity with various regional causes. With respect to the latter, political developments elsewhere in the Arab world and beyond triggered protests by Egyptian students, including: uprisings following the first Palestinian Intifada (Uprising) in 1987, protests in the early 1990s decrying Egypt's involvement in the 1991 Iraq War, protests in solidarity with Bosnia in 1995, and protests against the United States' bombardment of Iraq in 1998. Moreover, university and secondary-school students began large-scale demonstrations on September 29, 2000 against the visit of former Israeli Prime Minister Ariel Sharon to the al-Aqsa Mosque in Jerusalem – a visit that helped trigger the Second Intifada. And in March 2003, a large-scale student protest marched to Tahrir Square in Cairo to condemn the US invasion and occupation of Iraq.[53]

These commitments to democracy and to solidarity with regional causes did not generate mass uprisings, though, because students found themselves constrained from several perspectives. Although the General Union of Egyptian Students had been restored, it had no legal grounds for handling student regulations or funding, particularly following the severe tension caused by governmental interference in student elections in 1984–5.[54] In this context, Mubarak's regime utilized hitherto unavailable tools to limit the role of the student unions in arts and sports. It further amended the 1979 bylaw in 1984 in order to tighten the invasive influence of security forces on university campuses. More specifically, it amended the relevant article in the bylaw as follows: "In every university, a security unit shall be founded, as it will be tasked to protect the university facilities and its safety, which will be directly supervised by the university president." The inserted clause, "and its safety," despite seeming innocuous at face value, in practice gave the regime full license to ratchet up repression of students under the nebulous auspices of protecting the university's safety. Consequently, student activism was largely hindered,

[52] Abdalla, *The Student Movement and National Politics in Egypt*, 278.
[53] "Mathahirat Masriya did darb al-Iraq," *BBC News*, February 23, 2003, http://news.bbc.co.uk/hi/arabic/news/newsid_2791000/2791457.stm
[54] Abdalla, *The Student Movement and National Politics in Egypt*, 280.

and student unions became submissive and beholden to the will of university administrators – themselves appointed upon the approval of the State Security Investigation Service. Accordingly, the 1979 bylaw was referred to during the Mubarak years as the "State Security bylaw."[55]

Despite this hostile environment to campus activism under Mubarak, though, the same period proved one of increasing political influence for the Muslim Brotherhood in campus life. As discussed in the previous section, despite Sadat's initial embrace of Islamist student groups, his later years witnessed significant repression of his erstwhile allies, both inside and outside the university context. Nonetheless, the Islamists were ultimately empowered in the very same context of Sadat's intransigence, as evidenced by the results of the parliamentary, syndicate, and student elections.[56] The Islamist current also included politically quietist Salafis, as well as Jihadists like the Islamic Group (al-Gama'aa al-Islamiyya), but the Muslim Brotherhood was by far the largest faction within the broader Islamist bloc. The Brotherhood utilized this leverage within the broader Islamist political bloc to solidify its influence in the university activist scene during this period.

Between 1948 and 1989, Brotherhood-affiliated professors success-fully managed to join faculty members' clubs at their institutions, while Brotherhood-affiliated students won landslide victories in student elections in most universities.[57] In fact, Muslim Brotherhood-affiliated student groups in the 1980s had comparably more freedom than then deeply constrained Egyptian political parties and civil society outside the university milieu on the one hand, and than the broader student movement in the context of increased governmental restrictions later during the 1990s on the other.[58] In addition to protesting in solidarity with Arab and Muslim causes and on behalf of broader demands articulated by the student movement, such as the bylaw modification and expulsion of security forces from campuses, Brotherhood-affiliated student activists entrenched themselves more deeply in campus life through other educational, social, cultural, and religious activities, and through solidarity campaigns with Islamic countries such as Afghanistan, Bosnia, and Kosovo, among others.

---

[55] See *Student Rights and Freedoms*, 14–15.

[56] For more details on the rise of Islamists in the 1980s, see Hesham Al-Awadi, *The Muslim Brothers in Pursuit of Legitimacy: Power and Political Islam in Egypt under Mubarak* (I.B. Tauris; Reprint edition, 2014), 92–5; and Bradley, *Inside Egypt*, 58–9.

[57] Al-Awadi, *The Muslim Brothers in Pursuit of Legitimacy*, 122–3.

[58] See Mady, "Popular discontent, revolution, and democratization in Egypt," 313–37.

By the late 1990s and the early 2000s, to counter the increasing influence of the Brotherhood in campus politics, Mubarak's regime exerted considerable effort to establish pro-regime student groups under the aegis of the ruling National Democratic Party and the governmental Youth and Sports Agencies. The regime thus created and generously funded entities known as "Horus" student groups on university campuses, and encouraged them to intimidate the student body by silencing activists and deterring others from joining activist campaigns. However, these groups proved unsuccessful, as only reckless students joined them. In addition, the Mubarak regime intensively exploited university administrations and security apparatuses to undermine student political activities, and blatantly intervened in elections and nominations to political posts. To this end, the regime eventually deployed hired thugs (*baltajiyya*) to attack purportedly seditious students on campuses.[59]

On December 10, 2006, Brotherhood-affiliated students at al-Azhar University protested at the regime's violence with a mock military-style parade, replete with students dressed in military uniforms – a move that agitated both the government and political opposition alike, including leftists and liberals. This incident was known as having been spearheaded by "Azhar militias."[60] Although the Brotherhood attempted to alleviate the discord it created through this incident, to the point that the students involved apologized, the government used the incident as justification to mount a fierce propaganda campaign against Brotherhood campus activism. Swiftly, the Mubarak regime launched harsh raids in which hundreds of Brotherhood-affiliated students and dozens of Brotherhood-affiliated leaders and university professors were arrested, and prosecuted under the auspices of inciting violence and attempting to overthrow the political regime.[61]

After al-Azhar University's event, the security agencies disqualified Muslim Brotherhood-affiliated candidates from elections in 2007, leading to landslide victories by pro-regime student leaders. Protests erupted in al-Azhar University and then expanded to other universities. Brotherhood-aligned students, alongside faculty associated with the

---

[59] Personal observation by author, while serving as a faculty member at Alexandria University.

[60] Ahmad al-Bahiri, "'Militiayat Ikhwaniya' tasta'rada maharat al-qital dakhil jami'at al-Azhar," *Al-Masry al-Youm*, December 11, 2006, http://today.almasryalyoum.com/article2.aspx?ArticleID=40525

[61] Al-Awadi, *The Muslim Brothers in Pursuit of Legitimacy*, 209–10.

March 9th Movement for University Independence – the very movement founded in 2003 by Dr. Mohammad Abol Ghar and others, as discussed in the introduction to this chapter – suggested establishing alternative student unions in protest at the blackballing of Brotherhood and other opposition students from elections.[62] Informal elections were held across several universities in 2007, resulting in the election of alternative non-government-aligned unions. Nonetheless, the government dealt with the elections in Cairo University in 2007 using a new weapon, the *baltajiyya*, who would physically attack students and sabotage the elections, in addition to expelling students from universities and dormitories.[63]

As campus activism independent of the official pro-government student unions increased, the regime responded by issuing a new bylaw in 2007 that confirmed that official student unions were the only legitimate political entities on campus – thus invalidating the alternative informal unions discussed earlier. It also banned any factional, religious, or partisan gatherings, in addition to expanding professorial authority over student political activities.[64] On the other hand, despite these setbacks, during this same period, some professors resumed their political activities via faculty clubs that struggled against the regime's violations of academic freedoms, and actively opposed government attempts to rig faculty club elections in favor of pro-government electoral candidates. In 2003, professors affiliated with the March 9th Movement for University Independence were able to elevate several higher education challenges for public discussion, and in so doing objected to some suspicious projects advocated by Mubarak's regime, including its attempts to sell the historical facilities of Alexandria University and its public hospital, and the government's call for the privatization of education.

The university faculty further reasserted itself against threats by the Mubarak regime in 2006, when the Alexandria University Faculty

---

[62] Here it is interesting to note that, in this context, despite Dr. Abol Ghar's outright hostility to the Muslim Brotherhood in its totality in the aftermath of the 2013 coup, the March 9th Movement for University Independence proved willing here to ally with student activists aligned with the Muslim Brotherhood. For more on the complexities of the March 9th Movement's relations with the Muslim Brotherhood, see Benjamin Geer, "Autonomy and symbolic capital in an academic social movement: The March 9 Group in Egypt," *European Journal of Turkish Studies. Social Sciences on Contemporary Turkey*, no. 17 (December 19, 2013), https://ejts.revues.org/4780

[63] See "Observatory state of democracy," October 22, 2007, accessed December 20, 2015, http://www.mosharka.org/index.php?newsid=116

[64] For more details, see *Student Rights and Freedoms*, 15, 24–41.

Club insisted on conducting impromptu Club elections on the sidewalk opposite the club facilities, as the government had cancelled the official elections. This election, called "the sidewalk election," formed a board of directors composed of professors who belonged to various different political currents: the Muslim Brotherhood, leftists, and independents were all represented in this coalition. Moreover, the March 9th Movement for University Independence also mobilized faculty members in cooperation with students for a large-scale protest on April 6, 2009 – under the auspices of the April 6th Youth Movement – aimed at expelling university security forces, culminating in a lawsuit against the regime demanding an end to security force presence on university campuses.[65] However, the regime did not implement the ruling, interestingly enough, until the January 2011 revolution erupted.[66] Ultimately, security forces were expelled from the university in March 2011.[67]

In brief, since 2004, student activism during the Mubarak years had become an integral part of a broader trend in political opposition activism, initiated in particular by a cross-ideological populist movement known as Kifaya, Egyptian Movement for Change. Kifaya opposed Mubarak's attempts to extend his reign to a fourth term, and similarly opposed both his plan to bequeath the presidency to his son Gamal, and the constitutional amendments of 2005 and 2007 that in fact strengthened the absolute power of ruling party.[68] Kifaya's goals were broad, nationally driven concerns that gained appeal with all different political persuasions in the student activist movement. However, Mubarak ignored this movement and its populist demands, despite all indicators suggesting that protest against his regime would prove increasingly difficult to put down – including hundreds of yearly strikes; the emergence of the populist and non-ideological April 6th Youth Movement; in addition to other protest movements within different professional sectors including

---

[65] See, for instance, this statement from the April 6th Youth Movement's blog, detailing its partnership with March 9th: https://shabab6april.wordpress.com/2009/04/04/

[66] See on Academic Freedoms Abdel-Fattah Mady, *Kayf yomkn hemaya al-huriyat al-akademiyia* (How to protect academic freedoms), Aljazeera.net, August 27, 2012, accessed April 24, 2015, http://www.abdelfattahmady.net/opinion-articles/aljzeera/373-27-8-2012. html

[67] For more details, see Menna Omar, "Policing Egypt's universities: From campus to courts," *The Legal Agenda*, March 27, 2014, http://www.english.legal-agenda.com/article. php?id=600&folder=articles&lang=en#.UzQ9RqiSyyZ

[68] Al-Awadi, *The Muslim Brothers in Pursuit of Legitimacy*, 211

judges, laborers, lawyers, intellectuals, and university professors. In 2010, a cross-ideological alliance was also introduced via the formation of the "National Association for Change," comprised of all major political currents – including the Muslim Brotherhood.[69] Ultimately, these populist currents brewing in Egypt civil society – of which the student movement was a major catalyst – proved so overwhelming to the Mubarak regime that in 2011 they culminated in bona fide revolutionary upheaval. It is to this period and beyond that we shall now turn.

POST-JANUARY 25, 2011 REVOLUTION

As a preface, statistics regarding higher education during the period immediately preceding the eruption of the revolution indicated a steady increase in university student enrollment – but at the same time a remarkable decrease in the higher education budget. For instance, student enrollment in state- and privately owned higher educational institutions during the 2011–12 academic year totaled nearly 2.1 million, and in 2010–11 yielded around half a million graduates.[70] But, by contrast, budgets were limited, as expenditure on higher education (excluding al-Azhar) was nearly 13.5 billion Egyptian pounds in 2011–12. This figure represented nearly 25.1% of the nation's total expenditure on education and 0.9% of Egypt gross domestic product (GDP) – a marked decline from the 29.6% of total education expenditure and 1.2% of GDP spent on higher education in 2006–7.[71] This environment, then, characterized by increasingly bloated student enrollment coupled with an outright cutback in available resources, came to characterize the student activist milieu immediately preceding the 2011 revolution.

The developments of the student movement after the revolution can be examined in two phases: the first transitional phase, from the announcement of Hosni Mubarak's resignation as president on February 11, 2011 to the June 30, 2013 uprising against the presidency of Mohammad Morsi;

---

[69] See Mady, "Popular discontent, revolution, and democratization in Egypt," 329.

[70] Egyptian Ministry of Higher Education, *Statistical Yearbook*, 2011, accessed May 8, 2015, http://www.higheducation.idsc.gov.eg/front/ar/stat_popup_last.aspx?statistics_id=61

[71] Egypt's Central Agency for Public Mobilization and Statistics, *Education Statistics*, 2014, accessed May 8, 2015, http://www.capmas.gov.eg/pdf/EgyptinFigures2015/EgyptinFigures/pages/arabic%20link.htm

and the second phase, from the events of June 30, 2013, culminating in the overthrow of Morsi, until the time of this writing.

January 2011–June 2013

Student activism had no independent role during the January 25 revolution for one main reason: this revolution was deeply populist, and relied on Egyptian youth both inside and outside the university context. That said, students were nonetheless a crucial part of the youth protest movements, as universities and mosques were the starting point of many demonstrations that marched to public squares. In addition, January 25 coincided with the first term exams, followed by the mid-year holidays. Following the fall of Mubarak on February 11, 2011, revolutionary optimism permeated the university system as well, such that, a mere six days later, several thousand university faculty members organized a major conference dedicated to how the university could support the ongoing revolution. Jointly organized by the March 9th Movement for University Independence and the Islamist Academics for Reform (*gamaa'un men agl el-islah*)[72] – this conference set at Cairo University cultivated high expectations in university reform.[73]

Students thus responded accordingly, entrenching themselves in the post-revolutionary milieu to protest for deeply desired reforms, both in the university system and for the student movement. Rallying against the further dwindling resources allocated to higher education in light of escalating enrollments, and against the remaining specter of Mubarak loyalists in senior administrative posts, several student demonstrations erupted demanding the full ouster of the *ancien régime* from university life, and for tangible improvements in higher education. And on some metrics they proved successful: police security guards were removed from campuses, free elections for student unions were held for the first time in decades, as well as for administrative posts – which were previously

---

[72] It is worth noting that this conference on February 17, 2011 is yet another example of the March 9th Movement for University Independence partnering with Islamist-oriented forces, in contradistinction to its leader Dr. Abol Ghar's vehement opposition to the Muslim Brotherhood tout court in the aftermath of the 2013 coup.

[73] For more details, see Ursula Lindsey, "Freedom and reform at Egypt's universities," Carnegie Endowment for International Peace, September 4, 2012, accessed April 28, 2015, http://carnegieendowment.org/2012/09/04/freedom-and-reform-at-egypt-s-universities

granted by appointment. But protesters faced significant obstacles from achieving the totality of their desired reforms, namely the military junta under the Supreme Council of Armed Forces (SCAF) summarily refusing such demands, but also the heavily consolidated bureaucratic state apparatus, and the recalcitrant attitude of extant university faculty and administration, who often wound up reelecting Mubarak-era incumbents into their posts.[74]

Students faced similar difficulties in achieving the passage of a new student bylaw. Under the stewardship of SCAF, the minister of higher education drafted a new students' bylaw in February 2012 without student consultation as such. To be fair, this draft contained many positive developments, such as: the restoration of the political committee inside student unions; guaranteeing the students' right to elect their unions; depriving university administrators of authority in the formation of unions in instances in which runoff elections do not achieve at least twenty percent; the restoration of the General Union of Egyptian Students; and the addition of new procedures for transparency in elections and financial affairs. Nonetheless, students of all political persuasions were largely united in opposition to this draft bylaw, insofar as it was enacted without their consultation and contained other restraining articles.[75]

But this incident notwithstanding, unity among student activist blocs became elusive in the transitional period, with conflicts between the Islamist bloc and its secular opponents creating an increasingly polarized campus environment.[76] This became especially apparent during the reign of Mohammad Morsi, at which point the student movement was acutely divided between the Muslim Brotherhood and their opponents – which included leftists, liberals, and independents. Consequently, during the student elections of 2013, this political polarization permeating Egyptian campuses enabled oppositional political blocs to win in landslides in most universities. Moreover, this division in the student movement exacerbated major disputes over a new draft of the student bylaw issued by Morsi's government. While the new draft did ease many restrictions then being imposed on student political activity – such as the formation of a general student union, restoration of political and cultural committees,

<hr>

[74] Ibid., 9–14.
[75] "Waraqa mawqif hawla iqrar al-lai'ha al-tulabiya al-jadida bayna shari'ya iqrariha wa ashkaliyatiha al-qanuniya," Association for Freedom of Thought and Expression, February 26, 2012, http://afteegypt.org/academic_freedom/2012/02/26/525-afteegypt.html
[76] Lindsey, "Freedom and reform at Egypt's universities," 11–14.

and other new procedures for transparent elections – many students remained apprehensive because, as was the case under SCAF, this draft bylaw was issued without their consultation.[77] Moreover, many criticized this iteration for containing several nebulous articles that could ostensibly be interpreted in a way that would embolden repressive measures – for instance, insisting that unions commit to "the university laws and customs," and that student interaction with civil associations and institutions outside the university be "upon the permission of the specialized entities," without specifying those laws and customs or specialized entities as such.[78]

These disputes over the draft bylaw under Morsi were deeply motivated by divisions then extant in the student movement. But as we shall see in the next section, those divisions following the overthrow of Morsi and the new order under Sisi escalate to hitherto unforeseen levels.

Since June 30, 2013

Since June 30, 2013, divisions within the student movement have transcended the quotidian aspects of this or that particular political campaign, be it student bylaws or representation in elections. Rather, it has metastasized into systemic political polarization; drawing on the deepening divisions in Egyptian political society more broadly between supporters of the new regime and its opponents, student activism has been similarly divided across several lines, with student supporters of the regime – having been largely created and encouraged by the security agencies, as had been the case under Mubarak, Sadat, and Nasser previously – pitted aggressively against regime opponents. This increasing division even applies to the broader coalition of student groups that oppose the current regime: while the Muslim Brotherhood-affiliated entity known as "Students Against the Coup" is no doubt a key contingent of this coalition, it is joined by students of the Movement of Revolutionary Socialists, the Misr

---

[77] Abu al-Sa'id Muhammad, "al-Hakuma taqar al-lai'ha al-tulabiya al-jadida budalan min rais al-jamhuriya," *Al-Masry al-Youm*, January 11, 2013, http://today.almasryalyoum.com/article2.aspx?ArticleID=366969

[78] Muhammad Najy and Muhammad Abdel Salam, "Al-Lai'ha al-Tulabiya min al-'idad ila al-iqrar mazid min al-iqsa 'wa-l tahmish wa ghiyab al-shafafiya," Association for Freedom of Thought and Expression, January 20, 2013, http://afteegypt.org/wp-content/uploads/2013/01/afte001-20-01-2013.pdf

al-Qawiyya party, and the April 6th Youth Movement, among others.[79] All are deeply divided in their ideological orientation – the Socialist and April 6th Youth Movement blocs in particular have very little ideological affinities to the Brotherhood or Islamism – and thus in their proposed response in opposition to the coup.

That said, while these student blocs are all divided on how they envision a political solution to the disruption caused by the coup – for instance, on the possibility of the return of Morsi as president – they are united on the broader political goals of ending political repression against students in all its forms, and the reinstatement of academic freedom and the withdrawal of security forces on campuses. Undergirding this student coalition's political platform was the broader aim of opposing the new regime's incursion against the values of the January 25 revolution, the return of the Egyptian police state, and the concomitant crackdown on freedom and individual liberties. Campus activism under these auspices has been predominantly peaceful protest, including marches, human chains, and strikes.[80] The Muslim Brotherhood initiated many protests on campuses during this period, but was ultimately joined by other factions unaffiliated with the Brotherhood as such. The reason being, in the face of police brutality toward student activists on the one hand, and of a broader campaign of regime repression against any and all of its putative opponents on the other, even student activists with no ideological sympathies to the Brotherhood can and have come in the regime's crosshairs. In fact, it would be accurate to posit that the Sisi regime has exploited its war against the Muslim Brotherhood in order to dismantle student activism more broadly, and to eradicate whatever remained of academic independence and freedom.

Regime brutality against students cannot be overstated. Utilizing the full array of military power, including the use of tanks and live ammunition to storm into campuses and dormitories, the present regime's campaign against the student movement ostensibly exceeds all previous administrations in modern Egyptian history.[81] For instance, from November 2013

---

[79] Shahata Awad, "*Alharak Altollabi fi Masr* (Student Movement in Egypt)," *Aljazeera Center for Studies*, June 19, 2014, accessed April 25, 2015, http://studies.aljazeera.net/reports/2014/06/2014617121923939384.htm

[80] For more details, see Association for Freedom of Thought and Expression, "The Annual Report: Strangling of the Public Sphere," April 2014, accessed March 27, 2015, http://afteegypt.org/publications_org/2015/04/09/10013-afteegypt.html

[81] Shahata, Student Movement in Egypt.

to May 16, 2014 alone, twenty students were killed inside universities.[82] The Egyptian Association for Freedom of Thought and Expression, in its annual report for the year 2014, titled "Strangling of the Public Sphere," revealed an even starker picture: 2014 witnessed 88 incidents of breaking into governmental campuses and al-Azhar University by security forces, killing 12 students; 760 students were arrested; 673 were expelled, 400 of whom permanently; 23 were referred to military courts, and 31 were evacuated from dormitories, to name only a few such infractions.[83]

Regime repression against students also extends to abusive legislation. Following the ratification of a constitution that consolidated the sovereignty of the military over parliament, Sisi issued two presidential decrees, as well as a series of legal amendments, specifically designed to undermine student activism, including: a new student bylaw that wholly bans partisan political activism and grants the executive authority expansive regulatory powers; a return to the appointment system of university administrators (as of June 2014); amending university regulations at al-Azhar to allow for the expulsion of faculty who join political protests (as of September 2014); and a September 2014 presidential decree announcing that all public establishments – including university campuses – are heretofore subject to the authority of the military court.[84] Moreover, the regime annulled student union elections in both the 2013–14 and 2014–15 academic years, and the Court of Urgent Affairs issued a ruling in March 2014 stipulating that university security forces shall be reinstated.

Beyond legislative repression, the regime has embarked on a systematic campaign to vilify student activists in the media, through broadcasters demanding that security forces kill and oppress students and protesters, as justified in the name of stability and security.[85] In this same vein, Bahaa Taher, a prominent intellectual figure, called for the closure of campuses for two years.[86] Meanwhile, the regime has dissolved most of the board

---

[82] See "Awlaham Abdel Ghani wa-Akhiruhum Anas al-Mahdi 'huriya al-fikr' tanshir hasran bahalat wafat al-tulab khilal 'amayn dirasiyayn," Association for Freedom of Thought and Expression, May 17, 2015, http://afteegypt.org/academic_freedom/2015/05/18/10239-afteegypt.html

[83] Association for Freedom of Thought and Expression, "The Annual Report."

[84] Ibid.

[85] Many episodes of Egyptian television broadcasters in this vein are available on YouTube, such as: https://www.youtube.com/watch?v=0A61AEydFYo/, May 12, 2015.

[86] Muni Nur, "Usatidhat al-Jami'at radan 'ala fikra baha 'Tahir: al-Ghalaq laysa al-hal innama al-islah," *Akhbar Aladab*, May 3, 2013, http://www.dar.akhbarelyom.com/issuse/detailze.asp?mag=a&field=news&id=7920

of directors of faculty members' clubs and professional syndicates, following several humiliating incidents of security intervention in their internal affairs – in some cases outright threatening elected professors and professionals.[87] Some professors and intellectuals have consequently called for the formation of watchdog "patriot students" groups tasked with reporting their colleagues; some university presidents have taken pride in recruiting students as whistleblowers in this vein, as has the president of al-Azhar in the early 2014–15 academic year.[88] Universities have also spent millions of pounds on contracts with private security companies and on building laminated gates – all to the detriment of education, as evidenced by frequent campus closings and postponements of the academic term, and a palpable decline in research work.

CONCLUSION

This chapter demonstrates that student activism has played a palpable role in supporting liberties and democracy in Egypt since the early twentieth century until the 2011 revolution. This revolution was a remarkable opportunity for students to achieve a series of key demands: the amendment of the student bylaw to guarantee student political autonomy without security interference, alongside radical and qualitative reforms in the education system – both of which would have paved a way for the truly democratic society the 2011 revolution sought to attain more broadly. Regrettably, that noble ideal was shortchanged by the events of July 2013, wherein student activists faced harsh reprisals characteristic of regime violence against Egyptian civil society more broadly – including public institutions and nonviolent protesters.[89] In this return of the Egyptian

---

[87] In one case in Alexandria, the pro-government media accused Dr. Kamal Naguib, a well-known professor and board member of the Alexandria University Faculty Club, of being a member of the Muslim Brotherhood – despite his being a Christian. Based on correspondence with the author, while serving as General Secretary of the Alexandria University Faculty Club from March 2012 to September 2014.

[88] Ahmad al-Dasouqi, "Rai's Nadi Tadris 'al-Azhar' ya'taraf bil-tajassus 'ala talaba al-jam'iah," *Almalnews*, October 11, 2014, http://www.almalnews.com/Pages/StoryDetails.aspx?ID=184920#.VVZtnCFVhBc

[89] For more details, see Abdel-Fattah Mady, *Violence and Democratization in Egypt* (Dar Albashier, Cairo: Egypt, 2015), 8–13.

police state, there are several key implications for student activism, and its future role in cultivating democratization in Egypt.

First, it is imperative that we begin to view student activism as inextricably linked to broader political demands emanating from Egyptian civil society in general. Student demands for educational reform and academic freedom will simply not carry weight without a concomitant democratic bloc in Egyptian political life that can successfully transcend the partisan concerns of its constituent parties to articulate the aims of the January 2011 revolution. Political change in the student activist context must be accompanied by bona fide democratic change in Egypt to gain any meaningful traction.

Accomplishing as much, though, would necessitate that "liberal" as well as leftist forces in Egypt critically reevaluate their alleged commitments to bona fide democratic change. As we saw earlier with the example of Dr. Mohammad Abol Ghar, such forces have proven guilty of glaring double standards post-2013 in their handling of issues of human rights and democracy. If anything, the events of June 30, 2013 portend the lack of a truly "liberal" current in the Egyptian political landscape in the first place. Both before and after Morsi's election in June 2012, allegedly liberal and leftist figures expressed antagonism towards Morsi and the Muslim Brotherhood, having demanded a recall presidential election following Morsi's constitutional declaration in November 2012, rather than properly offering a political alternative to the Brotherhood in the parliamentary elections that were set to take place in late 2012 or 2013. Similarly, such a front collaborated with the Tamarod (Rebel) campaign that ignited the drive to topple Morsi – and which was later demonstrated to have links with deep state institutions.[90]

Yet these same "liberal" and leftist figures – alongside other political forces like nationalists and Salafis – for all their indignation against Morsi and the Muslim Brotherhood during their time in power, have

---

[90] See "Leaks from Sisi's office allege far-reaching UAE 'interference' in Egypt," *Middle East Eye*, March 1, 2015, http://www.middleeasteye.net/news/fresh-leaks-462283720#sthash. rTNVh6Wi.dpuf; and "tasribat jadida li-mudir maktab-l Sisi," *Aljazeera.net*, March 2, 2015, http://www.aljazeera.net/news/arabic/2015/3/1/%D8%AA%D8%B3%D8%B1%D9%8A %D8%A8-%D8%AC%D8%AF%D9%8A%D8%AF-%D9%84%D9%85%D8 %AF%D9%8A%D8%B1-%D9%85%D9%83%D8%AA%D8%A8-%D8%A7 %D9%84%D8%B3%D9%8A%D8%B3%D9%8A-%D8%AD%D9%88%D9%84- %D9%88%D8%AF%D9%8A%D8%B9%D8%A9-%D8%A5%D9%85%D8%A7%D8%B1 %D8%A7%D8%AA%D9%8A%D8%A9

proven oddly silent in the face of egregious abuses and political repression committed by the military order under Sisi since Morsi's overthrow. Many have actively supported the repressive measures of the current regime, including security repression of student and political activists, but extending beyond that to include the politicization of the judiciary, media campaigns against the opposition, and the repressive legislation mentioned earlier. Many have endorsed the regime's campaign of open season on Islamists, some having gone as far as advocating an exclusionist democracy without the Muslim Brotherhood, on the basis of Brotherhood members being unpatriotic, thus endorsing the present regime's campaign of "Debrotherhoodization."[91] Even a figure like Dr. Abol Ghar, for all his purported commitments to academic freedom, has otherwise given the Sisi regime a blank check for repression in all other arenas of Egyptian political and civic life. Suffice to say, for the university scene to be a true contributor to Egyptian civic life more broadly, such contradictions would need to be formatively addressed.

Substantive political change in Egypt more broadly, then, requires a democratic alliance or bloc, which could transcend the ideological affiliations of its component parties and thus truly express the interests of the January 25 revolution. To that end, democratizing Egypt necessitates that "liberal" and leftist forces address the double standards they have increasingly adopted with respect to individual liberties, democracy, and the rule of law. Such factions cannot achieve political success in the long term through the outright destruction of Islamist factions; instead, for liberal and leftist actors to gain purchase in Egyptian political life, they would need to work with the masses to offer a viable political alternative, and thus cultivate proper political platforms and credible party leaders. Moreover, Islamists would similarly need to recognize the need to fully engage collaborative partners, and recognize that freedom and democracy must take precedence over any ideological agenda, Islamist or otherwise.

As for the generals, they should realize that what happened in 2011 was a truly popular uprising that will never come to an end unless it leads to a modern state governed by a democratically elected government and accompanying institutions, in which neither the army nor any other unelected institutions have the upper hand. Change shall occur when the

---

[91] For instance, Moataz Abdel Fattah, *Risala ila al-safir al-almani bil-Qahira* (*Letter to the German Ambassador in Cairo*), *Alwatannews*, May 22, 2015, http://www.elwatannews.com/news/details/734230

generals understand that establishing civil control of the armed forces will eventually strengthen the state, the army, and democracy.

Moreover, the regional and international powers that support the current government should understand that times have changed and that the power of the masses and students, and their demand for freedom and dignity, can no longer be permanently halted by brute force, particularly when students and young people have access to technology and social networks. One cannot escape the negative repercussions that have been accumulating for decades due in large part to long-term Western support for despotic governments in Arab countries and double-standards toward democracy and human rights violations. Finally, student activists have to reunite behind a shared agenda that promotes democracy and human rights. There will be no freedoms and liberty in the university context if they are not accompanied in Egyptian civil society more broadly. Education reforms will never be actualized without elected and responsible political institutions.

Islam, secularism, and the state

8

Egypt's secularized intelligentsia and the guardians of truth

KHALED ABOU EL FADL

Initially, I was tempted to write an essay wrestling with the question of why the liberal and secular intelligentsia betrayed the Egyptian revolution. There is an extensive list of Egyptian intellectuals such as Saad Eddin Ibrahim, Ibrahim Eissa, Bassem Youssef, and many others who have carefully constructed themselves into emblematic figures standing for secular and liberal values. But what has transpired in Egypt from January 25, 2011 to date has cast serious doubt about the meaning and extent of both the secular and liberal commitment among the vast majority of the country's intelligentsia. There is little doubt that Egypt's intelligentsia betrayed the revolution that they claimed to celebrate and support. And there is no doubt that those who betrayed it the most are those who built entire careers bawling and orating about the modern nation-state, the citizenry, civic society, secularism, and democracy. But this intelligentsia ended up helping to uproot a budding revolution that still retained some degree of promise, replacing it with an inveterate condition of dreadful despair and wretchedness. Whatever one might say about the political order in Egypt before the military coup of 2013, at no point did the military regime of Abd al-Fattah al-Sisi embody the promise of liberal democratic values.

When it comes to Egypt today, one can speak of a mass of secularly minded or secularized intelligentsia whose thinking on democracy and constitutionalism is hopelessly opportunistic and muddled.[1] The most significant and all-pervasive reality about Egypt since 1952 and to this very day is that it is, as the political scientist Amos Perlmutter once described it, a "Praetorian State."[2] This means a state in which the military has become part of the bureaucratic state and a substantial force in creating and maintaining the middle class. In Egypt, the military is the only true sovereign and the de facto possessor and negotiator of legitimacy. The military has become like an octopus that has tentacles in every aspect of society, and, as such, it has become the ultimate arbitrator of wealth and legitimacy. Through the colonial era, a class of officers have ruled Egypt with mandatory powers, and, charged with administering the country for the good of its natives, they empowered themselves with a mythology akin to manifest destiny. In the name of progress and modernity, the colonial military administrators acted as a mandatory power charged with the advancement and civilizing of native peoples that are treated as though too immature to rule themselves. In 1945, the British Colonial Office wrote: "We are all in favour of freedom, but freedom for many of these territories means assistance and guidance and protection…What we can give them is liberty and free institutions. We can gradually train them in the management of their own affairs so that, should independence eventually come, they will be ready for it."[3] The paternalistic sentiment reflected in the above quote perfectly describes the attitude of so much of the Egyptian military, and, as we will see, also the secularized intelligentsia, toward shepherding the masses toward eventual self-rule and democracy. It is as though British colonialism succeeded in creating certain modalities of thinking in which the Egyptian military and secularized intelligentsia have been thoroughly indoctrinated since 1882.

The combination of colonialism and military rule established epistemic mindsets toward legitimacy, progress, nativity, culture, and religion. The one intransigent and interminable constant fact is that legitimacy is

---

[1] On the particularities and peculiarities of secularism in the Arab world, see Tariq Ramadan, *Islam and the Arab Awakening* (Oxford: Oxford University Press, 2012), 75–9, 85–9.
[2] See Amos Perlmutter, *Egypt: The Praetorian State* (New Brunswick, NJ: Transaction Books, 1974), depicting Nasser's regime, where the political leadership of the ruling class emerges from the ranks of the army, against the backdrop of praetorian political systems generally.
[3] Quoted in A. W. Brian Simpson, *Human Rights and the End of Empire: Britain and the Genesis of the European Convention* (Oxford: Oxford University Press, 2001), 292.

retained by those who have power and can yield coercive influence. This brutish proposition is completely at odds with the development of civic values or virtues.[4] The secularly minded or secularized intelligentsia, whom I will further discuss below, found itself in an onerous position. Armed with Western epistemological outlooks, they saw themselves as embodying the progressive forces of society – the *avant garde* leading their cultures toward modernity – and fending off the forces of reactionism and backwardness.[5] The prevalence of the logic of brute power and the persistence of the patriarchal logic of mandatory and supervisory roles over the citizenry created a true crisis in legitimacy. To be precise, the crisis was in articulating a coherent conception of legitimacy before a populace that had just made very costly sacrifices for a dignified life that would afford them the rights of citizenship.

The extent to which there was a real crisis of legitimacy was clearly evident in the pivotal days right before the military coup in Egypt. President Mohammad Morsi's last public speech focused on nothing but legitimacy, and the secularized intelligentsia did not seem to tire of defining, explaining, and expounding upon this key word. The amount of philosophizing that flowed endlessly from the pens and mouths of Egyptian intellectuals was truly dizzying, but it was also mostly incoherent and opportunistic. According to the pundits that filled every media outlet and journal, revolutionary legitimacy is different from electoral legitimacy but there is also constitutional legitimacy, which is different still from supra-constitutional legitimacy. The legitimacy of constitutions can be trumped by meta-principles, *grund norms*, or preemptory principles. But there is also legitimacy created by expectations and promises made during the electoral race, and conversely, the loss of legitimacy because of the failure to uphold those promises. Moreover, there is the legitimacy conferred and withdrawn by the guardians of legitimacy who are also the ultimate protectors of Egypt's sovereign state interests. But then there is the legitimacy of the streets and the legitimacy of the manifest destiny of Egypt in human history. There is also a lost legitimacy of an elected president who dared infringe upon the sanctity of the judiciary – something

---

[4] This is precisely why the minute two strangers quarrel in Egypt, instead of deferring to law, justice, or ethics, they will immediately claim to have connections in high places – connections that can yield the kind of compulsory power before which considerations of law, justice, or ethics can only submit.

[5] Remarkably, some of the secularized intelligentsia refer to the days of the Islamic civilization as '*usur zalamiyyah* (dark ages)!

like the religious idea of mortal sin. And then there is also the legitimacy of a judge, who remains a member of the judiciary, but is granted executive and legislative powers all at once. There is the legitimacy granted by a sincere commitment to democracy, and the illegitimacy of parties that should never have been allowed to form a political party because they are religiously based. There is the legitimacy of the social contract and the illegitimacy of those who are insincere in their commitment to the contract because they do not believe in the civic state and its legitimacy. There is the time-tested legitimacy of the guardians of liberal values – a legitimacy that trumps the illegitimacy of those who might believe in democracy but do not truly believe in liberal values.

The short of it is that, after a revolution that overthrew one of the oldest dictatorships in the Middle East, and after six different popular elections, the Egyptian intelligentsia seemed to be hopelessly chaotic in their understanding of what legitimacy is, and how one goes about acquiring it in a democratic system.

The truth is that the revolution of January 25, 2011 promised a complete paradigm shift in the way the Egyptian intelligentsia thinks about political legitimacy. The revolution created a hope, which now feels like a defunct dream, that Egyptians could learn the lesson taught by so many tragedies in human history. This lesson quite simply is that sovereignty belongs to the citizenry, and that the only source of legitimacy is the integrity and sanctity of the democratic process. No group and no person, whatever the imagined urgency or ultimate wisdom, has the right to shortchange or overrule the process. One truly hoped that the Arab Spring was the beginning of a new era in which it would be finally understood that sovereignty belongs to the people, and that the exclusive and sole way that the sovereign will can be expressed – and hence, the only way to gain legitimacy – is through the integrity of the process. The integrity of the political process must be defended above all. Civil society needs civic values, and civic values are upheld through a civil discourse that does not exclude or marginalize the other. Civic discourses cannot be navigated if the participants of the discourse get into the habit of using language to eradicate the other's worth, value, or dignity. Civic discourses try to search and achieve consensus over shared values, and strive to respect and tolerate values upon which people cannot agree. It had become all too common for liberal secular forces to refer to Islamists as traitors, murderers, fascists, and hoodlums, and, on the other side, for Islamists to question the faith, piety, and loyalty of their opponents. But in principle, regardless of how polarizing the discourse might have become, respecting the process was the only guarantor that there would be a non-violent and reliable way to challenge power, hold officials accountable, and establish legitimacy. If all else failed, civil disobedience would be the last resort because it can correct procedural deviations while remaining within the bounds of the civic order. Violence and forced military interventions de-legitimate the very logic of a civil order. The Egyptian military has practically colonized the country since 1952, and one did not need to be possessed of much probity to foresee that, once the military is called upon to save the country from a civilian government, the praetorian order would be bolstered and augmented more than ever before.

Even if it came in response to widespread grievances, the military coup was a fatal blow to the Egyptian Revolution. It was a fatal blow because it reaffirmed the politics of the old guardians in Egypt. It confirmed the traditional polarized, mutually exclusivist, and equally supremacist politics that has prevailed, not only in Egypt but also throughout the Middle East, since the colonial era. Unfortunately, the military coup and the return of the repressive security forces in Egypt came as a natural conclusion to the elasticity of the claims of legitimacy made by so many parties after the revolution. But more than anything else, it is the Egyptian secularized intelligentsia and the revolutionaries themselves that forced the revolution to commit suicide. This secularized intelligentsia – not only in Egypt, but also in the Arab world in general – has locked the region into a near-perpetual circle of self-defeatism because they appear incapable of understanding that nothing kills lofty ideas quite like the pragmatic hypocrisy of their bearers.

Hence, it is critical to understand that the failure above all else is the defeat dealt to the ethics of legitimacy. It speaks volumes that the grievances against Mohammad Morsi were that he tried to monopolize power, he failed to respect the rule of law as embodied in the judiciary, and he infringed upon the rights of dissenters. Yet the representative of the judiciary sitting as Egypt's interim president was blissfully not troubled by the unlawful closing of opposing media outlets, by the mass arrests and even murder of pro-Morsi advocates, nor by his own monopolization of legislative and executive powers deposited in him by the military. The secularized intelligentsia that presented itself as the upholder of civic and democratic principles during Morsi's rule celebrated the appointment of Mohamed El Baradei, who had not gone through a single electoral test of his legitimacy, and had been imposed upon the sovereign Egyptian people through military will. One cannot miss the paradoxical irony that the interim president Adly Mansour, sitting as a judge on the Constitutional Court, could not tolerate any degree of political intervention by a civilian president, but was not troubled by receiving his marching orders from the military.

The paradoxes and ironies that surrounded the theatrical days of interim President Adly Mansour pale in comparison to the atrocities and tragedies that followed when Sisi, who happened to be the leader of the coup, became firmly settled in power. It is no exaggeration to say that every offense which President Morsi was accused of has been blatantly, and often shamelessly, committed a hundred times over by President Sisi. After the horrifying massacre of hundreds of peaceful protesters in Rabaa and al-Nahda squares on August 14, 2013 – a massacre that is unparalleled in modern Egyptian history – the Sisi regime put into motion a campaign of terror in which all dissenters were either liquidated or imprisoned.[6] Kangaroo trials, extreme penalties, censorship, and many other human rights abuses reached levels that rivaled and even exceeded the most repressive leaders known to Arab history.[7] At the same time that the revolutionary youth who once supported Sisi's coup were processed before military tribunals, convicted, and sent to prison as a matter of course, the most notorious figures of the Mubarak regime and Mubarak himself were all acquitted in farcical trials. The Sisi regime not only achieved complete and total control over state- and privately owned media outlets, but a sustained campaign was launched to de-legitimate and demonize the revolution of January 25 and to elevate and sanctify the so-called revolution of July 3 (i.e. the date of the military coup). But the incongruities and anomalies do not end here. While Sisi spoke at great length about the threat of political Islam, and the evil of religiously based parties competing in the political process, not only did Sisi repeatedly invoke the support of the Grand Shaykh of Azhar Ahmed al-Tayeb and the Coptic Orthodox Pope Tawadros II, but the Salafi-Wahhabi Party El Nour was also recognized and allowed to compete in the parliamentary

---

[6] See Human Rights Watch Report, *All According to Plan: The Rab'a Massacre and Mass Killings of Protesters in Egypt*, HRW, August 2014, http://www.hrw.org/sites/default/files/reports/egypt0814web_0.pdf

[7] See Amnesty International Annual Report, *Egypt 2015/2016*, https://www.amnesty.org/en/countries/middle-east-and-north-africa/egypt/report-egypt/; Human Rights Watch World Report 2016, *Egypt: Events of 2015*, HRW, https://www.hrw.org/world-report/2016/country-chapters/egypt

elections. In the midst of this universe of tragic contradictions where a people are systematically degraded and abused in the name of a gradual ascension to the bliss of true liberty, what happened to the secularized intelligentsia? A few protested and suffered the ire of the repressive state; a few more fell silent; but most, accompanied by atonal narratives about the many shades of legitimacy, continued to support the Sisi regime.

All of this begs one basic and essential question: Why did the Egyptian secular intelligentsia betray their revolution and fall into such profound and blatant contradictions that they killed the infant revolution? To answer this question, we must go back in time and understand what can be described as the time-honored traditions of Egyptian politics. Long before the military coup, the secularized intelligentsia and some of their revolutionary partners destined the revolution to a painful suicide by indulging in what has now become an often-repeated offense. They imagined themselves as the one and only true possessors of legitimacy, not because they represent the sovereign will, but because they and they alone possess the civilizational and intellectual values necessary for a progressive order in which true democracy, unhampered by reactionary forces, can be achieved.

Since the age of colonialism, legitimacy has become an elastic word that is exploited to invent and repress history; to construct and de-construct identity; and to uphold and deny rights. Legitimacy is possessed by no one but claimed by everyone, and it is enforced only through sheer power. In the absence of a transparent and accountable civil process, those who believe that they are the de facto possessors of legitimacy massacre in cold blood, torture, maim, and commit every possible offense in the name of defending the existing legitimacy.

It is paradoxical, but very telling, that, long before the military coup, the secularized intelligentsia, whether on the right or left, adopted and promoted the claim that the Islamists were brought into power by the United States to implement an American agenda in the region. According to countless published articles and intellectuals appearing on privately owned television stations, the Muslim Brotherhood was but a pawn for American interests in the region. This conspiratorial framework was set out in great detail in numerous articles published in the opposition papers in which it was alleged that the United States brought Islamists to power in Libya, Tunisia, and Egypt and planned to bring Islamists to power in Syria so as to keep Arabs backwards and underdeveloped. Although no country has done more to undermine the Brotherhood in

Egypt than Saudi Arabia, and no country celebrated Sisi's ascendancy to power more than Israel, Egyptian secular intellectuals blissfully continued to claim that there is an Egyptian, Turkish, Qatari, and Israeli conspiracy to augment the United States' hegemonic power in the Middle East and to end any semblance of independence in the region. This conspiratorial view was repeated so incessantly and persistently to the point that one is reluctant to dismiss it as a propaganda ploy or simple rhetorical flare. Is it possible that the secularized intelligentsia truly believed that Sisi, who was trained and educated in the United States, and the likes of El Baradei, who served under Hosni Mubarak and who is more at home in the West than in Egypt, are capable of setting an independent course for Egyptian foreign policy? Is it possible that this secularized intelligentsia could not have noticed that, as soon as Morsi was overthrown, Saudi Arabia and UAE came forward to save the Egyptian economy with an unprecedented lucrative aid package? Shortly after Sisi came to power, Egyptian public television stations broadcasted state-sponsored public awareness messages in which Fox News and well-known Islamophobes were regularly quoted on political Islam and Islamists. Even more, well-known Islamophobic politicians were welcomed by Sisi in Egypt in highly publicized visits in which one of them compared Sisi to George Washington![8] Is it conceivable that the secularized intelligentsia failed to understand that the coup was very plainly and openly supported by pro-Israeli politicians and publicists on the far right and that this support in and of itself speaks volumes?

I am confident that the secularized intelligentsia had indeed noticed all of the above, however, the conspiratorial accusatory framework is a poorly intellectualized way of making a very important point, and that is: not just the Brotherhood, but all Islamists in the region, lack real legitimacy or at a minimum should lack legitimacy. Portraying the Islamists as part of a foreign conspiracy is driven by the indulgent need to cast the Islamists as

---

[8] Representative Louie Gohmert (Texas), Representative Steve King (Iowa), and Representative Michele Bachmann (Minnesota) were the Islamophobes who visited Sisi, and Louie Gohmert pushed the bounds of absurdity by comparing Sisi to George Washington. See David D. Kirkpatrick, "Visiting Republicans laud Egypt's force," *New York Times*, September 8, 2013, http://www.nytimes.com/2013/09/09/world/middleeast/three-us-lawmakers-visit-egypt-to-praise-crackdown.html?_r=0; Shazia Arshad, "'My enemy's enemy is my ally:' For Congress delegation to Cairo, that enemy is Islam," *Middle East Monitor*, September 10, 2013, https://www.middleeastmonitor.com/articles/americas/7308-qmy-enemys-enemy-is-my-allyq-for-congress-delegation-to-cairo-that-enemy-is-islam

outsiders to society. Accordingly, Islamists do not represent any type of traditional or native authenticity, but are agent-provocateurs manipulated by outsider forces. They exploit native symbols, but only to serve foreign agendas that have nothing to do with the material interests of the people they claim to represent. The tactic of claiming that Islamists are agents of foreign interests is not new. It has been used by every Arab dictator who has repressed Islamic groups since the 1950s. The secularized intelligentsia was forced to resort to it not only because they were incapable of galvanizing the electoral vote, but also because they themselves are alienated and poorly rooted in the cultures for which they claim to speak.

The colonial era witnessed the rise of a largely Western-educated class that was trained and weaned to form the necessary bourgeoisie that would service the state bureaucratic apparatus necessary for servicing colonial interests in the region. However, at that time, many of the Western-educated intelligentsia still enjoyed close ties to influential reform-oriented religious figures such as Muhammad Abduh (d. 1905). These religious figures worked to reconcile traditional Islamic values with the modern nation-state, democracy, and constitutionalism.[9] They also represented a symbolic link to historical continuity, and the legitimacy of tradition. The ability of the Westernized intelligentsia to negotiate grounds of commonality with religious intellectual forces granted them a relative degree of native legitimacy. Typically, this Westernized intelligentsia was thoroughly grounded in post-renaissance European thought, but knew precious little about the pre-colonial Islamic epistemic tradition. Indeed, this intelligentsia saw its own native tradition largely through Western eyes. In other words, what they understood or believed about Islamic history and thought came largely from the writings of Western orientalists. Even to this day, the general outlook of the secular intelligentsia – their understanding of the progression, trajectory, contributions, and the very worth of the Islamic tradition is derived almost exclusively from the writings of Western scholars on Islam. In the nineteenth and early twentieth centuries, the secular intelligentsia played a critical role in translating orientalist literature into Arabic and taught these sources in urban universities throughout Egypt. As such, they

[9] See Albert Hourani, *Arabic Thought in the Liberal Age, 1798–1939* (Cambridge: Cambridge University Press, 1983); Afaf Lutfi Sayyid-Marsot, *Egypt's Liberal Experiment, 1922–1936* (Berkeley: University of California Press, 1977); Abdeslam M. Maghraoui, *Liberalism without Democracy: Nationhood and Citizenship in Egypt, 1922–1936* (Durham: Duke University Press, 2006).

acted as a persistent bridge to transplanting and transforming Western views of Islamic history and thought to an internalized self-view in the consciousness of the urbanized elite.

The cooperative and friendly relationship of the Westernized intelligentsia with the reform and liberal-minded Islamic scholars did not last. With the rise of pan-Arab nationalism, and ideological movements such as Nasserism and Ba'athism in the 1950s, the dynamics between the Westernized intelligentsia and Islamic orientations changed in fundamental and dramatic ways. Arab nationalism adopted the rhetoric of religion as a fundamentally reactionary force pitted against a progressive force of national liberation. The secular intelligentsia, which at the time was largely leftist and socialist, legitimated and defended the repressive praetorian state as necessary for achieving progressive historical objectives. A very significant number of Egyptian intellectuals, such as journalist and political commentator Mohamed Hassanein Heikal (1923–2016), saw religion as a private and personal matter that should play no normative role in the public sphere. In reality, however, religion was not excluded from the public sphere, but it was allowed to exist only within the narrow space allowed it by the Arab secular state. The secular state created officially sanctioned podiums for religion, and, in effect, created an official state religion that rubber-stamped and legitimated state politics. At the same time, this state-sponsored religion lost its legitimacy on the ground, as the clergy of Azhar became salaried employees of the state. With the domestication of the native Azhari clergy, critical Islamic thought drifted into stale apologetics that placated and satisfied only the most uninspired and unchallenging intellects. This helps explain the powerful symbolism invoked when Sisi placed the Shaykh of al-Azhar and the Pope of the Coptic Church on either side of him when he announced his coup.

The 1967 defeat and the rise of Saudi-funded Wahhabi-Salafi movements in the 1970s heralded the death of pan-Arab nationalism, and challenged the privileged status of the Westernized Egyptian intelligentsia. While intellectually unsophisticated, Wahhabi-Salafi movements achieved something that the Westernized intelligentsia was no longer capable of doing, and that is to appeal to and galvanize the masses. After the cooptation of the scholars of Azhar by the state, and the death of the pan-Arab socialist dream, what captured the imagination of the masses was the impassioned rhetoric of the Islamic groups who recalled in the imagination of their audiences a time of glory when Muslims were powerful and respected, and when justice reigned.

The uncomfortable truth is that the Westernized intelligentsia continued to rely on the repressive state to continue in a privileged status. While Islamic groups appealed to the masses on the street by embracing many of their social and economic problems and by capturing their imagination with the promise of a regained glory, the secular intelligentsia had a very different path. For over four decades, the secular intelligentsia relied on the praetorian state to placate and repress the Islamists. But embracing the evolving language of the age, this intelligentsia adopted the Western language of democracy, pluralism, civil society, and human rights. While failing to understand or engage the aspirations of the masses, the secular intelligentsia adopted an increasingly elitist and even supremacist attitude toward Islamists. They borrowed the language of modernity, post-modernity, globalization, and the international community as a self-assuring and self-congratulatory discourse about their own ability to understand the complexity of the modern world, to rise up to the challenges of the globalization, and to move Egyptian society toward development and progress. Meanwhile, the gap between the rich and poor grew ever larger, and the economic problems of Egypt became more complicated.

The secularist and Islamist discourses grew ever more polarized. The secularists saw the Islamists as reactionary forces often describing them as *zalamiyyun* (of the dark ages or living in the dark ages), and the Islamists saw the secularists as essentially alien to the society they claimed to represent. The irony is that both parties spoke the language of democracy and civil rights, and both continued to believe that they represented the true and legitimate public good. In the name of democracy, Islamists won elections, and in the name of democracy the secular intelligentsia continued to rely on the repressive state as their guarantor against the reactionary Islamist forces.

A new emerging reality, however, had overtaken Egyptian society and marginalized all else. The military and security forces continued to enjoy the patronage of the United States, and control the institutions of the state. But Egyptian society was flush with Gulf money, and this created an odd and painful dynamic. Saudi Arabia continued to fund Wahhabi-Salafi movements, and, eventually, funded a number of privately owned satellite stations. However, other privately owned media sprang up that belonged to a class of investors with a complex web of interests involving Gulf money and Mubarak's state apparatus. Significantly, a large segment of the Egyptian secular intelligentsia relied on these profitable cultural venues for their very survival.

The Mubarak regime balanced the Islamist media with a secular media. The same balancing act is played by the Saudi government, which owns secular channels such as the rather racy MBC and plays them off against religious channels such as Iqraa. Importantly, the Mubarak regime had a complex network of incentives, rewards, and punishments for journalists, writers, media personalities, and everyone who could affect public opinion. Most of the secularized intelligentsia became clientele of the state in which they played the role of the loyal opposition. Their measured and domesticated opposition legitimated the repressive state apparatus that had become increasingly savage and brutal.

The Egyptian revolution was sparked by an idealistic group of youth who had lost faith in all the institutions of power. This youth was defiant, innocent, idealistic, and uncorrupted. But it was successful because the destitute masses had suffered enough. Once the alienated revolutionary youth took to the streets, they were joined by the destitute masses and the Muslim brotherhood. Initially, Saudi Arabia had its muftis issue a refrain to the Wahhabi-Salafi groups against rebelling against Mubarak. However, with the revolutionary fervor becoming like a tidal wave, especially after the resignation of Mubarak, the Wahhabi-Salafi groups had no choice but to go along with the pretense of being a part of the revolution.

The Egyptian revolution presented the arrogant and domesticated secularized intelligentsia with a true challenge. Suddenly, for the first time, they were presented with the task of practicing what they preached, and of speaking for the populace without the mediating role of the repressive state. Even when at times they defended the rights of a member of the Brotherhood or of an Islamist, the repressive state stood as an ultimate guarantor that the Islamists would never become too powerful. For decades, this intelligentsia theorized about the sovereign will, reactionism, progressivism, and the place of Egypt in world history, but, for the first time, they were forced to come face to face with, deal with, and explain themselves to the Egyptian people. For the first time, they could not simply dismiss the Islamists with contempt and arrogance, and they would have to figure out a native language – a language that did not simply transplant Western concepts, ideas, and historical movements but that would actually empower these ideas with meaning to the Egyptian people. Would the secularized intelligentsia be capable of working through the will of the people without guardian state institutions such as the army, police, or judiciary to package this will and present it in a palatable fashion?

Why did the secularized intelligentsia fear the Brotherhood so much? The Muslim Brotherhood had been the perpetual victim. Since 1954, there was no significant time that passed without the Brotherhood being persecuted and repressed in some fashion or another. Unable to depend on the powers of the state, the Brotherhood developed a network of charitable projects, and lived and preached among Egypt's disappearing middle class and impoverished masses. Like all wealthy Egyptians, the Brotherhood relied on Gulf money, but it was capital amassed when their members were forced to escape to Gulf countries during Nasser's regime (r. 1954–70). Under Sadat and Mubarak, many of those who lived in exile in Gulf countries returned to Egypt and focused their energies on entrepreneurial projects that capitalized on their Gulf connections. However, the Brotherhood had an odd love-hate relationship with Saudi Arabia. They clearly accommodated Wahhabi-Salafi Islam and benefited from Saudi largess in some contexts, but, at the same time, their brand of Islam was different. Unlike the Wahhabi-Salafi movement, they sincerely believed in democracy as the inevitable and Islamically acceptable system of government. They also rejected the infamous Wahhabi practice of *takfir* (or of calling their Muslim opponents infidels). Although Saudi Arabia had given quarter to the Muslim Brotherhood during the period of Nasserist persecution, Saudi's close ties to the Mubarak regime, Egypt's military, and the United States militated against this relationship. More critically, Saudi Arabia could ill afford the success and the inevitable spread of the revolutionary fervor of the so-called Arab Spring. Nothing could be more risky to the Saudi-supported brand of Islam and to the Saudi regime than an Islamic movement that would have successfully negotiated democracy. An Islamically inspired movement that could manage to adapt itself to a democratic political system would threaten to undermine the very ideological foundations that have sustained the Saudi regime since coming to power.

Because of its effective grassroots efforts in Egypt, the Muslim Brotherhood was well positioned to appeal to the electoral ballot. The secularized intelligentsia tried to put off an electoral showdown with Islamists for as long as possible. They openly complained that they had not had a chance to work with the masses, while the Islamists were adept at tricking and cajoling the simple-minded public that could not understand complex ideas such as constitutionalism and limitations on power. They tried in every way to dissuade the Supreme Council of the Armed Forces (SCAF) from holding a referendum that raised the ultimate question of the Islamic identity of the state. Many of them tried to convince SCAF that true democracy requires the banning of religiously based parties, and the prohibition of religious symbolism in elections. However, at that point, the military wanted a real sense of the pulse of the masses, and did not want to be dragged into a violent showdown with Islamists. The Islamists won the referendum of March 19, 2011, with seventy-seven percent of the vote. The parliamentary elections of November 28, 2011 were a landslide in favor of the Islamists, with the Brotherhood winning 43.4% and other Islamic alliances winning 25%. The Shura Council elections were also a landslide win with the Brotherhood capturing 58.3% of the popular vote.

Not only were the secularized intelligentsia and SCAF itself now worried, but the elite class of petty capitalists, who for decades had thrived only through a parasitical relationship with Mubarak's corrupt state apparatus, were apprehensive as well. On June 14, 2012, the Supreme Constitutional Court (SCC), staffed by Mubarak appointees, dissolved the entire parliament because purportedly the election laws discriminated against independent candidates. However, the Egyptian judiciary, which had gained a largely undeserved reputation for independence and integrity, could hardly be counted on as a neutral arbitrator between the Islamists and their opponents. The judiciary itself is but a part of the secularized elite that perceives itself as part of the progressive *avant garde*, protecting a native population against its own reactionary proclivities. After the scare of the parliamentary elections, on June 18, 2012, SCAF passed the infamous Revisions to the first Constitutional Declaration, insulating the armed forces from civilian oversight or accountability and granting the army veto power over the act of declaring war. A few days later on June 25, the SCC challenged the legality of the Shura Council, giving a clear indication that it too was likely to be dissolved.

The last remaining hope for the Islamists was the presidential elections, which were begrudgingly held by SCAF after repeated demonstrations and protests. Just in case the Islamist-dominated parliament would not be dissolved by the SCC, SCAF and the judiciary allowed General Ahmad Shafiq, Mubarak's last prime minister, to run against the Islamists despite the numerous corruption charges pending against him. Moreover, the old regime with its full network of petty capitalists put all its weight behind General Shafiq, who was reinvented by the privately owned media into a revolutionary figure who fervently believed in the rule of law. Considering that General Shafiq was given the full support of the Egyptian state and that the privately owned media launched a fully fledged attack on the

Brotherhood, the real surprise was that President Mohammad Morsi was still able to eke out a narrow victory of 51.7% against Shafiq's 48.3%. The presidential elections presented the secularized intelligentsia with a stark choice: they could support the old order or they could swallow the bitter pill of supporting an Islamist candidate. Most chose to do neither. But their sense of grievance and belief that the masses were not mature enough to decide the fate of the country through free elections was only reaffirmed.

Morsi and the Brotherhood gave their secular opponents a golden opportunity with his poor performance as Egypt's first freely elected president. Comforted by the repeated electoral victories, he moved against two bastions of privilege and power in Egypt – both secular, entitled, elitist, and deeply offended at having to limit their power. Egypt is the only purported democracy where it is a criminal offense to criticize the military or judiciary, and it is impossible to penetrate through the veil of immunity behind which corruption takes place.

Although the Islamists were able to pass the New Egyptian Constitution by a 63.8% vote on December 25, 2012, this was the last straw. The old regime with its unholy and somewhat psychotic alliances returned. The secularized intelligentsia once again manned all of the podiums provided by the privately owned media, the SCC kept rejecting draft after draft of the revised electoral law that was intended to save the Shura Council from being dissolved, and the military started negotiating with Washington, DC to remove Morsi from power. Most importantly, in my view, panicking from the new breed of democratic Islam, the Saudis waged a campaign of economic sabotage against Morsi's government, causing repeated power outages and gasoline shortages all over Egypt. And they opened their coffers to numerous writers and journalists for waging an incessant and sometimes irrational campaign against the Brotherhood.

The massive turnout of protesters against Egypt's elected president on June 30, 2013 came as nothing short of a real gift to the Brotherhood's opponents. Weeks before, the secularized intelligentsia had been openly calling upon the old guardians, i.e. the military and judiciary, to intervene to save Egypt's revolution. Reminiscent of the role they have consistently played since the colonial era, they called upon old guardians to save the country from the follies of its natives. The guardians of truth needed to reset the revolution on its proper course by undoing the results of all six elections, and by turning over the revolution to its rightful owners – the rightful owners being the possessors of the secular truth, that religion has no role in the public sphere, and that the masses need to be shepherded into a democracy rather than be treated as true sovereign agents.

The actual coup was a mere formality. The secularized intelligentsia, however, felt more empowered than ever before. Now, they badly wanted to believe that, in one year of Morsi's rule, they had finally achieved what they had failed to achieve since the colonial period, and that is mass appeal. This is why they jumped on the figure of thirty million people demonstrating in Tahrir as proof positive of the legitimacy of the secular project. It is this group in Tahrir Square and no other, so they believed, who were the indisputable source of legitimacy, and of what the intelligentsia knew all along, that Islamists should return to the periphery of power where they belong, and should be prevented by the old guardians from misleading the masses. This is why the secularized intelligentsia did not have a problem with the unlawful closings of the media outlets owned by Islamists and with the unjust arrests that included the speaker of the dissolved parliament and even the attorneys who represented the Brotherhood before the SCC. Paradoxically, it is the secularized intelligentsia that unwittingly admitted the empty circle in which they keep revolving. According to them, 1952 and 2013 were legitimate revolutions in modern Egyptian history – in 1952, the army rose against injustice and the people backed it up, and in June 2013, the people rose against injustice and the army backed them up! But the secularized intelligentsia fails to note that, in both 1952 and 2013, the army remained the ultimate arbiter of power and also the only force that invents and destroys constitutions, rights, and institutions at will. Indeed, it did appear that they were determined to repeat history once again. By celebrating the coup of 2013 just as they celebrated the coup of 1952, the Egyptian secularized intelligentsia demonstrated that they had learned nothing. This time, however, the folly of the secularized intelligentsia was far more serious. Nasser was a charismatic despot who sold the Egyptian people exciting visions of a bright future that never materialized. Sisi tried to do the same. He made a great deal of promises that could not be fulfilled, even with the full support of the United Arab Emirates, Saudi Arabia, Kuwait, Israel, and the United States. But Sisi is no charismatic leader, and in a short period of time, he over-taxed his allies with endless financial demands, while appearing unable or unwilling to control the bottomless pit of corruption that miraculously swallowed up all foreign aid given to the country since he took power. Shocked by the ferocity and unrestrained brutality unleashed by his regime, some secularized intelligentsia fell into dejected but complacent silence and others tried to exit the country, leaving the regime to its fate. The majority, however, continued to do what they have always done – no matter the level, scale, or degree of the repression, they continued to defend Sisi as an ambassador of peace who was left with no choice but to confront terrorism with decisive and overwhelming power. Not only the world, but also the average Egyptian understood that Sisi compensated for his lack of charisma and modest leadership skills with the infliction of unabashed violence against all those who dared to disagree or dissent. For all the talk about lofty principles, the secularized intelligentsia were at best the apologists for, and at worst the conspirators in, mass human rights violations that rise to the level of crimes against humanity. What perhaps came as a real surprise was that not only did Sisi lack charisma, but he also appeared to be a woefully incompetent ruler whose best moments were still worse than the performance of the elected President Morsi.

The Napoleonic invasion of Egypt in 1798 brought to the region an archetypal repetitive model. Inspired by the lofty ideas of Locke, Montesquieu, and Comte de Mirabeau, Napoleon and his savants made soaring oratory about the rights of man, and liberty, equality, and fraternity. The Napoleonic army and its savants felt that their civilizing mission was their call to destiny and their just cause. Because, in their eyes, their cause was so just and compelling, they reinvented life in Egypt, and invaded Palestine and Syria, all while committing atrocity after atrocity as if this was but a reasonable price to be paid for the sake of civilization and its lofty ideals. The French brutally put down an Azhari insurrection bombarding the Azhar mosque, and executed so many of the rebels to the point that eventually a guillotine was imported from France to dispatch the heads of the condemned more efficiently. Purportedly, the use of a guillotine was against French law, and was also an affront to French sensibilities that associated the hated instrument with the trauma of the Age of Terror in France.[10] The genesis of the grievous plight of the secularized intelligentsia can be traced back to the dynamics that started to take shape after the French occupation of Egypt. An elite group of individuals were so taken by the marvels of French culture, and the discoveries the French savants introduced into Egypt, that they internalized the perspective and outlook of the colonizer. They did so to such an extent that, while thoroughly enthralled

---

[10] Paul Strathern, *Napoleon in Egypt* (New York: Bantam Books, 2007), 385.

by the ideals of the culture of the colonizer, they became desensitized to the sufferings of their own native populations. It was not too long before they saw themselves as the inheritors of the elevated principles of the rights of man charged with the most sacred duty of becoming the guardians of civilization. These early guardians would uphold and protect the truth of civilization until their people matured enough to become worthy of the trust. A couple of centuries later, the guardians of civilization became the secularized intelligentsia of today. The reality is that, instead of being the progressive *avant garde* calling upon the people to change, the secularized intelligentsia has only succeeded in becoming part and parcel of the institutions and instrumentalities of despotism. I strongly suspect that democracy will never find its way to Egypt unless both the secularized intelligentsia and the Islamists recognize that there are invariable constituent elements to all democratic orders: the place of the military is in the barracks; individual rights are inviolable; the process is sacrosanct; and the people are the only true sovereign and the masters of their own destiny.

9

The truncated debate

Egyptian liberals, Islamists, and ideological statism[1]

AHMED ABDEL MEGUID AND DAANISH FARUQI

INTRODUCTION

[when asked what would have transpired had Morsi stayed on to complete his presidency] "They would have controlled the whole country. There would be Brotherhood in the media, Brotherhood in the Ministry of Culture, Brotherhood everywhere!"
– Alaa al-Aswany[2]

"The loss of life is tragic…But I'm sorry to say that the Muslim Brotherhood invited this. They wanted all of the time for this to happen…I don't accept that there are non-extremist elements to the Muslim Brotherhood."
– Mohammad Abol Ghar[3]

---

[1] The authors would like to express their deepest appreciation to Dr. Joel Gordon (University of Arkansas), Dr. William Reddy (Duke University), and Dr. Daniel Tutt (Marymount University) for their insightful commentary and feedback on previous chapter iterations.
[2] Negar Azimi, "The Egyptian army's unlikely allies," *New Yorker*, January 8, 2014, http://www.newyorker.com/news/news-desk/the-egyptian-armys-unlikely-allies
[3] Joshua Hersh, "Portrait of a Cairo liberal as a military backer," *New Yorker*, August 17, 2013, http://www.newyorker.com/news/news-desk/portrait-of-a-cairo-liberal-as-a-military-backer

For whatever the diversity of their political platforms, it would seem that an increasing number of Egyptian liberal figures have begun to define themselves and the worldview they represent precisely by what they oppose. Repeatedly emphasizing the existential threat posed by the Muslim Brotherhood to the future of Egypt, figures like Alaa al-Aswany, Mohammad Abol Ghar, and others have established themselves as operating in binary opposition to their arch nemesis, with the former committed to liberal democratic values and the latter committed to an insidious takeover of Egyptian state and society. Thus, so the argument would go, liberalism is both the binary opposition of and the antidote to the threat of Islamism.

Yet, despite the increasing prominence of this neatly packaged binary, in fact, liberals in Egypt have more commonalities with their Islamist interlocutors than they would willingly acknowledge. In this chapter, we argue that a distinct current of liberal thought in Egypt, despite its claims to be diametrically opposed to the Islamist project, nonetheless coalesces with the Muslim Brotherhood on one fundamental basis: that both streams of thought make the same subliminal assumptions about the role of the *state* in the polities they seek to articulate. Embedded in both the liberal experiment in Egypt alongside the Muslim Brotherhood is a statist mentality that grants absolute power to the sovereign, an essentially Hobbesian conception of the nature and role of the state as the sole and ultimate interpreter and implementer of the Egyptian social contract.

This statist posturing, moreover, is paradoxical on both fronts, insofar as it is at odds with the putative goals articulated both by liberalism and by Islamism in their competing visions for Egyptian political life: an all-encompassing inviolable sovereign state ostensibly compromises the liberal commitment to individual liberties and rational choice, as well as the decentralized model of governance typified of the classical Islamic civilization Muslim Brotherhood figures purport to be upholding. And as we shall demonstrate, the chauvinism and intransigence of the Muslim Brotherhood under its tenure in power in post-revolutionary Egypt, and the similar intransigence of Egyptian liberals in supporting a military-led counterrevolution and the concomitant crackdown on Egyptian civil society – most perniciously the support by many liberals of the mass killings of protesters in Rabaa and al-Nahda squares – cannot be fully understood without paying sufficient attention to how deeply embedded ideological statism is in the intellectual fabric of both groups.

Accordingly, we will begin by sketching a landscape of the genealogical development of Egyptian liberalism, from its auspices in the early twentieth

On the one hand, this trend of Islamic modernism gave rise to Hassan al-Banna (d. 1949), founder of the Muslim Brotherhood, who was deeply influenced by the writings of both Abduh and Rida. But on the other, Islamic modernism also gave rise to the very persuasion of Arab liberalism that is the focus of this study, perhaps best exemplified by the person of Ahmad Lutfi al-Sayyid (d. 1963), the putative founder of Egyptian liberalism proper and himself deeply influenced by the thought of Muhammad Abduh, this strand of liberalism adopted the modernizing agenda of Abduh and his fellow religious reformers, but denuded it of religious predilections as such. Accordingly, Egyptian liberals and their Islamist adversaries in the Muslim Brotherhood – at least in the group's founding figure of Hassan al-Banna – fall on different branches of the same intellectual genealogical tree. Needless to say, most contemporary liberals would be appalled at such an association – and perhaps justifiably so, given that Egyptian liberal thought radically diverges upon its very inception from the religious reform-oriented trend that came to inform al-Banna. But, as we shall see in more detail in the subsequent section, both nonetheless converge in sharing a reconciliatory posturing toward modernity – a posturing that comes to be fundamentally challenged in the person of Sayyid Qutb.

Yet, despite having emerged from the same intellectual pedigree as Islamic modernism, early twentieth-century Egyptian liberals of the persuasion we consider here were cut of a different cloth. Here we refer to literary figures and social critics such as Abbas Mahmud al-Aqqad (d. 1964), Tawfiq al-Hakim (d. 1987), Farah Antoun (d. 1922), Salama Musa (d. 1958), Shibli Shumayal (d. 1917), Muhammad Husayn Haykal (d. 1956), and most famously Ahmad Lutfi al-Sayyid (d. 1963), the *ustadh al-jil*, or teacher of the generation. In contradistinction to their Islamic modernist ancestors who, despite their clear admiration for European material progress, nonetheless committed to modernization through an *immanent* reform of their own religious tradition, figures in this vein instead were wholly committed to European ideals tout court. Many had spent considerable time studying in Europe, and were accordingly deeply versed in the philosophies of Rousseau, Montesquieu, Comte, the Mills, and Bentham, among others. And more interestingly for our purposes, they were also deeply versed in European writings on race and Orientalism by the likes of Ernest Renan, Gustave Le Bon, Hippolyte Taine, and Edmond Demolins. But whereas their intellectual ancestors, for example al-Afghani, went through painstaking efforts to argue against figures like Renan and their claims of the inherent irrationality of the Semitic mind, liberals of this coterie actively embraced such theories. And in so doing, they conceptualized modernist reform in Egypt as a wholly European phenomenon – which in turn necessitated wholly de-linking Egypt from its Arab-Islamic heritage.[5]

It is worth mentioning briefly that this particular strand of Egyptian liberalism was not all encompassing, that there remained Egyptian figures in the early twentieth century who espoused some kind of liberal reform but who nonetheless offered perfunctory concessions to the Egyptian nation's Arab and Islamic heritage – figures such as Qasim Amin (d. 1908), Huda Sha'rawi (d. 1947), Saad Zaghlul (d. 1927), and Tal'at Harb (d. 1941) would qualify. But this study concerns itself more specifically with the cohort of early liberal figures that Abdeslam Maghraoui refers to as "secular modernists," those who, following the lead of their figurehead Ahmad Lutfi al-Sayyid, channeled their liberal reform project into a distinctly Egyptian territorial nationalism that was necessarily disassociated from Egypt's Arab-Islamic heritage. Owing in part to their having adopted the premises of European racist scholarship decrying the inherent limitations of Semites and of Islamic civilization on the one hand, and in part to a desire to disassociate the then nascent movement of Egyptian nationalism from pan-Arab and pan-Islamic currents then extant in Ottoman lands on the other, these secular modernist liberal figures instead articulated an Egyptian nationalism that required reformulating the conception of Egyptian identity and citizenship on wholly new premises. Their antagonism towards religion was thus motivated by this desire to reconstruct Egyptian citizenship on European-inspired auspices – most notably by adopting the topos of Pharaonism as the basis of Egyptian identity, as a means of establishing a concordance between ancient Egypt and its known associations with ancient Greece, thus redefining modern Egypt as an intellectual heir of the West.[6]

More germane for our purposes, though, is how these figures articulated what Maghraoui calls "cultural preconditions of citizenship" into their liberal project. That is, despite the novelty of this European and secular model of citizenship these liberals espoused, their attempts to

---

[5] Abdeslam M. Maghraoui, *Liberalism Without Democracy: Nationhood and Citizenship in Egypt, 1922–1936* (Durham: Duke University Press, 2006), 66–7.
[6] For more on early Egyptian liberal flirtations with Pharaonism as the basis of Egyptian nationalism, see Israel Gershoni and James P. Jankowski, *Egypt, Islam, and the Arabs: The Search for Egyptian Nationhood, 1900–1930* (New York: Oxford University Press, 1986).

rescue an authentic Egyptian identity from the fetters of centuries of Arab and Islamic cultural imperialism did little to change the fact that the overwhelming majority of everyday Egyptians decidedly did not fit congruently with this newly envisioned European-inspired framework; a critical mass of Egyptians remained deeply beholden to Islam as a religious and cultural idiom, and to the Arabic literary and intellectual canon from which it originally was revealed. Yet as deeply elitist figures who viewed the masses as too backward and irrational to fit the proper (European and secular) mold of citizenship, secular liberals saw no need to convincingly demonstrate to the Egyptian masses why they should give up the allegedly incongruent or problematic aspects of their cultural heritage in exchange for this new enlightened conception of citizenship; they simply expected the masses to capitulate to the dictates of their liberal vision.

Indeed, many figures associated with this trend were quite explicit in their elitist paternalism, suggesting that the cultural and intellectual elite alone are capable of guiding the Egyptian nation toward its ultimate actualization.[7] This paternalism goes back to Lutfi al-Sayyid, who concluded, "given the irresponsibility of the common people the rule of the country should remain in the hands of the 'opinion makers' (*ahl al-ra'y*), whom he defined as large landowners or more generally as 'those who have a real stake in society' (*ashab al-masalih al-haqiqiyya*)."[8] Lutfi al-Sayyid's patronizing attitude toward the Egyptian public came to have significant currency in the subsequent generation of thinkers he nurtured, to the extent that this defining generation of Egyptian secular liberals came to endorse a top-down model of reform: emboldened by the European-inspired liberal worldview to which they subscribed, and ultimately enforced by the hands of the state. Maghraoui explains:

> There was thus no need to assess what aspects of native culture and moral values were illiberal or antidemocratic. Liberal advocates had a specific, ready-made, and expansive notion of the common good. But that is not all. They conflated the good with Western rationalism and unambiguously endorsed state intervention to pursue it. European scientific theories, the liberal reformers believed, provided

---

[7] There are some exceptions in this respect, particularly later figures like Taha Husayn and Salama Musa.

[8] Roel Meijer, *The Quest for Modernity: Secular Liberal and Left-Wing Political Thought in Egypt, 1945–1958* (New York: Routledge, 2002), 16.

a way of life different from, and better than, the dominant and irrational popular culture in Egypt.[9]

And herein lies the inherent statism of the Egyptian liberal project. Despite liberalism's doctrinal emphasis on individual freedom and on the protection of those freedoms from the caprices of an excessively invasive state, early twentieth-century secular liberals proved wholly willing to ally with the state apparatus to forcibly inaugurate their vision of cultural citizenship on an otherwise unwilling populace. These were not simply armchair theorists; in their writings – largely in newspaper columns – secular liberals actively endorsed the implementation of their vision of the public good through partnership with the public authorities:

> These were not just so naïve ideas totally removed from policies; liberal reformers called on the public authorities to play a dominant role. The police, schools, prisons, and hospitals were solicited again and again to enforce strict laws against unwelcome practices such as public celebration of saints, improper mourning, traditional attire, and other unhealthy habits.[10]

What is especially interesting is that many of the cultural practices liberals sought to extirpate through state intervention had no obvious relevance to citizenship eligibility as such. Sufi saint festivals (*mawlid*, plural *mawalid*), for instance, as celebrations of communal worship and spirituality, at face value have no bearing on the modern notion of citizenship whatsoever – particularly in light of developments in liberal theory that purport to allow for the toleration of religion, as articulated by figures like Locke and Kant. Yet liberal publications spared no effort to decry these festivals and demand that the state put a stop to them. Perhaps most intriguing of all, while their writings made no attempt to articulate why or how these celebrations compromised the political rights and responsibilities inherent in citizenship as such, liberals couched their admonitions of saint worship in the context of the European image of Egypt, and by extension the new self-image of Egypt they were trying to inculcate:

---

[9] Maghraoui, *Liberalism Without Democracy*, 88–9.
[10] Ibid., 89.

The quarter of Sayyidina al-Hussein and other sections of this district, such as Khan al-Khalili and al-Ghuriyya, are very famous among European tourists, who insist on visiting them. It is dishonorable and disreputable that European visitors see these embarrassing and repugnant sights, which confirm their ideas about Egyptians as a backward and ignorant people.[11]

Ultimately, then, early twentieth-century secular liberal thinkers in Egypt, as the basis of a territorial Egyptian nationalism, demonstrated a desire to cultivate a European-inspired conception of citizenship wholly denuded of Arab-Islamic baggage. But insofar as such a reform project had little purchase with the majority of Egyptians who would ostensibly constitute that political community, its architects were willing to advocate the force of the state to achieve it.

Yet, for all its promises, ultimately this elitist project of early twentieth-century Egyptian liberal nationalism proved unable to deliver on its promises to establish a politically independent and economically viable Egyptian nation-state. As Egyptians grew increasingly disillusioned with the "liberal experiment" in the 1930s, two movements emerged in response. On the one hand, this period witnessed resistance in the form of Islamism, most prominently in the founding of the Muslim Brotherhood in 1928 – about which we will spill considerable ink in the next section. On the other, though, grew a movement seeking to *deepen* the hitherto failed liberal experiment, through the framework of "the secular discourse of *radical* modernism" (emphasis ours), a modernism that differed from its previous incarnation in purporting to offer a more inclusive understanding of Egyptian political community.[12]

Perhaps most emblematic of this new trend of liberal thought was the Society of National Renaissance (Jama'at al-Nahda al-Qawmiyya), a liberal think tank that saw the paternalism of the previous generation of liberal thinkers as an impediment to the bona fide modernization of Egyptian political and social life. Accordingly, they rejected the romanticism of Pharaonism and other elitist forms of liberal nationalism, and maintained that the patronage and paternalism articulated by the previous

---

[11] "Al-Turuq al-Sufiyya: Mukhalafat Rijaluha li al-din, Wajib al-Mashikha wa Wajib al-Hukuma," *Kawkab al-Sharq*, November 6, 1926, I, quoted in Maghraoui, *Liberalism Without Democracy*, 99.

[12] Meijer, *The Quest for Modernity*, 22.

generation of liberals should be replaced with modern administrative institutions "that would establish a direct link between the state and the citizen."[13] By properly incorporating the multitude of social classes into the Egyptian political system, most notably through a more robust parliament based on the constitution of 1923, the Society maintained that Egypt would in turn cultivate a vibrant civil society that would serve as a guarantee of that political system, a bulwark against the power of the state on the one hand, and against the politics of patronage and paternalism on the other – that is, a self-regulating liberal order.

But to actualize such a robust expansion of civil society, this second generation of Egyptian liberals paradoxically had to *control* civil society through administrative and bureaucratic means. Merrit Butrus Ghali, a leading member of the Society, articulates in his seminal text *The Policy of Tomorrow* (published in 1938) that on economic matters he adheres to the nineteenth-century liberal premise that the economy is the purview of civil society, and that state intervention in the economic machine is rarely if ever justified. But he nonetheless assigns a remarkable role to the state in creating the *prerequisites* of that civil society, in cultivating a responsible citizenship that will be able to participate fully in civic and economic life:

> Areas of concern are the "major social and cultural problems, like national education and development of the national spirit, which may actually be even more important and more grave than the former [economic problems], although at times they do not call for attention and press for urgent solutions." Indeed, government officials should "devote themselves to the development of [the] national spirit among the people, which is their task *par excellence.*" Once government reform programs are implemented, the ultimate goal of the liberal reform program will have been fulfilled, and "*every individual would carry out his national obligation willingly without any need for check and control.*"[14]

Thus, through modernist reform, the second generation of Egyptian liberals saw the end result of their social engineering project as a wholly self-regulating balance between government and civil society. In contradistinction to the parochialism of the first generation of liberals, the

---

[13] Ibid., 38.
[14] Ibid., 52–3.

civil society envisioned by this new generation was not limited to the land-owning elite, but was open to the totality of the Egyptian nation – once it had properly imbibed the prerequisite liberal values, or the "national spirit" – that would fully integrate it into civic life. But to cultivate that national character, which would inevitably usher in a self-regulatory liberal society, Egyptian liberals of the 1930s and 40s paradoxically sought intervention from the increasingly powerful state apparatus – much in line with their predecessors in the early twentieth century, as we saw earlier.

This tendency proves especially palpable, moreover, in the context of the Egyptian peasantry. To fully integrate and civilize the country's rural population into participating in modern civil society, liberal reformers endorsed deeply invasive measures in housing and agrarian reform – going so far as proposing bona fide surveillance measures by semi-governmental institutions to ensure that newly reconstructed rural villages adhere to sufficiently modern standards in the most intimate aspects of daily life:

> "The purpose of this surveillance," Butrus Ghali maintains, "is to "promote in them national consciousness and social responsibility." Thus, the Institute's job is not finished with completion of the construction of the village. Its duties include the general supervision of domestic and social life in the villages; it would also be "concerned with the village house furniture and equipment and would assist villagers in obtaining them."[15]

Thus, despite the evolution of liberal thought in its move away from paternalism and toward a more unadulterated form of modernism, which once properly cemented would be inclusive of the totality of the Egyptian nation – including the peasantry – we nonetheless see consistency in liberal commitment to ideological statism.

This paradoxical reliance on state power to enforce a liberal project became even more palpable by the late 1940s, as liberals grew increasingly disillusioned with the existing political structure's capacity to implement reforms. Unable to secure purchase for their project from the large landowners and industrialists who continued to dominate the existing parliamentary system, liberals became increasingly desperate. The election of the Wafd Party in January 1950, and its concomitant refusal to implement key liberal reforms or scale back the powers of the monarchy

---

[15] Ibid., 55.

in favor of parliament – culminating in the 1952 burning of Cairo, the dismissal of the Wafd Party, and the return of martial law – was the last straw. Reflective of Egyptian political activism writ large during this impasse, which had by this point utterly lost faith in party politics, liberals in Egypt – as represented in this phase not only by the Society of National Renaissance, but also by leading liberal journalists of major newspapers and magazines like *Ruz al-Yusuf*, many of whose editors were originally trained at the Society's monthly *al-Fusul* – saw no options left to pursue their project through the traditional political channels.

Accordingly, liberal figures increasingly welcomed the idea of a left-wing reformist dictatorship, or a "just tyrant" (*al-musta'bid al-'adil*) to emerge and *create* the conditions for a liberal civil society, purge the existing political order of its corruption and patronage networks, and to then forcibly inaugurate the modernist reforms they sought. Consequently, Ihsan Abd al-Quddus, then editor-in-chief of *Ruz al-Yusuf*, could write in February 1952 that "Egypt is in temporary need of a dictator," one who will act "for the people, not against them, for and not against freedom; a dictator who will push Egypt forward and not hold her back."[16] Yet liberals endorsed the rise of a reformist dictatorship with reservations, recognizing the distinct possibility that such a dictatorship could prove uncontrollable. Accordingly, they maintained, "it would have to be a temporary regime that imposed reforms from above, to eliminate the 'grand families' (*buyutat*). Afterwards, this regime would have to step back, leaving a modernized country with a truly democratic, rationalist, political system."[17]

With the Free Officers Movement, it seems that liberals had their wish only partially fulfilled – their coveted dictatorship had arrived, but it proved anything but temporary. In response, in the early years of the revolution, most liberals did advocate that the military step aside and take on a civilian role by forming a political party and participating in free elections.[18] But by the March Crisis of 1954, a critical mass of liberal intellectuals were ultimately domesticated by the order, under the aegis of what Roel Meijer calls "authoritarian modernism." Which is to say, Nasser's radical nationalist overtures aimed toward social and economic development of Egypt into an independent and modern nation-state,

---

[16] *Ruz al-Yusuf*, February 11, 1952, p. 3, quoted in Joel Gordon, *Nasser's Blessed Movement: Egypt's Free Officers and the July Revolution* (New York: Oxford University Press, 1992), 33.
[17] Meijer, *The Quest for Modernity*, 145.
[18] Ibid., 156.

through meticulous technocratic state planning and industrialization, had considerable valence with Egyptian liberal intellectuals. Consequently, figures like Ihsan Abd al-Quddus, who by late 1952 was clamoring for a swift return to parliamentary politics,[19] are by 1955 and 1956 increasingly enthusiastic about Nasser's drive for industrialization, and in turn publish considerably in support of the regime's policies.[20] Democratic discourse is accordingly supplanted by calls for a "guided democracy," in which parliamentary politics are subjected to the rules of authoritarian modernism, dictated by technocratic arguments predicated on efficiency and authoritarian organization in support of modernization. Party politics is judged under these auspices not on whether it emboldens the self-regulatory civil society that liberals originally conceived, but on whether it supports the revolution and its modernist principles.[21]

Yet the reorientation of these liberal figures into Nasser's authoritarian apparatus is not entirely an about face; liberal intellectuals' embrace of Nasser's authoritarian modernism is wholly consistent not only with the modernist ethos that underpinned their project at its outset, but also with the commitment to ideological statism that they inherited from their intellectual predecessors of the early twentieth century. Thus, we see somewhat of a continuum in this particular strand of Egyptian liberal thought, whereby liberals in this vein, unable to garner popular support for a very elitist project of a renewed Egyptian consciousness – in the latter case through the topos of modernism – prove willing to ally with an all-powerful state to enforce it. Support by contemporary Egyptian liberals for the overthrow of Muslim Brotherhood-affiliated President Mohammad Morsi by the military establishment and the concomitant return to authoritarianism under Sisi – particularly given the inability of liberals to make meaningful gains in the electoral process, intimating precisely the lack of popular support that characterized earlier generations of liberal reforms – can thus be read as part of this continuum of liberal statism.

To be clear, though, the genealogy we describe here is *not* a linear or uninterrupted continuum, nor is it emblematic of Egyptian liberalism in its totality. As mentioned previously, this particular strand of deeply secular liberalism emerged in the early twentieth century alongside competing denominations of liberalism, those that either explicitly sought liberal

---

[19] Ibid., 153.
[20] Ibid., 186–7.
[21] Ibid., 213–14.

reform through the prism of Islamic thought (figures like Muhammad Abduh would qualify), or at the least offered some basic courtesy to the Islamic tradition (like Qasim Amin and others). Moreover, the category of "secular modernism," as articulated by Abdeslam Maghraoui to refer to the trend of liberalism we analyze here, does not offer us rigid and clear-cut distinctions between other trends in Egyptian liberalism. Indeed, these categories can occasionally prove porous and overlap with one another. Two examples prove especially illuminating in this respect. First, several major figures we otherwise associate here with "secular modernism" by the 1930s came to incorporate Islamic themes (*Islamiyyat*) into their work – most notably Muhammad Husayn Haykal, who eventually produced a series of works on Islamic history that seemed to glorify a Muslim past. On the one hand, this turn towards *Islamiyyat* in the 1930s gave rise to a thesis popularized by western Orientalists as a "Crisis of Orientation," whereby secular liberalism was being increasingly supplanted by reactionary religious impulses.[22] On the other hand, that thesis was ultimately rejected by subsequent generations of scholars, who instead read Haykal and others in this vein as using religious motifs and history in order to advance liberalism to the Egyptian masses.[23] While this does not wholly detract from the elitist proclivities of the secular modernist strand of liberalism discussed above, it does suggest that some figures representative of that trend did ultimately come to demonstrate *some* willingness to make their otherwise European-inspired political project more accessible and digestible to an Egyptian public. Second, for all their commitment to authoritarian modernism come the Nasser era, Egyptian liberals of the trend we consider here steadfastly rejected the doctrines of fascism and Nazism, and by extension the challenge such ideological forces posed to liberalism. Irrespective of their modernist blind spots, Egyptian liberals overwhelmingly opposed the allure of the equally technocratic and deeply reactionary form of modernism emblematic of the Third Reich.[24]

All of this is to say, we must recognize that the continuum we describe here within the secular modernist strand of Egyptian liberalism is not a

---

[22] See in particular Nadav Safran, *Egypt in Search of Political Community: An Analysis of the Intellectual and Political Evolution of Egypt, 1804–1952* (Cambridge, MA: Harvard University Press, 1961).

[23] See, for instance, Charles D. Smith, *Islam and the Search for Social Order in Modern Egypt: A Biography of Muhammad Husayn Haykal* (Albany, NY: SUNY Press, 1983).

[24] See in particular Israel Gershoni and James Jankowski, *Confronting Fascism in Egypt: Dictatorship versus Democracy in the 1930s* (Stanford, CA: Stanford University Press, 2009).

perfect one; exceptions have presented, and will continue to present, themselves, be it with respect to the tradition's commitment to secularism, or to authoritarian modernism. But even taking into account the exceptions of this clearly imperfect continuum, we nonetheless clearly see a statist ethos permeating this denomination of Egyptian liberalism. And in this sense, as we shall see in the next section, liberals have far more in common with their erstwhile Islamist enemies than they are willing to admit.

ISLAMISTS AND THE STATE: THE MODERNIST PARADOX

Islamists have tended to have an ambivalent attitude toward the idea of the modern state as the form proper of the body politic, and Islamist ideologues in Egypt are no exception. In this section, we will explicate further this complicated relationship between the Egyptian Muslim Brotherhood and the modern state, through the work of two of its most prominent figures: its founder Hassan al-Banna, on the one hand, and Sayyid Qutb (d. 1966), perhaps the most controversial theorist the movement has produced to date, on the other. By juxtaposing these two thinkers, in the first part of this section we will highlight a subtle yet critically important shift in the Brotherhood's attitude toward the concept of the state. Namely, the movement's relationship with the state is inextricably tied to its ambivalent intellectual and moral attitude toward Western modernity – an attitude that vacillates from willful embrace to a paradoxically incomplete repudiation. This problematic tension of the Brotherhood's relationship with modernity, moreover, in turn, gives rise to an equally problematic tension in its conception of and engagement with the state as constitutive of the Egyptian body politic. And it is only through this tension that we can make full sense of the Brotherhood's political comportment in the January 2011 revolution and the events that followed, as we articulate in the second section.

Islam and the question of modernity between Hassan al-Banna and Sayyid Qutb

Reading Hassan al-Banna's treatises one cannot miss their distinctly modernist tone. Following in the footsteps of his predecessors, Jamal al-Din al-Afghani, Muhammad Abduh, and Rashid Rida, al-Banna puts forward a vision for a social order and ideal governance that is rooted in the firm conviction that Islam is wholly compatible with the use of reason and science.[25] However, unlike Abduh and al-Afghani, al-Banna is not concerned with developing a new Islamic epistemology per se, whether by resorting to classical Islamic philosophy as in the case of the former or, as in the case of the latter, by calling for a quasi-Averroist engagement with the revelation privileging a rationally apodictic interpretation of religious rulings over purely literal ones.[26] Rather, al-Banna was specifically interested in fulfilling the dream originally articulated by his mentor Rashid Rida, of cultivating an Islamic legal and political theory that would be consistent with the demands of popular sovereignty characteristic of constitutionalism and the modern nation-state.[27] And most germane for our purposes, in the wake of this attempt, al-Banna assigns a considerable role to the state in securing the discursive and non-discursive conditions that would allow for a modern Islamic society to come to fruition.

In his treatise *Toward the Light*, after having emphasized the need for Islam as a guiding societal framework, given the moral incoherence of Western ideologies and philosophies, al-Banna moves on to offer specific policy recommendations to the then Egyptian monarch King Faruq. In the spirit of the tradition of advice-to-kings literature (*nasa'ih al-muluk*) prominent in medieval Islamic thought, al-Banna devotes a considerable section to practical steps for reform, giving the following admonitions on political, judicial, and administrative matters:

> ...An end to the party rivalry, and a channeling of the political forces of the nation into a common front and single phalanx... The diffusion of the Islamic spirit throughout all departments of the government, so that all its employees will feel responsible for adhering to Islamic teachings...The surveillance of the personal

---

[25] See John Esposito, *Islam and Politics* (New York: Syracuse University Press, 1991), 33–59. See also Hourani, *Arabic Thought in the Liberal Age*, 103–92; and Muhammad Qasim Zaman and Roxanne Euben, *Texts and Contexts from al-Banna to Bin Laden* (Princeton: Princeton University Press, 2009), 1–49.

[26] See Muhammad 'Imara, *Jamal al-Din al-Afghani Muqiz al-Sharq wa al-Gharb* (Cairo: Dar al-Shorouq, 1988), 265–80.

[27] See Muhammad Rashid Rida, *Al-Khilafa* (Cairo: Dar al-Nashr Liljami'at, 2013).

conduct of all its employees and an end to the dichotomy between the private and professional sphere...[28]

Similarly, on social and educational matters, as al-Banna categorizes them, he gives another set of prescriptions to the Egyptian monarch:

...Conditioning the people to respect public morality and the issuance of directives fortified by the aegis of the law on this subject; the imposition of severe penalties for moral offenses...The surveillance of theaters and cinemas and rigorous selections of plays and films... The expurgation of songs and a rigorous selection and censorship of them...The regulation of business hours for cafes; surveillance of the activities of their regular clients; instructing these as to what is in their best interest; withdrawal of permission from cafes to keep such long hours...Properly selecting whatever is being presented to the public whether songs, public lectures or general issues and using radio and television broadcasting in edifying the citizens patriotically and ethically...resisting bad habits whether economic or ethical and steering the public away from them like the habits associated with weddings, funerals, celebrations of the birth of religious figures, celebrating feasts, religious ritualistic ceremonies. The government should lead by example in properly straightening these bad habits...Consideration of ways to arrive gradually at a uniform mode of dress for the nation...[29]

There is an obvious Jacobin rationale governing al-Banna's thinking. He assigns the sovereign power the right to monitor almost every aspect of the private life of the individual. From his perspective, securing this role will guarantee that society will ultimately develop to the extent that it will be prepared to fully accept the return of Islam as the ultimate legal and moral referent governing Egyptian society. Thus, in al-Banna's vision the state plays a fundamental role in forging the moral sentiments, social objectives, and political vision of a proper Islamic society. This Hobbesian conception of an all-encompassing Leviathan state, moreover, is in full

---

[28] See Hasan al-Banna, "Toward The Light," in *Princeton Readings in Islamist Thought: Texts and Contexts from al-Banna to Bin Laden,* ed. Roxanne Euben and Muhammad Qasim Zaman (Princeton: Princeton University Press, 2009), 74.
[29] Ibid., 75–7.

accord not only with the colonial administration governing Egypt at the time, but also with the strands of Egyptian liberalism analyzed previously. Regarding the former, the British administration maintained a totalitarian form of rule over its colonial holding that granted it full bio-political governmentality, in Foucauldian terms.[30] And regarding the latter, as the previous section demonstrated, secular modernist currents in Egyptian liberal discourse gave rise to this same Leviathan by granting the state full sovereignty to forcibly eradicate allegedly problematic or offensive social and cultural practices in the name of cultivating the preconditions for proper liberal citizenship – despite those practices bearing no immediate relevance to citizenship as such, and despite this all-encompassing statist posturing being a fundamental contradiction of the basic assumptions of liberal theory about individuality and the protection of private life.

And just as this Hobbesian Leviathan proves contradictory from the liberal framework, it also radically contrasts with the classical view of Islamic governance in medieval and early modern Muslim societies. In this milieu, governmentality was primarily the purview of scholars – be it jurists, Sufi masters, or theologians – operating independently of the state.[31] Such independence from the fetters of the state apparatus, economically secured through the Islamic system of endowments (*awqaf*), afforded the cultivation and protection of a robust pluralism in Muslim legal and theological schools. This intellectual pluralism, argued medieval Muslim polymaths Averroes (d. 1198)[32] and al-Juwayni (d. 1085)[33] before him, accommodated the several different and often competing orientations of the members of the body politic and should thus be solemnly protected by the sovereign. Departing from this paradigm, al-Banna wanted the

[30] See Chapter 4 in Timothy Mitchell, *Colonizing Egypt* (New York: Cambridge University Press, 1988), 95–128. See Janice Bodey, "Purity and Conquest in Anglo-Egyptian Sudan," in *Dirt, Undress and Difference: Critical Perspectives on the Body's Surface*, ed. Adeline Masquelier (Bloomington: Indiana University Press, 2005). See also Chapter 7, "Reconfigurations of Law and Ethics in Colonial Egypt," in *Formations of the Secular: Christianity, Islam, Modernity*, ed. Talal Asad (Stanford: Stanford University, Press, 2003), 205–57; and Wilson C. Jacob, *Working Out Egypt: Effendi Masculinity and Subject Formation in Colonial Modernity (1870–1940)* (Duke: Duke University Press, 2011).
[31] See Wael Hallaq, *Introduction to Islamic Law* (New York: Cambridge University Press, 2009), Chapters 1–3.
[32] See Averroes, *The Decisive Treatise* (trans. Charles Butterworth) (Provo: Brigham Young University Press, 2001), 8–22.
[33] See Al-Juwayni, *Ghiyath al-Umam fi Iltiyath al-zulam* (Jeddah: Dar al-Minhaj, 2009), 160–203.

modernist state to be the tool for restoring the Islamic body politic, and the embodiment of the project of Islamic modernism envisioned by his intellectual ancestors Abduh and Afghani. And in so doing, al-Banna eschews the classical legacy of intellectual pluralism by offering the sovereign hitherto unimaginable authority over the public and private lives of subjects of his modernist Islamic state – which would necessarily render pluralism in the classical sense an impossibility. To put it more explicitly, the attempt of Hassan al-Banna to undertake a modernist reformation of Islam from a political perspective led him to embrace the modernist advocacy of the absolute power of the sovereign at the heart of the modern theory of the state, from Hobbes and Spinoza down to Hegel. In other words, al-Banna's interest in a modernist reconstruing of the role of the sovereign in order to construct an Islamic state was a reason for him to compromise the pluralism at the heart of the classical Muslim body politic. Al-Banna's line of thinking in this respect, moreover, comes to fruition when it is taken up by his successors, namely Sayyid Qutb. And Qutb's subtle reorientation of the question of the state becomes pivotal to the future reorientation of the Muslim Brotherhood project. It is to his work that we shall now turn.

In engaging Qutb's writings directly, we will also be reading Qutb in close conversation with Roxanne Euben, whose work has done much to inform scholarly reception on Qutb's thought and intellectual genealogy. This intellectual genealogy is crucial, moreover, in making sense of Qutb's understanding of the state. In *Enemy in the Mirror*, Euben argues that Qutb maintained a certain ambivalence towards the state.[34] Qutb took what Euben considered an anti-hermeneutical position, one in which he outright "[denies] that his own interpretation of Islam is an act of interpretation."[35] Instead, Islam for Qutb is a religious doctrine that is necessarily oriented to praxis, and thus may not be reduced to armchair theorizing; intellectualizing Islam in this respect then would be to engage in "a kind of scholastic sophistry" that would necessarily "rend the essential connection between Islam and action."[36]

Accordingly, Qutb rejects any speculation on the theoretical level about the nature of the Islamic state, its relation to the body politic, or how it will reflect a vision of the relation between the private and

---

34 Ibid., 73–88.
35 Ibid., 87.
36 Ibid., 78.

the public spheres. Similarly, he rejects any practical speculation about the institutions or methods of governance to be adopted by this state. Instead, Qutb contends that the general maxims of Shari'ah, such as the maintenance of social justice and fair distribution of wealth, suffice as guidelines for governance in any historical context. Islam should thus be understood as "an unchanging worldview that allows for variation in application depending on circumstances and needs," variation which precludes a specific blueprint of an Islamic state; "[t]here are no specifics to address, Qutb insists, because Islam is not theory, but practice."[37] That unchanging worldview, moreover, provides a trans-historical moral unity for human endeavors that the rationally based modern sciences cannot furnish. Thus Euben writes:

> ...all human knowledge...is by definition incomplete and fragmentary, a distortion of nature. Indeed, Qutb implicitly suggests that without the possibility of unitary knowledge – and in particular acknowledgment of a moral unity in terms of which we can organize human life – humanity is cut adrift, doomed to a knowledge that is purely positivistic and instrumental.[38]

Yet paradoxically, Qutb seems to be simultaneously maintaining a position similar to that of the early modernist Islamists and that of al-Banna, in arguing that establishing an Islamic state is the realization of the most important tenet of Islam, namely the sovereignty (hakimiyya) of God.[39] In this respect, Qutb writes:

> ...the divine character [of the Islamic system of governance] is achieved in Islam through monotheism manifested in attributed sovereignty to God. This is an essential part of Islamic monotheism. The Islamic system is singled out by this divine nature among other systems known by mankind, including the theocratic model. In the latter the ruler derives his authority from either clergy or from his divine right, as much as he is the vicegerent of God on earth. But the divine nature of Islamic governance has to do with the nature of the system itself, not the ruler or his authority. The ruler in Islam

---

[37] Ibid., 77.
[38] Ibid., 72.
[39] See Sayyid Qutb, Al-Mustaqbal li-hadha al-Din (Cairo: Dar al-Shorouq, 1993), 5–23.

does not derive his authority from the clergy or claim it by divine right. Rather he derives it from the free oath of allegiance pledged to him by his people. Similarly, he lays claim to the obedience of the people inasmuch as he applies God's Shari'ah.[40]

The realization of God's sovereignty, Qutb argues, is indeed the most important aim of any Muslim, let alone the hope of humanity for salvation from the moral decadence of modernity.[41] That said, even as Qutb leaves the contours of the Islamic system of governance upon which divine sovereignty would rest nebulously defined, several themes interspersed throughout his works allow us to speculate on the features of Qutb's Islamic state. For all his disdain for modern rationalism, his state would be committed to modern technology and scientific advancement, as well as to social justice and the eradication of poverty. Accordingly, Qutb's Islamic state is ultimately a *modern* state: "These speculative conclusions indicate that Qutb's Islamic state would not represent an attempt to recreate the structure and organization of seventh-century Mecca. On the contrary, they point to an embrace of many of the social and economic processes commonly associated with 'modernization' as defined by social science."[42] Thus, Qutb's thought reflects an ambivalent attitude toward modernity, which simultaneously offers a seeming endorsement of al-Banna's statist thesis, alongside a wholly contradictory aversion to modern rationalism.

In light of this ambivalence, Euben arrives at the conclusion that Qutb's anti-rational and anti-hermeneutical position gives rise to his constructing an alternative modernity rather than rejecting modernity altogether.

It is perhaps more illuminating to characterize Qutb's work as an embrace of the non-rational, that is, an argument for the authority of knowledge that is by definition beyond human reason... Understood in this way, in Qutb's work we are witnessing not anti-modernism but rather another perspective on and attempt to redefine what it must mean to live in the modern world, a

---

[40] See Sayyid Qutb, *Nahw Mujtama' Islami* (Cairo: Dar al-Shorouq, 1993), 152.
[41] See Qutb, *Al-Mustaqbal li-hadha al-Din*, 43–96.
[42] Roxanne Euben, *Enemy in the Mirror*, 83.

perspective that challenges the so called imperatives of modern rationalism in the name of other possible modernities.[43]

While Euben's point is convincing, we would like to highlight another possible interpretation of Qutb's ambivalent attitude toward the state and its modern genealogy. That is to say, as Euben astutely articulates, Qutb's hesitance toward the role of the state indicates a certain disenchantment with modernity. Euben diagnoses this disenchantment as a parting of ways with al-Banna and other modernist Islamists. What we would like to argue instead is that Qutb's position is a reflection of the broader failure of the metaphysical foundations undergirding the modern nation-state, a malaise that permeated the 1950s and 60s with the general aura of disenchantment with modernity and modern forms of metaphysics in the aftermath of World War II. There are many examples of this genre of thought but chief among them include Emmanuel Levinas's *Totality and Infinity*, and Hannah Arendt's *The Origins of Totalitarianism*. Qutb's work, having been produced under the yoke of Nasser's deeply authoritarian yet "modernist" police state, reflected that same disillusionment. If Qutb's ideas are read in the context of this era of disenchantment with modernity, we can shed new light on his call for a discourse that replaces the reconciliatory attempts of early modernist Islamists who, under the spells both of colonialism and of nineteenth-century scientism ardently sought to demonstrate the roots of rationalism as most palpably manifested in Islamic thought.

This discourse, moreover, would also be a rejoinder to Egyptian liberals who, despite their antagonistic relationship to religion and to Islamists, were responding to the same environment of scientism and social Darwinism – as evidenced by their embrace of Ernest Renan and other European Orientalists, as we saw in the previous section – and were thus part of the same reconciliatory project. Their reconciliatory approach differed only insofar as they excised Islam as the operational discourse from which to inaugurate a rational order, but were ultimately aspiring for the same reconciliation with modernity in Egypt. Thus, in his project Qutb rejects the posturing of both his Islamist genealogical ancestors *and* the secular liberals.

In contradistinction to his genealogical ancestors like al-Banna, Qutb reflected a more mature realization of the failures and limitations of the

---

[43] Ibid., 86–7.

modernist project. His antagonism towards Nasser's nationalism was an antagonism toward a self-defeated attempt by a Muslim state to revive an already thoroughly problematized modernist project that was (in his eyes) radically opposed to Islam, and by extension to Islam's inherent capacity to overcome the impasses produced by modernity. Though to be clear, that does not mean that Qutb's critique was simply an Islamized form of the postmodernist critique of rationalism. After all, postmodernism was a distinctly Western reaction to the failure of Western modernity. Qutb, by contrast, was interested in a *rational* displacement of the modernist project, which for him was inherently tied to colonialism and thus was inimical to liberty and individual freedom. This is rather evident in his critique of both liberal rationalism, and of Marxism and the historical materialism undergirding it, both of which he saw as obverses of the same phenomenon.[44] Qutb's modernist discourse is an expression of a strategic realism that echoes the realism and to some extent the pragmatism of al-Banna.[45] It is a method that accepts reality as it is, and then responds by radically transforming it.

However, the intellectual stagnation that plagued the Muslim Brotherhood and other Islamist movements since the late 1960s precluded any attempt at using Qutb's critique of modernity as a basis for a fully fledged Islamic political theory. Moreover, Qutb's own rather limited knowledge of the history and development of modernity on its philosophical and historical levels, to say nothing of his ultimately superficial understanding of the classical Islamic sciences, made his project especially inaccessible for future generations. What survived of Qutb was the radical tone that pervaded his rejection of Nasser's nationalistic modernism. Such radicalism ultimately left the Muslim Brotherhood with an ambivalent re-espousal of al-Banna's statist project, alongside the deep aversion toward modernity that they inherited from Qutb. While this aversion did not manifest itself violently in the discourse and practice of the Muslim Brotherhood itself, it definitely did so in the Jihadist movements that dogmatically adopted his thought. Furthermore, this ambivalent intellectual inheritance ultimately manifested itself clearly in the Brotherhood's handling (and mishandling) of the January 25

---

[44] See Sayyid Qutb, *Ma'rakit al-Islam wa al-Ra'smaliyya* (Cairo: Dar al-Shorouq: 1993), 36–62, 109–12.

[45] For more on pragmatism in al-Banna, see his epistle "Are We Practical People?" (*hal nahnu qawmun 'amaliyyun*), in *Majmu'at rasa'il al-Imam al-Banna* (Cairo: Dar al-Tawzi' wa-al-Nashr al-Islamiyah, 2006), 77–118.

revolution and the events that followed, most notably in its brief period of stewardship of the presidency under Mohammad Morsi. It is to this period that we shall now turn.

Egypt's revolution and the paradoxical heritage of al-Banna and Qutb

Following an era of brutal persecution under Nasser, the Muslim Brotherhood shifted gears to engage in strategic politics during the reigns of Sadat and Mubarak. In her important study *The Muslim Brotherhood: Evolution of an Islamist Movement*, Carrie Wickham characterizes this era of political pragmatism, which spanned around forty years between 1970 and 2011, primarily in terms of a series of tensions. The most salient of these tensions is that between self-assertion and self-restraint.[46] Wickham writes:

The arc of the Brotherhood's strategy during this period can be likened to the swing of a pendulum, seesawing between moments of self-assertion and moments of self-restraint. Moreover, the Brotherhood's trajectory did not trace a linear path toward greater integration into the political system. Instead it took the form of a sequence of fits and starts, its leaders continually recalibrating the terms of their engagement in an effort to expand their influence without jeopardizing the group's survival. More specifically, the Brotherhood's trajectory in the decade before the uprising arguably encompassed three distinct phases: (1) an initial period of guardedness in which the group attempted to recover from the repressive measures taken against it in the mid-to late 1990s (2000–2003); (2) a period of bolder self-assertion against the backdrop of a short-lived political opening (2004–5); and (3) a reversion to self-restraint following the onset of a new wave of repression (2005–10). Yet we can also discern a wider pattern in which a combination of external pressure and internal group dynamics worked to limit the pace and scope of "auto-reform."[47]

---

[46] See Carrie Rosefsky Wickham, *The Muslim Brotherhood: Evolution of an Islamist Movement* (Princeton: Princeton University Press, 2015), 97–119.
[47] Ibid., 96.

On the one hand, the Brotherhood sought to assure both the regime and secular forces within Egyptian society that it does not seek a monopoly of power. But on the other, it was keen to assert the power it had legitimately commanded as the most organized political movement in Egypt. We would like to contextualize this tension in light of the troubled heritages of al-Banna and Qutb articulated earlier.

In the wake of the January 25, 2011 revolution, this tension between self-assertion and self-restraint palpably characterized Brotherhood decisions and general policy. While Brotherhood youth and especially young women actively participated in the revolution from its outset, its leadership publicly announced taking part in the uprising only after being fully convinced that abstention is no longer viable from a pragmatic standpoint. In the two years that followed the ouster of deposed President Hosni Mubarak on February 11, 2011, this pragmatic attitude continued to be the hallmark of the Brotherhood politics, owing in large part to mounting pressure as it endeavored to establish an equilibrium between political ascendancy and (at the very least portending) political pluralism. On the one hand, as the biggest political organization in the country, the Brotherhood was forced to carefully manage the conflict with the deep state that had been governing Egypt for more than half a century, represented during this period by the Supreme Council of Armed Forces (SCAF). On the other hand, the Brotherhood needed to secure buy-in from other political players, reiterate their respect for pluralism, and eschew any pretensions to seeking to monopolize political power. [48]

This vacillation between self-assertion and self-restraint persisted, moreover, even after Morsi's ascent to power in June 2012. Despite having exercised firm political resolve to issue important rulings during his tenure – like his decision to order the retirement of both SCAF chairman Mohammad Hussein Tantawi and deputy chairman Sami Anan – Morsi was nonetheless continuously forced to capitulate to increasing pressures from the Egyptian deep state, and from secular political parties in the country. A key example of Morsi's capitulation in this respect was his eventual decision to backtrack on his own July 8, 2012 edict reinstating the hitherto dissolved (majority Islamist) parliament, in response to threats by the Supreme Constitutional Court (SCC) and SCAF.

Indeed, this impasse was emblematic of a greater refusal by the Egyptian deep state to fully transfer executive authority to the newly

---

[48] Ibid., 248–57.

elected president, most notably through an abrupt constitutional sup-plement announced by SCAF on June 17 – the second day of the presi-dential runoff – that, anticipating a Morsi victory, stripped the president of his authorities over matters of national defense and security, keeping those privileges under the purview of SCAF until the drafting of a new constitution. These sanctions on Morsi were backed, moreover, by mounting objections from secular political forces, who represent the core of the Egyptian economic and social elite.[49] Faced with pressures from at least three different political forces even before he formally assumed the presidency, Morsi was under considerable pressure to appeal to a broader constituency in Egyptian society, while at the same time being careful not to appear insufficiently committed to its Islamist base. Or, put another way, "[t]o win over its opponents without losing its supporters, the Brotherhood will need to walk a fine line, affirming its fidelity to the Islamic cause while honoring the democratic and inclusive spirit of the uprising that brought it to power."[50]

But did it succeed in doing so? Wickham ends her analysis by empha-sizing the Brotherhood's ambivalence, if not outright failure, to prop-erly respond to pressures for democratization. According to Wickham, despite making statements portending political and social inclusivity, the Brotherhood did not clearly and transparently articulate its stance toward the application of Shari'ah as it pertains to religious minorities.[51] Similarly, for whatever attempts Morsi made to assure women he had no intention of denying their rights, feminist activists grew increasingly concerned about women's rights and political representation under his tenure, particularly in light of a series of public statements by Morsi suggesting that men and women already have legal equality in Egypt, and that no additional reforms are necessary because laws protecting women's welfare are already in place.[52]

To further problematize the Brotherhood's internal contradictions, Wickham moves on to put the Brotherhood in conversation with more successful global Islamist currents. More specifically, she compares the failure of the Brotherhood to the relative gains made by other Islamist movements in Jordan, Morocco and Kuwait, emphasizing that these

---

[49] Ibid., 260–72.
[50] Ibid., 271.
[51] Ibid., 280–1.
[52] Ibid., 260.

groups succeeded in large part by successfully reconciling their Islamic values and conceptual orientation with the specific contours of the *modernist* state project in which they were operating.[53] The Brotherhood, by contrast, was not nearly as successful in reconciling that tension with the modern state. Thus, the Brotherhood's vacillation between self-assertion and self-restraint, as explicated by Wickham, can be better understood as symptomatic of its ambivalent relationship toward modernity in general, and to the state as a modern concept in particular – an ambivalence rooted in the tension produced by the overlapping projects of Hassan al-Banna and Sayyid Qutb.

Moreover, in addition to the practical tension Wickham articulates, Ashraf El-Sherif offers an additional major problematic that led to the downfall of the Muslim Brotherhood in Egypt – one that, we submit, is similarly a product of the movement's deeper epistemological ambivalence toward modernity.[54] Writing for the Carnegie Endowment as part of a series on political Islam in Egypt, El-Sherif attempts to diagnose what led to the Brotherhood's untimely demise only a year after it assumed the presidency. More specifically, El-Sherif argues that the Brotherhood's failure, even in the context of a hostile political environment, was primarily due to its own centralized authoritarian power structure, and its lack of any substantive democratic culture at an organizational level. El-Sherif ascribes this deficit in large part to what he characterizes as ideological hollowness, whereby the Brotherhood's emphasis on cultivating an enormous popular following – most notably through its famous charity networks – came at the expense of properly cultivating a clearly articulated ideological architecture for its broader "Islamic project." The nebulously defined ideology was helpful in allowing the Brotherhood to mobilize across wide segments of the Egyptian population that could have otherwise been alienated by excessively dogmatic positions, but it also prevented it from formulating meaningful ideologically grounded answers to the most fundamental questions plaguing Egyptian politics, like the relationship between Islam and democracy, pluralism, and civil society. These ideological deficiencies, El-Sherif continues, are emblematic of the Brotherhood's contradictory understanding of its own Islamic project:

---

[53] Ibid., 196–246.
[54] Ashraf El-Sherif, "The Egyptian Muslim Brotherhood's failures," Carnegie Endowment for International Peace, July 1, 2014, http://carnegieendowment.org/2014/07/01/egyptian-muslim-brotherhood-s-failure/i2bl

At the root of these deficiencies was the puritanical dream of an "Islamic state" that would resuscitate the Islamic caliphate and lead members of the Brotherhood toward the realization of their Islamic identity, salvation, and empowerment. In reality, however, the Brotherhood's concept of an Islamic state owes more to modernist ideas of a strong, authoritarian developmental state than to classical Islamic political thought. The concept of the Islamic state as the organizational embodiment of the Islamic order in the Brotherhood's doctrine is actually quite different from the concept of government in Islamic law. Historically, Islamic government was checked by other nonstate actors and enjoyed much less disciplinary and regulatory power over the population than the modern state does.

The Brotherhood understood the concept of Islamic identity in two parallel but contradictory ways: first, as an immobile set of religious attributes and cultural characteristics that the Islamic state needed to guard; and second, as a living set of political, social, economic, and cultural paradigms yet to be realized by the Islamic state. The two understandings were incongruous, but both implied that the Islamic state was the true representative of Islamic identity and therefore had a vital role to play in the defense and designation of that identity.[55]

According to El-Sherif there is an inherent paradox in how the Muslim Brotherhood conceptualizes its own project; beholden to the idea of an Islamic state, itself informed in large part by a romantic desire to restore Islam as the basis of political life, yet at the same time equally beholden to wholly modernist ideas that underpin this state. The Muslim Brotherhood's failure on the one hand to clearly articulate an interest in democratization, as manifested in its vacillation between self-assertion and self-restraint, and its similar failure on the other to adjust its politics and rhetoric to accommodate the new realities of post-revolutionary Egypt is inextricably connected to the paradox El-Sherif articulates.

Ultimately, though, this intellectual paradox, like the practical tension between self-restraint and self-assertion, is rooted in a deeper one: it is grounded in the historical tension between al-Banna's project of harmonizing Islam with modernity on the one hand, and the radical critique of

---

[55] Ibid.

modernity by Qutb on the other. The Muslim Brotherhood has proven guilty of many breathtaking failures during its history – particularly since 2011 – but perhaps its worst failure of all has been its inability to capitalize fully on either al-Banna's project or Qutb's project with any serious intellectual rigor. On the one hand, no real attempt was made to develop Qutb's radical critique of modernity into an alternative project that can slowly construct from within the modern condition a path to reverse it – on both discursive and non-discursive levels. On the other hand, the Brotherhood made no attempt to reconcile the Islamic legal and political corpus with modernity per al-Banna's vision.

And accordingly, the Brotherhood's failure to develop fully either of these nascent intellectual projects pushed it in the direction of an author-itarian form of modernism. As Carrie Wickham has argued, the partial success of other Islamist movements was proportionate with their success in developing a discourse and system of policies that utilizes Islamic values and concepts specifically within the framework afforded by modernist structural and discursive conditions. This is evident in the case of the Justice and Development Party in Turkey, as El-Sherif notes, and on a smaller scale in the case of Morocco and Kuwait, as Wickham notes.[56] Seeking to replicate the same successes won by these other Islamist groups, then, the Muslim Brotherhood in Egypt was driven toward a modernist path and hence toward a position that capitalizes on al-Banna and Rashid Rida's legacy of reconciling Islam and modernism. However, the lack of a fully fledged intellectual vision for such reconciliation, which, on the political level, meant lacking a vision of a *modern* Islamic state that builds on the particular immanent structural conditions and values of Egyptian society, led them to an authoritarian interpretation of this state. For only through authoritarianism can Muslims safeguard themselves against contamination by the harmful modern values so thoroughly chastised in Qutb's thesis.

In turn, this interpretation is indeed what the Muslim Brotherhood shares with the secular modernist vision upheld by many Egyptian lib-erals. Both camps lack any real intellectual vision about the concept and role of the state and how such a modern idea could respond to the norms they themselves claim to defend in the specific cultural and social con-text of Egypt. In the case of the Brotherhood, the intellectual poverty of their movement and its inability to critically wrestle with the theoretical

---

[56] See Wickham, *The Muslim Brotherhood*, 196–206.

projects inaugurated by al-Banna or Qutb led to an impasse that cannot help but support an authoritarian state. And in the case of the liberals, their similarly dogmatic commitment to ideological statism ultimately paved the way for its embrace of authoritarian modernism under Nasser, and most recently under Sisi.

CONCLUSION: POST-ISLAMISM AND POST-LIBERALISM AS POST-STATISM

In 1996, Asef Bayat published his quite influential essay, "The Coming of a Post-Islamist Society."[57] Building on Olivier Roy's thesis in *The Failure of Political Islam*,[58] and grounding his assertions on transformations then transpiring in Iran, Bayat argued that the failure of many Islamist movements as such does not necessarily indicate their demise. Rather, it indicates a radical transformation of their intellectual basis, ideological orientation, and social praxis. Subsequently, in 2013, Bayat argued that post-Islamism is a twofold term that refers to a *condition* and a *project* into which Islamism[59] has historically evolved.[60] The condition is one "...where following a phase of experimentation, the appeal, energy, and sources of legitimacy of Islamism are exhausted even among its once-ardent supporters. Islamists become aware of their discourse's anomalies and inadequacies as they attempt to institutionalize or imagine their rule."[61] The project of Post-Islamism, by contrast, refers to Islamists' "...conscious attempt to conceptualize and strategize the rationale and modalities of transcending Islamism in social, political, and intellectual domains."[62] However, this transformation that members of Islamist movements are undergoing or may undergo is "...neither anti-Islamic nor un-Islamic or

---

[57] See Asef Bayat, "The Coming of a Post-Islamist Society," *Critique*, 1996, 43–52.

[58] See Olivier Roy, *The Failure of Political Islam*, trans. Carol Volk (Cambridge: Harvard University Press, 1998), 194–204.

[59] Bayat defines Islamism as follows: "I take *Islamism* to refer to those ideologies and movements that strive to establish some kind of an 'Islamic order' – religious state, shari'a law, moral codes in Muslim societies and communities. Association with the state is a key feature of Islamist politics..." See Asef Bayat, "Post-Islamism at Large," in *Post Islamism: The Changing Faces of Political Islam*, ed. Asef Bayat (New York: Oxford University Press, 2013), 3.

[60] See Bayat, "Post-Islamism at Large," 3–32.

[61] Ibid., 8.

[62] Ibid.

secular."[63] Giving examples from the experience of the AKP in Turkey and how, for instance, it had to adapt economic policies that it originally saw as non-Islamic in order to adapt to the realities of modern politics, Bayat concludes that Post-Islamism is a category emblematic of the fundamentally changing conditions and nature of Islamist discourse, which to him seem rather inevitable.[64]

Building on Bayat's thesis, we would like to argue that the transformation that is likely to happen to the Muslim Brotherhood in Egypt in the near future, at least on the discursive level, is a turn toward post-statism. The tension we articulated earlier between the often-overlooked project of Qutb to displace modernity on the one hand and the project of al-Banna to mold an Islamic framework within the scheme of the modern state on the other is bound to resurface, both for Islamist actors in general and for the Muslim Brotherhood and other Egyptian Islamists in particular. For this tension to be reconciled, though, Islamists will ultimately need to reassess the question of *sovereignty* in the political project they are attempting to establish. Presently, owing to the intellectual impasse in which the Brotherhood finds itself between al-Banna's reconciliatory (yet deeply statist) Islamic modernism and Qutb's radical critique of modernity, its project ultimately grounds sovereignty in absolutist, statist terms. Overcoming this impasse calls for a serious subsiding of this modernist tension through a critical reengagement with the largely decentralized milieu of medieval and early modern Islamic governance – and by extension with the intellectual pluralism it helped preserve, as described earlier. Modern Islamists would need to examine this legacy and discern how, if at all possible, it may offer a vision for a way out of the crisis of sovereignty produced by the modernist – and, as Wael Hallaq recently argued, distinctly European – structure of the state upon which they presently ground their political project.[65]

The intellectual conditions for doing so, moreover, will prove more apposite moving forward. The reason being, this tension will now re-emerge in a wholly different context, in which the secular assumptions

---

[63] Ibid., 8.

[64] Ibid., 29.

[65] Hallaq moves on to argue that, insofar as the modern nation-state is predicated on a wholly European historical experience, it produces a political subjectivity that is fundamentally at odds with the subjectivity produced under an Islamic epistemic framework, thus rendering the conception of an "Islamic state" modeled on the modern nation-state paradigm an impossibility and an anachronism. See Wael Hallaq, *The Impossible State: Islam, Politics, and Modernity's Moral Predicament* (New York: Columbia University Press, 2013).

of the modern liberal state are being subjected to a radical critique in political theory and philosophy on the one hand,[66] and in social theory and anthropology on the other.[67] Moreover, the inevitable resurfacing of this tension will transpire in the context of an entirely new discourse on the advent of the post-secular, in which the return of religion and the metaphysical seem to be inevitable.[68] The implications of this new intellectual context and environment suggest that both the proponents of al-Banna's position and those of Qutb's project will comfortably share the common ground of a radical critique of Western modernity. In such a categorically different intellectual landscape, building an Islamic discourse on politics and governance will take on an entirely new form – one that must, if the project expects to have any long-term staying power, articulate political sovereignty in a way that departs from the absolutist statist auspices presently undergirding it.

Furthermore, there is an even more serious predicament facing liberals in Egypt, though it requires a more radical confrontation with the premises of their own discourse. Unlike early twentieth-century Egyptian liberals, who could complacently take the rational assumptions of liberalism as a political philosophy for granted, contemporary Egyptian liberals must adequately respond to the problems posed in recent decades to the very assumptions undergirding liberalism in the postmodern age. In this respect, liberalism as a worldview faces two fundamental challenges on the theoretical and practical levels. The key assumption grounding liberal theory more broadly – whether in the classical Kantian or more contemporary Rawlsian and/or Habermasian models – concerns the rationality of the liberal subject and society on the one hand, and, more importantly, the rationality of political judgment on the other. Granted, this spectrum of rationality varies dramatically, from an idealist, deontological form as in the Kantian assumption of the "Kingdom of Ends," to a more diluted form in the Rawlsian assumption of a minimal level

---

[66] See, for instance, the Agamben's critique of the failures of the modern liberal state and its contradictions in Giorgio Agamben, *Homo Sacer: Sovereign Power and Bare Life* (Stanford: Stanford University Press, 1998).
[67] See Talal Asad, *Formations of the Secular in Christianity, Islam, Modernity* (Stanford: Stanford University Press, 2003); and Saba Mahmood, *Religious Difference in a Secular Age: A Minority Report* (Princeton: Princeton University Press, 2015).
[68] See 'Part I' John Milbank, *Theology and Social Theory: Beyond Secular Reason* (London: Wiley-Blackwell, 2006), 7–48.

of reasonableness as a precondition for a well-ordered society.[69] In the Kantian model, autonomous members of rational, liberal societies will supposedly deal with each other as ends in themselves, according to the universal nature of the rationally based ethical maxims that Kant termed the categorical imperative.[70] The classical rational assumption of Kant's project – extending even to neo-Kantian formulations – was subsequently critiqued as utterly idealistic and completely impractical, which in turn called for a reconsideration of liberal theory.[71] In this vein, Rawls put forward his humbler choice of reasonableness as the basis for a contractual liberal society.

But Rawls' liberal theory is plagued with a series of blind spots. Namely, the assumption of a reasonable liberal subject presents problems in dealing with members of liberal societies who believe in metaphysical or comprehensive doctrines, to use Rawls' own language, and who thus cannot fully fit within the fetters of public reasonable discourse as Rawls defined – not to say that religion is inherently irrational or unreasonable. Religion has been a consistent thorn in the side of liberal theory in this respect, and the challenge it has posed to the liberal worldview has been exacerbated most recently by the rise of religious fundamentalism and the salient return of religion to politics in North America and Europe – especially in the aftermath of the fall of the Soviet Union. Jürgen Habermas, a scion in contemporary liberal thought, faces precisely this dilemma in his attempt to ground liberalism in a "universal pragmatics" as the basis of communication in rational societies. Indeed, Habermas has more recently recognized the limitations of his project to address or accommodate religion, and has thus begun to articulate dialogical conditions for the inclusion of religion, or its naturalization, in post-metaphysical and supposedly "rational" societies.[72] Habermas's latest intervention is by

---

[69] See Part I of John Rawls, *Justice as Fairness* (Cambridge: Harvard University Press, 2003), 3–38.

[70] For Kant's discussion of positive, intellectual freedom as the rational basis of the exercise of autonomy in an enlightened society and progress in history, see "What is Enlightenment?" "Idea for a Universal History With a Cosmopolitan Purpose," and "What is Orientation in Thinking?" in Immanuel Kant, *Political Writings*, ed. Hans Reiss (New York: Cambridge University Press, 2001).

[71] Consider Carl Schmitt's critique of liberal theorists in general and Neo-Kantian political theorists in particular in Carl Schmitt, *Political Theology* (Chicago: Chicago University Press), 16–52.

[72] See Jürgen Habermas, "Religion in the public sphere," *European Journal of Philosophy* 14, no. 1 (April 1, 2006): 1–25.

no means the final word in reconciling liberal rationalism's impasse on the question of religious metaphysics, but his recent turn to the subject of religion underscores that liberalism's rationalist assumptions can no longer be taken wholly for granted.

Moreover, liberal rationalism produces a second major contradiction, in the context of liberalism's incestuous relationship with corporate capitalism. In contradistinction to the classical assumptions of theorists of capitalism like Adam Smith and David Ricardo, the greedy pursuit of individual interests has proven largely resistant to rationalization as such. And in this sense, despite being a post-structuralist and thus unaligned with rationality as such, Alain Badiou depicts this internal contradiction rather accurately. In his essay "The Democratic Emblem," Badiou reconstructs the Platonic rational argument against the democratic soul in Books IX and X of the *Republic*, specifically in the context of the failure of liberal capitalism in the aftermath of the 2008 financial crisis – of which Badiou anticipates an inevitable recurrence. Here he articulates how the capitalistic nature of modern liberal societies ultimately gives rise to a fundamental contradiction with their own liberal assumptions. Capitalism makes the individual basis of choice not reason but the pursuit of immediate pleasure and selfish interest, that resists any rational *telos* that someone like Adam Smith tried to assume. About this nature of the liberal-democratic ethos, Badiou writes:

Democratic man lives only for the pure present, transient desire is his only law. Today he regales himself with a four-course dinner and vintage wine, tomorrow he is all about Buddha, ascetic fasting, streams of crystal-clear water, and sustainable development. Monday he tries to get back in shape by pedaling for hours on a stationary bicycle: Tuesday he sleeps all day, then smokes and gorges again in the evening. Wednesday he declares that he is going to read some philosophy, but prefers doing nothing in the end. At Thursday's dinner party he crackles with zeal for politics, fumes indignantly at the next person's opinion, and heatedly denounces the society of consumption and spectacle. That evening he goes to see a Ridley Scott blockbuster about medieval warriors. Back home, he falls to sleep and dreams of liberating oppressed peoples by force of arms. Next morning he goes to work, feeling distinctly seedy, and tries without success to seduce the secretary from the office next door. He's been turning things over and has made up his mind to get into real estate and go for the big money. But now the weekend has arrived, and this economic crisis isn't going away, so next week will be soon enough for all that. There you have a life, or lifestyle, or lifeworld, or whatever you want to call it: no order, no ideas, but nothing too disagreeable or distressing either. It is as free as it is unsignifying, and insignificance isn't too high a price to pay for freedom.[73]

Badiou insists that this contradictory nature, which he characterizes as false 'subjective mastery,' should provoke all liberal-democrats to revert to what he portrays – albeit from his distinctly post-structuralist Marxist perspective – as the original meaning of democracy. Badiou describes this meaning in terms of a full embracing of the immanent material force in the people, which does not assume any metaphysical ground. This in turn necessitates that politics, in a true sense of subjective mastery – which he defines as the mastery of thought and praxis – will come to "have independent value, obeying its own atemporal norms like science and art. Politics will not be subordinated to power, to the State."[74] Only by embracing an independent politics, unencumbered by the fetters of the state as such, can liberal-democrats resolve the contradictions of liberal rationalism produced by its flirtations with global capitalism, and thus make possible the restoration of "...the power of peoples over their own existence...From that perspective, we will only ever be true democrats..."[75]

Thus, the assumptions of liberal rationalism have left liberal theory more broadly with two major challenges: the inability to meaningfully and adequately address comprehensive doctrines like religious metaphysics on the one hand, and the outright undermining of those very rational foundations by the forces of global capitalism on the other. And a country like Egypt proves especially vulnerable to these two crises in liberalism: liberal rationality, as we have articulated throughout this chapter, has been deeply inhospitable to the crucial role religious metaphysics have played, and continue to play, in Egyptian society. And just as importantly,

---

[73] See Alain Badiou, "The Democratic Emblem," in *Democracy in What State?*, ed. Giorgio Agamben (New York: Columbia University Press, 2011), 13.
[74] Ibid., 14.
[75] Ibid., 15.

neo-liberal economic policies, from the Sadat era's policy of economic Opening (*al-Infitah*) of the country to the forces of global capitalism onward, have brought untold suffering on the middle and lower classes of Egyptian society.

Regrettably, though, contemporary Egyptian liberals have thus far proven unwilling to even acknowledge these two challenges in liberal theory, much less attempt to address them on either a theoretical or practical level – owing, we submit, to their dogmatic commitment to authoritarian modernism, and by extension to ideological statism. For, as we have seen, statism has consistently been the basis by which liberals have forcibly extirpated religious influences in public life in the name of maintaining a supposedly rational order. Furthermore, statism represents precisely the antithesis of the independent politics Badiou maintains is necessary to overcome the contradictions produced by liberal rationalism's incestuous relationship with global capitalism. Reconciling the liberal project in Egypt, needless to say, will necessitate addressing these challenges.

On what basis, then, will Egyptian liberals seek to find a new means of saving liberal theory in general? Will they reconfigure liberal rationalism altogether? And, if so, how will this newly reformed liberal rationality, if at all possible, yield a new view of the state? And to what extent will this new form of rational state succeed in addressing, rather than forcibly suppressing, the intellectual pluralism of the Islamic legal system articulated earlier? Put another way, saving liberalism in Egypt will require that Egyptian liberals find a proper basis for contextualizing liberal rationalism beyond its classical Protestant origins in Europe, in a way that does justice to the immanent social and cultural realities of Egypt. The liberal project in Egypt, as originally articulated by Ahmad Lutfi al-Sayyid, failed precisely because it ignored those immanent realities, attempting to forcibly superimpose the European experience on the Egyptian one. The past century of the Egyptian liberal experiment, culminating most recently in liberal complicity with the return of authoritarianism under Sisi in 2013, and the acquiescence of even the worst excesses of the new military regime – namely liberal support for the Rabaa massacre – adequately demonstrates that such an approach is bound to fail.

If these radical challenges are to be seriously accepted, Egyptian liberals may find it more edifying, paradoxically enough, to have a constructive dialectic with their erstwhile adversaries in the Islamists – who face a no less serious challenge of revisiting the origins of their political project and its ultimate aims. In so doing, it may very well be that both will inaugurate a new vision capable of transcending their statist myopia, and in turn initiate a new era that is not only, respectively, Post-Islamist and post-liberal, but ultimately post-statist.

SECTION IV

Egyptian liberals in comparative perspective post-2013

10

Conflict and reconciliation

"Arab liberalism" in Syria and Egypt

EMRAN EL-BADAWI

How did renewed autocracy in Egypt and civil war in Syria impact liberals differently? What lessons can be learned about the nature of liberalism in the greater Arab context from this comparative survey? This chapter seeks to answer these questions, first by following the reaction of liberals to the so-called Arab Spring, comparing a handful of intellectuals and academics in Egypt as well as Syria. The chapter goes on to focus on two of the most prominent liberals in each context, namely Gaber Asfour and Burhan Ghalioun. In each case, the role played by the armed forces vis-à-vis the public was critical to their rapid accession to power, and equally rapid fall.

INTRODUCTION

What affect did the recent Arab uprisings have on the region's liberals – especially those from Egypt and Syria? How did their intellectual activity before the so-called "Arab Spring" shape their behavior? What effect did military action have on this behavior? And finally can such a comparative analysis provide any lessons about the nature and prospects of liberalism in Egypt, and its context in the Arab world more broadly? Answering these questions draws attention to two democratically minded, politically active intellectuals from the Egyptian and Syrian context in particular. On the one hand, Gaber Asfour served as Egyptian minister of culture under Ahmad Shafiq in 2011 and maintains good relations with Abd al-Fattah al-Sisi's government. On the other, Burhan Ghalioun became the Syrian opposition's spearhead against President Bashar Al-Assad and the first president of the Syrian National Council (SNC) in 2011. Examining their political activity requires some discussion on the origins and history of "Arab liberalism" between its Egyptian and Syrian foci.

STATE ADVOCACY AND THE BEGINNINGS OF ARAB LIBERALISM

Liberalism is as old as the Egyptian state. The values of freedom (*huri-yyah*; *ahrar*) and equality (*musawah*) came to occupy the very crux of *al-libiraliyyah* in the context of modern Arab political parties, also beginning in Egypt.[1] The origins of liberal discourse can be traced to the unprecedented as well as rapid period of nation building under Muhammad Ali Pasha (d. 1850), who fostered the rise of a new class of Arabic-speaking intellectuals and entrepreneurs.[2] Inspired by a combination of British learning and French culture, Egyptian intellectuals and Syro-Lebanese entrepreneurs established the very rudiments of liberalism throughout the nineteenth and twentieth centuries, between the new khedival palaces of Alexandria and the ancient institutions of Cairo. New printing presses, newspapers, an overhaul of the legal and educational systems, and the beginnings of Arab nationalism coincided with rationalist Islamic reform in al-Azhar University. The pioneers of the modern Arab Renaissance or the Nahda hailed from both Egypt as well as greater Syria. Their ranks included Christians as well as Muslims. Foremost among them were Rifa'a al-Tahtawi (d. 1873), Butrus al-Bustani (d. 1883), Beshara and Saleem Takla (d. 1892), Abd al-Rahman al-Kawakibi (d. 1902), Muhammad Abduh (d. 1905), Huda Sha'rawi (d. 1947), Ahmad Lutfi al-Sayyid (d. 1963), Taha Husayn (d. 1973) and more. The "Nahda liberals" or

---

[1] Tawfiq al-Madani, "*Jadaliyyat al-intiqal min al-libiraliyyah ila al-dimuqratiyyah*," *Bawwabat al-sharq*, June 18, 2015.
[2] Cf. in relation Khaled Fahmy, *All the Pasha's Men: Mehmed Ali, His Army and the Making of Modern Egypt* (Cairo: American University in Cairo Press, 2002).

"classical liberals" were, and are still today, by and large members of society's elite, both educated in foreign schools and coming from wealthy, upper-class families advocating the burgeoning "Arab state" – especially Egypt – with whom it had close ties.

ACTIVISM AND STATE OPPOSITION: THE LATER DEVELOPMENT OF ARAB LIBERALISM

Once modern Arab states became independent during the mid-twentieth century, they faced innumerable challenges from within and without. The great external threat was the founding of an Israeli state. Internally, Arab states, including Egypt, underwent political, social, and economic upheaval. Foretelling events six decades later, the Free Officers, including future president Gamal Abdel Nasser (d. 1970), came to power through a military coup in 1952. Nasser would lay the foundations for the modern police state in Egypt, and throughout the region. His populism, nationalism, and socialist reforms, hailed by millions of his countrymen, weakened Egypt's wealthy landowners and mitigated their foreign predilections. Then came the devastating "setback" or *naksah*. Nasser and his allies from Syria and Jordan were defeated by Israel in the 1967 Arab-Israeli war. Following the military empowerment of the Arab state and its subsequent military failure, a new branch of Arab liberalism came into existence, based on opposing the power of the state and mobilizing progressive, democratic reform. Arab liberal activism was born.

Liberal activists include members of the middle and professional classes, former elites, an increasing number of women, and quite often exiles living abroad. Prominent women in their ranks include the medical doctor Nawal al-Saadawi in Egypt and the historian Madawi al-Rashid, whose tribe once ruled Arabia until its overthrow by the Saud family. There is, however, no firm line between liberal activism on the one hand and liberal advocacy on the other. The two camps exist in parallel under a broader umbrella called Arab liberalism, under which they share "liberal values," including secular governance and expanding women's rights for example. At any rate, the efflorescence during the Nahda and the protest after the *naksah* not only impacted Arab liberalism. It (re)shaped the defeated Arab states, including Egypt and Syria.

EGYPT AND SYRIA NO MORE

Since the brief stint of the United Arab Republic (UAR; 1958–61) stretching back to time immemorial, Egypt and Syria have been consistently united politically, and shared a unique set of political as well as cultural relationships.[3] These relationships began to diverge with the failure of the UAR in 1961 and the defeat of the Arab armies by Israel in the Six Day War in 1967. By 1970, the subsequent decline of Nasserism and pan-Arab nationalism ruptured the long-standing relationships between Egypt and Syria, and each nation forged its own political fate thenceforward.

In 1978–9, under President Anwar Sadat (d. 1981), Egypt made peace with the Arab enemy – Israel – and befriended its chief supporter – the US – from whom it began accepting $1.3 billion annually. By doing so, Egypt abandoned the dream of Arab union, opened up to foreign investment, boosted its tourist industry, and enjoyed a westward orientation.

Syria, on the other hand, doubled down on its passé Arab nationalist orientation. Following a coup in 1963, which was orchestrated by forces within Syria as well as Iraq,[4] the Baath Party came to rule along the regimented lines of a Soviet and later Russian model. That being said, President Hafez Al-Assad (r. 1971–2000) built Syria from the ground up. But he also closed off his country to foreign investment, completely eliminated any political opposition, especially the armed opposition of the Syrian Muslim Brothers, whom he crushed in 1982 along with thousands of civilians in the city of Hama. Denying Israel's existence and having no diplomatic ties with it became a staple of Syrian foreign policy. These

---

[3] Egypt and Syria have been united politically under most of pre-modern history, from the time of the Pharaohs and Hittites until the Mamelukes and Ottomans. About political and cultural relationships, see Marshall Hodgson, *The Venture of Islam*, Vol. 1 (Chicago: University of Chicago Press, 1977), 61.

[4] It is sobering, in light of the so-called Islamic State in Iraq and the Levant (ISIL, ISIS), to recall the cross-border political activism that gave rise to the Baath Party in both Syria and Iraq fifty years earlier. These channels of activism were established by the free officers of the Iraqi Baath Party in Baghdad, who rose to power in a coup in February 8, 1963, and immediately staged a follow-up coup in neighboring Syria in March 8, bringing a heavily militarized Baath Party into Damascus and the rest of Syria. Syrian Nasserists – the final link between modern Egypt and Syria – were driven out. For more on the rise of the Baath and fall of the Nasserists in Syria, see Patrick Seale, *Asad of Syria: The Struggle for the Middle East* (Berkeley and Los Angeles: University of California Press, 1995), 75–83.

historical developments had major consequences on the development of the region's liberalism.

Although Egypt and Syria came under the influence of opposing sides in the Cold War, there have been both continuities as well as disruptions with respect to how liberal advocates as well as activists have approached several political goals – especially preventing the spread of Islamic fundamentalism, ending autocracy and promoting democracy. In this vein, some are quick to point out the spread of political Islam in the region after the Iranian revolution (1978–9) yet forget the concomitant mobilization among both liberal camps especially in the 1990s and early 2000s, both in Egypt as well as Syria. In other words, prior to the Arab uprisings of 2011, a number of critical developments took place that would give shape to, and change the voice of, liberalism across the Arab world thereafter.

Given the increased Islamist activity, classical liberals in the form of public university professors challenged existing Islamic institutions, promoted secularism, and called for reform from deep within the Islamic literary tradition. This discourse pitted them squarely against Islamists, giving liberal advocates and the illiberal state a common enemy. This act of "reconciliation," which played out in the 1990s and early 2000s would repeat itself after 2011. Similarly, liberal activists took to the streets long before 2011. Their agenda of human rights and democracy, while not quite in line with illiberal Islamist politics, was a direct challenge to the secular but equally illiberal politics of the Mubarak or Assad governments. It was *these liberals* that joined the masses throughout the winter and spring of 2011, irrevocably coming into "conflict" with the state.

SILENCING LIBERAL ACTIVISM IN EGYPT, CA. 1979–2013

The tradition of classical Arab liberalism was maintained by academics and intellectuals. They remained statist and eventually came to oppose political Islam, rather than the state. In Egypt, the animosity between the two came to a head in the early 1990s. During a wave of Islamist activity and government crackdowns in Egypt, academics like Farag Foda (d. 1992) and Nasr Hamid Abu Zayd (d. 2010) published works promoting secularism and critical of established Islamic religious tradition and institutions. In response, extremists among their interlocutors assassinated the former in 1992 and divorced the latter from his wife *in absentia* in 1995 on charges of heresy.[5] It is imperative to recognize that neither Foda nor Abu Zayd was directly tied to the Mubarak government; they merely did not oppose it. While both academics were advocates of the modern nation-state, they were no fans of the Egyptian state itself. To complicate matters further, in the case of Abu Zayd it was the Egyptian state, through the appellate court of Cairo, that facilitated two injustices: (1) divorce by compulsion of the state; and (2) manipulation of *in absentia* judgment for a case with no crime.[6] For the Egyptian state, its relations with liberal advocates has typically been one of "convenience."

Toward liberal activists, however, the Egyptian state was more directly and decisively opposed. Activists including Nawal al-Saadawi and Saad Eddin Ibrahim challenged the cultural and political status quo, for which they were dragged through the courts and imprisoned. In the case of Saadawi, her feminism – especially her opposition to violence against women and female genital mutilation – would reap the anger of the Egyptian state. Her criticism of Islamic institutions in oppressing women would similarly anger Egyptian Islamists, who threatened her life. The year of President Sadat's assassination in 1981, she was found "in contempt of religion" and imprisoned for several months.[7] Similarly, in the case of Ibrahim, his opposition of Hosni Mubarak's government on grounds of human rights and his call for democracy was met with stiff opposition from the state. He was charged with "espionage" in 2000 (of which he was later acquitted), and with "defamation" in 2008, after which

---

[5] Important Azhari clerics including Muhammad al-Ghazali and Muslim Brotherhood personalities including Muhammad 'Amarah played a role in their persecution. For more on the clash between liberal academics and Islamist actors in Egypt during the 1990s, see Nasr Hamid Abu Zayd, *Al-Tafkir fi zaman al-takfir: did al-jahl wa al-zayf wa al-khurafah* (Cairo: Maktabat Madbuli Al-Saghir, 1995). It is also worth noting that the case against Nasr Hamid Abu Zayd was prosecuted under the auspices of *hisbah* legislation, a tool from medieval Islamic jurisprudence that I will explicate in more detail elsewhere.

[6] On the problematic nature of divorce from an apostate in modern states, see *Encyclopedia of Women and Islamic Cultures: Family, Law and Politics*, Vol. 2, ed. Suad Joseph and Afsana Najmabadi (Leiden: E.J. Brill, 2005), 8. Trial *in absentia* was established 1950–3 by Article 6, "Right to a fair trial," in the European Convention on Human Rights. It stipulates "everyone is entitled to a fair and public hearing within a reasonable time by an independent and impartial tribunal established by law." See the European Court of Human Rights, *European Convention on Human Rights* (Strasbourg: Council of Europe, 1998), 9, http://www.echr.coe.int/Documents/Convention_ENG.pdf

[7] For more on Saadawi's activism and imprisonment, see Nawal El Saadawi, *Muzakkarati fi sijn al-nisa'*, trans. Marilyn Booth, *Memoirs from the Women's Prison* (Berkeley and Los Angeles: University of California Press, 1986).

he went into exile. Despite his staunch opposition to Hosni Mubarak's government and his calls for democratization, Ibrahim safely returned to Egypt in 2010.[8] Ibrahim's and Saadawi's exile took them to the United States where they occupied important academic and research positions until returning to Egypt. The combination of (especially) Egyptian state repression as well as Islamist threats succeeded in keeping liberalism at bay for much of the 1980s until the early 2000s.

It would be safe to say that pent-up social and political unrest lead to an uptake in liberal activism in the early 2000s. For the first time in the history of an independent Egypt, a liberal activist challenged the police state and sought to supplant Mubarak's presidency through the democratic process. Ayman Nour, who founded the liberal al-Ghad Party in 2004, was the only politician ever to compete against Mubarak in presidential elections in 2005. After coming in second he was charged with "fraud" and imprisoned from 2005 to 2009. Were it not for his disqualification from the Presidential Election Commission – in part populated by pro-Mubarak cronies – he would have run for president in 2011–12. The al-Ghad Party, however, did spin off a much larger coalition of political parties under the leadership of Wael Nawara called the Network of Arab Liberals. The coalition rapidly grew into the Arab Alliance for Freedom and Democracy (AAFD), made up of more than a dozen parties from Egypt, Lebanon, Morocco, Sudan, and Tunisia.[9] But neither Nawara nor the AAFD capitalized on a post-Mubarak Egypt. The problem with this liberal activism is that, no matter its ambition within Egypt or other Arab societies, it was thoroughly incapable of mobilizing the masses. The members of progressive political parties were ostensibly too few, and occasionally divided, to have any lasting impact on society. Hamdeen Sabbahi, who frequented prison so often for his opposition to both Sadat and Mubarak, fared somewhat better. He founded the Dignity Party (hizb al-karamah) and came in third behind Mohammad Morsi and Ahmad Shafiq in the 2012 presidential elections. After the popularly supported military coup in 2013 and the overthrow of Egypt's first ever democrat-ically elected president, Mohammad Morsi, Sabbahi made another bid

---

[8] For more on Ibrahim's activism before and after the Arab uprisings, see Matt Bradley, "Military regime draws support from Egypt's liberals," *The Wall Street Journal*, January 12, 2014.
[9] For recent activity by the AAFD against fundamentalism, see Rimun Naji, "'Al-tahaluf al-'rabi lilhuriyyah' yu'ayyid hamlat almisriyyin al-ahrar 'watan did al-tatarruf'," *Bawabat Veto*, May 26, 2015.

for the presidency against Sisi in 2014, which he promptly withdrew. Since then, Sabbahi has tiptoed lightly through a political arena marked by renewed autocracy – a precarious existence for a liberal opposition figure in Sisi's Egypt. His intermittent silence and sporadic criticism of current policies must contend with the popular charisma of yet another president from the military. In the eyes of Sisi supporters – many of whom were relieved by the toppling of Morsi and the Muslim Brothers and who see the country's recent democratic experiment as a complete disaster – Sabbahi's unsuccessful presidential bid in 2012, campaign withdrawal in 2013, and sporadic criticism after 2014 are an unwelcome and dangerous political distraction. By 2014, the thorough silencing of liberal activism in Egypt would be encapsulated in the words of Sisi supporters to Sabbahi: "Sabbahi has no right to speak in the name of the Egyptian people!"[10]

ACTIVISTS IN CONFLICT AND ARTISTS IN RECONCILIATION, EGYPT, CA. 2013–

The narrative of the silenced liberal activist existed long before the fall of Mubarak in 2011 and continues until today. The relationship between liberal activism and the state is fundamentally one of "conflict." This is contrasted by the relationship between classical liberals and the state, which is characterized by support or at the very least "reconciliation" with the illiberal if not fully autocratic values of the state. They include intellectuals, authors, artists, actors, and other literary and creative personalities who enrich society through state institutions. By 2013, many of these personalities joined in the national campaign against all symbols of Morsi and the Muslim Brotherhood (MB), and commended Sisi and the military for saving their country.

There are reasons for this liberal support of the military against the Muslim Brothers beyond basic notions of classical liberalism defined above. Under the Muslim Brothers, a number of political and popular offenses took place that particularly threatened the arts. Their blunders in this respect include the executive restructuring of this arena by the then minister of the arts Alaa Abdel Aziz. The sacking of the director of the Cairo Opera House – an icon of Egyptian arts and a testament to the

---

[10] Muhammad Munisi, *"Ansar al-sisi li-sabbahi: lissah lik 'ayn titkallim?!," Al-Masri al-Yawm,* October 1, 2014.

country's classical liberal and modernist foundation – Ines Abdel-Dayem on May 30, 2013, and the refusal of her replacement Reda El-Wakil to fill her position, were the last straw.[11] In this context, it is little surprise that many prominent figures from within the Egyptian arts community took their antagonism of the Muslim Brotherhood to the extreme. Their ranks include the well-known novelist Alaa al-Aswany.[12] But they include equally famous artists such as the poet Ahmed Abdel Mu'ti Higazi, author Gamal El-Ghitani, actors Ahmed Bedier and Ilham Shahin, and of course the renowned academic and literary critic Gaber Asfour (about which see more below).

TEMPORARY RECONCILIATION WITH ASSAD, SYRIAN INTELLECTUALS, CA. 1982–2012

Between activists and advocates of the state, the story of liberalism in Egypt may be judged one of conflict and reconciliation respectively. In Syria, a number of politically active academics and intellectuals in the tradition of classical or Nahda liberalism contributed prolifically to an Arab liberal discourse, broadly speaking. Sadiq J. Al-'Azm provided a critique of Islamist politics and ideology in light of the violence that raged between the government of Hafez Al-Assad (d. 2000) and the Syrian Muslim Brotherhood throughout the late 1970s and early 1980s. Following Assad's decimation of the Syrian Muslim Brothers along with the city of Hama in 1982, 'Azm published his landmark *Critique of Religious Thought*.[13] During the 1980s and 90s, Tayyib al-Tizini and Muhammad Shahrur wrote equally important works on the role of government, society, and religion in the Arab world.[14]

The works of 'Azm, Tizini, and Shahrur criticize the failure of Arabism especially in light of the 1967 defeat, and the subsequent rise of opposing

---

[11] Richard Spencer, "Cairo Opera on strike in protest at Muslim Brotherhood sacking of director," *Telegraph*, May 30, 2013.

[12] Cf. Patrick Kingsley, "Alaa al-Aswany on why he had to support Egypt's military crackdown," *Guardian*, October 29, 2013; Negar Azimi, "The Egyptian army's unlikely allies," *New Yorker*, January 8, 2014.

[13] Cf. Sadiq J. Al-'Azm, *Naqd al-fikr al-dini* (Beirut: Dar al-Tali'ah, 1982), trans. *Critique of Religious Thought* (Berlin: Gerlach, 2014).

[14] Tayyib al-Tizini, *Fusul fi al-fikr al-siyasi al-'arabi* (Beirut: Dar al-Farabi, 1989); Muhammad Shahrur, *al-Dawlah wa al-mujtama'* (Damascus: al-Ahaly lil-Tiba'ah, 1995).

Islamist (mainly Salafist) identities. However, these academics and intellectuals criticized autocracy in the Arab world only in theory and without recourse to overthrowing the Assad regime specifically. The key is that no political challenge to the Assad government could be tolerated.[15] One may claim, therefore, that, like their Egyptian counterparts, Syrian intellectuals reconciled their liberal politics with an illiberal autocratic state.

While the term reconciliation may serve as a basic or operative term to describe the relationship between intellectuals and the state – in Syria, Egypt, and elsewhere in the Arab world – it does not tell the whole story. Nor does it encapsulate the nuances of the Syrian intellectual predicament as a result of the Arab uprisings in 2011. Contrary to the Egyptian example, Syrian intellectuals were much more divided on whether to support the Assad government or join the growing opposition. After 2011, Shahrur continued to offer criticism of Islamism but not Assad. Tizini called for Assad to step down while claiming, quite diplomatically, that his departure from power would be considered a "victory."[16] This and similarly artful and mixed signals were the limit of his later political activity. 'Azm, however, came out in vehement opposition to the Assad government, and on November 11, 2012 he joined ranks, in no uncertain terms, with the opposition body known as the Syrian National Council (SNC) in Doha Qatar.

As a brilliant intellect from Syria, and as a member of Damascus' most elite house (*Bayt al-'azm*), his opposition was an astonishing break with the status quo. It is, furthermore, proof that the relationship between liberals and the state in the Arab world is a complex continuum, and that given the necessary circumstances this relationship can transform drastically. It is 'Azm himself who most articulately explains the reasons for, and limits of, liberal intellectual reconciliation with autocratic states in Syria and Egypt, stating:

> I don't think anyone ever did a survey of Arab intellectuals to determine their views and positions. Such studies are rare in our part of the world. We rely on speculation, impressions and the spontaneous interpretation of events. If we think for example of an Egyptian intellectual living in a totalitarian system, he would have been forced

---

[15] Sadiq J. Al-'Azm would officially represent the Syrian Writers Union at the SNC meeting convened in Doha, Qatar on November 11, 2012.

[16] Rita Faraj, *"Tizini li al-ray, tanahi al-asad intisar lah,"* *Al-Rai Medi Group*, January 14, 2012.

to come to terms with that system. I do not believe that he served that system. I know from the experiences of many intellectuals that they had to make a number of compromises in order to continue working as university professors or writers – compromises that were however, in my opinion, not all that compromising.[17]

CONFLICT, EXILE AND CIVIL WAR: LIBERAL ACTIVISM IN SYRIA, CA. 2000–12

Given the absence of a real public sphere and the freedoms necessary to foster grassroots mobility, with respect to liberal activism in Syria there is deafening silence. There are no political parties of which to speak, and Assad's brutal secret police and intelligence network cut Syria off from the rest of the world, transforming it into the famed "kingdom of silence."[18] What scarce leftist and progressive activism survives within the country borders remains politically nationalist and frequently Marxist-socialist in orientation. The dearth of activism in Syria is complemented by a plethora of Syrian liberal activism in Paris, London, New York, and most anywhere else these activists have immigrated to willingly or as some form of exile.

The voices of democratization and critics of the Assad government have long since been exiled outside the national borders, thriving not within Syria but among the Syrian diaspora in Europe, the US, and elsewhere. The final hope of liberalization, reform, and legitimate reconciliation with the government came between 2000 and 2005 after Hafez Al-Assad died, leaving the presidency to his son Bashar Al-Assad – a seemingly more cosmopolitan, progressive leader many thought. However, the "Damascus Spring" came and went, leaving the exiled Syrian liberal opposition more embittered than ever. Their liberal political reform agenda, as well as their plans for economic liberalism became irreconcilable with the Assad government and, increasingly, with Syrian society more broadly. Liberalism swelled irrevocably into conflict. Like a volcano waiting to erupt, the battle on the horizon was between Syrian liberal

---

[17] Mona Naggar, "Interview with Sadiq Jalal al-Azm: A new spirit of revolution," *Qantara. de*, April 1, 2011.
[18] Wael Sawah and Salam Kawakibi, "Activism in Syria: Between nonviolence and armed resistance," in *Taking to the Streets: The Transformation of Arab Activism*, ed. Lina Khatib and Ellen Lust (Baltimore: Johns Hopkins University Press, 2014).

activists living in Europe and the US on the one hand, and Assad loy-alists living within Syria on the other. And it was Burhan Ghalioun at the helm of the liberal vanguard.

BURHAN GHALIOUN AND GABER ASFOUR, CA. 1990–2010

The professional careers and personal biographies of both Ghalioun and Asfour are comparable both in terms of length as well as their impact on liberalism in the region. Ghalioun was born in 1945, and Asfour one year earlier in 1944. Both are academics by trade, publishing in Arabic for an Arab audience. And most importantly, both academics served as political leaders in 2011. Ghalioun's interest in democracy and human rights took him to France, and more specifically to the University of Paris/La Sorbonne where he received a dual doctorate in the social sciences and humanities, and where he has worked since the 1970s. During this time, Asfour had obtained his doctorate in Arabic literature from Cairo University, joined its faculty, and remained in his home country of Egypt. Asfour remains a classic example of the Nahda liberal, whose nationalism and statism define his academic as well as political activity, whereas Ghalioun has always been a liberal activist first and an academic second. Before elaborating on the differences between the two, and how these differences conditioned their starkly opposite reactions to the Arab uprisings, it is imperative to share a few words concerning their common political goals between 1990 and 2010, i.e. two decades prior to the Arab uprisings.

As liberals in a single Arab context, both Asfour and Ghalioun strive toward creating a democratic society, eradicating Islamic fundamentalism, and fostering progressive, intellectual and humanistic values. Asfour, how-ever, argues for these values from within the Arabic and Islamic literary corpus. He had written a number of works in this vein, critical of Islamic fundamentalism and promoting an "Arab enlightenment," including *The Enlightenment Crisis* (*Mihnat al-tanwir*; 1993), *Combating Terrorism: A Selection from Contemporary Literature* (2003), and *In Defense of Women* (2007).[19] As a social scientist, however, Ghalioun argues for these same

---

[19] Gaber Asfour, *Mihnat al-tanwir* (Cairo: al-Hay'ah al-Misiryyah al-'Ammah lil-Kitab, 1993); *Muwajahat al-irhab: qira'ah fi al-adab almu'asir* (Beirut: Dar al-Farabi, 2003); *Difa'an 'an al-mar'ah* (Cairo: al-Hay'ah al-Misiryyah al-'Ammah lil-Kitab, 2007).

values principally through a political and social critique drawn from the European Enlightenment, rather than through the Islamic tradition proper. Prominent works from his oeuvre include *Assassination of the Intellect: The Crisis (mihnah) of Arab Culture between Salafism and Subjugation* (1993) and *The Arab Crisis (mihnah): The State versus the Nation* (2004). He was the one, furthermore, to write *A Manifesto for the Sake of Democracy* (1986, reprinted 1990, 2006) and the "textbook" so to speak on *Arab Human Rights* (1999).[20] However, for the purposes of deciphering the agenda shared by both Asfour and Ghalioun on the eve of the Arab uprisings, broadly speaking, some critical insights may be drawn from the titles selected above.

From the early nineties (1990 and 1993 to be specific) until 2003, both Asfour and Ghalioun emphasize that Arab societies are in a state of "crisis" (*mihnah*), namely a predicament of thought, culture, and identity. Both authors agree that the result of this crisis is Islamic fundamentalist discourse. However, Ghalioun adds the state's heavy hand – i.e. autocracy – as the other, graver, destructive outcome. This is a critical difference between the two and foreshadows their different trajectories in the wake of the Arab uprisings.

For Asfour and numerous other Egyptian liberals of his persuasion, there is only one existential threat – political Islam.[21] It is little surprise that Egyptian liberals were incensed by Islamic political actors in the country. These were namely the Muslim Brothers – the region's de facto popular as well as Muslim representative body – al-Azhar University, and (after 2011) the Salafists. The "editorial warfare" on the pages of *Al-Ahram*, for example, serves as ample evidence and expert witness to the rumblings of the invectives exchanged and legal actions taken between liberal-minded intellectuals and artists on the one hand and political Islamists on the other – long before Tahrir and Rabaa. One typical example features two editorials from 2007, one by Asfour and another by the poet Ahmed Abdel Mu'ti Higazi, which attack a bombastic Islamic cleric by the name of Yusuf al-Badri, calling him an "extremist" among other colorful epithets. Badri filed suit, based on Egypt's *hisbah*

---

[20] Burhan Ghalioun, *Bayan min ajl al-dimuqratiyyah* (Beirut: Mu'asasat al-Abhath al-'Arabiyyah, 1986); *al-Mihnah al-'arabiyyah: al-dawlah didd al-ummah* (Beirut: Markaz Dirasat al-Wihdah al-'Arabiyyah, 1993); *Huquq al-insan al-'arabi* (Beirut: Markaz Dirasat al-Wihdah al-'Arabiyyah, 1999); *Ightiyal al-'aql: mihnat al-thaqafah al-'arabiyyah bayn al-salafiyyah wa al-tab'iyyah* (al-Markaz al-Thaqafi al-'Arabi, 2004).

[21] See generally Asfour, *Muwajahat al-irhab*, 1–20.

ordinances against both[22] and was successful, ultimately requiring his defendants to pay substantial fines in reparation.[23] Such caustic battles between Egypt's left and the right were neither new nor particularly special. Over time, however, they did come to quintessentially define what "liberalism" in Egypt was, who the liberals were, and place them both in contradistinction with political Islam more broadly. During this time (1990–2010), one is hard pressed to find in the pages of *Al-Ahram* or otherwise any serious criticism of Mubarak's autocracy or corruption by Asfour or his liberal camp. The two were actually reasonably close and made up an important part of the political, cultural, and commercial elite that ruled the country. Asfour's liberalism ultimately defined itself so thoroughly in opposition to the illiberalism of Islamist currents that it came to lend its support – either implicitly or, as we shall see following the events of 2013, explicitly – to the equally illiberal Egyptian autocratic state. Under Mubarak, Asfour worked for several Egyptian state institutions, occupying prestigious offices in education, literature, publishing, and culture. His alliance lay quite naturally with the state with which he had a deeply positive and mutual relationship.

The situation was wholly different in the Syrian context. For Ghalioun and the liberal Syrian diaspora on the other hand, all Arab societies are "between a rock and a hard place." In the case of Syria, these poles are subservience to the Assad family on the one hand and the Salafists (specifically) on the other. Ghalioun's *Manifesto* thus systematically and directly criticizes the tenets of nationalist, Marxist, and Islamist political models.[24] Furthermore, his criticism came following the period known as the "Damascus Spring" between 2000 and 2001 when several Syrian liberals and opposition figures returned home to try their luck at activism under a new president, namely Bashar Al-Assad. It did not last. Ghalioun delivered a talk in September 2001 hosted by fellow activist Riyad al-Sayf.

---

[22] The origins of Egyptian *hisbah* laws and the *muhtasib*, a public and commercial investigator of sorts, are drawn from the Islamic legal principle of "promoting virtue and preventing vice" – the very same principle that in a different manifestation comes to inform the morality police forces (*mutawaeen*) of Saudi Arabia. For a more nuanced understanding of *hisbah* in a modern Egyptian context, drawing especially on the case of Nasr Hamid Abu Zayd (discussed earlier), see Hussein Ali Agrama, *Questioning Secularism: Islam, Sovereignty, and the Rule of Law in Modern Egypt* (Chicago; London: University of Chicago Press, 2012), 42–68.

[23] *"Taghrim 'asfur khamsin alf junayh li tadamunih ma' hijazi,"* *Middle East Online*, December 13, 2008.

[24] Ghalioun, *Bayan*, 161–71.

Hundreds attended. Syrian intelligence was alerted and immediately began its crackdown. Ten of the attendees, including Seif, received harsh prison sentences, and it was back to the police state.[25] This was followed in 2005 by a significant development, the "Damascus Declaration for Democratic National Change," a document with the outlines of a democratic constitution, criticizing the Assad government, and mapping out a gradual transition toward democracy, while respecting Islam as well as the diversity of the Syrian people.[26] Ghalioun backed the Declaration, which he saw as a Syrian grassroots political movement. It was also backed by Michel Kilo, the Christian human rights activist also living in France, as well as by Kurdish Syrian groups and – most significantly – the Syrian Muslim Brothers, an unlikely hodgepodge of Syrian opposition members.[27] Ghalioun's willingness to cooperate with an Islamic political group as notorious as the Syrian Muslim Brothers represents a major ideological compromise on his part. After all, Ghalioun believed in a civil path towards democratization, one informed not by Islamic tradition nearly as much as by European Enlightenment philosophy. The Syrian Muslim Brothers, by contrast, had taken to a full-blown Islamic insurrection by 1982. And as we shall see shortly, this unholy alliance only fanned the flames of the Syrian civil war beginning in 2011.

THE ARAB UPRISINGS, 2011

2011 proved to be the fateful year in which pent-up social injustice, endemic government corruption and Islamic fundamentalism shattered the very fabric of many Arab societies. Nowhere is this truer than in Syria wherein the region's bloodiest civil war has raged for approximately five years.[28] Despite escaping this destructive fate, Egypt has returned

---

[25] Amal Hanano, "Portraits of a people," *Jadaliyya*, October 11, 2011.
[26] Joshua Landis, "Damascus Declaration in English," *SyriaComment*, November 1, 2005.
[27] For more, see Joshua Landis, "Michel Kilo the patriot," *SyriaComment*, May 15, 2006; Robin Wright, *Dreams and Shadows: The Future of the Middle East* (New York: Penguin Press, 2008), 232–4.
[28] With a death toll of near 400,000 the Syrian civil war (2011–) has surpassed the death tolls for the North Yemen civil war (1962–70), Lebanese civil war (1975–91), Algerian civil war (1991–2004), and ongoing Iraqi civil conflict (2003–). See "320,000 people killed since the beginning of the Syrian Revolution," *The Syrian Observatory for Human Rights*, June 9, 2015.

to a stronger, more repressive form of autocracy under Sisi than under Mubarak. The objective here, however, is not to outline the historical development of the so-called Arab Spring, but rather to demonstrate the critical roles played by Egyptian and Syrian liberals, especially Asfour and Ghalioun, in shaping its outcomes. In both contexts there has been a single decisive actor, perhaps even a single decisive moment, upon which their activism or advocacy – and the fate of Arab liberalism itself – has been predicated: *military action*.

In order to appreciate the relationship of Egyptian liberals vis-à-vis military action, it is useful to start by examining this relationship in the Syrian context, and to continue following the course of Burhan Ghalioun, before turning again to Gaber Asfour in Egypt.

GHALIOUN AND THE SNC, 2011–12

The Syrian public was inspired by the peaceful protests at the heart of the popular revolutions in both Tunis (December 18, 2010) and Tahrir Square (January 25, 2011). Between February 4 and March 20, sporadic street protests turned violent and the full-scale government crackdown began in the city of Daraa. Details concerning whether protesters or the Syrian police "fired the first shot" remain controversial and are not central to the matter at hand. What is central is that by April/May the Syrian military began besieging cities throughout the country. They attacked the snow-balling armed opposition often located in civilian areas like mosques and private homes, killing hundreds and imprisoning thousands. On June 29, the brutality of the military crackdown and the rising civilian death toll led to army defections and the creation of the Free Syrian Army (FSA). By the end of the year, the Syrian civil war was in full swing, with jihadist groups on the rise.

It would be safe to say that the unexpected nature of the Syrian upris-ing and the rapid pace at which events unfolded caught all exiled Syrian activists, from the left and the right, completely off guard. Their country had gone from hopeful popular demonstration to armed rebellion in just five months. They needed to act, quickly and in unison. As a result, on August 23, the Syrian National Council (SNC) was founded in the city of Istanbul, with Ghalioun to be elected as its first chairman. As a broad political coalition, its national consensus charter lists "human rights, judicial independence, press freedom, democracy and political pluralism among its guiding principles" – precisely in line with the liberal project Ghalioun had been articulating for decades.[29] The SNC was expanded on November 11, 2012 in Doha, Qatar, into the larger National Coalition for Syrian Revolutionary and Opposition Forces (still abbreviated SNC).

Before proceeding with this discussion of the SNC, it is worth offering a caveat about its origins. Although it is common knowledge that this coalition came in response to the Syrian uprising, its deeper roots, established prior to the conflict, are often neglected. The SNC in 2011 formed directly out of the Damascus Declaration in 2005 and the Damascus Spring of 2000–1.[30] It was this Declaration that first galvanized and organized Syrian activists living abroad. Furthermore, a number of prominent signatories from 2005 resurfaced in 2011 and 2012, including Riyad al-Sayf. All this is to suggest a continuity between liberal currents inaugurated earlier during the short-lived Damascus Spring and in the Syrian uprising of 2011, a trajectory that is largely ignored. Having said that, by 2011, Syrian liberalism had become an opposition government in exile.

However, there were problems. By necessity, the SNC, like the Declaration before it, included the Syrian Muslim Brothers, whose historical track record was not only illiberal, but also included organized violence against the state.[31] Throughout 2011, the SNC hobbled along, cooperating with the FSA beginning in December of that year. This act was significant: however committed the SNC may have been as an (admittedly deeply problematic) incarnation of modern Syrian liberalism, it could only fully actualize that liberal project through strength of arms. In other words, Ghalioun's ability to convert his long-standing theoretical project of democratic liberalism into tangible outcomes in Syria was wholly contingent upon his and his coalition's ability to militarily defeat the Assad government. The SNC and its military wing, the FSA, were at the mercy of foreign funding, which all but dried up by 2012. And it

---

[29] "Q&A: Syrian opposition alliance," *BBC News*, November 16, 2011.

[30] AFB, "*Riyad al-sayf, ramz rabi' dimashq,*" *Jaridat al-Madinah*, November 7, 2012.

[31] It was Nasser, under the UAR, who first banned the Syrian Muslim Brothers, a policy that would radicalize the group and bring it into direct conflict with the Alawite minority of Syria, of whom the Assad family was a member. The seeds of the Nusra Front and ISIL/ISIS were sown by the Syrian Muslim Brothers three decades earlier, in their "long campaign of terror" from 1976 to 1982, in part aided by the Baath Party in Iraq. See Patrick Seale, *Asad: The Struggle for the Middle East* (London: University of California Press, 1989), 336–7.

was completely unwilling to undertake direct negotiation with Assad, stipulating that his resignation was a precondition to negotiations.[32] The SNC was simply no match for Assad's military as well as political resilience. In the coming years, Assad would garner the aid of Iran and Russia. And the meager FSA would be totally overwhelmed by the rise of well-funded, heavily armed, and better-organized jihadist groups. In the western half of Syria, these included a jihadist alliance fighting with the FSA, namely Nusra Front (Al-Qaeda in Syria), Ahrar al-Sham, Jaysh al-Islam, and smaller groups. In opposition to the FSA and its allies, as well as the Assad government was the so-called Islamic State of Iraq and the Levant (ISIL, ISIS) to the east.

Ultimately, the SNC's downfall was its weakness, before the rising tide of jihadism and political Islam on the one hand, and before the world community which it desperately needed on the other. The SNC was making strong demands from a rather feeble position. Their insistence on foreign (i.e. US) military intervention and their intransigence with respect to negotiating Syria's future with Assad (and Russia), while understandable in principle, lacked both credibility as well as strategy. The White House, fearing the rise of jihadist groups and the weakness of the SNC, was reluctant to recognize the SNC as the leadership of the Syrian opposition.[33] It also wavered incoherently with respect to arming Syrian rebels.[34] The SNC became internally fractious, incoherent, and ineffective. On May 17, 2012, Ghalioun stepped down as chairman. Liberalism was dead.

---

[32] "Syria opposition groups hold crucial Qatar meeting," BBC News, November 4, 2012.

[33] Scott Stearns, "Clinton: SNC no longer leads Syrian opposition," Voice of America, October 31, 2012.

[34] After the Obama administration's decision in 2011 to arm the Libyan rebels backfired, and the availability of heavy munitions caused a civil war in that country (ultimately killing US ambassador J. C. Stevens on September 12, 2012), the idea of providing heavy munitions to the Syrian rebels was debated intensely in Washington. Cf. Alissa Rubin, "Two senators say U.S. should arm Syrian rebels," New York Times, February 12, 2012; David Sanger, "Rebel arms flow is said to benefit jihadists in Syria," New York Times, October 14, 2012. In this context, the White House's policy to arm the "moderate Syrian opposition," beginning in 2013 and even after large-scale Russian intervention in Syria in 2015, is a (disastrous) compromise between Washington's hawks and naysayers. See Jim Acosta and Eugene Scott, "Obama: U.S. will keep backing Syrian opposition despite Russian intervention," CNN, October 3, 2015.

ASFOUR, THE MINISTRY AND EGYPT'S RETURN TO MILITARY RULE, 2011–14

In contrast to Syria, the development of liberalism in Egypt immediately after January 25, 2011 was a world apart. Activism flourished amid the police state. Millions of Egyptians took part in the twenty-two days of demonstrations and sit-ins taking place in Cairo's Tahrir Square. At the core of the youth demonstrating was a call for populist-style liberalism, "bread, freedom and human dignity (or social justice)."[35] Mubarak's brutal crackdown was overseen by his new interim prime minister, Ahmad Shafiq, but led directly by the minister of interior, Habib Al-Adli, and his security apparatus, i.e. police, intelligence, and armed gangs. The minister of media, Anas al-Fiqqi, was equally complicit in inciting violence against demonstrators through state-run TV. A total of 846 people died in Egyptian cities.[36] However, the critical mass of Egypt's students, activists, peasantry, labor unions, and (towards the end) the Muslim Brotherhood was irresistible, and by February 11 Mubarak was gone. He was deposed by the Supreme Council of the Armed Forces (SCAF), which fancied itself the protector of the people. The military would be their caretaker for the coming year and, as militaries are wont to do, it overstepped its bounds a number of times. But for now, it was celebrated as the savior of the revolution. "The army and the people are one hand," so they said.[37]

During the nascent weeks of the revolution, all of Egypt was in flux, its liberals included. Like their Syrian counterparts, the revolution was an opportunity to finally reject the status quo and establish a democratic society. On February 1, Shafiq offered Asfour the post of minister of culture for a new "salvation government," a completely unexpected if controversial opportunity. Asfour immediately accepted. He resigned ten days later, citing health concerns, which everyone understood to be a "save face" tactic. The truth as he claims was that he was shocked to find Mubarak's cronies, especially Fiqqi, desperately trying to cling to power,

[35] Wael Nawara, "Egyptian people tell Mubarak OUT," *The Huffington Post*, January 26, 2011.
[36] "Egypt unrest: 846 killed in protests – official toll," *BBC News*, April 19, 2011.
[37] See Robert Naiman, "Hand in hand, the army and the people are one," *The Huffington Post*, January 30, 2011, but also Max Strasser, "The army and the people were never one hand," *Foreign Policy*, January 24, 2012.

and he could not stomach being involved in such a government.[38] Asfour received harsh criticism from intellectuals, including Sadiq J. Al-'Azm, across the Arab world for involving himself with the final death throes of the Mubarak era – and justifiably so. 'Azm states:

> I do not want to take the intellectuals to task too strongly [about supporting their governments], unless the situation is crystal clear, as in the case of Jaber Asfour, former director of Egypt's Supreme Council of Culture and the last minister of culture under Mubarak. There was a time when he kept a certain distance between himself and the regime. But then that distance disappeared. It is impossible to respect such people.[39]

All criticism aside, however, Asfour was the perfect man for the job. After all he was a prolific author, as well as director of the High Council on Culture (1993–2007), an independent organization dedicated to promoting the arts and humanities, but also working closely with the ministry. The point is that this was the way Asfour could effect political change after the revolution. He served as minister of culture once again from June 17, 2014 till March 5, 2015. The question "why" Asfour would agree to serve as minister of culture under Mubarak and later Sisi is, like the contradictions of liberalism, a complex one to which we may never have a definitive answer. On the one hand, he was poised after a long and celebrated career to take on the challenge of reforming Egypt's cultural landscape from a position of authority. On the other hand, his raw ambition may have clouded his liberal values and severely tarnished his reputation as a liberal. I suspect the answer is a bit of both.

Other academics as well as activists without immediate ties to the government were equally active. Nawal al-Saadawi, the journalist Mona Eltahawy, and Khaled Fahmy, professor of history at the American University in Cairo (AUC), personally marched in Tahrir Square. Others took to the airwaves. On March 2, a televised debate hosted a discussion between Shafiq, the billionaire tycoon Naguib Sawiris, and the author Alaa al-Aswany on the current political state of affairs. Aswany was applauded by many (as well as criticized by some) for his relentless

[38] Ibrahim Sa'id, "*Jabir 'asfur: anas al-fiqqi kan ra'is al-junhuroyyah fi wujud ahmad shafiq*," *Bawabat Veto*, June 19, 2014.
[39] Naggar, "Interview with Sadiq Jalal al-Azm."

condemnation of Shafiq, under whom dozens of unarmed protesters were massacred.[40] Later that year, with a growing anxiety about Islamists, especially the Muslim Brothers, having carte blanche after decades of repression, academics like Sayyid Al-Qimany and Salafist clerics like Mahmoud Sha'ban would debate the concept of "civilian rule." On April 3, Sawiris, insofar as he can be considered a liberal, established the Free Egyptians Party, which actively opposed the Muslim Brothers. Unlike the Syrian context, any coalition between Egyptian liberal parties and the Muslim Brotherhood is simply unthinkable.[41] In this vein, the alliance between one-time presidential hopeful Mohamed El Baradei and the Muslim Brotherhood was ill-conceived and short-lived. Furthermore, once Morsi was elected president and enacted controversial executive powers, the alliance was all but over.[42] At any rate, it seemed for some time that, after seven thousand years of dictatorship, all sectors of Egyptian society were finally participating in the democratic process of political debate as well as trial and error. And liberals were playing an integral part.

RABAA

The following years proved to be more problematic for liberalism in Egypt. The first ever elected president of Egypt was a former member of the Muslim Brotherhood, Mohammad Morsi, and his own autocratic practices, overall mismanagement, and – more significantly – the simple fact that the Muslim Brothers and Islamist parties were thriving put liberals, artists, the elite, and large segments of the public in a state of panic. Through the Tamarod campaign, they all converged on Morsi and the Muslim Brothers. On July 3, 2013, army general Abd al-Fattah al-Sisi removed President Morsi from office and banned the Muslim Brotherhood soon after. At the time, only a handful of liberals openly protested taking

---

[40] Robert Worth, "The Arab intellectuals who didn't roar," *New York Times*, October 29, 2011.
[41] As the principal representative of political Islam, the Muslim Brothers have been particularly despised by the ruling elite since the Free Officers Movement in 1952, the UAR (1958–61), and the following decades where, as this chapter demonstrates, they were at loggerheads with a number of liberals, including Asfour, Higazi, Qimany, Abu Zayd, and others.
[42] Cf. Margaret Coker and Summer Said, "Muslim group backs secular struggle," *Wall Street Journal*, January 31, 2011; Erich Follath, "ElBaradei speaks out against Morsi: 'Not even the Pharaohs had so much authority,'" *Der Spiegel*, November 26, 2012.

such extreme measures at the risk of losing democracy. Among them was Amr Hamzawy, professor of political science at AUC and one of Egypt's strongest and ablest supporters of democracy, who unlike Asfour declined Shafiq's offer to serve as minister of youth in 2011. Instead, he opted to run for parliament. He won and served as an MP in 2012-2013, and was criticized by many for his condemnation of the popularly supported military coup on June 30, 2013. The same was the case for Mohamed El Baradei, former director general of the International Atomic Energy Agency (IAEA) and one-time presidential hopeful, who abandoned Egypt altogether following the military coup and the subsequent Rabaa massacre on August 14, 2013. The military killed over eight hundred demonstrators (some armed) and members of the Muslim Brotherhood calling for the return of Morsi to the presidency.[43]

If military protection of demonstrators in Tahrir allowed liberalism in Egypt to evolve, then its massacre of demonstrators in Rabaa completely reversed this evolution. The overwhelming majority of the country's liberals vilified the Muslim Brothers (see discussion earlier) and many went on to support Sisi's intervention, and later his presidency. Asfour, Aswany, Qimany, Higazi, and several others came down in support of Sisi. Their newfound enthusiasm for the youth (lukewarm in some cases) was overtaken by their decades-old mistrust of the Muslim Brotherhood. In the words of Asfour in an interview dated June 23, 2015, "Egypt was in dire need of Sisi!"[44]

Military autocracy was back with a vengeance, and the Muslim Brothers were driven underground once again. The critical mass of Egypt's liberals had yet again reconciled themselves with the status quo. They had "turned." Or did they? In light of Asfour's career and renewed armed opposition in Syria led by Ghalioun, this was very much a "return" to business as usual.

THE LIMITS OF ARAB LIBERALISM

The choices made by Gaber Asfour and Burhan Ghalioun following the Arab uprisings were experiments in testing the limits of Arab liberalism,

---

[43] Kareem Fahim and Mayy El-Sheikh, "Memory of a mass killing becomes another casualty of Egyptian protests," *New York Times*, November 13, 2013.

[44] Cf. eg. Fahmi al-Shishtawi, "Jabir 'asfur: misr kanit fi ashadd al-ihtiyaaj ila al-sisi," *Al-Fajr*, June 23, 2015.

the seeds of which were sown by their literati ancestors two centuries ago. These limits were first set by the political events of the later twentieth and early 21st centuries, and duplicated in the wake of the Arab uprisings, especially the popular revolution of 2011 and popularly supported coup of 2013. The definition of these limits are reflected in the actions – however disappointing they may be – of Egypt and Syria's foremost secular theorists and political activists. Asfour and Ghalioun are both leaders as well as archetypes in this regard. At the risk of overgeneralizing and succumbing to realism, many liberals in the Arab world have tread one of two political paths in the wake of the Arab uprisings: (1) working under military autocracy (Egypt); or (2) overseas mobilization (Syria mainly). It is little surprise given these hindrances that critics have bemoaned the "silence," "failure," or "destructive legacy Arab liberals."[45] In the case of Egypt especially, liberal support of the military state has made key figures complicit (through silence or explicit statements) in the Rabaa massacre of 2013, Israel–Gaza conflict of 2014, and Egypt's judiciary mass death sentences of Muslim Brotherhood members (and non-members!) in 2015.[46]

This begs the question, however implausible, had many of Egypt's liberals stood with the Muslim Brotherhood on democratic principles and actively resisted the heavy-handed military, would their legacy be any less problematic? It is unlikely. Given the unsuccessful El Baradei–MB alliance and the feebleness of the SNC in the Syrian context, a liberal coalition including an Islamist group as popular and forceful as the Muslim Brotherhood would sooner or later collapse, giving way to renewed military and jihadist interventions. Or depending on the scope of their collective resistance, especially if it were armed, either had them killed, exiled, or locked up in Egypt's crowded prisons, or even started a civil war – as in the case of Syria, Libya, and Yemen. For the "armchair academic," there may be a utopian democracy waiting at the end of popular revolution. But for the political opposition, feminist, secularist, religious skeptic, artist, and activist striving for human, civil, and LGBT rights on the ground, they are fighting a losing battle against a police state on the one hand and a religiously and culturally conservative society on the other. There

---

[45] Worth, "The Arab intellectuals who didn't roar"; Sohrab Ahmari, "The failure of Arab liberals," *Commentary Magazine*, May 1, 2012; Joseph Massad, "The destructive legacy of Arab liberals," *Electronic Intifada*, March 30, 2015.

[46] See in part Joseph Masad, "The destructive legacy of Arab liberals." Ibid.

is virtually no middle ground. Mubarak's chokehold on al-Azhar and the religious establishment, coupled with the influx of Wahhabi-trained scholars coming from Saudi Arabia, has all but dried up the "moderate Islam" (*al-islam al-wasati*) touted by al-Azhar.[47] Under Sisi and under the guidance of former Egyptian Mufti Ali Guma (among other state-supported clerics in the Arab world), al-Azhar became further entrenched in the politics of the state.[48] In this context, given their small numbers and the sheer absence of rule of law, liberals have been victim to martial law as well as *takfiri* fatwas. The resulting "brain drain" of Arab professionals has been staggering, and the dissolving of the Arab middle class has left the region's liberals starving and stranded.[49]

Since its inception, liberalism in Egypt has typically not been "by the people" nor "for the people," but rather in service of the state.[50] And since the state has been mired in a struggle for national identity (against Israel, the British, and the Ottomans), the military and security apparatus have dominated public life. Egypt boasts a truly proud and rich institutional history, making it the first modern state in the entire Middle East. However, its economy, universities, hospitals, opera houses, newspapers, and religious endowments are quintessentially appendages of the state.[51] Liberal academics (as well as religious clerics) are by default part of the state structure. They are an integral part of the elite, who are highly cosmopolitan, but also rather old fashioned and out of touch with the increasingly young, economically and culturally impoverished public. In this vein, one need not look further than the disparaging comments of admittedly older liberals against the demonstrations and sit-ins by the youth. Murad Wahbah, professor of philosophy at Ain Shams University, criticized the disruption of business and traffic in Tahrir, and claimed "these are a mindless people and revolution."[52] The Syrian poet Adunis similarly "found no satisfaction in what people had done," referring to

---

[47] Hani Nasira, "Salafists challenge al-Azhar for ideological supremacy in Egypt," *The Jamestown Foundation*, September 16, 2010.

[48] Mohamad Elmasry, "Ali Gumah: Sisi's most loyal Islamic scholar," *Middle East Eye*, June 27, 2015.

[49] Cf. in relation James Reinl, "Arab 'brain drain' accelerates after Arab Spring: UN," *Middle East Eye*, May 8, 2015.

[50] Cf. Abdeslam M. Maghraoui, *Liberalism Without Democracy: Nationhood and Citizenship in Egypt, 1922–1936* (Durham, NC and London: Duke University Press, 2006), 66–76.

[51] Fahmy, *All the Pasha's Men*, 93–124, 250–2.

[52] "*Murad wahbah: misr satantahi iza ata ra'is min al-ikhwan*," *Al-Arabiya*, April 22, 2012.

the demonstrations in Tunisia and Egypt as a "youth rebellion."[53] The teachings and tenets of liberalism, furthermore, are often perceived as foreign, hostile, or even confrontational to the public. On the streets of Cairo and Damascus, philosophy (*falsafah*) is often casually used to refer to nonsense, and secularism (*al-'ilmaniyyah*) is just as often associated with a reified school of religious heresy.

The Egyptian people have been excluded from the affairs of their own country by design. The popular revolution on January 25, 2011 and popularly supported coup on July 3, 2013 were the people's most vociferous cries to seize back control of their country. History teaches that the ebb and flow of revolution and counterrevolution while destructive is an integral part of creating political structures accountable to its people. The aftermath of the French Revolution in 1798–9 was a century of imperialist and republican autocracies. The Persian Constitutional Revolution between 1905 and 1907 led to the retrenchment of the Qajar dynasty. In this context, the long and bloody processes of political liberalization and Islamic reform started five years ago but have years or decades in which to come to fruition. Egypt walks a precarious middle way between the fragile democratic transition in Tunisia and civil war in Syria. Only once its liberals serve the people can Egypt, and the region as a whole, truly reap the benefits of an Arab Spring.

---

[53] Sinan Antoon, "Adunis, the revolutionary poet," Al Jazeera, July 11, 2011.

11

Egypt's new liberal crisis

JOEL GORDON

W hen historians consider the crisis of liberalism in Egypt, our gaze turns back to the second decade of the parliamentary era, a period of political unrest and intellectual upheaval in response to the unfulfilled promises of the 1919 revolution. For many, particularly the youth who came to be defined as the generation of the 1930s, this was an era of exhilaration and militant anthems. Few doubted that Egyptian liberalism was in crisis. Neither parliament nor the political parties had delivered democracy or independence. This failure produced deep divisions within the liberal intelligentsia, particularly over the issue of how to galvanize popular support within an increasingly fragmented body politic.

Looking back, from the perspective of the authoritarian state that emerged after the 1952 Free Officers revolution, Western Orientalists constructed a liberal "crisis of orientation" rooted in a perceived retreat from secular nationalist liberalism in favor of a growing socially conservative, defensive, and ultimately reactionary religious impulse. Hassan al-Banna's Muslim Brotherhood represented the definitive threat with its "mentality of Mahdism" that was "inspired and activated by a negative nationalism" rooted in "unwavering faith" that a "perfect Islam" provides all the answers to mankind's problems. But the emblematic figure of the liberal "crisis" was Muhammad Husayn Haykal, a prominent secular intellectual who produced a series of works on Islamic history that seemed to constitute an attack on Western ethics and culture and "contributed to the initiation of an era of great intellectual confusion." Standing firm, valiantly withstanding the tide but forced at times into tactical retreat, was Taha Husayn, himself clerically trained but dead set on combatting "a drift into intellectual chaos" and promoting an "unequivocal Western orientation."[1]

Subsequent generations of scholars rejected the binary of this crisis and painted a far more nuanced picture. Charles Smith reread Haykal as a committed liberal utilizing Islamic history to speak to the masses.[2] There is irony to be sure, as Haykal had abandoned the majority-based Wafd Party for the Constitutional Liberals, a minority party with a narrow, property-owning base. This suggests an alternative critique of Egypt's liberals as elitists detached from, even fearful of, mass culture, including popular religious expression.[3] For Haykal, the real crisis of liberalism was the consolidation of military rule by the new Nasser regime in 1954, which for him represented the rejection of liberal values by a new generation. For Israel Gershoni and James Jankowski, the test of liberal commitment has little to do with religious orientation, but rather how Egypt's liberals stood on the real issue of the day, the challenge to liberalism represented by fascism and Nazism: "the relationship between democracy and dictatorship; between an open, pluralistic society and a closed, totalitarian society; between a constitutional parliamentary multi-party system and an authoritarian one-party system; between individual freedom of expression and protection of civil liberties and rights and a police state...between racism and racial tolerance."[4] By their reading, Egypt's liberals passed the test, the familiar flirtations of rebellious officers with German agents notwithstanding.[5] Whether or not the liberal crisis of the parliamentary

---

[1] The primary proponent was Nadav Safran, *Egypt in Search of Political Community: An Analysis of the Intellectual and Political Evolution of Egypt, 1804–1952* (Cambridge, MA: Harvard University Press, 1961); quotes are from pp. 231–2, 173, 175.

[2] Charles D. Smith, "The 'Crisis of Orientation': The shift of Egyptian intellectuals to Islamic subjects in the 1930s," *International Journal of Middle East Studies* 4 (1973): 382–410; and *Islam and the Search for Social Order in Modern Egypt: A Biography of Muhammad Husayn Haykal* (Albany, NY: SUNY Press, 1983).

[3] Abdeslam M. Maghraoui, *Liberalism Without Democracy: Nationhood and Citizenship in Egypt, 1922–1936* (Durham, NC: Duke University Press, 2006).

[4] Israel Gershoni, "Egyptian liberalism in an age of 'Crisis of Orientation': Al-Risala's reaction to fascism and Nazism, 1933–39," *International Journal of Middle East Studies* 31 (1999): 553.

[5] Israel Gershoni and James Jankowski, *Confronting Fascism in Egypt: Dictatorship versus Democracy in the 1930s* (Stanford, CA: Stanford University Press, 2009).

era was fact or Orientalist fiction, it is clear that, by January 1952, the year Egyptians took to the streets to burn down central Cairo, many had lost faith in party politics and began to articulate the call for a "just tyrant."[6] The sentiment cut across political and social boundaries and produced the foundations for military rule that continues to dominate Egypt.

The liberal crisis that we examine today is, I would suggest, different. Rather than turning toward (or bowing to) religiously conservative social trends, those who have adopted the mantle of liberalism, who promote themselves as the exclusive progenitors – and therefore legitimate inheritors – of the 2011 revolution (and who have been so uncritically regarded as such), articulate a pronounced hostility toward Islamism that ultimately undercuts the ability to work together toward building a new political order – in effect, to share the revolution – despite divergent social agendas. While it is true that the Muslim Brothers did not officially join the movement in Tahrir Square until the protests had taken on a degree of momentum, it is also indisputable that many Brothers, especially younger members, had already decamped to Tahrir and other centers of popular dissent throughout the country. Whose revolution was it really? What happened between June 2012, when Egyptians freely elected Mohammad Morsi president, and June 2013, when many of those same voters returned to Tahrir Square to set in motion a series of events that, willingly or not, set the stage for military intervention, the arrest and deposing of Morsi, and the excommunication of the Brothers, defined legally as terrorists, from political life?

Both sides surely share blame, especially in so volatile a revolutionary moment. Having toppled a thirty-year dictator, can young self-identified secular revolutionaries be faulted for persisting in viewing the streets as the primary political stage? The Muslim Brothers in power proved at times to be equally intolerant, and their faith-based rhetoric, however exaggerated by opponents, raised concerns about the face of the new Egypt.[7] Yet they surely paid a price for having successfully exerted political muscle through the ballot box. It is worth noting that all Islamist forces, not only the Muslim Brothers, had "adopted party politics and

---

[6] Joel Gordon, *Nasser's Blessed Movement: Egypt's Free Officers and the July Revolution* (Oxford: Oxford University Press, 1992), Chapter 1.

[7] Mohamed Elmasry, "Unpacking anti-Muslim Brotherhood discourse," *Jadaliyya*, June 28, 2013, www.jadaliyya.com/pages/index/12466/unpacking-anti-muslim-brotherhood-discourse

democratic competition as a basis of their activism."[8] If secular liberals argue that the Islamists turned authoritarian, Islamist liberals can argue that, caught between the military, state security, a more conservative self-righteous Salafi bloc, and a secular intelligentsia that articulated its own exclusionary legitimacy as inheritors of a post-Mubarak Egypt, they had little chance to advance any agenda.

When anti-government demonstrators reoccupied Tahrir Square on June 30, 2013 (while Morsi supporters decamped at Rabaa Square in Heliopolis), they made what history may judge to be a Faustian bargain with the military. When we look back on these events, we may well reorient the liberal crisis from a defensive turn toward conservative Islamism to an unyielding dread of an Islamist threat that many had earlier blamed the Mubarak regime for cynically fomenting. Rather than judge the wisdom – or honesty – of those who so feared an Islamist turn under Morsi, I seek to understand the degree to which this dread turned so many liberals into "unlikely allies of the army."[9]

HEROES OF THE REVOLUTION

To fathom this new "crisis," I intertwine the pronouncements of two powerful voices of the "liberal" opposition, Alaa al-Aswany and Bassem Youssef. Neither should be regarded as an intellectual or necessarily a deep thinker. Yet their impact on popular culture as well as their global reach – one as a widely translated author and editorialist, the other as recipient of a prestigious international award for journalistic freedom, and guest, multiple times, on *The Daily Show*, as well as the subject of a stinging critique of the Egyptian government by its host, Jon Stewart[10] – is important. Al-Aswany's and Youssef's stories, as well as their artistic approaches, differ significantly. Each in his own way found himself facing a new public sphere in which rules had changed and political grounds

---

[8] Abdullah al-Arian, *Answering the Call: Popular Activism in Sadat's Egypt* (Oxford: Oxford University Press, 2014), 234; see also Hesham al-Awady, *The Muslim Brothers in Pursuit of Legitimacy: Power and Political Islam in Egypt under Mubarak* (London: I.B. Tauris, 2014).
[9] Negar Azimi, "The Egyptian army's unlikely allies," New Yorker, January 8, 2014, www.newyorker.com/news/news-desk/the-egyptian-armys-unlikely-allies
[10] Youssef won the 2013 International Press Freedom Award from the Committee to Protect Journalists. Stewart's defense of Youssef aired on April 1, 2013. He visited Youssef's show in June 2013, weeks before the military coup.

were fast shifting. Al-Aswany's championing of popular dissent against the Morsi government and later validation of the reassertion of military rule may well be a cautionary tale for those who seek to move Egypt forward toward a true democratic orientation. Youssef's meteoric rise and fall is the story of a suddenly open media with unprecedented freedom to pillory the ruler, one who happened to be an Islamist and, for a comic, an easy target.

Alaa al-Aswany – "Democracy is the answer"

Al-Aswany gained prominence in Egypt with the publication of his bestselling 2002 novel *The Yacoubian Building*, a blistering depiction of the reigning order in late-Mubarak Egypt. Translated into over twenty languages, the novel brought international fame. A 2006 film adaptation, featuring a bevy of super stars, brought him wider exposure. Already juggling dentistry and fiction writing, he became a regular op-ed columnist for *al-Dustour* (weekly) and *al-Shorouk* (daily), two privately owned newspapers associated with opposition to the regime. A collection of his pre-revolutionary columns have been translated into English for a volume that appeared in April 2011. These essays chronicle a society that had lost its way, mired in corruption, official indifference, and increasingly less concerned with veiling its violent underpinnings.[11]

Al-Aswany's primary targets were the regime and the likely succession of Hosni Mubarak's son Gamal as president. He emphasized national unity and anomie. The Muslim Brothers were part of the politically diverse campaign to thwart hereditary impulses: "Despite our political and ideological differences, we have come together to perform our national duty."[12] It was the regime that "has deliberately exaggerated the role and influence of the Muslim Brotherhood for use as a bogeyman against anyone who calls for democracy."[13] Ordinary Egyptians "usually have an infallible compass by which they determine the correct political position."[14] If the Brothers won open elections, "wouldn't that be the free

[11] Alaa al-Aswany, *On the State of Egypt: What Made the Egyptian Revolution Inevitable* (New York: Vintage, 2011).
[12] Ibid., 6.
[13] Ibid., 96.
[14] Ibid., 62.

choice of Egyptians, which we should respect if we are true democrats?"[15] Nonetheless, he concluded every essay, as he would through 2014 when he stopped writing, with the proclamation that "Democracy is the answer" (al-dimuqratiyya hiyya al-hal), an unveiled play upon the Brotherhood slogan, "Islam is the solution" (al-Islam huwwa al-hal).[16]

On January 25, 2011, al-Aswany concluded a writing session and turned on the news. Stunned by the size of the demonstrations, he headed to Tahrir Square and for the next eighteen days "lived" alongside millions of fellow Egyptians, only heading home for short breaks.[17] He was not the only celebrity on site, but he enhanced his popular standing with speeches and informal press conferences, and in the following months through writings and a famous television appearance in which he boldly confronted standing prime minister Ahmad Shafiq, who resigned the next day.[18] As with his literature, chastised by some as overly melodramatic and pandering, he spoke to a popular pulse. His English language fluency makes him particularly accessible to foreign reporters, and in the fall of 2013 he became a contributing editor and columnist for the New York Times. In late 2014, a second collection of essays appeared in English translation, this time replicated in strict chronological order.[19]

The latter essays provide a window into the evolution of his thinking between March 1, 2011 and June 16, 2014, revealing pendulum swings between optimism and pessimism, an escalating dread of what might constitute majority rule and, eventually, a confrontation with the realities of renewed military rule. There are several key themes that accentuate al-Aswany's – and by extension the liberal – predicament.

First is the suspicion, from the outset, that entrenched old regime forces would work to "abort the revolution."[20] On the eve of presidential elections, al-Aswany warned that "if it is not possible to impose their candidate, the military council will cause problems and total chaos that will prevent the presidential elections from taking place, leaving the military council in power indefinitely."[21] This fear vanished with the election of

---

[15] Ibid., 9.

[16] Regime banners often retorted: Islam is not terrorism (al-Islam laysa al-irhab).

[17] Al-Aswany, On the State, vii–ix.

[18] Wendell Stevenson, "Writing the revolution," New Yorker, January 16, 2012, 39.

[19] Alaa al-Aswany, Democracy is the Answer: Egypt's Years of Revolution (London: Gingko, 2014).

[20] Ibid., August 2, 2011, 89–93.

[21] Ibid., April 16, 2012, 230.

Morsi and the conviction that the new government, in cahoots with the old security apparatus, was moving to impose a dictatorship that was at once new – Muslim Brotherhood driven – and old. The speed with which al-Aswany adopted a hostile approach toward Morsi's rule accentuates the degree to which he held no faith that the president could speak to all of Egypt – something he challenged Morsi to do as part of a delegation that met with the new president right after the elections. He often rooted his critique of the Brotherhood in their deep past history more than their political evolution under Sadat and Mubarak: "Each time the Brotherhood participate in national movements, they will at some point break away from the national ranks and move closer to those in power, who inevitably use them to undermine the national opposition."[22]

It is a superficial reading at best, but a common narrative espoused even by radical Salafi critics and contains two primary themes. One emphasizes the violent wing of the movement and its militant proclivities; a second describes the Brothers' historical flirtations with power, particularly during the late liberal era, as endemic of a fundamental lack of commitment to democratic ideals. The Muslim Brotherhood "has always violated the national consensus and allied with despotic rulers against the will of the people.....Those adherents of political Islam will never shy away from forming an alliance with any power, no matter how oppressive or unjust, if it enables them to establish what they believe is God's rule."[23] Al-Aswany also characteristically prefaces talk of the Brotherhood with warnings about "Saudi" or Wahhabi Islam, painting their Islamist agenda in starkest colors and contrasting it to "the moderate Islam of the Egyptians."[24]

As he watched the presidential elections unfold, al-Aswany held his breath – and then his nose. "From the very beginning, the Muslim Brotherhood has put its political interests above the aims of the revolution," and now it outright lied, "went back on their promises" to not run a candidate and "obscured the truth."[25] At the same time, "The liberals and leftists must learn that the Muslim Brotherhood and the Salafists are not a bunch of reactionary fascists, but in fact are patriotic citizens who took part in the revolution and sacrificed martyrs. They also happen to

---

[22] Ibid., November 15, 2011, 145.
[23] Ibid., January 31, 2012, 185. This historical reading of the old regime was highlighted by Ayman al-Zawhiri in al-Hisad al-Murr: al-Ikhwan al-Muslimun fi Sittin 'Aman (Amman: Dar al-Bayariq, 1999), Chapter 1.
[24] Al-Aswany, Democracy, October 11, 2011, 127.
[25] Ibid., April 2, 2012, 220–2.

possess an Islamic political agenda, which we should respect even if we disagree with it."[26]

Al-Aswany, who supported the Nasserist candidate Hamdan Sabahi in the first round, feared that the deep state would fix the vote to ensure Morsi's defeat to Ahmad Shafiq in the runoff.[27] Nonetheless, he emphasized that, however "rigged" the process, the revolution "realised a great achievement in voting Shafik out of office and electing Mohammad Morsi." The new president's task "will not be easy because he is confronting the Mubarak regime which still controls the state and which I expect to put up stiff resistance to any change." Thus, Morsi "will need the support of all Egyptians, something he will only get if he is seen to be fighting for all of Egypt and not just for the Muslim Brotherhood."[28] "My 'violent feud' with political Islam should not stop me from helping them if they are injured or from supporting them if they wage a nationalist and legitimate campaign." The primary enemy remained the Mubarak regime.[29] Al-Aswany criticized "liberals and rightists who failed to realize that the core of the conflict" was now "between the elected president and a dictatorial power and whose hostility toward the Brotherhood has pushed them into supporting the military council against the elected president" – an argument he would later retract.[30]

Al-Aswany's conversion, which he attributes to Morsi's deceit, occurred over a three-month span. His initial charges related to the government's failure to curb the "brutal repression" of the Interior Ministry, the insular composition of Morsi's cabinet, the familiar control of state media, and the Islamists' domination of the Constituent Assembly.[31] In characterizing Morsi as a president for whom Egyptians had been "obliged" to vote, he ignored the broad base that voted for him out of ideological conviction.[32] After Morsi declared "quasi-divine powers" in order to curb the judiciary, he turned into a "dictator, therefore an enemy of the revolution" who was following instructions of the Brothers' Guidance Council "to placate the old regime instead of fighting it."[33] By the start of the New Year, al-Aswany

---

[26] Ibid., April 16, 2012, 230.
[27] Ibid., May 21, 2012, 244–8; June 4, 2012, 248–52; he later wrote that he had not voted for Morsi; ibid., September 24, 2012, 305.
[28] Ibid., June 25, 2012, 256–60.
[29] Ibid., July 9, 2012, 265–8.
[30] Ibid., July 16, 2012, 270–1.
[31] Ibid., September 24, 2012, 305–9.
[32] Ibid., October 8, 2012, 316.
[33] Ibid., November 26, 2012, 337–42. Mohamed Elmasry notes this as one of five

seemed to have lost faith in the democratic process: "how can we have elections when they are run according to a law passed by the useless upper house according to instructions from the office of the [Muslim Brothers'] supreme guide?"[34] After protests to mark the revolution's second anniversary turned violent, al-Aswany asked, "Why is Morsi killing Egyptians?"[35] By spring 2013, he proclaimed that Egyptians had traded "military fascism for religious fascism."[36] In a fanciful view back from the future, he predicted a second revolutionary "wave" that would topple Morsi – but through early presidential elections – and end Muslim Brother rule.[37] Soon after, the Tamarod petition drive to recall Morsi was in full swing. Al-Aswany now regularly described the Brothers as "full of treachery and opportunism," and a "secretive and fascist religious sect," with whom there could be "no dialogue or compromise."[38]

Early elections quickly vanished from the agenda as the stage was set for the mass gathering in Tahrir (June 30), the deposition and abduction of Morsi and suspension of the constitution (July 3), the clearing of Rabaa Square (August 14), and the decrees that followed. For al-Aswany, this constituted the corrective to a revolution long gone astray. The army had performed its "national duty" to crush a "delusional jihad."[39] Al-Aswany became an unapologetic international spokesperson for what he now termed the revolution's "third wave."[40] "We have finished with Hosni Mubarak, then Morsi's rule, now with political Islam," he told a German journalist.[41] Robert Fisk, one of many who challenged the legality of the intervention, described him as a "happy man."[42] The forceful clearing of Rabaa was "unavoidable" and the Muslim Brothers bore responsibility

"unfounded myths" promoted to justify Morsi's forceful removal: "Revisiting Egypt's 2013 military takeover," Al Jazeera English, June 30, 2013, www.aljazeera.com/indepth/opinion/2015/06/revisiting-egypt-2013-military-takeover-150630090417776.html

[34] Al-Aswany, *Democracy*, January 21, 2013, 366.
[35] Ibid., January 28, 2013, 367–71.
[36] Ibid., March 25, 2013, 404.
[37] Ibid., April 29, 2013, 420.
[38] Ibid., June 3, 10, 24, 2013, 435–53.
[39] Ibid., July 15, 2013, 459; July 22, 2013, 466.
[40] Ibid., July 29, 2013, 468.
[41] Jannis Hagmann, "Mubarak's regime remains intact," Qantara, July 23, 2013, en.qantara.de/content/interview-with-egyptian-novelist-alaa-al-aswany-mubaraks-regime-remains-intact
[42] Robert Fisk, "Alaa al-Aswany: The overthrow of President Morsi was not a coup, it was the third wave of Egypt's revolution," *Independent*, July 29, 2013.

for casualties. Critics of the action underestimate the threat posed by the "terrorists."[43] Eerily reminiscent of Islamist claims about anti-government protesters in late 2012, he related equally specious urban legends about a lawless, armed encampment. He supported the criminalization of the Brotherhood, equating this with European statutes against terrorism: "Egypt is waging a war against a criminal organization committed to terrorizing and killing innocent people, to bringing down the state and spreading chaos."[44]

However disillusioned he has grown with Abd al-Fattah al-Sisi – and that started well before Sisi was elected president in May 2014 – al-Aswany has not budged in his hostility to the Brotherhood, his reading of their history, and his depiction of Morsi as a dictator. What were Morsi's inexcusable – potentially "capital" – crimes as head of state? And how willing was someone like al-Aswany to allow an elected government, however inept in rule or unpalatable in agenda, to run its course, especially given he knew the entrenched security forces still pulled strings in the country? In his version of *Animal Farm*, published on the eve of June 30, the lion saves the jungle from savage wolves and evil sheep and then graciously returns to his den.[45] Should he be forgiven as blindly optimistic?

Bassem Youssef – one hour a week

A consistent concern articulated by liberals such as al-Aswany was that the Morsi government, by monopolizing power, would fundamentally change the face of culture in Egypt. Although the government did lend a friendlier ear to complaints about public decency in the arts, little of substance really changed. In early June 2013, prominent artists staged a sit-in to protest at the replacement of several key figures, including the director of the Cairo Opera, by the newly appointed minister of culture.[46] However, fears that the broadcast media would become fully faith-based proved to be totally groundless. Instead, the media experienced a dramatic opening – not totally,

---

[43] "Morsi critic: What happens in Egypt is not very clear abroad," NPR, August 15, 2013, www.npr.org/templates/story/story.php?storyId=212356278

[44] Al-Aswany, *Democracy*, August 19, 2013, 478–80.

[45] Ibid., May 27, 2013, 431–5.

[46] See Thoraia Abou Bakr, "Culture and lifestyle during Morsi's reign," *Daily News Egypt*, June 30, 2013, www.dailynewsegypt.com/2013/06/30/culture-and-lifestyle-during-morsis-reign/

but substantially – as old rules about public expressions of disagreement, and especially political satire, seemed to vanish in a renewed flood of private secular and religious channels.

The case of Bassem Youssef provides a notable – perhaps *the* notable – case in point. Youssef is a real product of the 2011 revolution, even more than al-Aswany. A heart surgeon by profession, he too went to Tahrir Square, where he helped treat the wounded. In May 2011, he began uploading five- to seven-minute segments of a program he called *B+* (after his blood-type) featuring satirical commentary mixed with snippets from daily media broadcasts.[47] As his weekly segments doubled in length, surpassing ten minutes by the eighth and final episode, his audience grew exponentially. During late summer, he inaugurated *al-Barnameg* (*The Show*) on a liberal private channel, ONTv. Episodes ran for approximately twenty-five minutes. In December 2012, he began his second season on a new network, CBC (in his opening episode he quipped it stood for "Choose Bassem Youssef") in the refurbished downtown Radio City Cinema and for the first time faced a live studio audience. The nods to *The Daily Show*, from the set to the edited news clips, down to Youssef's delivery and facial expressions were now striking. He is not Jon Stewart's only international clone, but he is arguably his closest.[48]

What allowed Youssef to flourish, in addition to his talent, were the new rules at play in television broadcast. The red line during the Mubarak era, whether in print or broadcast media, was criticism or satire of the standing head of state. After January 2011, that line evaporated. ONTv, Youssef's inaugural network, had gained particular notoriety in March 2011 for the live segment of the talk show *Akhar Kalam* (*Last Word*) on which al-Aswany confronted Ahmad Shafiq. Youssef aimed his satire at numerous targets, not only state officials but also fellow media figures, especially old regime holdovers. After June 2012, especially in his second season, a standing, elected president stood within his range. An unseasoned, uncharismatic, often tongue-tied politician, Morsi made an easy target. So did a wide array of fiery television preachers and Islamist-Salafi spokespersons, most of whom were not accustomed to such open mass-mediated mockery and close-cropped editing of their utterances.

Youssef had a field day poking fun at them, but how much of this fun was directed at rhetorical excess – and fumbling – and how much more

---

[47] See www.youtube.com/user/bassmyoussefshow/videos
[48] Episodes of the show as it evolved are easily viewable online, some with English subtitles.

generally at an Islamist worldview that had galvanized a large proportion of the Egyptian electorate? To what extent was Youssef propounding, even mimicking, a self-assured secular worldview, one in part bolstered by a proprietary hold on the "revolution" but also rooted deeply in the official secularism of the state?[49] Youssef's approach is zany but crafty. His editors are able to capture and/or edit people at their worst, and the rapid-fire delivery punctuated by a comedic pictorial depiction or a comic grimace leaves little room for pause.

During his first year's run, starting with B+, Youssef had lampooned exaggerated fears of Islamism, which his targets often lumped in with the threats of foreigners, Zionism, internet hackers, and sexual deviants. In his seventh, penultimate B+ episode, in April 2011, he announced that he had voted against the March 29 constitutional referendum, but insisted that its approval would not spell the end of the world, the presumed Islamic state that many dreaded. Instead, he criticized a prevailing "atmosphere of Islamophobia, Christianophobia, Liberalophobia, Democratophobia, any phobia you want." In an early ONTv episode of *al-Barnameg*, he even broke format to interview the Salafi comic Mohammad Tolba.[50] Nonetheless, following the presidential elections a year later, Youssef made less effort to promote bipartisanship; on the contrary, his subjectivity was pronounced, especially as the partnership that elected Morsi fragmented and the government found itself on the defensive.

Youssef asserts to this day that as a satirist his function is to poke fun at those in power. Early in his second season, in late 2012, as he came under increasing fire from government loyalists, he countered that he had only targeted the Brotherhood in five percent of his jokes (he was surely understating). He also noted that the rules governing satire had changed overnight. In the fifth episode of season two, he turned serious to conclude his opening segment:

> When we talked about…the old regime…sarcasm was funny. But with the Islamists in power and in parliament, and out in the streets, we shouldn't talk about them, because sarcasm has become taboo.…

[49] Joel Gordon, "Piety, youth and Egyptian cinema: Still seeking Islamic SPACE," *Islamism and Cultural Expression in the Arab World*, ed. Abir Hamdar and Lindsey Moore (London: Routledge, 2015), 103–19.

[50] www.youtube.com/watch?v=vuZ2qbLAEEE&feature=youtu.be/. He and Tolba appeared on stage together in late September 2012 at Ayn Shams University in Cairo, hosted by the Faculty of Engineering Student Union.

Make [Muhammad] el-Baradei president, Hamdan [Sabahi] prime minister, and the Copts the ruling party, and I'll talk about them every episode!

Why are most episodes directed against one group? And this is the last time I'll say it – because this group holds power, controlled the writing of the constitution, and holds the majority in parliament. Despite all this, they don't want us to talk about them![51]

He tried to remain critical of the troubling behavior (and laughable errors) of an opposition with which he openly identified: "We say provocative things too – we are impolite toward the other side and say things about them that shouldn't be said."[52] Yet he remained adamant that the binary opposition of "us and them" that so infected Egyptian daily life was rooted in an intolerant rhetoric espoused by the Islamists who characterized their antagonists as unbelievers: "That is why we deserve to be insulted and scolded, even if it comes down to beatings and torture and even, God forbid, murder."[53]

Youssef's targets (in addition to old state media stalwarts) were far more often the clerics and lay preachers on the new religious channels than Freedom and Justice Party or Muslim Brother spokespersons. He ridiculed outlandish claims that opposition protesters were sexually depraved – marching against the government armed with condoms and other birth-control devices – and/or homosexuals. He particularly defended the tenuous position of Christians, in a sinister voice comically elongating the Arabic plural (*masihiyin*). He took great pleasure in "mistakenly" posting images of Brotherhood leader Muhammad al-Badie as Egypt's president, underscoring a common liberal critique of where real power, and where Morsi's real loyalty, lay. Of course, Youssef took regular potshots at Morsi who, arguably, provided great comic fodder.

Underlying this was an ongoing contest over who could or should speak on behalf of religion. Youssef, who has always self-identified as a Muslim, held up clerical and lay antagonists to scorn, challenging their credentials, inferring that most Egyptians were comfortable in their religious skin and were in danger of having their faith hijacked. In one graphic, the Security Police (*Amn al-dawla*) were referred to as the Protectors of the

---

[51] *Al-Barnameg*, season 2, episode 5.
[52] Ibid., episode 4.
[53] Ibid., episode 5.

Brotherhood's "Call" (*Amn al-da'wa*). He was not, he insisted, insulting the faith. In a politically charged country, he was, however, insulting some of the faithful.

Bassem Youssef should be remembered, wherever his talents take him in the future, for bravely trying to straddle the divide between old regime media powers – and personalities – many of whom also sat in his crosshairs, and a new government, which happened to represent a worldview he found anathema. If he aimed his humor too widely, linking frenetic, sycophantic preachers and untrained spokespersons with serious political elders, he could be forgiven in part because of the haphazard way the process was unfolding. To those who complained, he asserted the sanctity of free speech. And with a self-deprecating twinkle of his eye, he asked, if it was so unfair, in the face of the non-stop, round-the-clock onslaught from the pro-government channels, to ask for one hour a week of alternative programming.[54]

It is vital to note that, despite calls for him to be shut down, Bassem Youssef remained on the air through the onset of the Tamarod movement, which he implicitly supported. In March 2013, he was called before a magistrate, and accused of insulting the president and religion, but the case did not proceed beyond a perfunctory fine. There is strong reason to believe that Morsi's advisors were embarrassed by the magistrate's action and unsure how to react. The outpouring of support for Youssef in the streets outside the precinct station where he appeared in compliance with the court order – sporting the oversized version of the ceremonial hat that Morsi had worn during a state visit to Pakistan and that Youssef had spoofed on air – demonstrated the scope of his impact.[55] Youssef continued his partisan spoofs right up to the moment when Egypt exploded. One of his last routines was a musical send-up of Morsi's fading appeal staged to imitate Nasser-era extravaganzas on national holidays. The song's chorus, "We chose him and we're stuck with him" (*ikhtarnah wa akhadnah*) spoke directly to the momentum of the Tamarod campaign, and verses reprised many of the themes Youssef had covered on his show, including clever puns relating to the Brotherhood and their religious call.[56]

---

[54] Ibid.

[55] Morsi wore the hat when given an honorary degree by the National University of Science and Technology. *Al-Barnameg*, season 2, episode 18.

[56] Joel Gordon, "Stuck with him: Bassem Youssef and the Egyptian revolution's last laugh," *Review of Middle East Studies* 48 (2014): 34–43.

Al-Barnameg did not air amidst the turmoil that followed. On July 16, two weeks after Morsi's arrest and nearly a month before Rabaa Square was cleared, he wrote a column for *al-Shorouk* (quickly picked up in translation by CNN online) in which he cautioned secular liberals to temper their "victory high"; those who justified, even celebrated the violent attack on Muslim Brotherhood supporters betrayed a "fascist" nature "no different from that of the Islamists who think that their enemies disappearance off this planet would be a victory for God." The Brothers, he cautioned, had "lost their moral compass a long time ago. Do you want to follow suit?" Youssef warned of a return to the security mentality of the 1990s.[57]

Youssef returned to the air in late October 2013. In his first episode, he tried to find humor in a country in which many had stopped laughing. He poked fun at both pro- and anti-Morsi camps' exaggerated estimates of their support in the streets the previous summer and parodied the ongoing debate over whether or not the army's intervention constituted a coup d'état. There was little humor to be generated, however, at the expense of a movement that had been brutally suppressed, not by people power, but armed force, and an elected president, however cartoonish, who now sat in prison. In the second half of the episode the show shifted gears to target, if indirectly, those who now held power, focusing on the grandiose proclamations and displays of affection for the army and General Sisi.

Towards the end of the hour, the show reprised a routine that aired in late 2012 in which supporting actor Shadi Alfons played a coquettish woman named Gamahir (a take on the "masses") calling in to the host of "*al-Barnameg* Love Line." In the earlier incarnation Gamahir had traded her "pilot" (*tayyar*, a reference to Mubarak) for a lover with an Islamist "bent" (*tayyar islami*).[58] Now she was separated from her husband and in love with an officer. To add spice to her new affair – and draw unmistakable parallels to real life, in which Morsi had appointed Sisi minister of defense – her husband had been the one who introduced her to her new lover. A series of gags ensued related to political discourse (the host asks if the officer's intrusion into her marital life constituted a "coup" and she retorts by accusing the host of disparaging the army) and, ultimately, punning Sisi's name, building to a bawdy climax, a double-edged mockery

---

[57] Bassem Youssef, "Egypt's secularists repeating Islamists' mistakes," CNN online, July 20, 2013, www.cnn.com/2013/07/19/opinion/youssef-egypt-political-upheaval/

[58] *Al-Barnameg*, season 2, episode 5; the two versions of *tayyar* come from different roots, with a different initial "t" but sound close enough to make the pun.

of public exhortations of the general's virility and of the prurience of Morsi and his movement.[59]

Youssef was clearly pushing the limits. His second show, taped the following Wednesday, was cancelled before airing on Friday night due to "editorial policy and contractual differences."[60] The single hour of broadcast political comedy that Youssef had asked for, granted for a turbulent year by the Morsi government, was no longer tenable. Alaa al-Aswany wrote about Youssef's predicament, circuitously admitting that the Morsi government had not pulled the plug because "everyone had stood up" to defend freedom expression. Now Youssef again stood accused of slandering the "leader of the nation," but times had changed. "We will not be able to build a modern nation unless Egyptians believe that they are all equal, and that they do not need a leader who is above accountability or sarcastic criticism, even if it is General Sisi himself."[61] The following spring, after Youssef's eventual return to the air, al-Aswany praised "Egypt's ancient snark" in a New York Times opinion piece. Egyptians, he wrote, often take refuge in satire when "other means of expression are blocked." The 2011 revolution "brought satire out in the open." He again invoked Bassem Youssef who, after ridiculing Morsi for a year, had turned his sights to Sisi. He ended on an optimistic note: "most Egyptians, in spite of their travails and problems, can still appreciate a good joke."[62]

Bassem Youssef tread lightly when it came to mocking Sisi. His edged his show more toward entertainment, but he could not ignore the outlandish claims, backed implicitly by regime officials, that military doctors had discovered a miracle cure for AIDS and cancer. A medical doctor by training, Youssef could not countenance such quackery, nor could he stand silent in the face of the rampant jingoism that such promises evoked. As the clock ticked down toward the promised delivery date, it also ticked for Youssef. On June 3, 2014, he announced that he could no longer bear the intensifying censorship and cancelled his show. Soon after, he left Egypt for the Gulf. The miracle cure for AIDS has slipped off the public radar, at least in broadcast media.

---

[59] Al-Barnameg, season 3, episode 1.

[60] Memorandum from CBC Network, October 27, 2013, displayed on the air during an interview with Yousry Fouda on Akhir Kalam (ONTv) broadcast on December 4, 2013, www.youtube.com/watch?v=ecwlx5SajVU

[61] Al-Aswany, Democracy, October 29, 2013, 519–20.

[62] Al-Aswany, "Egypt's ancient snark," New York Times, March 13, 2014.

Two weeks later, in what proved to be his last Egyptian column, al-Aswany wrote in the name of a "young revolutionary" turned political prisoner:

> Egyptians, I apologise for misunderstanding you; you didn't need a revolution, you didn't understand it and you don't deserve it. I'll leave you this stagnant water that we tried to clear for your sake and for which you accused us of being foreign agents and traitors.... Enjoy corruption, favoritism, crippled justice and the media that have programs prepared in the corridors of the State Security.[63]

Following this, he decided to take a brief pause from writing.

THE LIBERAL CRISIS RECONSIDERED

I began by questioning the "crisis of orientation" expounded by Western scholars looking at Egypt during the interwar period. For them, the crisis entailed an intellectual retreat by self-proclaimed liberals from core secular beliefs toward a defensive "reactionary" worldview couched in religious garb. In reality – I accept the arguments of Charles Smith and others – they sought outreach to a broader population; their sin was flying in the face of perceived notions of progress and modernity. In more recent decades, many outspoken liberals seemed to have embraced that binary of secular progress/religious reaction.

Alaa al-Aswany and Bassem Youssef strike me as representative of this newer liberal crisis. Each, in his own way, got swept along by a revolutionary moment of enthusiasm, fueled by the cumulative euphoria of the Arab Spring, the rapidity with which the dictator surrendered and the infectious camaraderie of Tahrir. Al-Aswany's accounts of standing in the crosshairs of snipers, an act he likened to playing Russian roulette, are chilling.[64] Youssef's eye for the absurd underscores the power of humor to advance politics. Still, both are culpable of solidifying boundaries between divergent worldviews that by summer 2013 became impenetrable. The writer, once hailed for a sympathetic literary portrayal of a jihadi militant, wound up caricaturing Islamists in ways reminiscent of Mubarak. The

---

[63] Al-Aswany, *Democracy*, June 16, 2014, 638–39.
[64] Stevenson, "Writing the Revolution," 39.

satirist occasionally, always gently, poked allies like Baradei and Sabahi. But in his campaign to make those in power appear ridiculous, he never found cause to again reach out, as he had prior to and early during Morsi's reign, to fellow comics who may have been bearded and to seek common ground through laughter. When, after Rabaa, he warned secular readers against a "victory high," he still rejected moral equivalency between the two camps. In an increasingly polarized country, the coalition that brought down Mubarak collapsed. Facing the specter of "Brotherhoodization" – arguably exaggerated – many secular "liberals" turned to a defensive, reactionary embrace of re-militarization, a new "crisis of orientation" from which Egyptians may well suffer for many years.

POSTSCRIPT: FIVE YEARS ON

In January 2016, Egyptians marked – they were not allowed to celebrate or demonstrate – the fifth anniversary of the overthrow of Hosni Mubarak and the *communitas* of Tahrir Square. Egypt's prisons hold some forty thousand political detainees, Muslim Brothers and their confederates, and a growing number of secular activists, many of whom have come to question the degree and speed with which they supported the military takeover of June–July 2013.[65] Alaa al-Aswany wrote his last *New York Times* op-ed piece in October 2014, a generic essay on "Traveling while Arab" with no nod to Egypt.[66] The English translation of his third novel, *The Automobile Club of Egypt*, appeared in 2015. A potboiler set in the waning days of Egypt's constitutional monarchy, the story makes only one passing, and historically dubious, reference to the most visible opposition movement in the country. One of his lead characters, who attends a meeting of a dissident organization, narrates: "There was a long agenda and a discussion of recent events, including the stance of the nationalist workers and the war against the independent trade unions being waged by the palace, the English, the minority capitalist parties and the Muslim Brotherhood, who were well known for their opportunism."[67] Fearing arrest, Bassem Youssef fled Egypt for Dubai following his

---

[65] Joe Stork, "Egypt's political prisoners," opendemocracy.net, March 6, 2015, https://www.opendemocracy.net/opensecurity/joe-stork/egypt's-political-prisoners
[66] Aswany, "Traveling while Arab," *New York Times*, October 14, 2014.
[67] Aswany, *The Automobile Club of Egypt* (New York: Knopf, 2015), 329. The original Arabic edition appeared in 2013, prior to the coup. For the historical role of the Brothers in

show's cancellation and forty-eight hours after a court found him liable for $15 million in court fees. He spent the spring of 2015 as a visiting fellow at Harvard University's John F. Kennedy School of Government. He has emerged occasionally to speak out against the Sisi regime and in January 2016 initiated a Twitter campaign to honor the memory of the revolution's martyrs, the incarcerated, and the disappeared.[68] He has kept his promise to not revive *al-Barnameg* outside Egypt. In February 2016, he signed on with Fusion Media Network to star in a new comedy series, *The Democracy Handbook*, a sendup of American, rather than Egyptian, politics and society. His "journey across the US," during which he "discovers that the land of the free and the home of the brave is actually much more a hotbed of corporate-owned politicians, and gun-toting racists," premiered on July 14 with ten episodes, each approximately five to six minutes long. Youssef introduces each episode by noting that,

> In my native Egypt I was a surgeon, until the Arab Spring, when I realized my country itself had fallen ill. So I created a comedy show to help the nation heal. The people liked it, but the government, not so much. And before things got worse, I left for the land of the free.[69]

Whether he can reinvent himself as an Egyptian-American social satirist in a much more competitive comedic political field remains to be seen.

---

trade unionism and labor organization, see Ellis Goldberg, *Tinker, Tailor and Textile Worker: Class and Politics in Egypt, 1930–1952* (Berkeley: University of California Press, 1986).
[68] Youssef admitted he fled in a recent interview (February 12, 2016) with Terry Gross on *Fresh Air*, http://www.npr.org/2016/02/06/465691577/fresh-air-weekend-bassem-youssef-homegrown-terrorists-babys-first-food/. He had previously denied this in interviews for the Egyptian press, "Bassem Youssef launches campaign for detainees, forced disappearance victims," *Egypt Independent*, January 19, 2016, http://www.egyptindependent.com//news/bassem-youssef-launches-campaign-detainees-forced-disappearance-victims
[69] Bassem Youssef, *Democracy Handbook*, fusion.net, http://fusion.net/series/democracy-handbook/

12

Egyptian liberals and their anti-democratic deceptions

A contemporary sad narrative

Amr Hamzawy

LIBERAL IDEAS AT A CROSSROADS

Over the past three years, liberal ideas in Egypt have been at a crossroads. Since July 3, 2013, countless "secular" political parties and movements have stood under their liberal banners in support of a military intervention into politics.

They supported the removal of an elected president, without early presidential elections. This was despite the fact that elections were a main demand of the crowds that filled the streets on June 30, 2013. They supported suspending the constitution of 2012 (my own opposition to it aside), and establishing an "Islamist free democracy" without recourse to a popular referendum and its ballot boxes. These liberal parties and movements are far removed from a real commitment to the principles and values of liberal democracy and, instead, appear quite ready to compromise them.

The majority of liberal politicians, intellectuals, and activists have been more than willing to cooperate with the de facto authority that imposed itself after July 3, 2013. In that time, Egypt has witnessed repeated oppressions: satellite channels were shut down, members and leaders of political parties and movements on the religious right arrested and abused, crimes of mass killing were associated with dispersing the Rabaa and al-Nahda sit-ins, and there is mounting evidence of systematic human rights violations. Yet, liberals have continued to work with Egypt's de facto authority. Most of their parties chose silence rather than condemn the repression.

The voices of the security state have been on the rise, inciting hate speech and exclusionary practices; they justify state violence, human rights violations, and the bypassing of rule of law. They have trampled over rights, freedom, and democracy in their path, and label all who oppose them, who have spoken out against stripping our society bare of its humanity, against abandoning consensus and social peace and police presence, as traitors. These forces and their media campaigns have overwhelmingly won popular support; as a result, the Muslim Brotherhood and their allies in the religious right continue to make irrational political decisions, and elements among them engage in acts of violence and incitement. The fact that most liberal parties and movements have abandoned the principles and values of democracy has only helped society accept the return of state security's repressive practices, and popularized statements like "the war on terrorism," "the security solution is the only solution," "it's necessary to exclude the religious right," and "human rights, social peace, transitional justice are luxuries that Egypt can't afford when it's facing terrorism," etc.

Egypt's post-July 3, 2013 authority has been initiating various total-itarian measures, ranging from introducing constitutional articles that make the army a state over the state and approving undemocratically spirited laws, to wide-scale human rights violations and the sustained politics of impunity. Yet, at this level as well, liberals have continued to cooperate with the powers ruling Egypt. By supporting the ascendancy to the presidential palace by the former minister of defense, Abd al-Fattah al-Sisi, they have contributed to the militarization of Egyptians' collective imagination, which began on July 3, 2013 – or, in other words, which began with the people's search for a "military savior," and has resulted in people engaging in a type of politics that overlooks civilians and civil democratic values.

Politics in Egypt has stepped beyond the bounds of human history that has shaped it through the past decades – types of government quite different from military rule, single party politics, the elite. The situation has stepped far beyond the bounds of contemporary human society, which has demonstrated the primacy of consensus, negotiation, and tolerance in stopping violence, the primacy of maintaining social peace, and building democracy. On the contrary, the vision of the military savior, the security state, and the popular discourse inciting hatred and exclusion negates key values of humanity, and the fact that liberal parties and movements have been politically engaged in the current moment represents their break from history and human values.

After July 3, 2013 and over the past three years, there has arisen a thick wall of isolation between most liberal politicians, intellectuals, and activists, and the very idea of liberal democracy in Egypt. They have abandoned the principles and values of democracy, compromised their moral and political credibility, accepted the negation of human values and the violation of rights and freedoms, and justified authoritarianism and a break with history.

Over the past three years, and in the context of this crossroads, liberal democratic ideas have returned to where they began in the 1970s – in universities, a few civil society organizations, and within groups of intellectuals, writers, human rights activists, and public figures. Over the course of the past three years, the new beginnings of the democracy movement's struggle have crystallized at the margins of politics and the margins of the public sphere.

Glimpses of it can be discerned among the workers demonstrating for their rights despite the repressive grip of the security state, and in initiatives coming from civil society, such as the "No to Military Trials for Civilians" group. Struggles associated with the renewal of the democratic idea on a small, citizen-centered scale have also grown, through self-criticism and the restructuring of relationships and intersections between rights and freedoms, elections and referendums, and legal and executive institutions that are both responsible and can be held accountable. The relationship between the army and a security apparatus that is neutral and committed to the rule of law, and citizens who maintain their dignity and participate in the way public affairs are managed are also being restructured, opening a new arena of intellectual reflection centered around civil–military relations.

Over the course of the past three years – and alongside the certainty that those upholding the liberal democratic idea in Egypt must distance themselves from the parties and groups that have failed the test of 2013 – the majority of liberal parties and groups have been engaged in grand deceptions to support the repressive regime that has come into being and to justify its wide-scale violations and abuses. Whether out of fear of the religious right, in seeking to secure their personal interests and stakes, or in upholding the duality of "protection in return of support" that the ruling regime usually promises through the gleam of brute force and systematic violations of the rule of law, liberals have been engaged in generating five grand deceptions that have enabled the new military autocracy to tighten its grip over state institutions, society, and citizens.

Indeed, these liberal-made grand deceptions are among the key factors that have allowed the new autocracy to entrench swiftly in Egypt from 2013–2015. It is thanks to these grand deceptions that Egypt's new savior in uniform and his establishment have been able to contain popular demands for a true liberal democratic order – defined by justice, rule of law, alternation of power, civic peace, and guarantees for personal, civil, economic, social, and political rights and freedoms. In today's Egypt, these grand deceptions have been quickly employed to "besiege" the concept of democracy in Egypt once again, and to pave the way for the continuous renewal of military autocracy and the ongoing subjugation of Egyptian citizens, Egyptian society, and the Egyptian state to the unilateral will of those in power.

GRAND DECEPTION ONE – SEQUENTIALISM

The first of these grand deceptions is that of "sequentialism," or the claim that transitions to democracy must first go through a phase of increasing economic and social development rates in order to overcome the crises of underdevelopment, poverty, illiteracy, and unemployment, to address massive gaps in income, and to improve the living conditions of the people and the level of educational, health, and welfare services provided to them.

According to this claim widely shared among Egyptian liberals, development will eventually be followed by the establishment of rule of law, rotation of power, guarantees for rights and freedoms, and other democratic principles. Of course, such developmental plans and efforts are viewed as impossible without the state, its grand investment projects, and its actors who are capable of undertaking and following up on such projects. As such, this deception of "sequentialism" propagates notions that run counter to the liberal beliefs centered around the leading developmental role of the market economy and the free enterprise of the individual, as well as the cognitive correlation between a small state and a civil society in which private property, rights, and freedoms are safeguarded.

Rule of law, rotation of power, and safeguards for rights and freedoms are considered, according to this liberal grand deception, to be the "luxuries of the rich and affluent," thus excluding the masses of the poor, illiterate, and unemployed – an understanding that has no intellectual roots in the world of liberal democratic ideas and that would be clearly more at home among Egyptian Marxist and socialist groups. Liberal sequencing in Egypt should occur, of course, according to the will of the ruling regime.

Many political science and economic studies have debunked the notion of "democratic sequentialism" – i.e. that development ultimately leads to democracy – due to the limited number of societies and states that have followed its prescribed trajectory since the 1950s, and to the significant specific conditions necessary for this theory to hold true (as were present in South Korea, for example). Thus, sequentialism is a deception and an illusion – albeit an illusion that is highly attractive to established authoritarian regimes. Indeed, the notion ignores the following three realities:

1. Societies and nations rarely develop along straight, uninterrupted lines. Nor do such developments generally go through definitive stages over time for which it is possible to apply set rules or calculations (as if transitions took place in engineering or scientific laboratories). It is thus impossible to define organized start and end points for democratic transitions and to determine the steps that could be expected to lead states from development to democracy.

2. Ruling regimes and elites allied with them are accustomed to controlling and subjugating citizens, society, and the state. Their refusal to establish rule of law, rotation of power, and guarantees for rights and freedoms stems from the fact that their continued existence, as well as their ability to exert their unilateral will and protect their interests, fundamentally depends on the continued absence of democracy. As a result, they desperately defend existing authoritarian arrangements and fiercely combat popular demands for democracy. They continue to resist democracy even when development plans succeed in overcoming the crises of underdevelopment, poverty, illiteracy, and unemployment and in improving the living conditions of the people – although this has not occurred in a sustainable manner in Egypt since the 1950s.

3. The continued absence of democracy strips state institutions and bodies, as well as other public and private institutions and even some civil society organizations, of the ability to manage their own affairs and, thus, the ability to administer the affairs of citizens independently from the authorities. As a result, authoritarian regimes become the sole frame of reference for the society and the

state, and experience dealing with these regimes is the only thing that can be relied upon by individuals and groups seeking to attain certain goals.

GRAND DECEPTION TWO – NOTHING IS MORE IMPORTANT THAN...

The deception of sequentialism is not fundamentally different from a second deception also widely generated by Egyptian liberals: the deception that democracy must be postponed because "nothing is more important than such and such issue at this time." This second deception justifies putting off the establishment of democracy, rule of law, rotation of power, and safeguards for rights and freedoms for the sake of the ruling regimes' objectives that are formulated as sweeping slogans. Indeed, respective ruling regimes tend to link these objectives in an exclusive manner to "national interests" and "the public good," and in doing so do not allow for these objectives to be expanded upon or amended. Rather, these objectives solely reflect the trajectory set forth by the rulers and their allied elites.

For this reason, the deception of a "necessary postponement of democracy" has been propagated in Egypt since the 1950s by successive ruling regimes and by the economic, financial, and administrative elites allied with them – the latter of which are embedded in the bureaucracy of the state institutions and bodies, and of the influential public employment sectors. Since the 1950s, many different issues have been used to complete the argument that democracy must be postponed because "nothing is more important than such and such issue." The issues that have completed this argument have included: national independence, development and preparing the people to practice democracy, socialism, the liberation of Palestine, confronting Zionism and imperialism, the battle to liberate Sinai, economic well-being, stability, the preservation of the national state, and now the war against terrorism.

These issues have thus been claimed to be equivalent to "supreme national interests" and "the objectives of the current period," which could not be expanded upon or amended, in order to eliminate any competing goals, values, or principles that are not sanctioned by successive ruling regimes.

Since the 1950s, such claims have been used not only to justify postponing democracy, but also to artificially circulate a negative view of the principles of rule of law, rotation of power, and safeguards for rights and freedoms. According to this view widely shared by Egyptian liberals, implementing such principles at the respective current time, in the worst case, would prevent Egypt from protecting its "national interests" and from achieving the "objectives of the current period" and thus such principles must be overlooked. At best, this view claims that principles of democracy are a "luxury that cannot be afforded due to the dangers, threats, and challenges facing the nation." Again, such "luxuries" must be postponed, and voices and groups calling for them must be silenced.

In all cases, this negative vision, which fundamentally contradicts liberal democratic ideas, completely denies any positive correlation between rule of law, rotation of power, and safeguards for rights and freedoms, and societies' abilities to achieve national independence, development, progress, economic well-being, and civic peace – despite the existence of convincing, credible evidence for such correlations in the histories of many peoples around the world, including some similar to ourselves in Egypt.

GRAND DECEPTION THREE – THE NOTION OF NATIONAL NECESSITY

The current despotic regime in Egypt and the elites allied to it depend heavily on the propagation of the liberally produced grand deceptions of sequentialism and postponing democracy. In turn, these grand deceptions are utilized among Egyptian liberals to produce a third deception that contributes to the current siege on the concept of democracy in Egypt; the deception of "national necessity."

Through this deception, the new military autocracy can effectively ensure its continued grip on power. Prior to and following the summer of 2013, I consistently warned of the authoritarian trend that lies behind the claims that the military intervention in politics and the coup of July 3 were "acts of necessity" and that the former minister of defense, Field Marshal Abd al-Fattah al-Sisi, was participating in the presidential elections as the "candidate of necessity," later to become the "president of necessity" following the announcement of the election results in 2014.

These claims of "necessity" are truly authoritarian in nature, as they – in the best of cases – justify departing from democratic mechanisms in the summer of 2013, based on the pretext that there was no alternative to an intervention by the military establishment in politics, even when the alternative of holding early presidential elections certainly was possible. In the worst of cases, such claims of "necessity" effectively strip citizens of the right to freely choose their leaders through elections by legitimizing the presidential candidate backed by the two strong state institutions, the military and the security apparatus as a matter of "national necessity."

Moreover, the deception of "national necessity" produced by Egyptian liberals has effectively prevented at least some Egyptian citizens from freely expressing their opinions about the orientations and actions of the national savior in uniform who has ascended from the ministry of defense to the presidential palace, and who has been portrayed in the human and most integral embedment of the notion of "national necessity." As such, the right to peacefully oppose the president and the executive branch of government is virtually eliminated. Indeed, opposition is immediately framed as a betrayal of the exigencies of the "national necessity," just as the right to seek alternative orientations or modes of action is falsely labeled either an act of "conspiracy against the nation," "ignorance of the nation's greater interests," or "futile idealism." Individuals who express such opposition or seek such policy alternatives are discredited, defamed, or labeled as traitors.

The most belligerent use of the grand deception of "national necessity" by Egyptian liberals was related to their endorsement of the former defense minister Abd al-Fattah al-Sisi's run for president. His candidacy was undemocratically propagated as an "act of necessity" and his involvement in mass killing, human rights violations, and repressive measures immorally justified by liberal parties and movements.

The deception of the "candidate of necessity" reduced Egypt and its societal and political affairs to one person, the hero-savior, the savior in uniform being introduced to the public prior to the presidential elections as "the only candidate" capable of "rescuing the nation from the current danger" and "the last hope" for "saving the nation from the evils and harms of the enemies, inside and out" and achieving its greater goals and objectives.

Here, the pro-Sisi liberal politicians, intellectuals, and activists used his affiliation with the military establishment to inject the image of a strong and capable leader. They intentionally conflated his military role with involvement in politics and matters of governance, and, in doing so, laid the foundations for the "candidate of necessity" deception.

Pro-Sisi messages, heard widely on public and private media outlets during the presidential elections, invoked a litany of slogans and stereotypes to imply the former defense minister is the only one who is able to "save the ship of state, battered by storms of internal and external conspiracies"; "confront and defeat terrorism"; "guarantee efficient state institutions and vital services because his career is rooted right at the heart of the military institution"; "achieve a cohesive state and society following the chaos of the past few years and the destructive roles played by the Muslim Brotherhood and by pro-democracy traitors"; "implement a real reform program adopted by state institutions and backed by a popular majority yearning for a strong president"; "transcend the current exceptional situation of danger and crisis," and many others.

It is worth mentioning that private media outlets were identifying with the emerging national savior either because they have been under the control of the security apparatus, or because of the organic bond between the economic and financial interests that own private media outlets and the power centers in the military establishment and in the entrenched security apparatus.

The "candidate of necessity" deception stifled the people's voting preferences in the presidential elections by eliminating in practice the right of Egyptians to cast their vote freely among diverse presidential candidates, and excludes any real chances of competition outside the electoral process. If we take these facts into consideration, in light of Egypt's current situation of military–security dominance since the summer of 2013, the decay of politics, prevalence of one voice, compounding violations of human rights, freedoms and the constitution, and oppressive, undemocratic laws passed in recent months, the "candidate of necessity" deception was an additional step in a series of acts diverging from the course of democracy.

Such a deception, which Egyptian liberals helped produce and sustain, reintegrated tyranny and autocracy. In the wake of the presidential elections, the "candidate of necessity" deception was an additional step in entrenching the new autocracy and justifying its crimes; it was soon to be followed by the propagation of a set of sub-deceptions such as the "inspiring leader," "eternal leader," "president's party," "president's achievements," "the need for the president to stay in his position because there's no alternative," and others, which by design promote tyranny and silence citizens.

Egyptian liberals have been trying to turn back the hands of time. Voices that in the 1950s, 1960s, and following decades promoted the myth of the "president of necessity" and "eternal leader" resurfaced today to play the same role through the "candidate of necessity" deception.

Remarkably, this occurred after the January 2011 revolution that sought to keep pace with modernity, seeking justice, rights, freedom, rule of law, and rotation of power, then democracy and development. It is as though the results of the 1960s, 1970s, and later decades were not catastrophic for Egypt and did not lead to tyranny, and the lack of justice, rights, freedom, and development that ignited the January 2011 revolution. It is as though tyranny and its accompanying deceptions did not testify to the experience of countries near and far that failed to overcome their own crises. These countries failed to safeguard the cohesion of the state and communities whose sovereignty, stability, security, civil peace, and coexistence are threatened by unjust, violent, and oppressive autocratic rulers, far more than internal and external conspiracies, whether real or fabricated.

This prevalence of one voice in post-July 3, 2013 Egypt paved the way for the suppression of opposing visions and ideas. Therefore, it was morally and intellectually shocking to take note of liberals arguing, in justifying the deception of the "candidate of necessity," that there was no contradiction between the elevation of the former defense minister to a national savior and competitive conditions in the presidential elections in 2014. They even linked his expected ascendancy to presidential power to the objectives of democracy, rule of law, rotation in power, safeguards of human rights and freedoms, and pro-reform sentiments. In complete disregard for human history and for liberal democratic ideas, these arguments put forward by Egyptian liberals supposed that authoritarianism will lead to a democratic outcome, and that it is possible for tyranny to establish the deception of "national necessity," and then to confine them to a set period of time and move beyond them once the society is developed and citizens are enlightened.

GRAND DECEPTION FOUR – RELIGION AND POLITICS

The fourth grand deception produced by Egyptian liberals and contributing to dismantling the very idea of liberal democracy has been the religionization of politics and the politicization of religion. This deception that it is acceptable to use religion for political gains stems from the corrupt implication of religion in matters of rule and in the affairs of the state and society. Liberals, opposed to the Muslim Brotherhood and other movements within the religious right-wing spectrum, have defended the current regime taking advantage of religion, as well as using religious spaces and symbols, to lend a false "holiness" or untouchability either to the savior in uniform who is not only on a mission to save the nation but is also actively saving religion – the state-sanctioned discourse of moderation and renewal in religious thinking, or to the orientations and actions put forward by the savior – even when they entail clear human rights violations and repressive measures.

This corrupt use of religion by ruling regimes in Egypt dates back even further than the 1950s. To this day, official religious institutions are implicated in such schemes that abuse religion for political purposes. Groups and currents of the religious right have also attempted to use religion for their political benefit. Such groups' alleged monopoly on absolute truth eliminates space for democratic engagement on matters related to power and rule, the state, and society, for it disallows diversity, plurality, difference of opinion, peaceful opposition, and the right of citizens to freely choose their leaders and to freely express their opinions within the framework of rule of law, rotation of power, and guarantees for rights and freedoms. However, the new element in the post-July 3, 2013 setting has been the liberal involvement with producing and propagating this deception.

The deception – that it is acceptable to use religion for political gains and in doing so introducing the dynamics of religionizing politics and politicizing religion – grants legitimacy to the current ruling regime and helps it to a social effectiveness that is difficult to deny. It does so, even as the regime subjugates Egyptian citizens, society, and state institutions to its unilateral will and fiercely fights popular demands for democracy. Indeed, official religious institutions and their ranks and files – both Muslim and Christian – are accustomed to bestowing such religious legitimacy on the rulers and to renewing the formulations of this legitimacy to keep pace with changing events and to fit diverse "saviors" who come to power, along with their orientations and actions.

As for groups and currents of the religious right, they also thrive on the regime-sanctioned and liberally produced deception of religionizing politics and politicizing religion. It has always allowed them in moments of social ascendency to express condescension toward those who differ from them and to disregard the exigencies of citizenship and safeguards for citizens' rights and freedoms, even as they strive to align themselves with the idea of democracy. In moments of decline, such groups adopt a disastrous narrative that runs between peaceful opposition to the injustices and violations to which they are subjected and oppressive, totalitarian, extremist narratives that are hostile to the "other" – no matter who the "other" is – in order to justify extremism, violence, and bloodshed, a dynamic that is today taking hold in the Egyptian Muslim Brotherhood. In all cases, the very idea of liberal democracy is eclipsed, and those who truly seek democracy are marginalized.

GRAND DECEPTION FIVE – THE STATE ABOVE EVERYONE AND EVERYTHING

It is a wild turn of contemporary history that Egyptian liberals find themselves, in their attempts to promote the new autocracy, praising Nasserism and the Nasserite experiment of the 1950s and 60s.

Amid the grating cries of today's agents of darkness, who propagate the fascist slogan "you are either with us or against us," who serve the "sultan," and not surprisingly buy into the deal of "obedience to the regime for protection and revenues"; amid the voices that justify injustices and violations of human rights and freedoms, and the economic and financial elite who perpetually seek to protect their privileges by supporting the new autocracy; amid of all these, Egyptian liberals have been vested in producing and propagating a fifth grand deception – the deception of the supremacy of the state, which justifies abandoning democracy and the continued dominance of the military establishment and security apparatus over the society and the citizenry.

It is in relation to this fifth grand deception that Egyptian liberals come to praise Nasserism. Joined of course by leftists, liberals of today put forward an idealistic and romantic recollection of the 1950s and 60s, and a depiction of those decades to the public as an extended era of national independence, rejection of domination by other countries, economic prosperity, and social modernization, with social justice policies that defended the poor, under the leadership of the military establishment and a single, heroic military leader, commander, and savior.

On the one hand, this idealistic and romantic recollection of the 1950s and 60s downplays the catastrophic breaches of human rights and freedoms, which are falsely described as either necessary for national independence and social justice or as mere errors that could have been avoided. On the other hand, there is a dearth of critical evaluation of Nasserism, which was founded on autocracy, the military establishment's intervention in politics, and the predominance of the intelligence and security agencies. Nasserism weakened civil institutions, which became iron cages of bureaucracy that lacked efficiency and bred routine, corruption, and nepotism. It crippled the rate of economic growth and the mechanisms of sustainable social modernization, most notably higher education, large- and small-scale investment in scientific research, the democratic partnership between the state and public activity, and the independent role of the private sector. It cancelled politics and criminalized pluralism. It also cost Egypt a catastrophic military defeat in 1967.

The idealistic and romantic recollection of the 1950s and 60s by Egyptian liberals dresses up the idea of autocracy in the false robes of the "just dictator" and the "strong state." It justifies the military establishment's intervention in politics – old and new, and the predominance of the intelligence and security agencies as the direct results of the weakness of the civil, political, and economic elite, and of the necessities of national security and preserving the cohesion of the nation-state. It blames local or foreign conspiracies or "the avoidable mistakes of the savior," like the breaches of rights and freedoms, for the lack of growth and modernization and the catastrophic military defeat. The truth that this idealistic and romantic recollection denies in today's Egypt is that all of the dangerous violations and breaches mentioned above were the inevitable result of the autocracy established in the 1950s and 60s. After all, in the twentieth century that autocracy inevitably thwarted the very goals it had promised its droves of crushed and broken citizens. In the end, it did nothing to preserve national independence, to promote development and modernization, to create a country with strong institutions that abide by the constitution, the rule of law, or the standards of efficiency and fairness, or to foster a productive and educated society that ensures citizens' economic, social, and political rights.

An additional element of the deception of the supremacy of the state is connected to a claim that is contradicted by Egyptian history from the 1950s until the January 2011 revolution. In essence, it is that the arrival of former President Anwar Sadat to office in 1970 made a break from the powerful state of the Nasserist period, which only grew during the three decades under former President Hosni Mubarak. On the one hand, this creates a distinction between Nasserism – which strove for a strong state tasked with achieving national independence, development, modernization, and social justice, and was biased toward the poor and low-income – and the regimes of Sadat and Mubarak – which are accused of pushing the Egyptian state toward subordination to international powers, ignored development and modernization, and turned against the poor and low-income in favor of an alliance between the regime and the revolution, and of a corrupt and exploitative economy. On the other, it offers the public reductionist explanations for this distinction that revolve around the "correct" choices of the heroic military savior in ensuring the strength of the state and the "incorrect" choices of the presidents who came after him, as well as the central role of the military establishment and nation's public sector in the 1950s and 60s and its subsequent regression in favor of the "civilian," economic, financial, and security elite in the 1970s and afterwards.

But this claim of a complete break between Nasserism and the eras of Sadat and Mubarak denies the objective truth that the role of the military in the state, society, and politics has not decreased since the 1950s. Rather, the overlap between the military and civilian elite has grown for reasons concerning the interests of the government and the revolution. Furthermore, none of the economic or social policies toward the public sector or in support of the poor and low-income has changed; the state institutions have only become less capable of effectively implementing them, after years of corruption, nepotism, and administrative exploitation of society's resources. The predominance of the intelligence and security agencies has not changed since the 1950s, and neither have the breaches of rights and freedoms. National independence took a hard hit in 1967, and, though the Egyptian administration (and the military–civilian collaboration) reclaimed its land after the 1973 victory, the government surrendered to Western subordination and largely relinquished its national and pan-Arab role.

It is absolutely impossible to argue that Nasser's decisions were "correct" while the decisions of his successors were "incorrect." Some of their decisions were essentially the same, such as the oppression, restrictions on freedoms, and the practices of the state security apparatus. Others began under Nasser and continued under his successors. These included the tyranny of bureaucracy and the inefficiency of state institutions and executive and administrative agencies. They also included the domination of the "trusted" elites (military and civilian) over their knowledgeable, intellectual, thoughtful, and experienced counterparts to the degree of producing corruption, nepotism, and laziness. A last category, however, did differ, whether partially – as in the case of the presidents' economic models, social attitudes, and weight of the public and private sectors – or completely – as in the case of their regional and international policies. Egypt has yet to completely break away from Nasserism and its disastrous consequences, including militarization, the absence of democracy, and a crippling lack of development.

The third element of the deception of the supremacy of the state relies on people's false perception that reproducing the attitudes and policies of the 1950s and 60s is the way out of our current failures and crises, and that "the candidate of necessity" in 2014 turned "president of necessity" in 2015 is the only person capable of moving Egypt in that direction of rescuing its state.

Liberal politicians, intellectuals, and activists involved in perpetuating this deception differ in their explanations for the current crises and failures. Some believe they are connected to the weakness of the nation-state and the weakened capacities of its institutions and agencies. Others treat the crises as synonymous with the absence of development and social justice. A third group believes that they are the result of the corruption of the political elite and the wickedness of the economic and financial elite. A final group blames them on local and foreign conspiracies, which plague Egypt and threaten its sovereignty, national security, and civil peace.

They trick people by suggesting that reproducing the "strong state" of the Nasserite decades would be a way out of all these failures and crises, while they know that the fruits of the 1950s and 60s were far from sweet. They suggest that more government intervention would lead to development and social justice, while they do not call for fighting corruption or rein in the wicked economic and financial elite. They trick people by claiming that only a heroic savior from the military establishment is capable of protecting the nation-state, fostering development and social justice, and frustrating local and foreign conspiracies. It is as if the nation-state is the priority of the military and no one else, and that, in the minds of civilians, development and social justice are mere luxuries.

It is as though the military and their allies in the intelligence and security agencies held a monopoly on fighting both local and foreign conspiracies. It is as though the autocracy connected since the 1950s and 60s to presidents with military backgrounds had not weakened the state with its absence of democracy, the rule of law, justice, and freedom, and had not derailed development and social justice for the benefit, profit, and gain of the ruling military-security sector and corrupt economic and financial elite. It is as though surviving amid regional disintegration and fighting was conditioned on abandoning the need to build a democratic nation-state, society, social justice, and a legitimate government that adheres to the rule of law and the principles of transparency and fairness. After all, these are all ideas that autocracy throws to the wind.

Finally, Egyptian liberals vested in the deception of the state *Ueber Alles* put forward an additional element focused on the notion of a "direct relationship" between the heroic savior with a military background and the common people, who have no need for political entities, parties, or civil society organizations as mediators, or for legal or popular monitoring of the government.

The masses are portrayed as capable of transcending such limitations due to their hero's deep love for the public and their limitless trust in him; they identify with their hero, who has been chosen by fate. This element offers the public a simple, fascist approach to governance, power, and politics. In this approach, once again in a wild turn of history employed by liberals, politics is essentially dead and the ruling regime thrusts its hand deep into the state and society without supervision or control. Autocracy is justified and allowed to monopolize the discourse in the name of the public and the masses – while the individual citizen is crushed – and to make claims that it is impartial, pure, and the embodiment of their hopes and dreams. A few of the false statements that date back to the Nasserite period, for instance, include that political parties were forums for private, special interests, or that all different types of civil society organizations were under the control of foreign powers which determined their priorities and activities, or that the tools and mechanisms of popular and legal monitoring of the government remained ineffective as long as the ruler himself did not endorse them. As with Abdel Nasser, a rose-tinted picture of a heroic military savior has been painted in the public imagination. Today's savior is capable of transcending party limitations, gaining control of the foreign-influenced civil society, and transparently communicating with the public and the masses. What allows him to do so is his ability to monitor and hold others accountable. This rose-tinted picture goes hand in hand with the sales pitch that the military establishment is the only institution that can stop the political entities and parties toying with the nation and quarantine the damage caused by civil society organizations, which it accuses of working against the state to fragment society. Then, in the name of the direct relationship between the heroic savior and the public (the connections of love and trust) and in the name of the military's necessary role to defend the state, it justifies autocracy, militarization, the absence of democracy, the oppression of civil society, the disappearance of the individual citizen, and the weakness of legislative, executive, and judicial institutions and agencies meant to monitor the ruler and hold him accountable.

As with the other deceptions, the grand deception of the supremacy of the state, with its many elements and diverse contexts, has one goal: to justify autocracy and convince the public that it must inevitably accept the dominance of the military establishment and, for that matter, the security apparatus over the state and society, and support its heroic savior. Liberals have been engaged in this truly undemocratically spirited deception in spite of the bitter fruits of the Nasserite period in the 1950s and 60s. The fundamental difference is in the situation today, the tragedy of romanticizing the past, the disastrous reduction of the state to one institution and the nation to one ruler who is neither monitored nor held accountable, the danger of allowing the regime and the corrupt economic and financial elite allied with it to gain more power, and the delusion that those who oppose the regime and the savior are abandoning the defense of the nation or following foreign agendas.

CONCLUDING REMARKS – FASCIST TECHNIQUES STEPPED UP

However, confronted with an unprecedented and documented accumulation of human rights violations, including crimes such as extra-judicial killings, forced disappearances, and torture practices, many Egyptians between the summer of 2013 and the summer of 2016 have come to perceive the military autocracy for what it is: a brutal regime keen on defending the privileges of the army generals, the security and intelligence services, and the corrupt financial and economic elites allied to them. Such an altered perception has led to the gradual erosion of the persuasive power of liberal elites supportive of the military autocracy. Among other reasons, it has also led to the rise of nonviolent protest activism – according to the Egyptian nongovernmental organizing Democracy Index, 3,691 protest activities have been reported in 2015. The population segments participating in the protests have also grown more diverse – students, informal groups of young Egyptians, industrial workers, civil servants, medical doctors protesting at police brutality, victims of human rights violations, and Muslim Brothers. At least in two cases, the 2015 killing of a citizen who was in police custody in the southern city of Luxor and the

2016 killing of a citizen by a policeman in a Cairo neighborhood (al-darb al-ahmar), massive popular protests against police brutality erupted and prompted the military autocracy to either start legal investigations against the police personnel involved in the violations or to promise accountability and improvements in the performance of the police.

Faced with the popular realization of its failure, the growing aversion against human rights violations, and the dwindling approval rates of the self-proclaimed savior president, the military autocracy has fashioned alternative techniques to convince Egyptians either not to discontinue supporting the official policies of the government or not to develop their disenchantment into active opposition followed by a search for an alternative to a failed government. In a way, these techniques have come to supplement – if not to replace altogether – the anti-democratic deceptions of the liberal elites, whose credibility has been eroded in the eyes of many Egyptians.

While noting that such techniques do not precede the use of state-sponsored repression to subdue citizens, and scare them from the consequences of opposing the president or his government, they are all based on a conscious attempt by the military autocracy to ridicule politics, discredit civilian politicians, and suggest to Egyptians that only the generals are able to run the country.

In this regard, one of the most prevailing techniques is the continuous extension of "enemies and conspirators" lists in the government rhetoric and discourse. In the summer of 2013, supporters of the Muslim Brotherhood represented the core of the nation's enemies and conspirators who were made responsible for the upsurge in terrorism, for the failure in terrorism-combating efforts, and for the absence of improvement in the living conditions in Egypt. The Brotherhood was accused of nurturing ties to terrorist groups in Sinai and elsewhere. It was publicly defamed for "plotting" to sabotage the national economy and to disrupt development efforts. In the downward stratification of enemies and conspirators, the Muslim Brothers were followed by pro-democracy and human rights activists who opposed the military coup of July 3, 2013 and spoke up against human rights violations perpetuated by the autocracy. They, in spite of their sheer weakness and due to the collective hysteria that followed the coup, were described as "dangerous traitors and collaborators" and a "fifth column" acting against the nation and its security and stability.

In 2016, the "enemies and conspirators" categories have been extended to include wide segments of the population which refuse to remain silent in the face of violations and injustice. University students, young activists, industrial workers, and civil servants are accused of conspiring against the nation because they either demand an end to human rights violations or peacefully protest against the loss of their economic and social rights. Medical doctors, whose syndicate organized wide-scale peaceful protests after various doctors became victims of police brutality, are accused of "national treason" and are defamed as "collaborators" of the banned Muslim Brotherhood. Eruptions of popular anger and protest due to the accumulation of human rights violations – especially extra-judicial killings and torture practices – are blamed on "conspiracies" of regional and international actors opposed to the Egyptian autocracy. The governments of Qatar and Turkey, Hamas, Western governments, and the forces of international terrorism are accused of stirring up popular protests in Egyptian cities and of using misled masses to undermine the stability of the state, to challenge national security, and to impose on Egypt the fate of a failed country similar to that of Iraq, Syria, and Libya.

Legions of "enemies and conspirators" are being held accountable for Egypt's ongoing crises. They – Muslim Brothers, human rights activists, students, workers, and average citizens – are responsible for terrorism in Sinai, not that the military autocracy is stumbling in its terrorism-combating policies because of the unilateral dependence on security measures and the wide-scale repression inflicted on the population of Sinai creating a local environment conducive to terrorism and violence. They are also responsible for the deterioration in economic and social conditions – conspiring all the way from bringing down the value of the Egyptian pound against the US dollar and creating a foreign currency crisis to flooding big cities, such as Alexandria, through the subversive activities of underground groups. Not that the military autocracy is also stumbling in its social and economic policies due to the obsession with "Grand National Projects" that are not economically sound, because of the lack of transparency and the free flow of information, which are essential to successful development efforts, because of the environment of fear that undermines the private sector and citizens' initiatives, and because of the lack of rational debate and freedom of expression, which are vital assets to align people and government in combating economic and social crises.

A second prevailing technique in the government rhetoric and discourse feeds on the ever-increasing societal polarization and hate speech in Egypt. Representatives of the military autocracy, government officials, and media apologists of the self-proclaimed savior president dehumanize

355

opponents and delegitimize the act of nonviolent opposition in itself. Putting forward arbitrary accusations regarding the identity of those involved in acts of terrorism, the (as of 2016 still) minister of justice, Judge Ahmad al-Zind, announced in a TV interview that members of the Muslim Brotherhood and supporters of the movement are not "true Egyptians," and described them as "elements that do not deserve to live among us." Subsequently, he topped his Nazi-like rhetoric with a call to collectively execute the Egyptian Muslim Brothers as an act of revenge for the victims of terrorism. The minister of justice made no reference in this regard to due process, legal safeguards of human rights and freedoms, or to the rule of law.

Mr. al-Zind's hate speech is indicative of the wider dehumanizing techniques used by the military autocracy. By no means is such a technique restricted to collective accusations and calls to acts of revenge leveled against the Muslim Brotherhood. Since the summer of 2013, similar accusations and calls have been heard in relation to pro-democracy and human rights activists. Also, they have been effectively used against the limited number of writers who refused to remain silent in the face of repression or to submit to the military autocracy. As promoters of ter-rorism and violence, as sympathizers of the Muslim Brotherhood, and as traitors of the nation true liberal writers have been defamed and repressive measures implemented against them – varying from imprisonment to travel bans – justified.

The fact that this dehumanizing technique feeds on societal polari-zation and has disastrous repercussions on the Egyptian social fabric, on the dissemination of feelings of anger and vengeance among the victims, and on the nature of the public space, which has come to be permeated by hate speech and other hysteric sentiments, does not seem to caution the military autocracy. Nor do the erosion of the notion of rule of law and the threatening collapse of popular trust in the state and its institu-tion, both of which emanate from the wide-scale repression and injustice perpetuated by the autocracy, seem to caution them.

Far more important in the autocracy's short-sighted approach to Egyptian social and political realities is the use of the dehumanizing technique to delegitimize the act of nonviolent opposition and to justify state-sponsored violence and human rights violations. Far more important for the self-proclaimed savior president is to ridicule politics by means of dehumanizing all potential participants in politics who are not willing to serve the autocracy or to submit to its hegemony over state and society.

Using the dehumanizing technique to defame opponents and to ridicule politics and its potential participants also results in pushing the autocracy's denial of Egyptian social and political realities to new heights. In the world of the autocracy, there is no repression, nor injustice. Alleged victims of human rights violations are fabrications of enemies and conspirators who seek to undermine the nation, the state, and national security. Then, when violations become documented through the personal testimonies of some of the victims and through the efforts of their family members, their defenders, and some independent human rights organizations to document the injustice they have been facing, the military autocracy launches government officials and media apologists to justify the state-sponsored violence either by framing the violations as individual cases of abuse of office committed by a small group of policemen who "will be subjected to scrutiny and accountability" or by describing them as acts of legitimate self-defense in the face of conspiracies and subversive activities. Harassed medical doctors, imprisoned industrial workers, students participating in peaceful protests to denounce repression and violations, and tortured-to-death citizens are alternatively accused of plotting to overthrow the government, to wipe out the state, to violate "true Egyptian ethics and morality," or to undermine the glory and inevitable success of the savior president.

In a last step of madness, the dehumanizing technique of the military autocracy leads government officials and media apologists to resort, when other deceptions and techniques are rendered no longer sufficient, to justify state-sponsored violence and crimes as legitimate acts of "liquidating enemies of Egypt." In this regard, wide segments of the population are constructed as enemies of the nation, in a manner similar to twentieth-century National Socialist anti-Semitic constructs of German citizens of Jewish religious affiliation as well as to xenophobic constructs of Muslims and Arabs in discourses of radical right-wing movements in the contemporary West.

A third prevailing technique generated by the military autocracy to supplement or replace the meanwhile less convincing anti-democratic deceptions of liberal elites is to ridicule politics and to suggest to Egyptians that their country can only be ruled by the army generals. This technique relies on systematically undermining civilian institutions and civilian elites. The state gets reduced to its ascribed mighty core related to the military establishment, the security services, and the intelligence community.

Civilian institutions within the state apparatus, especially the state bureaucracy at the national level as well as local administrative bodies, are portrayed as being dependent on the military-security core of the Egyptian state both in historical developments and in contemporary realities. With regard to the three branches of government, the same duality of the mighty military–security core and dependent civilian components get reproduced, and the executive branch of government that is controlled by the generals is empowered over the legislative and judicial branches. So, the legislative and judicial branches of government are subjected to the dominance of the military-security core. Furthermore, the current legislative assembly has been composed on the watch of the security and intelligence services, with almost one-fifth of its members being retired army and police officers, while judges who have been joining the judiciary since the 1970s come from the ministry of interior and are being positioned to preside over key criminal tribunals in which members of the Muslim Brotherhood and other "enemies" of the military autocracy are being trialed.

Finally, other, civilian elements of the legislative and executive branches of government are reduced to ineffective components that need to be controlled and contained. The ultimate outcome is to reduce civilian elites to individuals driven by personal interests, and to groups incapable of tackling bread and butter issues or of delivering food to the tables of Egyptian families. The ultimate outcome is to ridicule civilian elites, to ridicule politics, and to deprive Egyptians of their legitimate quest for an alternative to the generals' administration.

In this context, the technique regarding the dominance of the military-security core and the weakness of civilian institutions and elites employs a set of arguments ever-present in the rhetoric and discourse of the Egyptian autocracy. Examples of such arguments can be discerned in key phrases systematically propagated in statements by government officials and media apologists: "the president is working singlehandedly, other state institutions undermine his success"; "the president and the army are working hard to rescue the nation, whereas parliament and the state bureaucracy are consumed in either nonsensical debates or petty demands"; "the Egyptian state would collapse if it was not for the army and security institutions safeguarding its stability and cohesion," etc.

The predominance of the army generals, the security and intelligence institutions, and their extended representation in the legislative and judicial institutions leads to ridicule politics and ultimately aims at depriving Egyptians of their right to free choice between alternatives visions, ideas, policy proposals, and serious politicians.

Ultimately, similar to the grand anti-democratic deceptions of liberal elites, the depressing reality of the military autocracy with its perpetuated wide-scale repression and its failure in tackling the country's economic and social problems will undermine the persuasive power of the techniques of leveling conspiracy accusations, dehumanizing opponents, and ridiculing politics. It is only a question of time.

Conclusion

Does liberalism have a future in Egypt?

EMAD EL-DIN SHAHIN

C an we imagine a future for politics in Egypt without liberals and liberalism? Egypt's political community is diverse and pluralistic, with competing and overlapping presences across liberal, Islamic, Arab nationalist, and socialist persuasions, to name a few. The liberal stream needs to remain an integral part of Egypt's political and social landscape. Yet, even after successive decades of the liberal experiment in Egypt, Egyptian liberalism has failed to attract a broad political and social currency, or infuse its ideas into the mindset of viable political parties. January 2011 provided a unique moment for liberals to cultivate key political capital, but this opportunity was regrettably squandered. Rather than gain political ground, or consolidate their presence by building durable institutions, liberals instead fell into fragmentation, entrenched themselves in conflicts with Islamist forces, and resorted to myopic identity politics, all of which coalesced into wholly unnecessary polarization of the Egyptian political landscape. As a result, liberal representation and performance in the post-January 2011 electoral process was dismal. Liberals continue to be viewed with suspicion, their role as a credible opposition increasingly suspect, particularly after their support for the military coup of July 2013.

Presently, Egyptian liberalism faces a serious crisis, which if left unresolved casts serious doubt on its future viability.[1] Constructing a meaningful future for liberals in Egypt will require that liberals themselves recognize this crisis, and take the necessary steps toward its resolution. This crisis can perhaps be best encapsulated by the infamous appearance of liberal icon Mohamed El Baradei alongside both the Shaykh of al-Azhar and the Coptic Patriarch, as well as a representative of the conservative Salafi trend, during the pronouncement of the Coup Communique on July 3, 2013 – thereby demonstrating a complete disregard for the liberal narrative's purported commitment to a civic state based on neither religion nor militarism. Indeed, the chapters in this book offered considerable explication of these disappointing contradictions, and in so doing raised concern about the existence of true liberals and liberalism in Egypt.

Liberalism in Egypt presently exists in the form of liberal ideas, scattered and eclectic, that have not coalesced into a coherent liberal trend or stream that represents a wide segment of Egyptian society. What is needed, then, is a brand of liberalism that is grounded in the nuances and particularities of Egyptian society, and constructs an *indigenous* liberal model with its own creative frame of reference, moral values, inclusive political orientation, and economic vision – one that advocates social justice rather than the unfettered free market. Fortunately, though, Egyptian liberals do not need to start from scratch in reconstituting their project, and thus in resolving this crisis. Liberals have a rich legacy of "liberal nationalism" to build upon, but the onus is on them to relate convincingly to that century-long legacy and indigenize its primary strengths.

A LIBERAL LEGACY

Put another way, if we expect to build a democratic future in Egypt, it would be folly to discredit liberals and liberalism altogether. In fact,

---

[1] Al-Sayyid Amin Shalabi, "Liberalism and its dilemma in Egypt," *Al-Ahram Online*, May 30, 2016, http://www.ahram.org.eg/Wafyat/395388/%D8%A7%D9%84%D9%84%D9%8A%D8%A8%D8%B1%D8%A7%D9%84%D9%8A%D8%A9-%D9%88%D9%85%D8%A3%D8%B2%D9%82%D9%87%D8%A7-%D9%81%D9%8A-%D9%85%D8%B5%D8%B1.aspx; Abdelghaffar Shukr, "The future of the liberal stream in Egypt," al-Badil, April 3, 2009, http://www.copts-united.com/Article.php?I=39&A=1340; Amr Hamzawy, "The crisis of Egyptian liberalism and its reconstruction," *Shorouk*, July 31, 2013, http://www.shorouknews.com/columns/view.aspx?cdate=19062016&id=a0d3b570-7511-4607-94bf-e2df2be150ab

to build roots for liberal ideas and promote support for a democratic culture, it is necessary to highlight Egypt's liberal legacy, albeit a weak one with recognizable deficiencies. That legacy, replete with a yearning for freedom, rights, and political participation and representation, is well established in Egypt's modern history. The liberal narrative in Egypt begins as early as the nineteenth century with Rifa'a al-Tahtawi (d. 1873). Contemporary liberals present Tahtawi as the founding father of secular liberalism in Egypt. Yet, in fact, Tahtawi remained a distinctly Muslim reformer who remained faithful to the Shari'ah, his absolute monarch and patron Muhammad Ali, and own indigenous values, despite his admiration for certain European liberal ideas. He tried to find roots for European ideas in Islam. Tahtawi translated the French Constitution of 1814 and the *Déclaration des Droits de l'Homme et du Citoyen* of 1789 into Arabic. Subsequently, the country had its first constitution and a Shura Council of Representatives in 1886. Liberal parties mushroomed from the beginning of the last century and Egypt lived a parliamentary experience till 1952.

Like Islamic activism, Egyptian liberal nationalism was the twin child of Islamic modernism. Jamal al-Din al-Afghani (d. 1897) and Muhammad Abduh (d. 1905), the founders of the Islamic modernist trend, diligently sought to synthesize a long list of liberal values within an Islamic framework: reason and rationalism, progress and change, nationalism, civic virtues, popular will, restrictions on sovereign powers, political representation, and civil rights. Their disciples, however, took the ideas of the Islamic modernist project into considerably different directions, one textual and the other liberal/secular. The former culminated in fundamentalist and/or politically activist strands of Islam, represented by the Muslim Brothers. The latter, on the other hand, produced a liberal Egyptian nationalism, which later evolved into secular liberalism. This bifurcation has polarized Egyptian intellectual and political life ever since, until today.

Understanding this background in the development of Egyptian liberalism is crucial for making sense of its limitations and of its ultimate future. Egypt has witnessed three denominations of liberalism throughout its modern history: nationalist, secular,[2] and neo-liberal. As these

---

[2] A large number of the advocates of secular liberalism were associated with the Liberal Constitutionalist Party that split from the Wafd Party in 1922. This split took liberalism in a new direction. Its intellectual leaders advocated secularism and Westernization as the philosophical basis for the reconstruction of Egyptian society, viewing a wholesale adoption of a Western social and cultural framework as the antidote for the country's social and

different strands of liberalism are explicated in detail in several chapters in this book, I will focus here on the first, as it remains the most capable of fostering a distinctly Egyptian model of liberalism moving forward – even with its serious shortcomings. This strand of liberalism was central to the movement for national independence and hence enjoyed popular support, all while avoiding outright hostility to the identity and values of Egyptian society. Yet insofar as nationalist liberalism evolved within a distorted democratic context, it was not able to produce a coherent intellectual and socio-economic program. Consequently, later secular liberals criticized liberal nationalist Saad Zaghlul (d. 1927), the leader of the Wafd Party, for his conservatism and his inability to "liberate the Egyptian mind." Zaghlul's cardinal sin, secular liberals maintained, was his criticism of Ali Abd al-Raziq's book *Islam and the Fundamentals of Governance* and Taha Husayn's *The Future of Culture in Egypt*, the former advocating a separation of religion and state, and the latter advocating a wholesale embrace of European lifestyle and values.

Yet despite those limitations and a lack of a coherent intellectual vision, the liberal legacy in Egypt nonetheless made formative and lasting contributions to Egyptian society. Continuing the reformist trend it had inherited from the Islamic modernists, liberals highlighted the need for social reform at the religious, educational, and political levels of Egyptian society, promoting values of freedoms of thought, religion, and expression, individual rights, the rights of women and minorities. Egypt's "Liberal Age,"[3] as Albert Hourani has called it, institutionalized these ideals through the founding of the Egyptian University (later renamed Cairo University), the modern Egyptian nationalist movement, the 1923 liberal constitution, a nascent parliamentary system and culture with incipient political parties, a relatively free and bustling press,[4] and Egyptian economic companies to back the struggle for the country's independence.

---

political ills. They were deeply critical of many aspects of religion and Egyptian popular culture, and called for its replacement with particular Western mores, like the donning of European clothing and the establishment of the Latin alphabet. In so doing, secular liberals caused much consternation with many of their fellow Egyptians, who then as now have come to associate liberalism with Westernization, and even with outright atheism.

[3] This phrase comes under severe criticism because of the use of the term "liberal" while Egypt languished under the yoke of both British occupation and autocratic kings.

[4] For more on the centrality of the press in the early Egyptian liberal project, and its ultimate failure to live up to those ideals in the context of the uprising of 2011 onward, see Mohamad Elmasry's chapter in this volume, "Myth or Reality?: The Discursive Construction of the Muslim Brotherhood in Egypt."

Towering liberal figures, such as Ahmad Lutfi al-Sayyid, Muhammad Hussein Haykal (d. 1956), Taha Husayn (d. 1973), Abbas al-Aqqad (d. 1964), Ahmad Amin (d. 1954), Ahmad Hasan al-Zayyat (d. 1968), Tawfiq al-Hakim (d. 1987), Naguib Mahfouz (d. 2006), and many others enriched Egypt's literary and artistic life for decades to come, and enshrined Egypt as the cultural center of the Arab word. Liberal ideals, moreover, had a formative impact on the modern Egyptian judiciary system, which until recently was firmly grounded in liberal ideals and individual rights.[5] Suffice to say, for whatever its blind spots, Egyptian liberalism nonetheless bequeathed modern Egypt a meaningful legacy, that could pave the way for a more robust liberal polity moving forward. This, however, would require elevating liberalism from a scattered set of disparate ideas into a political force with popular currency.

NEW BEGINNINGS

At present, liberalism in Egypt faces several challenges that prevent its transformation into a bona fide popular intellectual and political trend. Aside from the fact that the Egyptian bourgeoisie class is predominately not liberal, and has often allied with the authoritarian state under Sadat and subsequently Mubarak, liberalism suffers at the levels of personalities and leadership, orientation and practices. Few liberal figures are willing to acknowledge the crisis of liberalism in Egypt in this respect.[6] Liberals in general demonstrate a tendency to blame others for their shortcomings and for their inability to compete with other political forces – particularly Islamist movements like the Muslim Brotherhood. They accuse the Islamists of undermining their ideas and deliberately distorting their liberal message, and of inaccurately associating them with moral per-missiveness and aversion to religion. They further attempt to victimize themselves by suggesting that successive authoritarian Egyptian regimes had targeted and repressed liberals and excluded them from the politi-cal process, in favor of the Islamists. Some liberals go as far as to blame the deficiencies of Egyptian culture and the paltry level of education of

---

[5] For more on liberalism in the Egyptian judiciary, see Sahar F. Aziz's chapter in this volume, "(De)liberalizing Judicial Independence in Egypt."
[6] See Ayman Nour, "The crisis of Egyptian liberalism and its representatives," https://www.facebook.com/dr.Aymannour/posts/10152408772511318

the Egyptian populace for the inability of their political project to gain firmer grounding, suggesting that these handicaps render most Egyptians ill-equipped and unprepared to properly appreciate liberal ideas.

The crisis of Egyptian liberalism thus starts with the liberals themselves. In fact, it has become increasingly difficult to identify precisely who constitutes a "liberal" in contemporary Egypt.[7] Today's liberals are diverse and heterogeneous in their intellectual and philosophical orientations, incorporating under the broader aegis of liberalism a strange confluence of Nasserites, leftists, Arab nationalists, Islamists, human rights advocates, former security officers, and even "eradicationists."[8] As the liberal intellectual Wahid Abdelmaguid explains, "liberals in Egypt are not one trend. They embrace extremely broad and general principles – to the extent that some are close to the left, while others are to the extreme right."[9] Naturally, it thus becomes difficult to identify a consistent liberal stance at the level of ideas and practices. In some cases, liberals have articulated scattered ideas and contradictory positions that are dictated by personal or partisan interests. Al-Nida al-Jadid, an organization established in 1991 to represent liberals and liberal ideas, was a serious attempt to unite liberals, but was not properly institutionalized and thus could not survive its founder Said al-Najjar. Most recently, the National Salvation Front – a coalition of political parties established in part by Mohamed El Baradei in opposition to then President Mohammad Morsi's November 22, 2012 constitutional declaration – was the closest manifestation of a liberal political apparatus, given the participation of many prominent liberals. However, that coalition's role in undermining Egypt's democratic transition and giving rise to the coup of July 2013 reveals the internal contradictions that continue to plague Egyptian liberals.

Indeed, at their most basic intellectual and philosophical orientations, liberals differ considerably over fundamental issues. They maintain widely

---

[7] Amr Hamzawy, "The liberals in Egypt," *Shorouk*, October 31, 2015, http://www.shorouknews.com/columns/view.aspx?cdate=31102015&id=179ef7f5-7d0e-4e59-8a29-c85b6fcce17b; "Liberals from home," *Shorouk*, January 22, 2012, http://www.shorouknews.com/columns/view.aspx?cdate=22012012&id=e6d01467-cb4d-4e5a-8aa6-1665392e57e2; and "Dictatorship in the name of liberalism," *Shorouk*, January 22, 2012, http://www.shorouknews.com/columns/view.aspx?cdate=18012012&id=65d328b0-0a55-49ec-b8ec-2a589c8bd17f

[8] This term refers to political actors who are extremists and are willing to physically eliminate their opponents.

[9] Wahid Abdelmaguid, "Who are the liberals in Egypt," *Al-Ahram*, September 19, 2011, http://www.ahram.org.eg/archive/Issues-Views/News/102230.aspx

differing positions on the social scope and dimensions liberalism ought to maintain in Egyptian society (social liberalism versus neo-liberalism); the concept of individualism in a predominantly collective culture; individual freedoms and public rights; the identity of the Egyptian state; the role of religion in state and society; their relations with Islamists; and their relations with the state. Accordingly, liberal forces and parties are struggling to identify their own platform, which in turn presents a significant obstacle to liberalism becoming a popular and effective intellectual and political trend in Egyptian society. The future of liberalism in Egypt will thus depend on the liberal project adequately addressing certain shortcomings at its basic intellectual, political, and societal levels.

Reconcile with Egyptian cultural identity and social values

As mentioned previously, liberal nationalism emerged from the mantle of Islamic modernism, and was not immediately dismissive of religion; in so doing, it was able to maintain popular currency, and offered formative contributions to Egyptian civil society. But in contradistinction to this accommodationist posturing by liberal nationalists, secular liberals instead have long been waging the same futile wars and "intellectual battles" against the very social values and core beliefs that Egyptians hold dear. Time and again they raise the same controversial issues without offering meaningful resolution or providing viable alternatives: the role of religion in state and society, the place of the Shari'ah in the legal and social structures, the nature and authority of the Quran, the secularity of education, literary and artistic freedoms, the role of religious institutions, women's rights, veiling, civic marriage and divorce, establishing the authority of reason and science over society and their supremacy over religion, the purported backwardness of Egyptian culture and society, among others. Accordingly, it is little surprise that secular liberals have failed to gain popular support.

Liberalism as a political project simply cannot succeed when it overtly declares war against the very values and belief system constitutive of the society in which it operates. Yet for decades liberals in Egypt have done precisely that, viewing religion and Egyptian society's traditional culture as the basis of its underdevelopment, and relentlessly attempting to overhaul the education system to resocialize Egyptians into proper liberal subjects. Yet forced social engineering, as the experience of the French in Algeria adequately demonstrates, is an exercise in futility. Whether liberals approve or not, Egyptian society remains a predominantly religious one, and Islam provides a fundamental basis of its identity, moral values, and core belief system. Today's liberals in Egypt thus need to make a historic compromise with the questions of religion and of Egyptian social and cultural identity, in the same way Islamists need to make a similar compromise with the questions of modernity and liberalism. This can be accomplished very conceivably by assimilating elements of the Islamic discursive tradition that can help contextualize liberalism's basic ideals, drawing on Islam's emphasis on human dignity, individual responsibility, equality, pluralism, and respect for the law. Put another way, liberals need to abandon their attempts to forcibly uproot religion and the allegedly backward aspects of Egyptian cultural identity, and instead adopt a model of synthesis, following in the footsteps both of their Islamic modernist and liberal nationalist predecessors.

Properly define liberalism

Ironically, despite liberalism's lengthy track record in modern Egyptian history, the concept of liberalism remains ambiguous and inaccessible to average Egyptians. Prominent liberals recognize this failing, acknowledging that "Arab perception has not formed a clear understanding of the meaning of liberalism,"[10] and admitting to the "urgent need to explain what liberalism is and the ways to implement it."[11] Osama al-Ghazali Harb asserts that "this thought [liberal] until this current moment [1990s] seems besieged and unable to crystalize itself."[12]

As liberalism remains nebulously defined, moreover, its objectives and goals increasingly run the risk of being articulated in reductionist and formulaic ways that do little justice to the true aims of the project. Under these auspices, some liberals engage in false marketing of liberalism,

---

[10] "The state of liberalism in Egypt," *al-Bayan*, December 22, 2013, http://www.albayan.co.uk/rsc/print.aspx?id=3188

[11] Ahmad al-Shazly, "Egyptian intellectuals circle around 'liberalism,'" *Middle East Online*, February 3, 2015, http://middle-east-online.com/?id=193360

[12] Nahed Ezzeddin, "The liberal stream and human rights," NHRC, May 11–12, 2008, http://www.nhrc-qa.org/ar/%D8%A7%D9%86%D8%B4%D8%B7%D8%A9-%D9%88%D9%81%D8%B9%D8%A7%D9%84%D9%8A%D8%A7%D8%AA/%D8%A7%D9%84%D9%85%D8%A4%D8%AA%D9%85%D8%B1%D8%A7%D8%AA-%D9%88%D8%A7%D9%84%D9%86%D8%AF%D9%88%D8%A7%D8%AA/

unconsciously vulgarizing and misrepresenting its tenets in an attempt to make it seem more appealing to the masses. Liberalism is often idyllically portrayed as a magic wand that can effortlessly provide solutions for all the ills plaguing Egyptian society, and as an end in itself – despite the fact that these caricatured depictions often lack much content. Substantive engagement with Egypt's core political and social challenges is thus replaced with empty sloganeering, as the following examples demonstrate: "Liberalism is the element that provides security for all the segments of society…A garden that can contain all types of flowers and thorns";[13] "Liberalism is a clear and a straightforward approach to grant the human mind and thought a true opportunity to rid itself from its problems and crisis";[14] "The objective of liberalism is to liberate the mind [and achieve] economic and social growth."[15]

In a similar vein, liberalism is often arbitrarily juxtaposed with other modern ideological persuasions such as modernity, secularism, and democracy, in an attempt to establish a casual and deterministic relationship between what are wholly distinct orientations. For instance, to add additional mystique to liberalism under Enlightenment auspices, the renowned liberal intellectual Shaker al-Nabulsi sees modernity as the essence of liberalism, describing it as "an electric current that lights the dark corners."[16] In a Hobbesian manner, he preaches for the Leviathan by declaring that "the decisive victory of modernity will only come through a consolidated sovereign…"[17] offering Napoleon in France, Muhammad Ali in Egypt, Ataturk in Turkey, and Bourguiba in Tunisia as illustrative examples. Yet given the fact that none of those figures would properly qualify as a liberal, Nabulsi's attempt to draw a causal connection between liberalism and modernity is ultimately contrived. Similarly, other liberals attempt to conflate liberalism with secularism, despite the two orientations bearing no inherently causal relationship: "democracy will only be achieved through adopting secularism, separating religion from the state, separation of religion from politics. Religion has never experienced

---

[13] Nabil Sharaf al-Din, "The crisis of liberalism in Egypt," *Al-Masry al-Youm*, December 12, 2008, http://today.almasryalyoum.com/article2.aspx?ArticleID=192575

[14] al-Shazly, "Egyptian intellectuals circle around 'liberalism.'"

[15] Ibid.

[16] Shaker al-Nabulsi, "The necessity of the Sultan to achieve modernity," *Ilaf*, December 22, 2008, http://elaph.com/Web/ElaphWriter/2008/12/393223.htm

[17] Ibid.

democracy. Secularism is the same, its rules are the same. There is no moderate secularism and radical secularism."[18]

Moreover, in addition to being reductionist and misleading, these liberal narratives fail to look critically at the contradictions that wholly permeate liberal societies. Similarly, they fail to recognize or acknowledge the multiple permutations that exist within the domains of liberalism, modernity, democracy, and secularism; accordingly, they remain unable to properly articulate how to orient those ideological persuasions in a way that does justice to the particularities of Egyptian society. For liberalism in Egypt to have a meaningful future, liberals will need to temporarily step back from their ongoing skirmishes with Islamists, and instead direct their energies inward, and invest in building an intellectual framework for a distinctly *Egyptian* liberalism. They need to clarify and explicate its main tenets, and its relation with the Western experience with modernity. And more importantly, they need to adequately persuade Egyptians why, if at all, they should give secularism, Westernization, and neo-liberalism a priority over Islam and their indigenous social and cultural identity. And if they cannot successfully persuade Egyptians on this front, they need to modify their definition and articulation of liberalism in a way that does sufficient justice to those concerns.

Disengage from the authoritarian state

Despite portraying themselves as the antithesis of, and bulwark against, authoritarianism and the arbitrary caprices of the state, Egyptian liberals have an established track record of colluding with the autocratic Egyptian state. In fact, many have considered the state apparatus the only viable vehicle ultimately to implement their reform project. Tahtawi was a

---

[18] Omayma Abboud, "The concept of reform in the neo-liberal Arab discourse," *al-Tajdid al-Arabi*, September 4, 2005, http://www.arabrenewal.info/%D9%83%D8%AA%D8%A7%D8%A8-%D8%A7%D9%84%D9%85%D9%88%D9%82%D8%B9/11099-%D9%85%D9%81%D9%87%D9%88%D9%85-%D8%A7%D9%84%D8%A5%D8%B5%D9%84%D8%A7%D8%AD-%D8%A7%D9%84%D8%B3%D9%8A%D8%A7%D8%B3%D9%8A-%D9%81%D9%8A-%D8%A8%D8%B9%D8%B6-%D9%86%D8%B5%D9%88%D8%B5-%D8%A7%D9%84%D8%AE%D8%B7%D8%A7%D8%A8-%D8%A7%D9%84%D9%84%D9%8A%D8%A8%D8%B1%D8%A7%D9%84%D9%8A-%D8%A7%D9%84%D8%B9%D8%B1%D8%A8%D9%8A-%D8%A7%D9%84%D8%AC%D8%AF%D9%8A%D8%AF.html

loyal custodian of the autocratic and absolutist state of Muhammad Ali. Similarly, the Umma Party established by Ahmad Lutfi al-Sayyid and Abduh's disciples in 1907 was well received and encouraged by Lord Cromer, who viewed them as the real stakeholders in Egypt and the country's future elite. They in return viewed the presence of the British as a benevolent occupation that worked for the interest of the country. This relationship also provided them with protection against the National Party of Mustafa Kamil (d. 1908) and Muhammad Farid (d. 1919), which called for immediate independence from the British and for keeping links with the Ottoman Sultan. Owing to their reformist orientation, many of the early liberals assumed high positions within the state apparatus. Likewise, the Liberal Constitutional Party, the rival of the Wafd Party, drew close to the British to support it against the overwhelming popularity of the Wafd Party. Finally, even under the Nasserite regime major liberal intellectuals and writers, despite the increasingly authoritarian and illiberal tenor of Nasser's rule, nonetheless agreed to serve in his state apparatus and his cultural and media institutions.[19]

Under the rule of Mubarak, moreover, many liberals continued this posturing of remaining hand in glove with the state apparatus. Accordingly, liberals were largely not at the forefront of the protest movement during that period, with the exception of the al-Ghad Party and, at a very late stage, the Democratic Front (whose founder was a former member of Mubarak's National Democratic Party). Ironically, some liberals went as far as considering Gamal Mubarak a "crystallization of a national liberalism in a new phase and a new thinking."[20] Hazim al Biblawi, a presumably liberal figure who following the coup of July 2013 became interim prime minister, is a testament to this proclivity, and years earlier offered a succinct explication justifying liberal collusion with the state. In 2005, while Mubarak was still in power, Biblawi articulated two main challenges to Egypt's successful

---

[19] For more on liberal collusion with the authoritarian Egyptian state, see the chapter by Ahmed Abdel Meguid and Daanish Faruqi in this volume, "The Truncated Debate: Egyptian Liberals, Islamists, and Ideological Statism."

[20] Hani Nusayra, "Do not look for liberalism in Egypt but for liberals," al-Hayat, April 10, 2009, http://daharchives.alhayat.com/issue_archive/Hayat%20INT/2009/4/10/%D9%84%D8%A7-%D8%AA%D8%A8%D8%AD%D8%AB-%D8%B9%D9%86-%D8%A7%D9%84%D9%84%D9%8A%D8%A8%D8%B1%D8%A7%D9%84%D9%8A%D8%A9-%D9%81%D9%8A-%D9%85%D8%B5%D8%B1-%D8%A8%D9%84-%D8%B9%D9%86-%D8%A7%D9%84%D9%84%D9%8A%D8%A8%D8%B1%D8%A7%D9%84%D9%8A%D9%8A%D9%86.html

transition to a robust liberal system: the dearth of liberal leadership and the inability to organically produce new ones on the one hand, and the increasing popularity and looming threat of anti-liberal Islamists on the other.

To address this impasse, Biblawi maintains that actively advocating liberal reforms might backfire by benefiting and emboldening anti-liberal forces; instead, he proposes that the best course of action to facilitate a liberal transition, bafflingly enough, is to throw support behind Mubarak, going so far as refraining from fielding a candidate to run against him in the forthcoming presidential elections. This strategy, he concludes, would best allow for promoting liberal freedoms and constitutional reforms, and for eliminating exceptional restrictive measures during Mubarak's new term.[21] Given his willingness in 2005 to accommodate the authoritarian Egyptian state as a necessary fulcrum for advancing the liberal project, Biblawi's role in 2013 as head of the post-coup cabinet that orchestrated the worst massacre against political protesters in modern Egyptian history becomes far less surprising.

Liberal embrace of the returned authoritarian state following the coup of 2013, from their participation in the National Salvation Front coalition that emboldened military intervention in the first place, to their involvement in the post-coup administration and the fifty-member committee that wrote the post-coup constitution, fundamentally tarnished the credibility of the liberal project, and raises serious questions about its future viability. To overcome this crisis of legitimacy in the future, liberals must fundamentally rethink their association with the authoritarian Egyptian state. Namely, they need to disengage from the state as an interlocutor, and instead build their own independent institutions that promote their vision. Granted, institution building is indeed difficult under the yoke of a repressive state – a fact liberals regularly point out – but even then, other forces, namely the Islamists and the April 6th Youth Movement, have managed to build meaningful independent institutions under those very same circumstances, while simultaneously keeping a degree of distance from the state. Liberals must do the same.

---

[21] Hazem al-Biblawi, "The road to liberalism," *Al-Ahram Online*, March 13, 2005, http://hazembeblawi.com/%D8%A7%D9%84%D8%B7%D8%B1%D9%8A%D9%82-%D8%A5%D9%84%D9%89-%D8%A7%D9%84%D8%AF%D9%8A%D9%85%D9%8
2%D8%B1%D8%A7%D8%B7%D9%8A%D8%A9-%D8%A7%D9%84%D9%84%D9%
8A%D8%A8%D8%B1%D8%A7%D9%84%D9%8A%D8%A9/

Overcome liberal elitism

Liberals often blame society at large for the failure of liberalism to take hold in Egypt. As mentioned earlier, liberals often maintain that the core values of Egyptian society conflict with the fundamental tenets of liberalism, particularly democracy, human rights, rationalism, secularism, and liberal citizenship.[22] Seeing the two value systems as fundamentally incompatible, some liberals have expressed concern at the idea of having the illiterate Egyptian masses participating in the electoral process. Some have proposed voter disenfranchisement, by granting the vote of the illiterate Egyptian masses half the value of the literate elites; others have gone further by suggesting banning the masses from voting altogether. This elitist posturing, moreover, has characterized Egyptian liberalism since its early inception, with Ahmad Lutfi al-Sayyid and his colleagues having disenfranchised Egyptians who owned less than fifty feddans from voting. Liberal elitism has always been predicated on an implicit, and sometimes explicit, paternalism, in which liberal elites alone warrant trusteeship over Egyptian society. Despite their putative rejection of absolute truths, Egyptian liberals nonetheless present their project as an inerrant truth. As one liberal claims, "liberalism is a clear and a straightforward approach that grants the human mind and thought a true opportunity to rid itself from its problems and crisis."[23] In presenting liberalism as so manifestly just that it alone can bring Egyptian society to salvation, liberals by extension present themselves as uniquely qualified to chart Egypt on the proper path to redemption – thereby alienating themselves from the very society over which they have become the self-appointed messiahs.

If liberalism expects to have a meaningful future in Egypt, liberals must overcome this alienation by reminding themselves that they in fact remain part and parcel of the society they continue to criticize, and commit to being leading agents in the production of its values and political orientations. Egyptian liberals thus must produce leaders that can properly connect with the Egyptian "masses" ('awam) and "mobs," appreciate their chosen priorities, and inspire them to adopt a liberal vision for the future. They must thus maintain a strong presence in professional syndicates and in the student movements. Additionally, liberals must build substantive

---

[22] Ezzeddin, "The liberal stream and human rights."
[23] al-Shazly, "Egyptian intellectuals circle around 'liberalism.'"

institutions and organize a popular base that is both committed to liberal ideals and is willing to actively advocate for their implementation.

Put another way, Egypt needs a viable liberalism, and a national liberal stream. Whether liberals can cultivate that coherent national stream, and thus ensure its future viability, though, will depend on its cultivating a coherent political and cultural bloc that adheres to liberal ideals and demonstrates consistent liberal practices. One main task in that respect would be to reconcile the liberal project with Egyptian social and cultural identity and with Islam, and to properly contextualize the intellectual narrative of the liberal project in a way that properly speaks to the concerns of the masses. Ayman Nour, the leader of al-Ghad Party, envisions "an Egyptian liberalism that does not clash with religion or human moral values; does not oppose human rights and does not side with wrong."[24]

If liberals fail to properly reorient their project in this respect, then the crisis facing Egyptian liberalism will further entrench itself, and will become increasingly difficult to resolve in the future. The reason being, liberals no longer carry monopoly over the use of purportedly liberal terms and concepts. Other political forces, despite not necessarily being liberal as such, are advocating these same political values – and are perhaps more successfully reaching the masses of Egyptian society. One obvious implication of this development is that liberals and their political discourse stand to be marginalized. The democratic process will further alienate them, because their elitism and alienation from the base of Egyptian society precludes them from winning elections or from offering a viable counterweight to the Islamists. Egyptian liberals can no longer hide behind the authoritarian state to force an otherwise unwilling Egyptian populace to adopt its programmatic agenda. They must instead construct a broad and unified political vision, and cultivate durable independent institutions that support that vision – or else remain stuck in the morass of alienation from Egyptian society, and continue to be cavalierly dismissed by the masses at the ballot box.

---

[24] Nour, "The crisis of Egyptian liberalism and its representatives."

About the contributors

AHMED ABDEL MEGUID is an assistant professor at the Department of Religion, Syracuse University. He earned his BA at the American University in Cairo and his MA and Ph.D. in philosophy at Emory University. His research draws on Islamic and German philosophy, focusing on metaphysics, epistemology, and social and political philosophy. He has published and has forthcoming articles in the *European Journal of Political Theory*, *Oxford Journal of Islamic Studies*, and *Philological Encounters*. He is presently finalizing a monograph on the philosophical anthropology of Ibn al-'Arabi, provisionally titled *Symbolic Meaning and Imagination: Ibn al-'Arabi and the Synthesis of Islamic Theories of the Self*, and is also working on a manuscript on modal logic in classical and early to late modern Sunni theology and philosophy, provisionally titled *Modality and the Problem of Skepticism versus Foundationalism in Sunni Epistemology*.

KHALED ABOU EL FADL is the Omar and Azmeralda Alfi Distinguished Professor in Islamic Law at the University of California, Los Angeles (UCLA) School of Law. He holds a BA in political science from Yale University, a JD from the University of Pennsylvania Law School, and an MA and Ph.D. in Islamic law from Princeton University. He is the author of fourteen books including *Rebellion and Violence in Islamic Law* (Cambridge University Press, 2001), *Speaking in God's Name: Islamic Law, Authority and Women* (Oneworld Press, 2001), and, most recently, his magnum opus *Reasoning with God: Reclaiming Shari'ah in the Modern Age* (Rowman & Littlefield, 2014).

SAHAR AZIZ is an associate professor at Texas A&M University School of Law and a nonresident fellow at the Brookings Doha Center. Professor Aziz's scholarship lies at the intersection of national security and civil rights law with a focus on how post-9/11 laws and policies adversely impact racial, ethnic, and religious minorities. She is also an expert on the Middle East wherein she focuses on the relationship between authoritarianism and rule of law in Egypt. Professor Aziz has been featured on CNN, CSPAN, Fox News, Russia Today, and Al Jazeera America, and she has published commentaries on CNN.com, *The New York Times*, the Carnegie Endowment for International Peace, the Middle East Institute, the *World Politics Review*, the *Houston Chronicle*, *The Guardian*, the *Christian Science Monitor*, and *Huffington Post*.

EMRAN EL-BADAWI is program director and associate professor of Middle Eastern Studies at the University of Houston. He is also the founding executive director and treasurer of the International Qur'anic Studies Association. Dr. El-Badawi has published articles in English as well as Arabic. His book on *The Qur'an and the Aramaic Gospel Traditions* (Routledge, 2013) was a finalist for the British-Kuwait Friendship Society Book Prize. He is currently co-authoring a textbook on *A History of the Classical Middle East* (Cognella, forthcoming), and his future projects will research liberalism in the Arab world as well as the contribution of eastern church laws to the Shari'ah. Dr. El-Badawi received his Ph.D. in Near Eastern Languages and Civilizations from the University of Chicago.

MOHAMAD ELMASRY is an associate professor in the Media and Cultural Studies Program at the Doha Institute for Graduate Studies and an assistant professor in the Department of Communications at the university of North Alabama. In 2009, Dr. Elmasry received his Ph.D. in mass communication from the University of Iowa, where he was a presidential fellow. His Ph.D. dissertation examined constraints on news production in Egypt. Dr. Elmasry held assistant professorships at Qatar University from 2009 to 2011, and at the American University in Cairo from 2011 to 2014. His research on Arab press systems, the sociology of news, and news and race has appeared in refereed scholarly publications, including the *International Communication Gazette*, the *International Journal of Communication*, *Journalism Practice*, the *Journal of Middle East Media*, the *Journal of Arab and Muslim Media Research*, and the *Global Media Journal*. Dr. Elmasry is also a political and media analyst, specializing in Egypt. He writes regularly for Al Jazeera English and the *Middle East Eye*, and has also written for *Muftah*, *Religion Dispatches*, *Open Democracy*, *PULSE*,

The Immanent Frame, Jadaliyya, and *Egypt Independent.* He has appeared regularly on local and international television, radio, and internet news networks, including CNN International, BBC World News, BBC World Service Radio, Al Jazeera English, Al Jazeera America, Al Jazeera Live Egypt, Huff Post Live, NTV (Turkey), ARD (German Public Television & Radio), A9 Television Istanbul, SVT (Swedish TV News), and ABC News Australia Radio, among other networks.

DALIA F. FAHMY is an assistant professor of political science at Long Island University and a senior fellow at the Center for Global Policy. She has published several articles in academic journals focusing on democratization and most recently on the effects of Islamophobia on US foreign policy. Dr. Fahmy's forthcoming book explores the rise and fall of the Egyptian Muslim Brotherhood. She is also co-editor of *International Relations* (Kendall Hunt, 2017). Her current research examines the intellectual and political development of modern Islamist movements. She has been interviewed by and published in various media outlets including ABC, CNBC, MSNBC, CNN, the *Huffington Post,* Al Jazeera, and *The New Middle East.*

DAANISH FARUQI is a doctoral candidate in history at Duke University. His work deals with Islamic political thought, and currently focuses on the nexus between Sufi mysticism and political activism. Additionally, he has worked extensively on modern Arab intellectual history, and on reformist Islamic thought through the prism of objectives-based legal theory (*maqasid al-shari'ah*). A former Fulbright scholar, he has spent several years in the Arab Middle East as a researcher and journalist. In addition to his scholarly work, he regularly writes for the global press, having published in Al Jazeera, *Common Dreams,* and *Religion Dispatches,* among other media outlets.

JOEL GORDON is professor of history, former director of the King Fahd Center for Middle East Studies at the University of Arkansas, and a research affiliate of the Center for Middle East Studies at the University of Denver. He is the author of three books – *Nasser's Blessed Movement: Egypt's Free Officers and the July Revolution* (Oxford University Press, 1992), *Revolutionary Melodrama: Popular Film and Civic Identity in Nasser's Egypt* (Middle East Documentation Center, 2002), and *Nasser: Hero of the Arab Nation* (Oneworld, 2006) – as well as numerous articles on Egyptian political and cultural history, particularly film, television, and popular music.

AMR HAMZAWY studied political science and developmental studies in Cairo, The Hague, and Berlin. After finishing his doctoral studies and after five years of teaching in Cairo and Berlin, Dr. Hamzawy joined the Carnegie Endowment for International Peace (Washington, DC) between 2005 and 2009 as a senior associate for Middle East Politics. Between 2009 and 2010, he served as the research director of the Middle East Center of the Carnegie Endowment in Beirut, Lebanon. In 2011, he joined the Department of Public Policy and Administration at the American University in Cairo, where he continues to serve today. Dr. Hamzawy also serves as an associate professor of political science at the Department of Political Science, Cairo University. Most recently he is a visiting scholar at Stanford University's Center on Democracy, Development, and the Rule of Law (CDDRL).

His research and teaching interests as well as his academic publications focus on democratization processes in Egypt, tensions between freedom and repression in the Egyptian public space, political movements and civil society in Egypt, contemporary debates in Arab political thought, and human rights and governance in the Arab world.

Dr. Hamzawy is a former member of the People's Assembly after being elected in the first parliamentary elections in Egypt after the January 25, 2011 revolution. He is also a former member of the Egyptian National Council for Human Rights. Dr. Hamzawy contributes a daily column and a weekly op-ed to the Egyptian independent newspaper *Shorouk* and a weekly op-ed to the Arab newspaper *Al-Quds al-Arabi*.

ANN M. LESCH is emeritus professor of political science at The American University in Cairo, where she was dean of the School of Humanities and Social Sciences and associate provost for international studies. She previously taught at Villanova University, worked in New York and Cairo for the Ford Foundation, and represented the American Friends Service Committee in Jerusalem. She was president of the Middle East Studies Association and of the Sudan Studies Association and director of the Palestinian American Research Center. Dr. Lesch has published numerous books and articles on Palestinian and Sudanese politics as well as on Egypt. Her latest articles include "Parliament without Politics: The

Effort to Consolidate Authoritarian Rule," The Foreign Policy Research Institute (FPRI), 2016; "Egypt: Resurgence of the Security State" (FPRI), 2014; "The Fluctuating Roles of the Military in Egypt," *Journal of South Asian and Middle Eastern Studies*, 2015; and "Egypt's Spring: Causes of the Revolution," *Middle East Policy*, 2011.

ABDEL-FATTAH MADY is an associate professor of political science at Egypt's Alexandria University. He joined the Woodrow Wilson International Center for Scholars as a visiting scholar from September 2015 to May 2016. He also served as a visiting scholar at University of Denver, spring 2015. In 2004, he was a recipient of the John Randolph Haynes and Dora Haynes Fellowship for social research. He received his BA and MA in politics at Alexandria University, Egypt, with a further MA and Ph.D. from Claremont Graduate University, USA. His research focuses on regime transitions and democratization, Islamic political movements, civil education and human rights in the Arab region, and the Arab-Israeli conflict. He is the author and editor of several books, including *On Reform and Revolution in Egypt* (2015), *Towards a Historical Democratic Front in the Arab Countries* (Beirut, 2010), *Arab Regime Transitions* (Beirut, 2009), *The Concept of Democratic Elections and Arab Elections* (2010), and *Religion and Politics in Israel* (1999), as well as numerous articles appearing in *Democratization*, the *Arab Journal of Political Science*, *Contemporary Arab Affairs*, the *Arab Future*, *Arab Politics*, among other publications. He is currently involved in projects in Egypt, USA and Switzerland. He can be reached at: www.abdelfattahmady.net / Abdelfattah.Mady@gmail.com

HESHAM SALLAM is a research associate at Stanford University's Center on Democracy, Development, and the Rule of Law (CDDRL), and serves as the Center's associate-director of the Program on Arab Reform and Democracy. He is also a co-editor of *Jadaliyya* ezine. His research focuses on Islamist movements and the politics of economic reform in the Arab world. Dr. Sallam received a Ph.D. in government and an MA in Arab studies from Georgetown University.

EMAD EL-DIN SHAHIN is the Hasib Sabbagh Distinguished Visiting Chair of Arabic and Islamic Studies and a visiting professor of political science at the School of Foreign Service at Georgetown University. He is also a tenured professor of public policy at the American University in

Cairo (on leave). Shahin holds a Ph.D. from the Johns Hopkins School of Advanced International Studies, and an MA and BA from the American University in Cairo. He has taught in leading universities including Harvard, Notre Dame, George Washington, and Boston University. Shahin was a Distinguished Visiting Scholar at Columbia University and public policy scholar at The Woodrow Wilson International Center for Scholars. His research and teaching interests focus on comparative politics, democracy and political reform in Muslim societies, Islam and politics, and political economy of the Middle East. He has authored, co-authored, and co-edited six books, and has more than fifty scholarly publications including journal articles, book chapters, and encyclopedia entries. His publications include *Political Ascent: Contemporary Islamic Movements in North Africa*; co-editorship with Nathan Brown of *The Struggle over Democracy in the Middle East and North Africa*; and co-authorship of *Islam and Democracy* (in Arabic). He is the editor-in-chief of *The Oxford Encyclopedia of Islam and Politics* and co-editor with John L. Esposito of *The Oxford Handbook of Islam and Politics*.

Index

References to notes are indicated by n.

Abdalla, Ahmed 203, 208 n. 29
Abdel Aziz, Alaa 298
Abdel Aziz, Zakaria 98, 101
Abdel-Dayem, Ines 299
Abdel Fattah, Alaa 88 n. 12, 114
Abdel Fattah, Moataz 197
Abdel-Khaleq, Farid 66
Abdel-Qouddous, Mohamed 74
Abdelrahman, Dina 189
Abduh, Muhammad 11, 12, 243, 255, 256, 292, 363
Abdullah, Talaat 107
Abol Ghar, Dr. Mohammad 4, 7, 9, 17–18, 231
  and Muslim Brotherhood 253–4
  and SDP 48
  and universities 200–1
Aboul Naga, Fayza 134, 139, 161
Abu Hasira, Rabbi Jacob 156
Abu Saeda, Hafez 124, 125, 137, 145
Abu Zayd, Nasr Hamid 295–6
Abul Fotouh, Abdel Moneim 43–4, 192
  and student movements 69, 70, 71, 72, 73, 74
Al-Adli, Habib 309
Adunis 314–15
advocacy organizations 127–30, 132, 158–60
al-Afghani, Jamal al-Din 11, 255, 363
Ahmad, Eqbal 27
Al-Ahram (newspaper) 16, 303, 304
Ahrar al-Sham 308
Al Fan Midan (Art in a Square) 152
Al Jazeera 113, 154, 163
Alexandria University 207–8, 209, 210, 221–2

Ali Pasha, Mohammed 202, 292
Amin, Nasser 139
Amin, Qasim 15, 257
Anan, Sami 276
Andalus Institute for Tolerance and Anti-Violence Studies 133
anti-protest law 112–13, 114
Anti-Torture Task Force 132
Antoun, Farah 256
April 6th Youth Movement 2, 6, 149, 151, 193, 227
al-Aqqad, Abbas Mahmud 256
Arab Alliance for Freedom and Democracy (AAFD) 297
Arab Center for the Independence of the Judiciary and the Legal Profession (ACIJLP) 137, 139, 140, 143
Arab-Israeli war (1967) 208, 209, 214, 293, 294
Arab Penal Reform Organization (APRO) 165
Arab Socialist Union (ASU) 32–3, 64, 68, 74, 79
Arab Spring 21, 238, 247, 291, 306, 313
Arab Women's Solidarity Association (AWSA) 123
Arabic Network for Human Rights Information (ANHRI) 128, 136, 158, 166
armed forces 56, 179, 207–8, 231–2, 236
  and Muslim Brotherhood 58–9, 60
  see also Supreme Council of the Armed Forces
arts, the 151–2, 298–9, 326–7, 365, 367
Asfour, Gaber 21, 292, 299, 302–3, 304, 312
  and government 309–10